Sex Differences in Cognitive Abilities

Third Edition

Sex Differences In Cognitive Abilities

Third Edition

DIANE F. HALPERN
California State University,
San Bernardino

Psychology Press
Taylor & Francis Group

New York   London

Psychology Press
Taylor & Francis Group
270 Madison Avenue
New York, NY 10016

Psychology Press
Taylor & Francis Group
27 Church Road
Hove, East Sussex BN3 2FA

© 2000 by Taylor & Francis Group, LLC
Psychology Press is an imprint of Taylor & Francis Group

Printed in the United States of America on acid-free paper
10 9 8 7 6 5 4 3

International Standard Book Number 13: 978-0-8058-2792-7 (Softcover)
International Standard Book Number 13: 978-0-8058-2791-0 (Hardcover)

Cover: Graphite drawing of the shared labyrinthine brain by California artist, **Robert Perine**, creator of The Tribes of Xyr and sometimes graphic designer.

Library of Congress Cataloging-in-Publication Data

Halpern, Diane F.
    Sex differences in cognitive abilities / Diane F. Halpern.—3rd ed.
        p. cm.
    Includes bibliographical references and index.
    ISBN 0-8058-2791-9 (hardcover : alk. paper)
    ISBN 0-8058-2792-7 (pbk. : alk. paper)
    1. Cognition. 2. Sex differences (Psychology). 3. Sex role. I. Title.
    BF311 .H295   2000
    155.3'3—dc21   99-0484-53

Visit the Taylor & Francis Web site at
http://www.taylorandfrancis.com

and the Psychology Press Web site at
http://www.psypress.com

For Sheldon, my first husband and best friend;
For Evan, "my son, the dentist;"
For Karen, who my son the dentist had the good sense
to marry and bring into our family
and to the many children in the Los Angeles
public schools that she teaches;
For Jaye, my daughter and college student who has
all the choices in the world ahead of her;
For the many students and teachers who aren't afraid
to ask tough questions
This book is lovingly dedicated to you.

Contents

Preface to the Third Edition

What is the meaning of differences and why are we so afraid of them? These decep-
tively simple questions are at the heart of this book. Of course, females and males
differ in some ways and are similar in others, but where are the differences and the
similarities, and how can we make sense out of them? Perhaps there are even more
fundamental questions that need to be asked first: Why is it important to know about
differences? Are answers even possible given the many ways that belief systems bias
the conclusions that we make and the decisions about what we want to know? All of
these questions have a long and turbulent history entangled with beliefs about the appropriate roles of men and women and the political and economic ramifications of
the way we answer them. The questions and answers are philosophical, empirical,
political, historical, and interesting to large numbers of people both inside academia
and in the real world that exists beyond the ivy curtain. Those opposed to research on
sex differences fear that it will legitimize false stereotypes, obscure similarities, and
provide fuel for those determined to convince the world of the inferiority of females
or be used in ways that discriminate against males. As I write this preface, the new,
repressive government in Afghanistan has forbidden all girls and women from attending school or working outside the home. I hope that this stunning act of discrimination will be history by the time you are reading this book. But, it does underscore
an important reality, the potential for the misuse of information on cognitive sex differences is cause for concern; no wonder so many people are afraid of any research
that examines group differences.

   In writing about such a sensitive and politically explosive topic, I have tried to
present the most recent findings along with some age-old questions about "maleness" and "femaleness" in as fair and unbiased way as possible. I wanted to go beyond the pop culture version of sex differences that is presented on talk shows and
in the usual array of books found in many book stores to provide a reasoned and

empirical view of one of psychology's most fundamental topics. Of course, by definition, none of us can see our own blind spots, so I am certain that many readers will see biases, especially if the information provided or the way it is presented does not agree with their own favored point of view. Following the publication of previous editions of this book, I received mail from many readers—some praising my fair-mindedness and the clear way in which I presented information (funny, but I remember these the best), but others taking exception to the way a particular area of research or theory was interpreted. I was pleased to find that the criticisms came from all ends of the political spectra, which I interpreted to mean that I had done a fairly good job of angering all sorts of people. In other words, I had succeeded at interpreting the huge and diverse literature. I hope that this edition comes even closer to achieving that goal.

The years since the publication of the second edition of *Sex Differences in Cognitive Abilities* have seen an explosion of new theories and research into the many questions about sex differences in cognition. New techniques for peering into the human brain have changed the nature of the research questions that we can ask and the kinds of answers we can expect. There have been surprising new findings about the influence of sex hormones throughout the life span for both women and men. Readers are warned that the burgeoning area of cognitive neuroscience is still in its own perinatal period, which means that inferences about the brain bases of cognition are extremely fragile and likely to change as the field develops. There has also been a rapid increase in the number of studies that examine unconscious and automatic processes that influence how people think when they become aware of category variables like one's sex, race, or age. The most important advance since the publication of the second edition of this book is the renewed emphasis on the continuity of environmental and biological variables, a perspective that blurs the distinction between these two types of influences. The psychobiosocial model that I advocate discards the nature–nurture dichotomy and replaces it with a continuous feedback loop in which nature and nurture are inseparable. I hope that this reconceptualization of the variables that influence who we are and how we develop will move us away from the nature–nurture tug-of-war to a more holistic and reciprocal view of human cognitive development.

ACKNOWLEDGMENTS

My sincere thanks goes to those unsung heroes who have read and commented on some or all portions of this book as it progressed through numerous drafts. I am enormously grateful for the insights of Dr. Marcia Collear at Middlebury College, Dr. Ann Gallagher at the Educational Testing Service, and Dr. George Spillach at Washington College. I also thank numerous students who have helped with this edition, especially (soon-to-be-Ph.D.) Mary LaMay at Loma Linda University. Each of these wonderful scholars gave generously of their time and expertise and, each of these special people provided encouraging feedback and helpful ideas throughout the writing process.

The contributions of many students who have influenced my thinking and writing are gratefully acknowledged, both those who have asked the "really tough questions" in my own classes and those who used earlier editions of this book in classes taught by other instructors. I am grateful to all of you who have written and e-mailed from many different places in North America and from numerous countries around the world. Your thoughtful comments, kind words, and unique international perspectives are sincerely appreciated.

Preface to the Second Edition

It seems that everyone has strong opinions about the ways in which females and males do and don't differ. Television talk show hosts and guests regularly "debate" (read, that try to out-shout each other), research findings dot the front pages of newspapers, and the rest of us talk, listen, and argue about the many questions about sex differences and similarities.

Yet, despite all the heated rhetoric, few people outside of academia are aware of the way in which psychologists, biologists, sociologists, and researchers from almost every other discipline have studied the questions about sex differences and similarities and the kinds of answers they have provided. In this book, I synthesize and summarize the enormous research literature that pertains to the ways males and females differ in their cognitive abilities. The intended audience for this book is anyone who wants to read a thoughtful analysis of the complex issues involved in asking and answering multifarious questions. A basic-level background in psychology, biology, and research methods will help readers with some of the more technical points, but readers without such a background can follow the main points. Upper division undergraduates and beginning graduate students should benefit the most from reading this book as they have already addressed some of the issues in their other courses.

I hope that every reader will take away something of value from this book—a new idea, a different way of conceptualizing the issues, a more open mind, an appreciation for the immense complexity of the issues involved, a more thoughtful approach to complicated problems, a framework for interpreting the quality of evidence, an understanding of the way societal values influence the way questions are posed and the type of answers we get, and the knowledge that there is a reciprocal relationship among psychological, biological, and societal influences that makes simple answers to complicated questions simply wrong. This is a long list of desired outcomes, but if most readers gain in at least one of these areas, then, I have successfully accomplished the goals that I set for myself when I began writing.

ACKNOWLEDGMENTS

This is my favorite part, the opportunity to thank the many wonderful colleagues who helped me with this book. I am grateful to Dr. Claire Etaugh at Bradley University and Dr. Nora Newcombe at Temple University for reading an earlier draft of the entire book. Their insightful comments have greatly improved the text. Dr. Neil Campbell from the University of California, Riverside, Dr. Michelle Paludi from Hunter College, Dr. Anne Petersen from Pennsylvania State University, and Dr. JoAnna Worthley from California State University, San Bernardino, all read chapters and generously shared their expertise with me. Of course, I would like to be able to attribute any errors that exist in the text to them, but, unfortunately, I will have to assume this responsibility.

Many colleagues have written to me to share their research and to comment on the myriad of issues. I thank them and the many other researchers whose work I have cited. I also thank my wonderful family, my husband Sheldon and my children Joan and Evan, for "being there" and for acting as sounding boards as I read my way through a mountain of literature and asked them to consider the many questions pertaining to sex differences in cognitive abilities.

Preface to Volume 1

It seemed like a simple task when I started writing this book. All I had to do was provide a comprehensive synthesis of the theories and research concerning the causes, correlates, and consequences of cognitive sex differences and make some meaningful conclusions that were supported in the literature. My interest in the area grew naturally out of several years of teaching both cognitive psychology and psychology of women to college classes. The idea that women and men might actually think differently, that is have different preferred modes of thinking or different thinking abilities, came up in both classes. At the time, it seemed clear to me that any between-sex differences in thinking abilities were due to socialization practices, artifacts and mistakes in the research, and bias and prejudice. After reviewing a pile of journal articles that stood several feet high and numerous books and book chapters that dwarfed the stack of journal articles, I changed my mind. The task I had undertaken certainly wasn't simple and the conclusions that I had expected to make had to be revised.

The literature on sex differences in cognitive abilities is filled with inconsistent findings, contradictory theories, and emotional claims that are unsupported by the research. Yet, despite all of the noise in the data, clear and consistent messages could be heard. There are real, and in some cases sizable, sex differences with respect to some cognitive abilities. Socialization practices are undoubtedly important, but there is also good evidence that biological sex differences play a role in establishing and maintaining cognitive sex differences, a conclusion that I wasn't prepared to make when I began reviewing the relevant literature.

The conclusions that I reached about cognitive sex differences are at odds with those of other authors (e.g., Caplan, MacPherson, & Tobin, 1985; Fairweather, 1976). There are probably several reasons why the conclusions in this review are different from the earlier ones. I believe that the data collected within the last few years provide a convincing case for the importance of biological variables, and that earlier reviews were, of course, unable to consider these findings, Other reviewers were sometimes quick to dismiss inconsistent theories and experimental results as symptomatic of a chaotic field of investigation. If they had reviewed the inconsistencies, they would have found that many of them are resolvable and that some of the theories and research could be eliminated because they had become outdated or had not received experimental support, thereby reducing the dissonance in the literature. Although there is still much that we don't know in this area, plausible conclusions based on the information that is currently available can be made.

This book was written with a broad audience in mind—bright undergraduates and graduates and their professors and general readers who are intrigued with the questions and answers about cognitive sex differences. It could serve as a supplemental book in many courses in psychology and other fields. The other issues raised in this book are appropriately addressed in introductory psychology, sociology, education, philosophy, human development, and biology courses. It is also appropriate for advanced courses in sex roles, sex differences, human genetics, child and adult development, education theory and research, social psychology and physiological psychology because of the broad perspective needed in understanding cognitive sex differences.

The topics addressed vary in their complexity, with brain-behavior relationships more difficult to explain than psychosocial influences on the development of cognition. My goal was to make even the advanced topics in biology and statistics comprehensive without oversimplifying multifaceted relationships or losing sight of the fact that the problems are complex. The topics addressed in this book go far beyond the usual "pop" coverage found in the popular press. I hope that despite my efforts to emphasize serious research and conceptual issues, I have been able to convey to readers some of my fascination with one of the most controversial and politically charged topics in modern psychology, the psychology of cognitive sex differences.

1

Introduction and Overview

CONTENTS

1

A HOT ISSUE IN CONTEMPORARY PSYCHOLOGY

*The difference between male and female is something
that everybody knows and nobody knows.*
—Money (1987, p. 13)

"Congratulations, you're the parents of a beautiful baby _____." I don't believe that there are new parents anywhere who wouldn't hold their breath until the missing word was filled in. Anxious friends and relatives await the momentous news about the new young person—is it a girl or a boy? The critical importance that we attribute to a newborn's sex reflects more than a curiosity about the shape of its genitals; it reflects a fundamental belief that the life of the newborn will differ in essential ways depending on whether it's a girl or it's a boy. But what are those beliefs and what is the evidence that supports them?

The questions of sex differences have been a consuming interest of psychologists and other social scientists for many years. Virtually every journal in every area of specialization, including the popular press and stories in nonprint media, contains reports of research on differences between women and men. More than 20 years ago, one observer noted that "women have become the latest academic fad" (Westkott, 1979, p. 427). More than 10 years ago, Jacklin (1989) described the study of sex differences as a "national preoccupation." Interest in the topic continues to mushroom. Spence (1993) estimated that 35,000 to 40,000 articles on gender were published in social and behavioral sciences journals between 1967 and 1993. The study of sex differences is surely a growth industry that has been fueled by recent advances in brain imaging and a new understanding of the reciprocal relationship between biology and environment. But the topic of sex differences isn't just "hot" in the sense of fashionable; it is, in fact, inflammatory. The answers we provide to questions like "Which is the smarter sex?" or "Do girls have less mathematical ability than boys?" have implications for present and future societies. The questions are important, and no one is taking the answers lightly.

Baby Blues cartoon. Reprinted with special permission of King Features Syndicate.

The political climate with regard to the questions of sex differences and the appropriate roles for men and women has been combative in the approximately 30 to 35 years since the women's movement began shaking up U.S. society. During the intervening decades, women have been entering traditionally male occupations at an increasing rate, and to a lesser extent, men have assumed a greater role in child care and homemaking (U.S. Bureau of the Census, 1997). In contrast, the Equal Rights Amendment, a failed attempt to constitutionally mandate equality between the sexes, is often relegated to a footnote in U.S. history texts. Apparently, Americans either are opposed to social changes in the roles played by men and women in contemporary society or believe that an amendment ensuring equal protection is unnecessary. The international picture is much the same—a contradictory mix of evidence showing that the lives of males and females are becoming more similar in some areas (e.g., more females are entering traditionally male occupations), increasingly disparate in others (e.g., the proportion of women in governmental positions of power has substantially decreased in countries that were formerly Soviet), and also staying much the same in other areas (e.g., the incidence of many mental illnesses remains overwhelmingly higher in males or females, depending on the type of illness).

Political commentators, late-night talk-show hosts, teachers, and the rest of the population have wrestled with issues such as whether women should be permitted to participate in combat (Are women too weak for the physical and psychological rigors of war?), whether women could be good vice presidents or presidents of the United States (Are they too emotional to make reasoned decisions?), whether men should be given equal consideration in child custody suits (Are most men as able as most women to assume the primary role in parenting?), whether the number of women in the sciences can be substantially increased (Are women less able to comprehend advanced scientific concepts?), and whether men are naturally too aggressive to be trusted with world peace (Would there be fewer wars if women ran the military?).

Few areas of study engender as much controversy and acrimony as the questions about sex differences. The way we answer these questions will have extensive influences on the way we live our lives and the way we govern society. My goal is to change not only how you answer these questions but also how you ask them. Perhaps the way we pose questions about sex differences contributes to the controversy and acrimony. Instead of assuming the perspective of which sex is better for a particular task or which sex has more of some hypothetical ability, there is a less polarizing approach to the many questions that society asks about the nonreproductive differences between men and women. The focus of the sex differences questions needs to change from "Who is better?" to "Where and when are meaningful differences found?".

Despite my plea for a more rational approach to questions of sex differences, there are some harsh realities that always cause an emotional response. Consider these grim facts:

1. *The Wage Gap.* A substantial wage gap exists when women and men are compared, even when controlling for critical variables such as education, age, and length of employment. For example, the median weekly wage for full-time workers in the United States in 1996 was $557 for men and $418 for women (U.S. Bureau of the Census, 1997, p. 431). The wage differential widens as the status of the position increases. In 1993, men with some postcollege education earned $53,000 annually compared with $38,000 for comparably educated women (Educational Testing Service, 1996). Jacobs (1995), in a review of sex segregation in the workplace, concluded that overall, "women working full-time and all year earn three-quarters of the take-home pay of their male counterparts" (p. 9). When I was in college in the late 1960s and early 1970s, many students wore buttons that read "59 cents" as a symbolic reminder of the amount that women were paid for every dollar men were paid. These pins are now out-of-date, but the gap has closed only slightly in the three or more decades since then.

2. *Poverty.* More than 60% of all adults living below the poverty line in the United States are women. (Contrary to common stereotypes, the majority are White women.)

3. *Corporate Positions of Power and Leadership.* Among Fortune 500 companies in 1995, only five presidents or chief executive officers were women and only 2% of all executives just below the chief executive officer were women (Heilman, 1995).

4. *Political Positions of Power and Leadership.* At the start of 1998, there were only 5 "heads of state," 4 "heads of government," and 10 foreign ministers who were women among the 191 countries in the world (Wright, 1997). At that time, female politicians were on the periphery in every major world power, with none as powerful as Britain's Margaret Thatcher, India's Indira Ghandi, or Israel's Golda Meir had been in the past.

5. *Psychiatric and Behavioral Disorders.* There are many psychiatric diagnoses that are primarily or exclusively applied to either females or males. For example, 90% of eating disorders such as anorexia occur in females. Panic disorders (with agoraphobia) are three times more common in women than in men. In contrast, the ratio of males to females diagnosed with attention deficit disorder with hyperactivity ranges between 4:1 and 9:1, depending on the setting; the ratio of males to females with mental retardation is approximately 1.5:1; only 2% to 4% of all people in treatment programs for pathological gambling are women; and schizoid disorders, transient tic disorders, stuttering, pyromania (fire setting), and antisocial personality disorder are "much more common in males" (American Psychiatric Association, 1994).

6. *Crime Statistics.* Approximately 95% of all prisoners in the United States are male. Males account for 91% of all arrests for murder and (nonnegligent) manslaughter, aggravated assault, and robbery (U.S. Bureau of the Census, 1997). The only major crime categories in which the percentage of females exceeds that of males are prostitution and, for juveniles, runaways.

7. *Professional Sports.* One-hundred percent of the professional baseball, football, and soccer players at the major-league level are male. The first female professional basketball league is a recent addition to professional sports.

8. *Everyday Activities of College Students.* College men spend much more time exercising, partying, watching television, and playing video games than college women (37.2% of men spend 1 or more hours per week on video games compared with 6.8% of women; Astin, Sax, Korn, & Mahoney, 1995). Women in college report that they spend much more time on household and child-care responsibilitites, reading for pleasure, studying, and volunteer work. On average, female and male college students live systematically different lives despite the fact that much of the time they attend class and do homework.

9. *Selective Infanticide, Abortion, and Rates of Literacy.* Worldwide, the "apartheid of gender" is responsible for the deaths of millions of females (U.S. Committee for UNICEF, 1993). The selective abortion of female fetuses and infanticide of female infants have resulted in 100 males for every 92 females in India and 100 males for every 28 females in rural China, with disparate sex ratios favoring males in many other countries in the world (Morrison, 1995). In discussing the missing females from the world population, Morrison (1995) commented, "Cultures that consider a double-X chromosome a deformity may be committing gender genocide" (p. 5). According to estimates from UNICEF, "More than a million children die each year because they are female" (U.S. Committee for UNICEF, 1993). UNICEF reports also estimate the literacy rate for females at two thirds that of males because worldwide 20 million more girls than boys are denied access to school.

Data of this sort demonstrate that women and men in contemporary industrialized societies and in most, perhaps all, other places around the world can expect to live qualitatively different lives solely on the basis of whether they are male or female. What is it about femaleness and maleness that determines, among other things, how much money you are likely to earn; the type of job you are likely to have; the type of psychiatric disorder you are likely to manifest; the type of sport you are likely to play; and, for some, whether you will be allowed to live? Being female or male is a central fact in all of our lives.

In the midst of all of this brouhaha, psychologists and other social scientists have amassed mountains of data about sex differences in the belief that the answers can be determined in a scientific manner. The purpose of this book is to review the data that pertain to sex differences in cognitive abilities and the theories that have guided the way the data are collected and interpreted. The goal is to provide an up-to-date synthesis and summary of this highly complex and controversial area of research.

Should We Study Sex Differences?

Scholarship on gender is all too often dismissed as politicized mythology
—Eagly (1990, p. 560)

There are controversies in every area of research about the way the research is conducted, the interpretation of the findings, and the theoretical and practical significance of the results. But, unlike other areas, this field faces the issue of whether sex differences research should be conducted. Many psychologists are opposed to any comparisons of women and men, especially when differences are found, fearing that the data will be interpreted and misused in ways that support a misogynist agenda or unwittingly provide support for the idea that there are "proper roles" for men and women. Lott (1996) answered this question with a resounding "no." She argued that identifying differences "obscures the complexities of human experience [and] reinforces existing political arrangements that maintain gender dichotomies" (Lott, 1996, p. 155). Such fears are understandable given the many social inequalities such as "mommy tracks" (career paths for women who will be devoting time and energy to their families and, therefore, supposedly, are better served with less demanding work assignments and lowered career aspirations than their male counterparts) and "glass ceilings" (artificial barriers to career advancement) that work against women (Kitzinger, 1994). Outspoken critics claim that all sex differences research is inherently sexist and that the results legitimize negative stereotypes of women (Hare-Mustin & Marecek, 1994; Hollway, 1994). McHugh, Koeske, and Frieze (1986), for example, argued that sex differences should be reported only under limited circumstances because of the problems inherent in studying and reporting sex differences. Baumeister (1988) adopted the more extreme position that researchers should cease reporting any between-sex comparisons.

The argument for limited reporting is that spurious findings of sex differences (a concept that is explained more fully in chap. 2) create an emphasis on the way women and men differ while slighting the multitude of similarities. The reason for never studying sex differences is that such studies are inherently sexist and fail to address the vast range of differences within each sex. In contrast, others have argued that the biological and social variables that vary as a function of one's sex are a critically important area of psychological inquiry, and for this reason, comparisons between females and males should become a routine part of scientific reports (Eagly 1990, 1994). Not surprisingly (this is a book on sex differences), I find the reasons in favor of studying sex differences most convincing. These reasons have been persuasively articulated by Eagly (1994, 1995). First, arguments against studying sex differences often are based on the implicit assumption that if the truth were known, women's deficiencies would be revealed. This is simply not true. Much of the research has documented areas in which women, as a group, excel. A point that is made in numerous places throughout this book is that differences are not deficiencies, and it is only through a careful study of differences that similarities can be revealed.

Sex differences research is not inherently sexist—it is the only way that we can empirically determine if common beliefs and stereotypes about males and females have any basis in fact. The only alternative to knowledge is ignorance. And ignorance does not counter stereotypes or dispel myths. If there were no sex differences research, we would never know that females earn much less than males or that males are much more likely than females to be diagnosed with certain mental illnesses. High-quality research is the only way that we can determine whether and when females and males are likely to differ. It is the only way that we can reject false stereotypes and understand legitimate differences.

THEORETICAL APPROACHES

Feminists be bold! Let us be active, smart scientists who welcome new research findings and who enter the theoretical fray as powerful contenders.
—Eagly (1994, p. 513)

Research on the many questions regarding sex differences in cognitive abilities has been guided by the theoretical perspectives of the investigators. I am reminded of the old tale of the blind men and the elephant. According to this tale, three blind men heard about an animal—the elephant—that was unknown in their country. Eager to learn more, they set out to study this strange and mythical animal. Coming on the elephant, one blind man reached out and grasped its thin, hairy tail, leading him to conclude that the elephant was a thin and hairy animal. A second blind man walked into the elephant's solid leg and exclaimed that the elephant was like a tall and sturdy tree. The third blind man was enveloped by its muscular trunk and shrieked that the elephant was pliable and strong, with a playful personality. Which of these blind men captured the true nature of the elephant? Perhaps we are like these blind men, trying hard to understand the true nature of a "beast" that is many different things, depending on our perspective, and all of us missing the most essential characteristics of the beast that we are striving to understand.

The framework in which a research question is posed, data are collected, and, most important, the data are interpreted is critically important in determining the answers. A broad overview of four dominant theoretical approaches can serve as a guide to this academic and political domain.

Nature–Nurture Controversy

Nature is a political strategy of those committed to maintaining the status quo of sex differences.
—Money (1987)

Even in an area as complex and replete with contradictory results as the study of sex differences in cognitive or thinking abilities, there are a few facts that virtually everyone agrees on. These facts concern the sex-related differences in the daily activities of a majority of women and men in contemporary Western cultures and other parts of the world. The majority of mathematics, science, and engineering majors in coed colleges are male, whereas the majority of elementary school teachers, nurses, and secretaries are female. When one parent assumes the job of primary homemaker, it is almost always the mother. The vast majority of professions and avocations are composed of a clear majority of one sex. For many professions, sex segregation has been increasing in recent years. For example, nearly three fourths of all public school teachers are female, with the percentage of male teachers at the lowest value since the National Education Association began collecting data in 1961 (Grace, 1992). In 1991, only 12% of elementary school teachers were male, down from 17.7% only a decade earlier. In fact, few sex-neutral occupations come to mind. The important questions for experimental psychology are (a) do these differences in activities reflect sex-related differences in cognitive abilities and, if so, (b) are the cognitive differences due to factors that are inherent in the biology of maleness and femaleness or to differential sex-related experiences and expectations?

The second question is a familiar one to psychologists: Does nature or nurture play the greater part in the differences under study? When applied to differences in cognitive abilities, the question becomes controversial and politically charged. Like all loaded questions, the answers sometimes backfire. The implications of the way psychologists answer this question are similar to those about racial differences in intelligence. Results could be, and have been, used to justify discrimination and affirmative action on the basis of sex.

The nature–nurture dichotomy has guided much of the research in the area of sex differences. Proponents on each side of the issue stack up their data, hoping to overwhelm the opposition with the sheer weight of their evidence. Arguments on the nature side of the question point to the folly of denying that the biological manifestations of manhood and womanhood influence how we think and act. The nurture side is quick to point out that individuals develop in a societal context that shapes and interprets thoughts and actions in stereotypical ways.

Nature–Nurture Interactions

Of course, few modern psychologists maintain a strict "either/or" position. The naturally gifted poet and author, for example, will never develop this gift if denied an education. The gift will never be recognized if publishers refuse to publish the creative work. Nature and nurture must operate jointly in the development of cognitive abilities. When we say that nature and nurture interact, it means that specific combinations of each "independent variable" cause a result that would not be predicted from either variable alone. Thus, for theoretical purposes, this model assumes that nature and nurture are independent and that certain combinations produce unusual results. For example, if you were lucky enough to receive genes for high intelligence and were raised in an environment favorable to intellectual development (perhaps a home with many books and college-educated parents who spend time with you), then you might develop into a genius—far beyond a level that would be predicted from either your nature alone (genetic inheritance) or your environment alone (intellectually stimulating home). Other specific combinations (e.g., genetic inheritance for low intelligence combined with an environment that is not conducive for intellectual development) also would be expected to be important determinants of an individual's level of intelligence by those who support an interactionist position of nature and nurture.

Although most researchers agree that the better question is how much do nature and nurture contribute to the development of cognitive abilities, it is virtually impossible to devise measures that allow for a direct and independent comparison. In addition, nature and nurture are not independent. Nature and nurture are like conjoined (Siamese) twins who share a common heart and nervous system. How could we ever decide where one twin ends and the other begins? Thus, although virtually all researchers pay lip service to interactionist positions, their research is, in fact, focused primarily on either biological (nature) variables or environmental (nurture) variables. We are both biological and environmental beings—our biological potential develops within an environment, despite the fact that researchers often interpret variables that influence development as being primarily due to one or the other. The nature–nurture controversy has been debated for more than 2,000 years without resolution because it is essentially unanswerable. Yet, it has served as a framework for much of the sex differences research.

Heredity/Environment cartoon. Copyright © Leo Callum (1985).

Evolutionary Psychology

The furor may be inevitable.
—Gelman et al. (1981)

The nature–nurture controversy erupted into a full-scale war when E. O. Wilson "sought to establish sociobiology 'as the systematic study of the biological bases of all social behavior'" (as quoted in Bleier, 1984, p. 15). Sociobiology, now more commonly called "evolutionary psychology," is a subdiscipline within biology that attempts to use evolutionary principles to explain the behavior of humans and other animals (Daly & Wilson, 1999). It has been growing in popularity over the past decade, with adherents from several different academic domains taking this perspective outside of the academic domains of biology and sociology and moving it into other areas including anthropology, history, and geography, among others. The term *evolutionary psychology* has evolved as the general label for psychological theories grounded in the Darwinian principles of reproductive fitness. According to this theory, a species is fit if it reproduces well. A major tenet of evolutionary psychology is that there are genetically programmed universal traits that improve the probabilities of producing many viable offspring. Given the basic assumptions of sociobiology, women, for example, should have a genetically determined predisposition that makes them better at child care because they are the ones that gestate and nurse the young of our species. Like the female members of other species, women purportedly possess a "maternal instinct" because such an instinct would be beneficial to the survival of the species. According to this theory, women without these instincts would not be threatened, but their children would have lower survival rates, and therefore fewer of these "nonmaternal" genes would be passed on to subsequent generations. Eventually, all offspring from these women should disappear. Men, in contrast, inherit a genetic predisposition that makes them prone to infidelity because multiple sexual encounters is a good reproductive strategy for males. Evolutionary psychology has enjoyed a tremendous increase in popularity in the past several years (Buss, 1995; Geary, 1998). It is probably more accurate to think of evolutionary psychology as a broad framework for understanding Darwinian-based psychological principles instead of as a single unified theory. Several different explanations, rooted in the idea that contemporary human sex differences have an evolutionary basis, have been proposed. Although each of these positions is discussed in more detail in later chapters in this book, an overview of each is useful for understanding how explanations of sex differences that are offered by evolutionary psychologists differ from those that are offered by other theoretical perspectives.

Differences Between Monogamous and Polygynous Species.   One theory of the evolutionary bases of human sex differences focuses on how sex differences vary across species with respect to their mating strategies. For example, Gaulin and his colleagues (Gaulin, 1995, Gaulin & Fitzgerald, 1989; Gaulin, Fitzgerald, & Wartell, 1990; Gaulin & Wartell, 1990) have studied sex differences in spatial abilities in two species of voles (rodents), one of which is monogamous (mates with only one member of the species) and one of which is polygynous (mates with more than one member of the species). They found that only the polygynous species shows sex differences in spatial abilities. Gaulin argued that polygynous male voles have larger home ranges than monogamous male voles because the polygynous species needs to roam farther to find multiple mates. For polygynous male rodents, superior spatial skills would provide a reproductive advantage. For the monogamous species, the males and females have the same home range, and, therefore, as predicted from this theory, there are no sex differences in spatial skills for these rodents. Gaulin hypothesized that human males developed excellent spatial abilities (along with the underlying neuroanatomical structures for superior spatial abilities) during human evolutionary history because human males, like polygynous male rodents, with these abilities would be better at life skills such as hunting and finding mates and therefore would have higher reproductive rates.

As additional support for this evolutionary perspective, Gaulin (1995) examined the hippocampus, a portion of the brain that underlies spatial cognition. He reported that there are no sex differences in the size of the hippocampus in monogamous species of voles, but for polygynous species of voles, the males have larger hippocampi (plural of hippocampus) than do the females. Sherry, Jacobs, and Gaulin (1992) concluded that "because sex differences evolve slowly, any findings of sex differences in neuroanatomy and related cognitive function are especially strong evidence of adaptive modification of the brain" (p. 300).

Although much more research is needed to determine if sex differences in other animal species are correlated with whether the males have a large or small home range or whether the species is monogamous or polygynous, it is still a long leap to extrapolate findings of this sort to the complex environment of humans. It also seems that this explanation would require the assumption that humans are more like a polygynous species of rodents than a monogamous one.

The Hunter–Gatherer Hypothesis

Generalizations to human behavior from our closest relatives ignore 5 million years of exuberant evolutionary development of the human brain.
—Bleier (1978, p. 161)

Another theory grounded in evolutionary psychology is based on the division of labor in earlier human societies. Proponents of this position maintain that because men were the hunters in primitive hunter–gatherer societies, they needed better spatial skills than the women who performed the gathering tasks; therefore, men evolved to be genetically superior in spatial ability. To be successful in "bringing home the bacon" or the bison, male hunters had to be able to maintain their orientation while pursuing prey over unfamiliar territory. According to this line of reasoning, genes coding for spatial ability would be an evolutionary advantage. In contrast, the female gatherers had to remember the location of edible plants from season to season. In support of this idea, Silverman and Eals (1992; Eals & Silverman, 1994) and Silverman and Phillips (1993) found that women are better at tasks that require memory for location and men are better at tasks that require mental transformations of spatial displays. They concluded that through the evolutionary pressures of adaptation, males developed brain structures that supported the cognitive and motor skills needed in navigating large areas and killing animals and cognition in females evolved in ways that supported effective gathering.

There are numerous problems with attempts to explain findings of contemporary sex differences in cognitive abilities with reference to behaviors that were adaptive in hunter–gatherer societies. Spatial skills, for example, also were needed for gatherers who often had to travel long distances to gather food. In addition, there were many hunter–gatherer societies in which women hunted (e.g., the Pygmies of the Zaire rain forest and the Tiwi of the Bathurst Islands; O'Kelly, 1980). Women in these earlier societies had to weave the baskets needed for efficient gathering (a complex spatial skill). Pontius (1989) described the daily activities of women in a 20th-century hunter–gatherer society (nonmissionized nomadic Auca Indians of the Amazon) as heavily reliant on the use of spatial skills: "The women, with amazing skill, fold a whole howler monkey to fit into a relatively small pot or two turkey-like birds into a pot which seems just large enough for only one bird. This skill implies accurate visualization of the body size of the animals in relation to one another and to the pot. Such spatial visualization is also used to a lesser degree in the knotting of hammocks from lianas" (p. 57).

Biologically Primary and Secondary Domains.   A third theoretical perspective that attempts to explain human sex differences in cognition using the rubric of evolutionary psychology was proposed by Geary (1995a, 1996d). Both Gaulin's (1995) extrapolations from monogamous and polygynous voles and Silverman and Eals' (1992) extension of the division of labor in hunter–gatherer societies were used to explain human sex differences in spatial ability. Unlike these other perspectives, Geary's theory was proposed as an explanation for cross-national patterns of sex differences in mathematical abilities, although this third perspective also relies on sex-related spatial ability differences at its conceptual core.

Geary (1996) made a distinction between cognitive skills that are "primary," that is, they were shaped by evolutionary pressures and therefore would be found across cultures and developed universally in children's play, and cognitive skills that are "secondary," that is, they are found only in technologically complex societies—skills like reading and spelling that are important in school but would not have evolved in hunter–gatherer societies. Geary maintained that there are no sex differences in biologically primary mathematical abilities such as counting or understanding basic concepts in comparing quantities. According to Geary, sex differences are found only on those mathematical abilities that are biologically secondary, abilities like solving mathematical word problems and geometry. He suggested that sex differences in spatial cognition could be the underlying factor in explaining the differences that are found in some types of math problems.

Numerous respondents raised objections to Geary's (1996) evolutionary-based explanations for sex differences in some math problems: (a) The extensive overlap in math abilities for females and males cannot be explained with this theory (Casey, 1996b), (b) the relationship between spatial abilities and mathematical problem solving is tenuous at best (Dowker, 1996), (c) both sexes are equally responsive to education and training (Baenninger & Newcombe, 1996), and (d) some sex differences are found prior to formal schooling and on supposedly biologically primary tasks (Stanley & Stumpf, 1996).

Critiques of Evolutionary Theories

A comprehensive understanding of human differences requires us
to think more integratively about the multiple causal influences
on our contemporary behavior.
—Schaller (1997, p. 1379)

Although theories that posit evolutionary origins for complex human behaviors offer interesting alternatives to nature–nurture dichotomies, they are untestable, and they ignore large bodies of data that do not conform to these explanatory frameworks. Virtually any finding can be "explained" post hoc by hypothesizing how it might have been advantageous to hunter–gatherers. In a somewhat humorous attempt to demonstrate this point, Cornell (1997) used the tenets of evolutionary psychology to explain surprising sex differences in a hypothetical society. In this mythical society, women were stronger and more sexually aggressive than their timid male counterparts. Of course, such behaviors could easily be predicted by using the logic of sexual selection. Because the males rarely engaged in the reproductively important task of child care, they never developed the skills needed to defend their offspring. Fleeing from danger would be a more adaptive response for males, when viewed from this explanatory context. Similarly, sexually aggressive females would be better able to evaluate potential mates and could convince many men that any child they bore was biologically the men's offspring. This sort of tongue-in-cheek exercise shows the weakness in the post hoc explanations of evolutionary psychologists.

Evolutionary theories ignore the fact that women have always engaged in spatial tasks and that they often had to travel long distances to gather food. There is also archeological evidence that women played significant roles in hunting and warfare (Adler, 1993). Basket weaving and cloth- and shelter-making work are spatial tasks that were very important to the survival of a community because success at gathering depended on the quantity and strength of the baskets, and the protection afforded by clothing and shelters was critical. In addition, the visual–spatial tasks that show the largest sex differences favoring males, like mental rotation, are performed in small areas (paper-and-pencil tasks), which are qualitatively different from finding one's way over miles of territory, although post hoc explanations could be thought up, such as the possibility that cognitive maps of three-dimensional space require implicit rotation skills, the ability to assume different perspectives, and so forth.

Another critique of evolutionary theories of human behavior is that they heavily rely on dubious analogies from other animal species to make their point. As Weisstein (1972) noted, this is the same as concluding "that it is quite useless to teach human infants to speak since it has been tried with chimpanzees and does not work" (p. 218). None of these criticisms are meant to deny the importance of evolution or the possibility that there are many human traits that have been molded over time in ways that support survival. However, we are still a long way from systematically relating evolutionary forces to contemporary sex differences in cognition (Eagly & Wood, 1999).

PSYCHOBIOSOCIAL HYPOTHESES

Of all the discoveries that have poured out of neuroscience labs in recent years, the finding that the electrical activity of brain cells changes the physical structure of the brain is perhaps the most breathtaking.
—Nash (1997, p. 10)

Psychobiosocial hypotheses offer an alternative conceptualization to the nature–nurture dichotomy, to the interaction of these two forces, and to evolutionary theories that posit Darwinian adaptation by our prehuman and early human ancestors as the reason for contemporary sex differences in humans. The psychobiosocial hypothesis is based on the idea that some variables are both biological and social and therefore cannot be classified into one of these two categories. Consider, for example, the role of learning in creating and maintaining a (average) difference between females and males. Learning is both a socially mediated event and a biological one. Individuals are predisposed to learn some topics more readily than others. A predisposition to learn some behaviors or concepts more easily than others is determined by prior learning experiences and the neurochemical processes that allow learning to occur (release of neurotransmitters) and change in response to learning (e.g., long-term potentiation and synaptic changes in areas of the brain that are active during performance of a task; Posner & Raichle, 1994). Thus, learning depends on what is already known and on the neural structures and processes that undergird the learning and remembering processes. Of course, psychological variables like interest and expectancy are also important in determining how readily information is learned, but interest and expectancy are also affected by prior learning. The model that is being advocated is predicated on an integral conceptualization of nature and nurture that cannot be broken into nature or nurture subcomponents. Neural structures change in response to environmental events, environmental events are selected from the environment partly on the basis of predilections and expectancies, and the biological and socially mediated underpinnings of learning help to create the predilections and expectancies that guide future learning.

Instead of perceiving nature and nurture as "independent variables," psychobiosocial hypotheses recognize that nature and nurture are inextricably entwined. Biology responds to the environment, and people adjust and select their environment to make it compatible with their biological propensities. Consider the biological question of whether male and female brains tend to differ in their organization of functions, a topic that is discussed in considerable detail in later chapters in this book. Brain differences develop in the context of a socialization process

(Petersen & Hood, 1988). There is a large research literature documenting the effects of different environments on the morphology of the brain (Spear, Spear, & Woodruff, 1995). Diamond (1988) found that when rats were reared in either enriched or impoverished environments, their brains manifested systematic differences in cortical thickness and weight, the branching of dendrites (parts of the neurons), number of glial cells (nourishing tissues), and cell size. Furthermore, even in old age, the brain was altered in response to changes in the environment. The brain has an enduring capacity to form new synapses (Greenough, 1986; Greenough & Black, 1992; Nelson, 1999). The vast majority of the 1,000 trillion synapses (connections) that a newborn's billions of neurons will make are determined by early experiences (Lach, 1997). Thus, even if we were to conclude that there are structural differences in male and female brains, we would not know whether such differences are due to sex-related biological mechanisms or occur as a response to a socially differentiated environment or, as is more likely, some combination of the two.

The turbid relationship between nature and nurture is muddied even further when we consider that the links between cognitive performance and its underlying biology are only loosely conceptualized (Petersen & Crockett, 1987). All behavior results from the joint action of biological, psychological, and social influences. Suppose, for example, a reciprocal and interactive process such that some biological characteristic of maleness (e.g., hormone concentrations) creates a slight advantage on spatial tasks and that, because of this slight advantage, males seek more spatially related activities that society, in turn, encourages as sex role appropriate. This hypothetical sequence could create an even greater difference in the biological underpinnings of spatial ability because of the spatial nature of the activities in which males engage (e.g., playing with building blocks). When viewed from a psychobiosocial perspective, the same variables are both cause and effect. Brain alternations result from different life experiences and different genetic propensities, and they affect future behavior, which, in turn, influences further brain development. This circular pattern is depicted in Fig. 1.2. In this way, biological, psychological, and societal factors could operate in concert to enhance an initially small differences between the sexes. Similarly, they also could reduce an initially large difference between the sexes.

One of the most eloquent commentaries about the nature–nurture controversy and the joint action of many variables was made by Reinisch, Rosenblum, and Sanders (1987):

> Consider the hoary, always dying, but never dead, pseudoquestion of the role of nature and/or nurture in determining the most commonly observed masculine and feminine characteristics. ... Culture may seek to diminish, exaggerate, ignore, or even reverse the impact of these biological factors. ... Nevertheless, although the pathways from genes to behavior may be extremely complex in all organisms ..., culture and experience act on a given constellation of capacities and propensities present at the start of the whole process, even when that interactive process is seen as beginning prior to conception. (pp. 5–6)

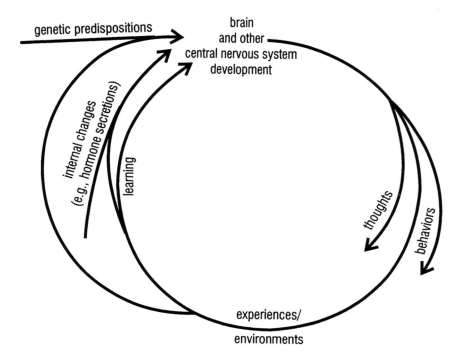

FIG. 1.2.   A schematic diagram of a psychobiosocial model in which nature and nurture are continuous and inseparable. Notice that thoughts and behaviors, which are biologically mediated processes arising from brain activity, alter the environment experienced by individuals, which in turn alters brain development and other internal processes (e.g., hormone secretions). Genetic potential also can be affected by some environmental stimuli (e.g., some drugs), causing changes in biological processes (e.g., signs of aging), which in turn alter the environmental experiences to which each individual is exposed.

THE NOTION OF COGNITIVE ABILITIES

Cognitive psychology is the branch of psychology concerned with how people think, learn, and remember. The ability to think, learn, and remember is, in turn, related to the concept of intelligence. Although intelligence has been defined in many ways (see Halpern, 1996c; Neisser et al., 1996), it is used in this context as the raw material or "stuff" of thought. It is frequently conceptualized as a limited quantity within each individual that is developed more or less fully depending on environment.

Intelligence—Singular or Plural?

One view of intelligence is that there is a single "general" factor, known in the literature as g for short (Spearman, 1927). This approach is contrasted with the view that intelligence is made up of a number of separable factors (Thurstone, 1938). The debate over the structure of intelligence, that is, whether it is best conceptualized as a single factor or as several components that are relatively independent of each other, may be psychology's longest running and most acrimonious controversy. The research literature addressing the question of whether it is more accurate to think of intelligence as a single or a multifaceted trait spans the past 100 years and shows no sign of abating. There is some evidence that intelligence can be thought of as a general trait, at least for some purposes, but there is also good evidence that there are separable components or cognitive abilities. (Brody, 1992, presented an excellent and balanced overview of the issues and evidence that bear on this problem.) At the heart of the intelligence controversy are methodological issues such as how to best define and measure intelligence. The research literature shows that there are differences in the ability to reason abstractly and to process information accurately and quickly and that when we examine performance on complex tasks, meaningful, separable factors emerge. In an extensive review of the literature, Brody (1992) concluded that "the structure of ability tests supports a hierarchical model of ability with g at its apex" (p. 49). Thus, he concluded that intelligence consists of a single factor that can be broken down into separable components—sort of a compromise position between the single-factor and multiple-factors theorists. Many contemporary psychologists believe that intelligence is not a unitary concept, although there is considerable disagreement as to the number and nature of the separable factors (Neisser et al., 1996; Sternberg, 1988).

It is constructive to think of intelligence as consisting of several intellectual abilities that are related to each other but yet somewhat different. The number and nature of these component abilities are frequently identified with a mathematical procedure known as *factor analysis*. Factor analysis is a useful descriptive technique that allows researchers to discover clusters of correlated variables. These clusters of variables, known as factors, can be thought of as the underlying dimensions of intelligence. Intelligence was one of the first interests of early psychologists, and there is probably more written about intelligence than any other topic in psychology. In a classical factor-analytic study of intelligence, Thurstone and Thurstone (1941) administered 60 different ability tests (e.g., arithmetic, spelling) to eighth-grade students. They found that scores on these tests formed three sets of clusters or factors that they called Verbal, Number (Quantitative), and Perception (Visual–Spatial) factors. Modern psychologists concerned with cognitive sex differences still refer to these same three factors. In the years since 1941, several other models of intelligence have been proposed, but the notion of multiple intelligence is still widely supported (e.g., Cattell, 1963; Guilford, 1967; Sternberg, 1996).

One of the most influential conceptions of intelligence was posited by Gardner (1983). In his seminal book, *Frames of Mind,* Gardner proposed seven different

intelligences: linguistic, logical–mathematical, spatial, musical, body–kinesthetic, interpersonal, and intrapersonal. Gardner relied on multiple sources of evidence that these are seven distinct components of intelligence or, as he called them,
"frames of mind." Each of these seven abilities responds selectively to localized
brain damage (suggesting localization of brain function). There are autistic savants who excel in only one of these areas and are dysfunctional in the other areas
and exceptional prodigies with extraordinary ability in only one of these areas.
These abilities are differentially valued in different societies, and they conform to
commonly held intuitive notions about the way people differ.

Gardner's (1983) seven intelligences are a good starting point for a discussion
of sex differences in cognitive abilities. Much of this book reviews the literature
pertaining to his first three intelligences: linguistic (or language), logical–mathematical (or quantitative), and spatial. Sex differences in musical ability are considered only briefly because of the paucity of high-quality research on this ability.
There undoubtedly are sex differences in bodily–kinesthetic ability, but like the
other "intelligences," the nature of these differences must depend on the way
bodily–kinesthetic ability is measured. If we were to consider the complex, grace-
ful movements of ballet dancers, we would find that although there are numerous
outstanding male ballet dancers, the vast majority of accomplished ballet dancers
are female. Alternatively, if bodily–kinesthetic ability is assessed as running speed
or ability to pass a football, then males would appear more talented. There are also
some areas of bodily–kinesthetic ability in which males and females have similar
levels of performance, such as long-distance swimming. Thus, it seems that females and males may excel at different types of bodily–kinesthetic performance
depending on an interaction of physiological capacity and the opportunities provided by society for fully developing one's potential. Bodily–kinesthetic ability is
a good example of two points that I emphasize repeatedly throughout this book:
The evidence available suggests that there are sex differences, but (a) there is considerable variability within each sex, and (b) it would be foolish to try to decide
which sex is "better" at tasks that require bodily–kinesthetic ability. The fact that
differences probably exist doesn't mean that one sex is the "winner" and the other
is the "loser." Differences do not require a value judgment.

Interpersonal intelligence is defined as the ability to determine the moods of
others. By contrast, *intrapersonal intelligence* is knowledge of one's own feelings.
It seems reasonable to conclude that there are sex differences in these areas as well.
In a review of the literature on nonverbal communication (one measure of understanding the moods of others), Hall (1985) concluded that women, on average, are
better at decoding nonverbal communication. Intrapersonal intelligence is more
difficult to assess because only each individual knows his or her own feelings.
Common stereotypes reveal the belief that women are "more in touch with their
own feelings than men are with their own feelings," but there is very little research
on this topic.

In this book, I focus on the first three of Gardner's (1983) categories of intellectual abilities because linguistic, quantitative, and spatial are the three ability fac-

tors in which sex differences are most frequently reported. They are the only areas in which the literature is large enough and the research is rigorous enough to permit a detailed review with conclusions.

Assessment of Cognitive Abilities

Underlying abilities are abstract constructs. They are what psychologists believe they are measuring when they administer certain tests. But not all tests measure abilities. In fact, it is very difficult to devise a test of ability that isn't also measuring achievement. An achievement test measures what an individual knows (and is willing to reveal) at the time of the test. For example, if I wanted to know how much mathematics you know, I would give you a mathematics achievement test. If you had very few mathematics courses in high school, then I would expect that you wouldn't know much about the type of mathematics taught in the high school courses you didn't take. You wouldn't be able to solve trigonometry or calculus problems, for example. This doesn't mean that you couldn't solve these problems with appropriate instruction, nor does it necessarily mean that you would have difficulty learning these mathematical concepts. A low score on this test would mean only that you can't solve the mathematical problems at the time of the test.

Ability tests attempt to assess the likelihood of your being able to succeed at certain tasks in the future if you received proper instruction and if you were motivated to learn and demonstrate the skills needed to perform the task. A low score on a mathematical ability test, for example, is meant to imply that you are less able to learn certain advanced concepts such as calculus or other higher mathematics than someone obtaining a higher score. It can be loosely thought of as the ability to benefit from instruction in a certain area.

There are, however, several important *ifs* in ability testing. Suppose, for example, a young man who believes that language fluency is a "sissy trait" is tested in the area of verbal ability. He certainly would not be motivated to perform well on this test, leading the researcher to conclude that he has little verbal ability. Consider some of the other assumptions implicit in ability testing. We test mathematical ability by presenting individuals with mathematical problems to solve. Wouldn't someone who had taken more or better mathematical courses be expected to answer more questions correctly than someone with a poorer mathematical education background? In other words, aren't we also measuring achievement? To some extent, we are always measuring achievement whenever we try to measure ability. This is a troublesome problem for psychologists who want to understand possible sex differences in ability. In U.S. and other Western societies, girls typically take fewer advanced mathematics courses and receive less encouragement to excel in mathematics than boys. Females may take fewer advanced mathematics courses because they have less mathematical ability, because they *believe* they have less mathematical ability, or because they get fewer rewards for studying advanced topics in mathematics. How can we ever be certain that what we are labeling sex differences in ability aren't really sex differences in achievement? We can't. The blurry distinction between ability and achievement means that we have to be very careful about the conclusions that we draw from tests that show sex differences.

A pure measure of cognitive ability would separate what each of the sexes in fact does (achievement) from what each of the sexes can do (ability). This is not yet possible. Instead, we must rely on the only available data that we have. But, we also need to be careful about the kinds of extrapolations we make from them. Just because tests given in the 1980s or 1990s or into the single-digit decade of the 21st century show sex differences doesn't mean that tests in the year 2010 or beyond will. The term *cognitive abilities* is used throughout this book because it is the term that is commonly used in the literature, but readers should not hesitate to question whether ability or achievement is actually being measured.

Tests of cognitive abilities, like all tests, contain a "margin of error." That is, they are not perfectly accurate in the kinds of predictions that they make. A good test of mathematical ability, for example, should predict fairly well an individual's ability to acquire mathematical concepts. Ideally, it should be validated by actually comparing scores on the test with achievement in future mathematics courses. Unfortunately, this is rarely done. More often, these tests are validated by comparing scores on one mathematical ability test with scores on another mathematical ability test. If, in general, the scores are in accord, we can probably conclude that they are measuring the same construct, but we still cannot say much about the predictive value of either test or the meaningfulness of the construct we've just measured. The construction of valid and reliable tests is a complex statistical endeavor. Some of the tests cited in the cognitive sex differences literature have poor or unknown psychometric properties (reliabilities and validities). These tests should be considered only as ancillary evidence for or against a particular position and not as primary evidence because of the questionable nature of their construction.

In all psychological measurement, there is always a gap between the test result and what it signifies. Test results are interpretable only to the extent that a plausible theory can link them to meaningful constructs. Although mountains of data exist that address the questions of cognitive sex differences, there are few good theories that can synthesize and interpret the empirical results. Thus, although we can talk about sex differences on various tests, we can't always interpret what these differences mean.

Cognitive abilities are theoretical constructs that represent the underlying components of intelligence. The quality of a construct in the sex differences literature can be assessed by how well it passes three tests:

1. If sex differences are found consistently on several different tests that tend to cluster or load onto a single factor (signifying a construct), then we have reason to believe that, in general, the sexes perform differently on whatever these tests are measuring. This first step provides converging evidence from several tests that sex differences exist with respect to the construct being measured.

2. If, in addition, we can use these tests to predict performance on a task that requires the skills we believe that the tests are measuring, then the construct is useful.

3. If an empirically supported theory or theories have been devised to explain why sex differences exist in the ability being measured, then the construct and the theory that incorporates it have explanatory power.

The ability to explain phenomena is a major goal of research. The third requirement is needed to make the construct theoretically meaningful and is the most controversial and difficult of the conditions to satisfy.

VALUES AND SCIENCE

We do not have to ask for the head circumference of women of genius—they do not exist.
—Bayerthal (1911, cited in Janowsky, 1989, p. 257)

Political and ideological positions are intertwined when psychologists and others venture into studies of group differences of any sort. The question is not whether individual and societal beliefs influence the scientific methods but when, how, and how much.

The Myth of Objectivity

All knowledge is constructed and the knower is an intimate part of the known.
—Belenky, Clinchy, Goldberger, and Tarule (1986, p. 137)

When most of us first learned about the scientific method, sometime back in junior high school, we were told about the disinterested researcher who objectively and methodically goes about the business of collecting data with the goal of revealing truth. For those of us involved in research, the imagery that this description brings to mind is somewhat humorous. Although it is true that researchers collect data, very little of what most of us do could be considered "disinterested." Whatever the topic, few researchers who invest their energies in an experiment are neutral with respect to the type of outcome they expect or want. This is especially true in an area like cognitive sex differences, where there is so much at stake and where the potential for misinterpretation and misuse of experimental outcomes is so great.

There are numerous ways in which personal beliefs and values can influence the experimental procedure. Researchers make many decisions in the course of conducting an experiment, and the way in which the decisions are made can deliberately or unwittingly bias the results. Although this topic is covered more extensively in chapter 2, let's think about a few of these decisions now: the question under investigation, the traits and abilities that are assessed (e.g., visual–spatial memory, interpersonal skills), the way participants are selected (e.g., retarded as well as normal participants), the type of measurement used (e.g., continuous or discrete), the kinds of items used on tests (e.g., multiple-choice or essay), how to analyze the data (e.g., multivariate or univariate, parametric or nonparametric tests), the number of participants to include in the study, and whether to focus the discussion on significance levels or effect sizes. If I were interested, for example, in showing that there are no sex differences in mathematical ability, then I would want a sample in which women with high mathematical ability were included because I would want an overall high score for the women. I could opt for discrete measurement; the test items that I would select would have to include examples drawn from typical female experiences; I could use nonparametric tests, which are typically less powerful (less likely to reveal group differences); and I would want to use a small number of participants. Decisions concerning what to focus on in the discussion could be made post hoc depending on whether they would support or detract from my favored view. None of this is dishonest (although the use of a less powerful or inappropriate statistical test is very close to dishonest), nor are all of the decisions devious, especially if all of the relevant information is provided in the write-up of the experiment. In fact, the decision to include test items from typical experiences of girls would make it a fairer test than including examples exclusively from typical boy activities. This discussion is not intended to show that research or researchers are "bad." An experiment is the most objective method for providing answers to questions. It is important to keep in mind, however, that even our most objective method can be slanted in ways that support the researcher's favored outcome.

In a discussion about the relationship between values and science, Wittig (1985) stated, "Knowledge about behavior is constructed, not merely deduced. Such constructions are affected by the historical, personal, social, and cultural context. Judgments of the meaning, validity, and usefulness of a particular analysis of human behavior are themselves socially influenced" (p. 803). It is important to remember that research is conducted in a social environment. The kinds of questions that we ask and the kinds of evidence we are willing to accept depend on their compatibility with the prevailing social view and each researcher's personal views on the topic.

Modern researchers can laugh at the evidence Broca provided in 1861 to support his contention that Blacks and women were intellectually inferior. According to Gould (1978), Broca won an epochal debate on this topic by citing the following evidence: "In general, the brain is larger in mature adults than in the elderly, in men than in women, in eminent men than in men of mediocre talent, in superior races than in inferior races" (p. 44). Broca failed to consider the relationship between body size and brain size and had no data at all on his "inferior race–superior race" distinction. Yet, many 19th-century academics and physicians willingly accepted his "data" as support for the view that they favored on this issue. We can only imagine 21st-century researchers laughing at our own naivete in the way we sought to understand cognitive sex differences. In Shields' (1980) cogent discussion of the subservience of science to social values, she explained that the 19th-century belief that women were intellectually inferior to men because of their smaller frontal lobes in their brains was replaced later in the century with the belief that the parietal lobes were the true seat of intellectual prowess. Not surprisingly, the following report was published soon after the discovery of the importance of the parietal lobes: "The frontal region is not, as has been supposed, smaller in women. ... But the parietal lobe is somewhat smaller, a preponderance of the frontal region does not imply intellectual superiority ... the parietal region is really the more important" (Patrick, 1895, as quoted in Shields, 1980, p. 489).

How We Explain

[An] event simply activates a stored explanation.
—Krull and Anderson (1997, p. 2)

How do we explain events? This broad question has become the focus of psychological research as investigators probe the way we make causal attributions. The study of explanations as a field of inquiry is important because it may shed light on the types of explanations scientists and laypersons offer and accept for the many questions about sex differences.

Most people probably have noticed that the overwhelming majority of secretaries are female and the overwhelming majority of auto mechanics are male and have arrived at an explanation for these disparities in sex ratios. When psychologists talk about "explanations," they are referring to judgments about causality (Krull & Anderson, 1997). They found that sometimes explanations are generated automatically, relying on one's dominant beliefs about the world. If you generally believe that social forces are powerful, then you quickly and effortlessly interpret the finding that most secretaries are female and most auto mechanics are male as being caused by societal factors such as sex role stereotypes and cultural norms. You are not likely to even consider other possibilities. If the explanation you arrived at is satisfactory to you, and if you do seek evidence to check your explanation, then you are more likely to focus on evidence that supports the explanation you are considering than evidence that does not support it. Of course, these same processes of explaining are at work for those who automatically prefer a different sort of explanation, such as the idea that males are, on average, inherently better able to learn mechanical information and females are, on average, better at typing and organizing an office. Because people strive to maintain consistency in their beliefs, it is easy to understand why so few people ever change their preferred explanations, even when new sorts of data are being accumulated at a rapid rate, as in the area of sex differences. I urge all readers, regardless of their preferred type of explanation, to keep an open mind and to carefully weigh all of the evidence. Knowledge about sex differences in cognition is increasing exponentially, so if you have not reconsidered your explanations of complex sex-related findings, please try to apply the same standards of argument and evidence to preferred explanations as you apply to those you do not like.

Feminist Scholarship

Feminism is a perspective, not a method or a topic.
—Crawford and Kimmel (1999a, p. 3)

In recognition of the fact "that science played handmaiden to social values" (Shields, 1975, p. 739), several psychologists have suggested that sex differences researchers adopt a "feminist scholarship" approach (Crawford & Kimmel, 1999b). One of the goals of feminist scholarship is the recognition and elimination of the "androcentric bias in both content and method" in traditional research (Lott, 1985, p. 156). Men and women who ascribe to the philosophy of feminist research are careful to consider the importance of context or situational variables as potent influences on the results they obtain from research. Sex is not only a participant variable but also a stimulus variable, when viewed from this perspective. Women and men may respond differently in certain situations because the other people in those situations are responding to them in a sex-differentiated manner. In other words, women may perform differently from men on a certain type of task because the other people in the setting are giving them more or less encouragement to perform that task than they are giving to the men.

Feminist research is based on the belief that the world is determined by the categories that we use to define it (Unger, 1989). It recognizes the role of values in research and is deliberately grounded in feminist values (Crawford & Kimmel, 1999a, 1999b). Feminist psychologists reject the idea that a distinction can be made between what is being studied and the person doing the study; they emphasize the notion that the beliefs of the researcher influence the way abilities and traits are interpreted (Valentine & Brodsky, 1989). For example, if you believe that women are more likely to gossip than men, then you will interpret objectively identical behavior by a man or a woman differently—the man's behavior is less likely to be labeled as "gossip" than is the woman's behavior. In this case, any sex differences in the task performance should be attributed to sex as a stimulus variable rather than to sex as a participant variable.

Feminist psychology has a "new" masculine counterpart as the psychology of men and "men's studies" is emerging as an academic area worthy of study in its own right (Doyle, 1995). One of the newest divisions (interest areas) of the American Psychological Association, the largest professional association for psychologists, is "Psychology of Men." "Promasculinists," like their feminist counterparts, tend to emphasize the importance of context variables. There is no single "men's movement" any more than there is a single feminist perspective on complex issues. In many ways, the two perspectives are complementary in that they emphasize social and cultural factors that proscribe male and female roles.

Advocates of feminist scholarship and the newer "promasculine scholarship" use nontraditional methods, such as personal reflection, in addition to traditional mainstream methods to examine qualitative differences in the psychology of maleness and femaleness. They sometimes prefer lengthy individual interviews in attempting to understand a phenomenon. Feminist scholars of both sexes are concerned with similarities as well as sex differences. In a survey of feminist psychologists, Ricketts (1989) found that they tend to prefer external or social determinants of human behavior rather than internal or biological determinants. A feminist epistemology also contains a conscious awareness of the way sexist assumptions and other stereotypic beliefs guide the kinds of research questions that are investigated and the varieties of evidence researchers are willing to accept. Like all good researchers, feminists examine the quality of the data that are collected and the logic that links the data to a conclusion. Of course, they are no freer from their own personal biases than researchers with other epistemological beliefs, but hopefully they are more aware of them and attempt to state them explicitly for others to examine—an important fact in itself.

A Question About Answers

In thinking about the nature of explanations, I caution readers not to expect simple explanations for phenomena as complex as sex differences and similarities in human cognition. Most readers prefer a single and simple answer—especially if you are reading this book as part of an academic course for which you also are concerned with putting a "right answer" on a test or a paper. But there may not be a single "right answer," or if there is, it may not be the kind of answer that you are expecting. I always tell my own students that all complex questions in life have exactly the same answer. They like the part where they can use the same answer on every essay question in every class. The correct answer is "it all depends." The only problem with this answer is that you then have to explain what "it" depends on. When do different sorts of variables affect cognitive abilities, can differences be eliminated or magnified with experience, are there any meaningful differences, and why are these important questions to explore? Each of these many questions has different sorts of answers and explanations. The ability to cite evidence for many sides of controversies and to understand how each might be part of an answer is a hallmark of advanced understanding. I return to the question of answers again at the end of this book. But, be forewarned: Don't expect simple answers to the many complicated questions about sex differences in cognitive abilities.

POLITICAL AND SOCIAL RAMIFICATIONS

Information about one component of the gender stereotype heavily influences inferences about other gender-related attributes.
—Kite, Deaux, and Miele (1991, p. 19)

There are many commonly held stereotypes about differences between women and men. Women, for example, are usually perceived as being less intelligent than men (Broverman, Vogel, Broverman, Clarkson, & Rosenkrantz, 1972). Many people also believe that women should be less intelligent than men. In a survey of school teachers, Ernest (1976) found that both male and female teachers believed that boys were superior to girls in mathematical ability. We know that teachers sometimes act in ways that convey these beliefs to the children in their classrooms (Sadker & Sadker, 1985). Suppose that after a careful review of the literature, these stereotypes were found to be true! Teachers would knowingly or unknowingly increase the way they encourage and discourage different areas of intellectual development in their students depending on the students' sex. Advocates of sexual prejudice and discrimination could justify their beliefs and actions by an appeal to scientific findings. The social and political ramifications of such conclusions cannot be ignored.

The Bugaboo of Biological Explanations

It was almost taboo to talk about gender difference in the brain.
—George (as quoted in Foote & Seibert, 1999, p. 68)

For many, it is frightening, and perhaps even un-American, to consider the possibility that even a small portion of the sex differences in cognitive abilities may be attributable to biological factors. This is probably because many people confuse biological contributions with the idea of an immutable or unavoidable destiny. Suppose, for example, that after reviewing the literature, I were to conclude that males really are superior in mathematics and that sex-differentiated hormones or brain organizations are implicated in these differences. This does not necessarily reduce the importance of psychosocial variables, nor does it imply that the differences are large or that the differences could not be reduced or eliminated with appropriate instruction. What such a conclusion does do, however, is create the potential for misquotation, misuse, and misinterpretation in an attempt to justify discrimination based on sex. Perhaps the very publication of such research results creates a considerable risk.

Part of the fear of biologically based explanations of human sex differences in nonreproductive areas such as cognition is confusion about the term *biology*. Readers with expertise in the biological sciences may find this idea funny or strange, but for many people without this sort of expertise, biology really does mean destiny, which is why biological hypotheses are greeted with suspicion and hostility. We are biological organisms, so at some level, whatever it is that makes us who we are is biological. But, this statement doesn't say much. Readers are urged to keep the psychobiological perspective in mind as they read through this book. Life experiences change our underlying biology—they shape and reshape the brain, and the brain, in turn, influences life experiences. In addition, our thoughts, which spring from biological processes, can change our brains. We are also social organisms who are affected by environmental variables—variables that include the nutrients, pesticides, and calories in the foods we eat, the experiences to which we are exposed, and the experiences that we choose for ourselves. If we can reeducate the general public to understand these relationships, there would probably be less fear of biological research into the many questions of sex differences.

Censorship in Science

There is perhaps no field aspiring to be scientific where flagrant personal bias, logic martyred in the cause of supporting a prejudice, unfounded assertions, and even sentimental rot and drivel,
have run riot to such an extent as here.
—Wooley (1910, cited in Russett, 1989, p. 155)

The question that is being raised is whether there should be censorship in science, even self-imposed censorship, when results are likely to be misused. However, the danger inherent in censorship is far greater than the danger in publishing results that could be used for undesirable purposes. The answers provided in this book to the questions of sex differences are complex and contain many qualifiers. Readers who read only the chapters on biological hypotheses or only the chapters on psychosocial hypotheses without reading the final chapter that integrates both approaches will go away with different erroneous conclusions about the area. Quotations taken out of context can be used to support virtually any position because all sides of the issues have been considered and because it is possible to find research results to support almost any theory. The misrepresentation of biologically based explanations contributes to the chilly academic climate that women face in advanced courses in mathematics and that men face in "nurturing" fields like nursing and social work. Keep in mind that results obtained from groups of males and females do not justify discrimination against individuals. Nor can we afford to confuse what has been with what could or should be. Sex differences that exist at the start of 21st-century American society do not necessarily exist in other societies or in the American society of the future.

Sex Differences—Good and Bad

Beliefs about the desirability or usefulness of sex differences research often depend on the topic being investigated. For example, research that showed that women's risk of heart attack rises after menopause or that women metabolize alcohol differently than men is usually hailed as beneficial. Similarly, Gilligan's (1982) book on sex-related differences in modes of thinking and reasoning about moral issues and the association of these modes with male and female "voices" has been embraced as a best seller. In contrast, carefully executed research on sex-related differences in mathematical reasoning ability (e.g., Benbow, 1988) has generated hundreds of pages of vitriolic criticism (e.g., most of an entire issue of the journal *Behavioral and Brain Sciences,* Fausto-Sterling, 1985; Halpern, 1988). Why are differences in moral reasoning that are based on minimal support hailed as beneficial and differences in mathematical reasoning dismissed and belittled as sexist (Tiger, 1988)?

In an eloquent discussion of this question, Kenrick (1988) explained, "Advocates of this ideological approach have often used a two-front denial strategy. The first line is to deny that there are any substantial gender differences in behavior. This failing, the second line is to assume, a priori, that any differences that are demonstrated do not have a biological basis" (p. 199). It is important that each reader attempts to keep an open mind in considering the research and the way in which it is interpreted. To do anything less is self-deceptive.

TERMINOLOGY

The terms we use to convey ideas reflect our own biases about the topic being discussed. I have argued elsewhere that different images and meanings are evoked depending on the choice of words that is selected to convey our thoughts (Halpern, 1996c). Consider, for example, differences among the terms *senior citizen, old man,* and *golden ager.* Although, in some sense, these three terms can be considered synonyms, each conveys a somewhat different meaning. There is a reciprocal relationship between thought and language. The words that are used in the sex differences literature also influence how we think about the issues and the research results; therefore, I have decided to explain why I selected certain controversial terms.

Sex and Gender

> *Gender depolarization would ... require a psychological revolution*
> *in our most personal sense of who and what we are as males*
> *and females, a profound alteration in our feelings about the meaning*
> *of our biological sex and its relation to our psyche and our sexuality.*
> —Bem (1993)

Some psychologists prefer to use the term *sex* only when they are referring to biological distinctions between males and females while reserving the term *gender* to refer to the psychological features or attributes associated with the biological categories (e.g., Deaux, 1985; Unger, 1979, 1989). Gender used in this way refers to societal definitions of female and male traits and abilities (Goodnow, 1985). Levy (1989) articulated this distinction as follows: "The term *sex* is used to refer to the grouping of people into the two distinct biologically defined groups of female and male. Gender, in turn, refers to the social categorizing of individuals based on social standards and ascriptions" (p. 306). I have decided to use the term *sex* to refer to both biological and psychosocial aspects of the differences between males and females because these two aspects of human existence are so closely coupled in our society. It is frequently difficult to decide if the differences that are found between females and males are due to biological (*sex*) differences or the psychosocial concomitants (*gender*) of biological sex. I cannot argue, on the one hand, that the distinction between environmental and biological variables is often artificial and that nature and nurture are inseparable and then, on the other hand, use different terms to refer to each class of variables.

The use of the term *sex* is not meant to imply that biological variables are more important than psychosocial ones or that the results being discussed are caused by differences in genes, hormones, sex glands, or genitals. The point that biological manifestations of sex are confounded with psychosocial variables is made repeatedly throughout this book. The use of different terms to label these two types of contributions to human existence seemed inappropriate in light of the psychobiosocial position that I have taken in several places throughout this book.

Language purists probably will agree with my choice of the word *sex* instead of *gender. Gender* was originally a grammatical term used in languages that make a distinction between feminine and masculine nouns. It is not related to maleness or femaleness even in these languages. *Gender* is also sometimes used as a euphemism for the word *sex* because of the possible physical overtones implied by *sex*. Thus, for several reasons, *gender* seems to be an inappropriate label for the differences between females and males.

I also understand that language is a living phenomenon and that the meanings of words change over time. Increasingly, *gender* is being used to refer to a host of variables that seem distinctly biological. Pearson (1996) wrote that the term *gender* is being used to refer to the molecular biology of plants, insects, flatworms, crustaceans, rodents, and even sphincter muscles. It is difficult to see how any of these referents are influenced by societal expectations of appropriate behaviors. The distinction between these two terms is becoming increasingly difficult to understand. Pearson (1996) provided this example from a scholarly paper: "In humans and other mammals, chromosomes determine gender. In other species, sex is controlled by temperature or even the social environment" (p. 330). Given the confusion about these two terms, readers may understand my decision to stick with the term *sex,* regardless of the purported cause of any differences.

Sex and Sex-Related

Other psychologists have urged that the term *sex-related* differences be used instead of *sex* differences to emphasize the fact that many of the differences that are reported are correlates of the biological distinctions between females and males and are not necessarily due to biological differences (e.g., sex differences in cognitive abilities are not caused by the differences in female and male genitals; Sherman, 1978). Once again, the objective of this distinction is to separate biological and psychosocial determinants of between sex differences. Although I am aware of the consciousness raising aspect of this distinction, I have decided to use the shorter term *sex differences* in recognition of the close relationship between biological and psychosocial variables, using the term *sex-related differences* only occasionally for emphasis. The preference for the term *sex differences* is not meant to imply a preference for biological explanations.

Abilities, Skills, and Performance

Because there is considerable disagreement about how well various theories can explain sex differences and whether sex differences could be eliminated with appropriate instruction, other researchers have suggested that the term *abilities* should be replaced with other more neutral terms like *skills* or *performance* (Sherman, 1977). Once again, this distinction is based on the notion that the word *abilities* is suggestive of biological or immutable differences whereas the terms *skills* and *performance* are not. These three terms are used interchangeably throughout this book. The use of the term *abilities* is not meant to imply that the trait under discussion is either biologically determined or genetically linked. Abilities are developed in a social context, which includes opportunities for learning, cultural roles and values, the physical environment, and individual differences.

Pronouns

Traditional English usage has required that the masculine pronoun *he* be used whenever the sex of the referent is unknown. The male bias in our language and particularly the use of the male pronoun to refer to either females or males are discussed more fully in chapter 5. Psycholinguistic research has shown that listeners tend to think of males when the male pronoun is used (Hamilton, 1988; MacKay, 1983; Merritt & Kok, 1995). It seems that, at least among Western populations, the male is perceived as normative, and the use of the pronoun *he* is literally assumed to refer to a male referent. For this reason and because of my personal dislike for this convention, I have rejected the exclusive use of the masculine pronoun and have alternated the use of female and male pronouns throughout this book whenever the sex of the referent is unknown. Sex-neutral plural constructions (*they*) also have been used when they didn't interfere with the topic being discussed, although recent research has shown that using *they* to refer to a singular referent whose sex is unknown can create the presumption that a male is being discussed (Foertsch & Gernsbacher, 1997).

SELECTIVE NATURE OF ALL REVIEWS

The purpose of this book is to provide a comprehensive review and synthesis of the research and theories that pertain to the questions of cognitive sex differences. Tens of thousands, maybe even hundreds of thousands, of journal articles and books have been written that address this topic. Different experimental methods sometimes have been used to answer the same questions, and the answers don't always agree. Different results frequently have been obtained with the same tests, and similar results have been interpreted in different ways by different experimenters. Decisions have to be made continually as to which research is important and good. In an area as large as this one, only a subset of all of the available information can be presented. In addition, new knowledge is accumulating at an unprecedented rate. Thus, this review, like all reviews of the sex differences literature, is necessarily selective.

I'd like to take this opportunity to apologize to the many researchers who have published in this field but whose research has not been cited. In deciding which research to include in this review, I followed a few basic guidelines. I decided to include research that is representative of many experiments when several similar investigations were reported on the same topic (e.g., many researchers have found that spatial skills can be learned), to include pivotal or important research that helped to clarify a theoretical position or to choose between two or more alternative interpretations of research, and to devote more space to the controversies than to the areas in which a consensus has been reached. I also attempted to maintain a balanced view in this highly controversial area of psychology. This means that I probably will manage to offend almost every reader as I explore alternative explanations of research findings and the theories that guide the research. I also believe that the answers we accept as true today probably will seem outdated and sometimes will be proven wrong in several years. There are no final answers; only the questions endure.

ABOUT THIS BOOK

This introductory chapter is designed to set the stage for an examination of sex differences in cognitive abilities. Research methods and philosophies that determine how we answer the questions of cognitive sex differences are discussed in chapter 2. It is unusual to include a research methods chapter in a book on cognitive sex differences. It is included here in the belief that readers need to understand how the research questions were answered in order to understand the answers. Readers with a good background in experimental methods and statistics can skip or skim this chapter before going on in the book. Chapter 3 examines the question of whether sex differences in cognitive abilities exist, and, if so, are they large enough to be theoretically or practically important? Chapters 4 and 5 consider hypotheses concerning genetics, hormones, and brain–behavior relationships devised to explain cognitive sex differences, and chapters 6 and 7 consider learning, sex role pressures, and cultural norm hypotheses. Competing and complementary research and theories are integrated in Chapter 8, along with some closing thoughts for assimilating this large body of information.

2 Searching for Sex Differences in Cognitive Abilities

CONTENTS

2

THE NEED FOR RESEARCH

This study may generate more heat than light.
—Gunter and Gunter (1990, p. 367; conclusion from an experimental study on the domestic division of labor)

The first step in our quest to understand if, where, and when sex differences in cognitive abilities exist is an examination of the experimental and statistical procedures used to provide the answers. The kinds of questions we can ask about sex differences and the answers we get depend on the experimental and statistical methods used in research. The goal of this chapter is to consider the research issues that are important in evaluating the proliferating literature in the area of sex differences. Some of the issues are relevant to evaluating research claims in any area; others are unique to research about sex differences. The issues range from the basic assumptions underlying hypothesis testing to methods of integrating results across multiple studies. Readers with little or no background in statistical and research methods may have difficulty grasping some of the more technical explanations in this chapter; however, the general principles should be easily understandable to all readers. Reports of the actual research on sex differences are presented in chapter 3, and research and theories designed to explain why differences exist are presented in chapters 4 through 7. As you see in these chapters, not all of the researchers have used the techniques that are identified as desirable or necessary to reach a defensible or valid conclusion. Consumers of psychological research need to understand the strengths and weaknesses of different types of research and research practices. The validity of the conclusions from any study rests on the quality of the research from which they were generated.

Why We Need Research

There are many areas of psychological inquiry in which emotions run high. When this happens, research results that support a favored point of view are greeted with enthusiasm, and those that don't are often dismissed as irrelevant, flawed, or biased or simply are ignored without any justification. In general, most people are far more distrustful and critical of research when it yields results that they don't like than those times when research results support conclusions that they believe to be true. Scarr (1997) made this point in her discussion of the public's response to a series of eight studies on the effects of working mothers on their children. Like many of the topics discussed in this book, most people have strong feelings about the effects of maternal employment on children. How can we know, as a general principle, if having a working mother harms (or helps) a child, holding other variables like parenting styles, involvement with children, and socioeconomic status constant? This is a difficult question to answer, and it is only through multiple large-scale studies with many different children and family situations that an answer about maternal employment can be obtained. None of the eight studies that Scarr reviewed found any evidence for the generally accepted conclusion that infants suffer negative consequences when their mothers are employed outside of the home. When Scarr appeared on National Public Radio to discuss these findings, her adversary made an emotional appeal in which she said that she felt the pain of the infants whose mothers went to work all day and that she would be their voice. The audience was apparently swayed by this eloquent and moving appeal; many agreed that the opinion of this single speaker was as valid as the results obtained from hundreds of infants in eight separate studies. Like many of the topics addressed in this book, the question of whether maternal employment has negative effects on young children is controversial and important. How can we find the best answer to important, complex questions, for which "best" is defined as the answer that most closely captures reality? Should we rely on anecdotes and gut feelings, or should we rely on the findings from multiple studies with careful controls?

Readers need to appreciate the critical importance of high-quality research in answering complex questions, but they also need to be able to distinguish good research from shoddy research and valid conclusions that are supported by data from those that are not. Most readers are eager to "get to the heart" of the matter and read the conclusions that researchers have obtained, but the conclusions are only as good as the research that generated them, and for this reason, our quest to understand when, where, why, how, and how much males and females differ and are similar begins with an overview of research and statistical methods.

A number of years ago, I had a conversation about the nature of sex differences with a member of an Eastern fundamentalist religion. There were no unresolved questions for him. One of the tenets of his religion was that women are best suited for home and child care whereas men are best suited for the intellectual and physical work needed to support a family. For him, any research on this question would have been superfluous because the answers were God given. Of course, not everyone shares his religious beliefs. I later learned that some members of his religious sect doubt his interpretation of the religious principles. For most of us, the many questions pertaining to sex differences require an empirical test; they are not taken on faith. An empirical test requires collecting information in as unbiased a manner as possible and then carefully scrutinizing it in accord with the rules of evidence to determine what, if any, conclusions can be drawn. Research methods provide the tools for understanding the relationships between variables, in this case, between sex and cognitive or intellectual abilities. The experimental method is a potentially objective method that allows researchers to confirm or disconfirm their hypotheses or beliefs. I have described the experimental method as "potentially objective" because it is impossible for research ever to be totally objective. The very questions in which researchers are interested and the way in which they construct hypotheses and decide what variables to measure are contaminated by their beliefs, prejudices, and societal values. We all view controversial issues from our own point of view, so it should be no surprise that we often do not "see" the same issues or pose the same problems. The hostile and politically charged climate surrounding sex differences research has called into question the possibility of ever obtaining bias-free research. Although many people are distrustful of research results and, as discussed in chapter 1, research is certainly not value-free, the scientific method is still the most objective, unbiased, and systematic approach available for finding answers to questions. As a way of knowing, the scientific method is much less biased than any alternative method for understanding the relationships between variables in the social or physical world.

There are several different ways of conducting research, each of which has advantages and disadvantages. Let's consider how various research methods can influence the type of information they yield.

TYPES OF RESEARCH INVESTIGATIONS

There are many different ways of collecting data that relate to research questions. Although we expect to find converging evidence for conclusions using data generated with different methods, the method sometimes influences the results and conclusions in unexpected ways.

Anecdotal Evidence and Surveys

Most people have strong beliefs about sex differences. Stop and ask almost anyone about sex differences with regard to a specific ability—math, for example—and you're likely to get an answer like this one: "Of course, boys are better than girls in math. Both my sons did well in math, but my daughter just hated it." (Notice that this answer switched from performance in mathematics to attitudes toward mathematics.) Or, you might get an answer like this one: "Personally, I think that women are better at math than men. My husband always depends on me to balance the checkbook." There is a tendency for people to rely on and to prefer personal anecdotal answers to questions instead of general ones derived from large samples. This preference reflects a well-documented bias in favor of using one's own experiences in understanding human behavior (Dawes, 1994; Gilovich, 1991; Holland, Holyoak, Nisbett, & Thagard, 1986). Many people find a single anecdotal example more persuasive than a series of well-documented research findings. The tendency to rely on a single example to formulate general laws about human behavior is called the "I know a person who" phenomenon. This is a strong, pervasive, and seriously flawed way of understanding behavior. Unfortunately, research statistics are faceless and bland and are no match for the personally relevant experiences of each individual.

> If you doubt the powerful influence of single examples, try this miniexperiment: Tell several people that the recent winner of a prestigious mathematics contest (make up a serious-sounding name for the competition, like the Mathematics Scholars Program) was a 10th-grade girl. Tell them also that numerous researchers have found that high school boys outscore high school girls on tests of mathematical ability. Now, ask them if the fact that a female won a prestigious contest in mathematics weakens the conclusions from the research studies. You'll find that many people, especially those who are not familiar with the research method, are willing to discount the results from numerous studies because of a single example that is contrary to the research results.

There are many problems with anecdotal answers or conclusions that are based on a single example. First, our own experiences and those of our friends and families may not be typical of people in general. We may be generalizing to all or most males and females from atypical observations. Second, they are biased in predictable ways. Our memories are fallible and may be influenced by our beliefs and expectations. There is a wealth of evidence in the social psychological literature that shows that stereotypes are difficult to disconfirm because we select and remember information from our environment that is constant with our beliefs (e.g., Halpern, 1985). Third, anecdotal evidence lacks precision. You might remember that your brother got higher grades in mathematics than you did, but you might not remember how much higher. Most important, such evidence can rarely be used to determine cause. Did your sister perform poorly because she lacked ability or because she was discouraged from performing well? Despite the typical reliance on personal experience to formulate general laws of human behavior, only systematic investigations of large samples of data that are representative of the population we want to know about (in this case, all men and all women) can provide answers to questions relating to sex differences.

Carefully controlled research also is needed because of the human tendency to reject results that are not in accord with our belief biases. Consider a letter to the editor that appeared in *The Chronicle of Higher Education*. The letter was written by an assistant professor of physics in response to an article about sex differences in spatial skills. Asaro (1990) wrote that the notion that men have better spatial skills than women is "another of the erroneous stereotypes" (p. B4). You should be wondering, "What is the strength and nature of the evidence that supports Asaro's conclusion?" The only evidence given by Asaro was that she observed no sex-related discrepancies in spatial abilities in her personal experience. An "alarm" should go off in your head every time someone offers a conclusion about all women and men based solely on his or her personal experience. Anecdotes and case studies can be a rich source of ideas for future, better controlled research, but without the strength of well-designed studies, they are more likely to reflect personal biases and predilections than reliable findings that can be generalized to the broader population.

Another weak type of evidence for understanding the nature of sex differences comes from survey data. Surveys can take many forms. Sometimes, surveys ask what skilled activities you perform well or poorly. If more women than men were to report that they write poetry well, would you be willing to consider this finding as support for the notion that women have better poetry or language skills than men? I hope not, because differences in self-reports may not reflect differences in actual abilities. The unreliability of self-report data is well established across many fields of study. It is possible that more women report that they write poetry well because it is a more socially acceptable trait for women. It is possible that comparable numbers of men also write poetry equally well but they are unwilling to admit it.

Sometimes, surveys involve simple head counts of the number of women and men in a selected category. For example, virtually every such survey finds that there are many more men than women in math-related occupations such as accounting, mathematics, and physics. Head-count surveys may provide interesting information about "how many" and "how much," but they can never tell us why each sex has disproportionate representation in certain occupations. Are there more male mathematicians because men have greater mathematical ability or because it is more difficult in our society for women to gain access to these occupations? Although anecdotes and surveys may seem intuitively appealing, they are limited in the type of research question for which they can provide answers.

However, like anecdotes and case studies, one advantage of surveys is that the results can be used to suggest topics for future research. Fennema and Sherman (1977, 1978), for example, began an extensive series of studies by conducting surveys on attitudes toward mathematics among high school girls and boys. They found that girls perceived mathematics to be less useful than boys did and, in general, maintained less favorable attitudes toward the study of advanced mathematics. Numerous researchers used these results as a springboard for further studies. Sherman (1980), for example, found that among equally able girls, perceived usefulness of mathematics and confidence in learning mathematics were significant factors in determining their enrollment in mathematics courses.

Correlational Approaches With Nonrandom Assignment of Participants

In a correlational approach, the relationship between two or more variables is examined. Suppose, for example, that you read a newspaper report on the relationship between marijuana use and scholastic aptitude that argued that marijuana has a deleterious effect on scholastic aptitude on the basis of the finding that Scholastic

Assessment Test (SAT) scores declined during the years that marijuana was in heaviest use and SAT scores increased when marijuana use declined. This argument is based on the negative relationship between SAT scores and marijuana use; when marijuana use increased, SAT scores declined, and when marijuana use decreased, SAT scores increased. Let's suppose that the data in support of this claim are correct. Can you find anything wrong with this line of reasoning? What is missing is the causal link. It is incorrect to infer that marijuana use was responsible for the rise and fall in SAT scores. It is possible that a third variable, for example, changes in the economy, was responsible for the increase in marijuana use and the decrease in SAT scores. (Perhaps when the economy is tight, students take school more seriously and have less money to spend on drugs, with the reverse pattern occurring in a booming economy.) It is also possible that changes in SAT scores caused the changes in marijuana use. Maybe when students perform poorly on the SAT, they smoke more marijuana, and as their scores improve, they smoke less marijuana.

The problem being raised here is commonly known as "causal arrow ambiguity." The coincidence of changes in two variables does not provide support for the notion that one variable is responsible for the concomitant changes in the second variable. To determine if marijuana smoking caused changes in SAT scores, students would have to be assigned at random either to smoke or not to smoke marijuana for a predetermined period of time. If we found that the group who smoked marijuana scored, on average, significantly lower on the SAT than the group that didn't smoke marijuana, then we could conclude that marijuana smoking is deleterious to SAT performance. Unless participants are randomly assigned to conditions, it is likely that students who voluntarily smoke marijuana differ in many ways from those who don't (e.g., differences in socioeconomic status, attitudes toward illegal drugs, parental control). It is possible that any or all of the other differences are responsible for the decline and subsequent increase in SAT scores.

Most of the research on sex differences does not use the random assignment of participants to conditions because it usually is not possible to intervene in people's lives and change their life experiences. Sex differences research often involves studying males and females the way they are, that is, without experimental manipulations. For example, suppose an investigator reports that the ability to visualize objects in space is positively correlated with the amount of male hormones present during prenatal development. Such a result constitutes only weak evidence for the hypothesis that the prenatal concentration of male hormones causes good visual–spatial ability because of the problem of causal arrow ambiguity. It is possible that many children with high levels of prenatal male hormones also have different home environments or different socioeconomic backgrounds than children with low levels of prenatal male hormones. Or, more likely, males not only have prenatal male hormones but also have life experiences that encourage the development of spatial skills. How can we determine if it is the life experiences, the prenatal hormones, both, or some third unidentified variable that is responsible for the good spatial ability? Alternative explanations are possible whenever participants are not randomly assigned to experimental conditions. All research based on naturally occurring events without experimental manipulations is necessarily confounded (i.e., more than one variable changes at the same time; in this case, the biological determinants of an individual's sex vary along with sex-related life experiences) and cannot provide causal information.

Correlational data with nonrandom assignment can provide a stronger case for causation if the results are in accord with a highly plausible theory and when other sorts of data provide converging evidence for the relationship being studied. Suppose, for example, there is reason to believe that if male hormones are high during fetal development, then the neurons in the area of the brain specialized for vision show a more complex pattern of dendritic growth with more interconnections with other neurons. If this theory were true, then the finding that high concentrations of prenatal male hormones are positively correlated with the ability to visualize spatial objects would provide corroborative evidence that these hormones underlie spatial visualization abilities. This is a totally fictitious theory that I devised to make the point that research conducted with nonrandom assignment of participants in conjunction with a strong theory provide better evidence for causation than the research alone. In this case, data involving nonrandom assignment of participants would serve to corroborate other empirical sources of support for the theory. In fact, any report of sex differences without a theoretical underpinning to explain why the sex differences occurred should be viewed with skepticism. Like survey results, serendipitous findings can be valuable if they are used as an impetus for additional research and if they can be incorporated in a testable theory.

All research results are necessarily probabilistic, which means that sometimes sex differences occur in experiments by chance. If all of the human research conducted included a test for sex differences, many spurious reports of sex differences would clutter the literature. It is prudent to consider any atheoretical reports of sex differences as chance findings until they are replicated and cast in a theoretical framework.

If correlational data can be used to support a "highly plausible theory," the problem remains of determining what makes a theory "highly plausible." The mere existence of a theory is not sufficient. A theory needs to be supported empirically with research conducted in multiple settings, using different samples of participants, and different measurement techniques before it gains the status of *highly plausible*. It also needs to fit within an existing framework of facts and beliefs. There are many theories about sex differences in male and female brains, for example. Yet, these theories are surprisingly mute on the mechanisms that underlie these differences. Like the proverbial chain, a theoretical network is only as strong as its weakest link. A strong theory can explain and predict the causes, correlates, and consequences of cognitive sex differences.

Observational Techniques

With observational techniques, researchers literally look at behaviors, usually in real-world situations. Suppose that you were interested in knowing if young girls really differ from young boys with respect to aggression. You could observe the playground behavior of young children, keeping a tally of the number of aggressive acts committed by boys and girls. One of the advantages of this technique is that you would be actually observing real behavior rather than relying on some secondary technique like asking girls and boys about how aggressive they are. However, this technique has many of the same problems associated with it as those noted in previous sections. Even if you found that boys (or girls) committed more aggressive acts, observation can never provide an answer as to why these sex differences occur. There are also other drawbacks to this technique. Observations are never really objective because we tend to see what we expect to see. If a girl pushes a child on the playground, it may appear less aggressive to an experimenter than when the same push is done by a boy. It is also likely that children behave differently if they know that they are being observed. Thus, by observing the behavior, the researcher may actually have changed it. The choice of where to observe behavior also becomes important. A researcher may find sex differences on the playground but not in the classroom or on the soccer field because much of our behavior is context-dependent.

True Experiments and Quasi-Experiments

Most researchers consider the experiment as the method of choice for determining cause. In a "true" experiment, the researcher has greater control over the variables because participants are assigned at random to experimental and control groups. Consider the hypothetical example (given earlier) of the relationship between prenatal hormones and spatial visualization ability. In a true experiment, the researcher would select the participants, in this case female and male fetuses, assign them at random to either high-hormone or low-hormone conditions by administering drugs to their mothers, measure their spatial visualization abilities later in life, and examine the neural structures in the part of the brain that is presumably affected by the hormones. The underlying assumption is that large groups of participants selected at random are more or less equivalent with respect to the variable of interest, in this case spatial visualization ability. If we systematically vary only one aspect of their lives (prenatal hormones) so that overall the two or more groups differ only in this way, we can attribute any major differences between groups to this "treatment." Presumably, there would be rich and poor, smart and dull, and tall and short children of each sex in each group, but the only consistent between-groups difference would be the nature of the variable the researcher has manipulated.

The major difference between a true experiment and the correlational approach discussed earlier is the random assignment of participants to manipulated conditions. Random assignment allows the experimenter to control the variable of interest so that any systematic differences between the groups are attributable to the manipulated variable. The underlying rationale is that people differ from each other in many ways. If we assign people to different treatment groups at random, then preexisting group differences would be unlikely because people of all sorts should be found in each of the groups. It then becomes more likely that any difference between the groups is due to the treatment. Thus, only a true experiment that randomly assigns participants to conditions allows the experimenter to infer cause.

Very few true experiments with humans are ever conducted in the area of sex differences. Obviously, we cannot vary the concentration of selected hormones that certain fetuses are exposed to before birth. Such interventions would be unethical and unconscionable. Instead, we must take people "as they come" and lose the control that is needed to understand causal links. A paradox in sex differences research is that the major variable of interest—being female or male—is never assigned at random. If we find that women perform a task, on average, better or worse than men, we still can't answer the question, "Why?" There are many variables that covary (or go along) with biological indicators of sex in our society, such as hormone concentrations, social expectations, power, status, childbirth experiences, and learning histories, to name a few. Given that so many variables are confounded with sex and that sex is never randomly assigned, causal attributions for any between-sex difference are difficult to support. This is an important point because all sex differences research with humans is basically correlational in nature; true experiments are conducted only with nonhuman mammals and other animals. Researchers can never be certain if any between-sex differences are due to the biological aspects of sex, psychosocial concomitants of sex, the interaction between them, or some unidentified factor.

Because participants can never be assigned at random in sex differences research, a somewhat less stringent procedure for examining cause is sometimes used. Quasi-experiments, like true experiments, involve some sort of experimental manipulation, but do not randomly assign participants to groups. An example of a quasi-experiment might be to provide an educational or counseling program to a group of females who score poorly on mathematics tests in order to reduce "math anxiety." In interpreting the results, the experimenters would determine if the girls scored significantly higher on the test of mathematics ability after they received counseling to reduce their math anxiety. Research of this sort must also include a control group, in this case a group of females who score low in mathematics but do not receive the counseling, so that meaningful comparisons can be made. An experimental design of this sort involves a manipulation (the counseling to reduce math anxiety), but the participants were already identified as females who score low on tests of mathematics. This experimental design allows the researcher to examine causality (math anxiety possibly caused the low mathematics scores) but does not permit strong causal statements.

The fact that biological sex creates very different environments for males and females from the moment of birth means that differences in biological sex are always associated with different environmental experiences. Distinguishing between nature and nurture as the more probable cause of sex differences is so difficult because of the confounding of nature and nurture. This is particularly germane to the controversies surrounding cognitive abilities. I return to this theme in several places throughout this book because it is critical in understanding the etiology or origin of sex differences.

Comparisons of Research Methods.   Hendricks, Marvel, and Barrington (1990) suggested a "methodological cube" for summarizing the differences among research designs. Their cube is shown in Fig. 2.1. As you can see in this figure, descriptive, correlational, quasi-experimental, and true experimental designs differ in the kind of information they provide. Research designs also vary as a function of setting (laboratory or field) and the way the data are collected (observation or self-report). These three dimensions form the axes or edges of the cube. As you read about the research that is described in the following chapters, keep these variables in mind because they determine the kinds of inferences that we can make from the data.

Factor Analytic Approaches

Traditionally, a common method of studying human cognitive or intellectual abilities has been the factor analytic approach (e.g., Thurstone & Thurstone, 1941).

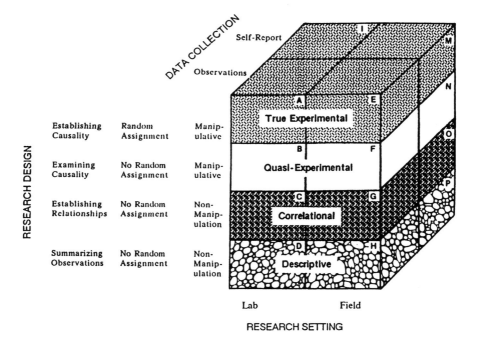

FIG. 2.1.   Methodological cube of group research methods. From B. Hendricks, M. K. Marvel, & B. L. Barrington, 1990, *Teaching of Psychology, 17,* p. 79. Copyright 1990 by Lawrence Erlbaum Associates, Publishers. Reprinted with permission.

The underlying rationale for this approach is that cognition is not a single homogeneous concept. Most psychologists believe that there are several cognitive abilities and that individuals can be skilled or unskilled in one, some, or all of them. Although there is an intense debate among psychologists over the question of whether all of these abilities are related to a single intelligence factor (Brody, 1992), one of the most common theoretical distinctions is between verbal and spatial abilities.

One way to test hypotheses about sex differences in factor structures is to give a large number of women and men several tests of verbal abilities (e.g., vocabulary comprehension, verbal analogies) and spatial abilities (e.g., using maps, solving jigsaw puzzles). If these four tests are really measures of two different abilities, then through the statistical technique known as factor analysis, two factors or underlying dimensions will result from the data analysis. The first factor, which we believe represents verbal ability, will be created from the vocabulary comprehension and verbal analogies test scores, and the second factor, which we believe represents spatial ability, will be created from the using maps and solving jigsaw puzzles test scores. (The actual mathematical principles and procedures involved are not germane to the purpose of this discussion and, therefore, are not described. The interested reader is referred to Tabachnick & Fidell, 1996, for a lucid discussion.) If we obtained the same two factors for both our sample of women and our sample of men, then we would conclude that women's and men's cognitive abilities have similar factor analytic structures. Suppose, by contrast, that we found that only one factor emerged for our sample of women. This would mean that these four tests had a single underlying dimension for women. (Another way of thinking about this hypothetical result is that all four tests were measuring the same unitary construct.) If our sample of men yielded two factors from these tests and our sample of women yielded only one factor, then we would conclude that there are sex differences in cognitive processes.

Only a handful of studies have actually used factor analytic techniques to compare the cognitive structures of men and women. This is an important approach because it poses the more fundamental question of sex differences in the organization and structure of cognitive abilities as opposed to asking which sex is better at a given ability. For this reason, it's a good technique for examining differences.

VALIDITY, FAIRNESS, AND BIAS

Many of the studies that are reviewed in later chapters in this book are based on comparisons of average test scores for males and females. Throughout our lives, but especially during the school years, we take many tests. Some of these tests are "high stakes," that is, they are the basis for decisions that affect lives—who gets into college or professional school, who graduates, or who gets a job or a promotion. For most of the high stakes tests, there are multiple group differences, or "on average" differences—differences that vary as a function of sex, racial or ethnic group, socioeconomic status, major in college, and geographic region, among others (Willingham & Cole, 1997). Does the fact that there are group differences mean that the tests are biased? Increasingly, this question is being asked in the courts and in state and federal legislatures. The stakes are high, and there are "winners" and "losers" in the sorting process, so it is not surprising that many of those involved are highly critical of society's reliance on any standardized testing that shows group differences.

Questions about bias and its flip side, fairness, depend on how these terms are defined and how test scores are used. Fairness is a statistical concept and a matter of societal values, and frequently these two types of fairness are at odds with each other. In general, tests are used for two purposes: to assess past learning and to predict the future. Standardized college entrance examinations, such as the SAT and the American College Test, measure the level of ability that has been developed up to the time the test is taken (Hunter & Schmidt, 1996), and on the basis of this index of prior learning, predications are made about probable success in future learning tasks. This is one type of validity, called *predictive validity*. For statisticians, psychometricians (people who measure psychological constructs like intelligence or personality), and other sorts of testing experts, a measure is fair or free from bias if it predicts success on some criterion variable equally well for people from different groups (Halpern, 1996b). Thus, if a test were designed to predict success in college, and "success in college" were measured as grade point average, a fair test would predict college grade point average with the same degree of accuracy for all groups. On the basis of this definition, we would conclude that such a test is fair or unbiased because it has approximately equal predictive validity for all groups (Brody, 1992).

Although fairness and bias are abstract statistical concepts, in reality they have a very different meaning to those who are not testing experts. For the general public, bias and fairness are tied to concrete circumstances. In general, selection tests seem unfair to those who are not admitted to a desirable program or who are denied a good job, and they seem fair to those who "get in." Studies have shown that judgments about the fairness of affirmative action policies vary depending on whether one's own group is going to obtain the benefit of the affirmative action (Graves & Powell, 1994). Perceptions about the fairness of selection tests often lie in the special interests of the beholder. For this reason, Messick (1995) urged that we consider the social consequences of a test along with other validity and fairness-related issues.

UNDERSTANDING RESEARCH RESULTS

Scientific inquiry is a voyage of discovery toward a horizon, beyond which yet another horizon beckons.
—Myers (1998, p. 29)

Many of the questions pertaining to sex differences and similarities relate to the general principles of the scientific method. A firm foundation in the underlying assumptions of and rules for scientific inquiry is a necessary prerequisite for a critical analysis of the research literature.

The Logic of Hypothesis Testing

A researcher searching for sex differences is really considering two mutually exclusive hypotheses. The first hypothesis is that there are no differences in the overall population between males and females with respect to the variable being studied and, therefore, any differences found between the two samples are due to random error or chance differences in the samples selected. This hypothesis is called the *null hypothesis*. The competing or alternative hypothesis is that there really are differences in the population between women and men and these differences are reflected in the sample of males and females that is being studied. The researcher uses statistical tests to decide if any between-group differences are likely to have occurred by chance. If the tests show that the differences between the samples of women and men probably are not due to chance factors, then the experimenter can reject the null hypothesis and accept the alternative hypothesis. Thus, we formulate conclusions in a somewhat backward fashion. We conclude that the alternative hypothesis is probably true by deciding that the null hypothesis is probably false. In hypothesis testing, demonstrations of sex differences rely on a clear-cut set of procedures that involve deciding that the null hypothesis (the one that states that there are no sex differences) is probably wrong, and therefore the competing hypothesis that sex differences exist is tentatively considered to be more correct.

The Problem of Null Results

What about failures to reject the null hypothesis? Any serious researcher in the field of sex differences is also concerned about similarities. How can she or he conclude that there are no sex differences? This is a much more difficult problem and one that is particularly troublesome for research in the area of sex differences. Unfortunately, we can never accept the null hypothesis. The best we can do is fail to reject it. The strongest statement that can be made from failures to reject the null hypothesis is that the data don't support the notion that sex differences exist. We cannot conclude that differences don't exist. There are two reasons why failures to find differences can't lead to the conclusion that there are no differences: statistical (the alternative hypothesis is not precise enough to permit the computation of the probabilities needed to reject it) and logical. (A more detailed explanation of the statistical reasons is beyond the scope of this book. Readers who have not had a course in statistics or experimental methods have to take it on faith that there are mathematical reasons why claims of no sex differences can't be accepted statistically. Interested readers are referred to Cohen and Cohen, 1983, and Howell, 1992.)

Consider a simple example that should help to clarify this point. Suppose you formulate the hypothesis that girls are better than boys at spelling. In this case, the null hypothesis is the one that predicts that there is no difference between boys and girls in their ability to spell. To test this hypothesis, you could collect the spelling tests from a third-grade class and tally the number of words spelled correctly, on average, by the girls and by the boys in this class on this test. You could then conduct a statistical test to determine if the results you obtained are unlikely to have happened by chance. Researchers usually set a chance criterion at 5%. If the results would occur by chance less than 5% of the time when the null hypothesis is true (i.e., there really is no difference in the spelling skills of the boys and girls), then you would reject the null hypothesis and conclude that something other than chance is happening and there really are differences between the sexes in their ability to spell correctly.

What if the statistical test showed that you could not reject the null hypothesis? You could not then conclude that there really are no differences in spelling ability between the boys and girls. It could be that these differences don't show up on spelling tests when the words were just studied but would show up on other measures of spelling, or that the test was too easy or too hard to show differences (almost everyone got all of the words right or wrong, so there was so little variability that no conclusions can be made), or.... The list of possible reasons why you failed to find sex differences is virtually endless. All that you can conclude is that you failed to reject the null hypothesis, not that the null hypothesis is true. The scientific method is one reason why researchers focus more on sex differences than between-sex similarities.

It may seem that studies that don't show sex differences should "cancel" studies that do show sex differences. Assuming the studies were well conducted, those that find sex differences (positive studies) carry more weight than those that don't (negative studies) because it is always possible that the negative studies were not sensitive enough to detect a difference. Too few participants, a poor test, plain old sloppy research, or numerous other problems can lead to false negatives. Thus, in the logic of hypothesis testing, we can never directly prove a null hypothesis. We can only disprove or reject the null hypothesis (the one that states that there are no sex differences), which in turn allows us to accept a mutually exclusive alternative hypothesis (the one that states that there are sex differences). (See Rozeboom, 1960, for a classic discussion about the failure to reject the null hypothesis.)

Most sex differences researchers are as interested in discovering similarities between females and males as they are in discovering differences; yet, it is axiomatic that they can never conclude that differences don't exist. Consider an experiment conducted by Seth-Smith, Ashton, and McFarland (1989) in which they reported that there are no sex-related differences in brain organization for verbal functioning. Although their study was well designed, they used only 10 college males and 10 college females. Their sample size was too small and too restrictive (college students only) to conclude that there are no sex differences in brain organization. The strongest statement that can be made from studies like this one is that the researchers failed to find differences with the specific sample and experimental procedures that they used. We cannot use these results to conclude that there are no differences. The logic of hypothesis testing is the backbone of the experimental method, and it does not permit a similarities conclusion.

Rosenthal and Rubin (1985) distinguished between the use of the experimental method to establish facts and its use to summarize research. They argued that it is virtually impossible to establish facts with any single study. In their view, a research report is publishable "if it contributes important evidence on an important scientific question" (Rosenthal & Rubin, 1985, p. 527). I believe that their point is especially relevant to research on the nature of sex differences. Although it may not be possible to prove that sex differences in a particular area don't exist because of the strict logic of hypothesis testing, it is important to know if large numbers of researchers fail to find sex differences. If, for example, we knew that 95 out of every 100 investigations of mathematical sex differences failed to find differences, this information would certainly cause us to alter our conclusions about this area.

What about the studies that report sex differences? If half of them find that females are superior and half find that males are superior, it seems likely that experiments that report differences are "statistical errors." That is, they may have occurred just by chance. Alternatively, suppose that all of the studies that report differences find that one sex is consistently scoring higher on one type of mathematical test. This sort of evidence would suggest that the positive results are not occurring by chance and that differences may be specific to one type of test—for example, geometry—or to one subpopulation—for example, children.

There are some experimental and data analytic techniques that allow researchers to investigate similarities. Murphy (1990) suggested that if the focus of a research program is similarities, the researcher could specify a range of outcomes that would be consistent with the hypothesis that there are no differences. For example, if I wanted to show that there are no sex differences in intelligence, I could give a large sample of women and men an intelligence test. I would have to specify a priori (before the data are collected) that if the average difference between the sample of females and males is less than two points, this result would be consistent with the hypothesis that there are no sex differences. It is also important to consider the size of the difference, a very important topic that is discussed in more detail in a later section in this chapter. There are also measures of concordance or similarity that can be used to provide evidence of similarity (e.g., correlations, Cronbach's alphas, factor loadings).

The Debate Over Null-Hypothesis Significance Testing

In recent years, numerous statisticians and researchers have been engaged in a debate over the underlying principles of "null hypothesis significance testing" (Cohen, 1994; Frick, 1996; Hagen, 1997; Rosnow & Rosenthal, 1996). Part of the debate is over the idea of a null hypothesis—whether it is ever possible to have zero differences between two groups (e.g., if we were to measure the spelling ability of every girl and boy in the world, could it ever be possible that there would be absolutely no difference at all between these two groups?)—and part of the debate concerns the misuse and misunderstanding of hypothesis testing. Even if a researcher concluded that the results he or she obtained are "statistically significant" (not likely to have occurred by chance if the null hypothesis were true), this does not mean that the difference between the girls and boys was large enough to be important or meaningful. I return to this point in chapter 3, in which I present results about sex differences in overall intelligence.

Sampling Issues

There are several sampling pitfalls that are exacerbated in or unique to sex differences research. Five of these issues are considered here: comparable between-sex samples, sample size, inappropriate generalizations, age by sex interactions, and replication samples.

Comparable Between-Sex Samples.   Sex differences research is concerned with ways in which women and men, on average, differ. Although we may want to know about all women and men in North America or in the world, we can only collect data from a sample or subset of the population in which we are interested. The people we actually use in our study must be representative of the population we want to know about if our generalizations are to be accurate. Consider the issue of mathematical ability. One common approach to the question of whether males or females exceed in mathematical ability is to administer mathematical aptitude tests to males and females who have attained a given level of mathematical training. For example, a researcher might give an aptitude test to all students in a high school calculus course and then compare the scores obtained by the girls and boys. The major problem with this sample is that there may already have been considerable self-selection of participants before entry into the calculus class. If mathematical ability is possessed by more boys than girls, then the attrition rate in mathematics courses should be higher for girls than boys, with the result that fewer girls persist in mathematics courses. A study of high school calculus students would then be sampling only an extreme group of mathematically gifted or persistent girls (e.g., perhaps the top 10% of all girls) and a less extreme group of boys (e.g., perhaps the top 25% of all boys). As noted earlier, studies like this one do not permit any causal statements because the participants are not assigned at random to math classes. It is impossible to know why sex differences that might emerge from this study exist. They could be due to some factor or factors inherent in the biology of maleness or femaleness, to societal expectations, or to a host of other possibilities.

There is no single satisfactory way to resolve the problem of how to sample the sexes so that bias is eliminated. The logical alternative to sampling girls and boys with an equivalent number of mathematics courses is to sample the sexes without regard to the number or type of mathematics courses they have taken in school. The obvious disadvantage to this plan is that any differences that might be found would most likely be attributable to the differences in mathematics education.

Similar sampling issues arise with other cognitive abilities as well. One partial solution is to use statistical control in the form of partial correlations and analysis of covariance procedures. These techniques allow the experimenter to *hold constant* the effect of a variable, such as the number of mathematics courses taken by each participant. These procedures statistically allow the researcher to ask a question like, "If boys and girls had taken the same number of mathematics courses, would we still find differences in mathematical ability?" Although these statistical approaches represent an improvement in the way we find answers to sex differences questions, they are also flawed. The use of analysis of covariance, for example, requires certain mathematical properties that are rarely true of any data set (e.g., linear effects across all groups, covariate unaffected by the treatment, homogeneity of between- and within-groups regression). (Readers with an advanced background in statistics are referred to Evans & Anastasio, 1968, and Harris, Bisbee, & Evans, 1971, for classic discussions of the use and misuse of analysis of covariance.)

Statistical techniques that control for sampling differences do provide some useful information. For example, they could show that sex differences in mathematical ability tests can be explained on the basis of course taking alone. Despite these advantages, research that utilizes statistical control procedures still begs the basic question of why there are differences in mathematical achievement tests and in the number of mathematics courses taken by boys and girls. It's like asking if poor people would vote like rich people if they weren't poor. Even if the researcher found that they would, this result would be of little immediate value because the poor people are still poor and therefore will continue to vote for issues that concern the poor, despite the statistical control we've gained over our data with this technique.

Quite simply, the results obtained from any study depend on the participants who are selected for the study, among many other variables. People vary along countless dimensions—educational level, age, socioeconomic status, and motivation, to name a few. It is important to keep the nature of the sample in mind when interpreting research results.

In sex differences research, there is no easy answer to the dilemma of sampling. If you were interested in determining whether cognitive abilities vary over the menstrual cycle, who would be the appropriate comparison group? Would it be women who are not menstruating (either because they have reached menopause or because of a hysterectomy or medications that suppress the cyclical change in hormone concentrations), or would it be a group of men? Studies that have investigated the possibility that women become more aggressive during the premenstrual phase of the menstrual cycle seem to ignore the fact that men commit many more acts of aggression every day of the month.

Sample Size.   A second sampling problem in sex differences research concerns sample size or the number of participants we need to include in an experiment. In general, large samples yield good estimates of population parameters (true values in the population). One of the major factors concerning sample size is the amount of variability in the population from which the sample is drawn. If the population has little variability (i.e., there is very little spread among the scores) then a small sample will provide a good estimate of the population parameters, whereas a population with considerable variability (i.e., scores are spread out and do not cluster tightly around a mean value) will require a larger sample size to obtain stable estimates of its parameters. One theory in the sex differences literature is that male performance is more variable than female performance. (This hypothesis is discussed in more detail in chap. 3.) If this hypothesis were true, then we would have to sample more males than females to obtain the same level of confidence in our statistics. This is virtually never done in practice, nor have I ever seen it addressed as a sampling issue.

The number of participants selected for a study has important implications for the conclusions we can draw. Although large samples are desirable because they yield good estimates of population parameters, they also virtually ensure that statistically significant sex differences will be found. For mathematical reasons, small samples are less likely to provide evidence of sex differences than large ones. Many of the studies that fail to find differences use a small number of participants. The experimenter who is honestly seeking answers to sex differences questions has to be concerned with sample size. Far too frequently, the issue of sample size is ignored or resolved on the basis of a hunch or intuition. Ideally, all sex differences research (and other research) should begin with an estimate of the size of the sex difference effect that would be important to detect. For example, a researcher studying sex differences in intelligence might decide that a sex difference of less than two IQ points would not be important in understanding differences in cognition. The two-point difference would then be converted into an "effect size" (discussed in more detail later in this chapter). It is then a simple procedure to solve a mathematical equation for determining how many participants should be included in the experiment. Details of this procedure are presented in most standard statistical texts (Cohen & Cohen, 1983; Howell, 1992). Unfortunately, this method of determining sample size is rarely used.

Sample size is a critical variable in determining whether the results of a study will show statistically significant differences between males and females. In general, a small sample will make it less likely that an experimenter will obtain statistically significant results, and a large sample makes it more likely that an experimenter will obtain statistically significant results. It is important to keep this mind when you review the experimental literature. The fact that statistical significance depends so heavily on sample size is one reason why there seems to be so many contradictions in the research literature.

Inappropriate Generalizations.   A third issue in sampling concerns the use of atypical populations. Very frequently, researchers sample from abnormal populations to formulate conclusions about normal women and men. This approach is most commonly used in research that examines the effects of chromosomes and hormones on the cognitive abilities of normal women and men. The reasoning behind this approach is that by examining what happens when something goes wrong (e.g., the effect of extremely high concentrations of male hormones on developing fetuses), we can understand the role of the variable being investigated under normal circumstances (e.g., the effect of normal levels of male hormones on developing fetuses). There is an obvious flaw in this approach. First, abnormal populations differ from normal populations in many ways. An infant exposed to abnormal concentrations of prenatal hormones may develop a masculine body type or may receive specialized medical care or unusual treatment by family members. The secondary effects of the hormone anomaly may affect the variable under investigation, and these effects could be mistakenly attributed to the hormone rather than the experiential factor. Thus, it is not possible to isolate the influence of hormones per se. In addition, abnormal hormone levels (or chromosome patterns or any other variable that is atypical) may have effects that are unrelated to the effect of normal hormone levels (or chromosome patterns). Research with abnormal populations can provide supporting or confirming evidence for a hypothesis but cannot be used as the primary support for a hypothesis.

Researchers concerned about understanding human sex differences often conduct their research with other animal species. The major difficulty is generalizing from rats or monkeys to humans. We know that hormones, for example, play a greater role in the behavior of nonhuman species than they do in humans, whereas cognitive and social variables are more important in determining human behavior. Generalizing from animal research to humans is also difficult because contradictory results are obtained with different species and different breeds within a species. Thus, although animal research can provide information that is interesting in its own right, extreme caution is urged when extrapolating the results to humans. For example, Janowsky (1989) studied the brain mechanisms that underlie song behavior in canaries. Male canaries, but not females, exhibit a complex learned song behavior. When researchers administer testosterone (a male hormone) to female canaries, female canaries develop the song behavior of male canaries. Research of this sort suggests that testosterone plays an important role in the development of canary song behavior. We cannot use this sort of data to conclude that testosterone is important in human verbal behavior because there are too many differences between human and bird brains and between canary songs and human verbal behavior. Nevertheless, this research is not useless. It does suggest that, at least for some animals, testosterone plays a role in vocalization. Like research with abnormal human populations, research with nonhuman animals can provide supplemental support for relevant hypotheses and can suggest new areas of research, but it cannot support a hypothesis without more relevant evidence.

Age by Sex Interactions.   Another issue in selecting participants is age. It is likely that some sex differences change over the life span and in different ways for each sex. A difference may be nonexistent in childhood, emerge during puberty, and disappear again in old age. Some abilities decline at different rates for elderly men and women. The answers we find to sex differences questions are age-dependent. Research that utilizes only young adults in college (the favorite participant pool of academics) will undoubtedly fail to capture the age-dependent nature of any differences that exist.

Age is a complex variable because it is confounded with cohort variables. A 75-year-old woman spent her young adult years during the horrors of World War II and may have received very little formal education, and if she drives a car, she probably learned later in life than most 75-year-old men. If we were to find that older women are less able to read maps than an age-matched group of older men, it would be difficult to disentangle the effect of sex from the effects of aging, a lifetime of sex-differentiated experiences, and systematic differences in formal education.

In general, researchers have tended to ignore the developmental nature of adult age differences in cognition. Overwhelmingly, college students have been used as participants in cognitive research. Thus, we also know very little about sex differences in cognition for the majority of the population who never attended college (e.g., most waiters and waitresses, truck drivers, barbers, manicurists, janitors, salesclerks). Because our cognitive abilities do not remain static throughout the life span, generalizations about sex differences that may be true at adolescence or young adulthood may be false for midlife or older adults. The elderly remain one of the most understudied populations for cognitive sex differences, despite the fact that understanding sex-related developmental differences is crucial in an aging society and the proportion of the population that is elderly is increasing at a rapid rate.

Replication Samples.   Because all research is necessarily probabilistic, spurious reports of sex differences sometimes are found in the literature. The ultimate test of whether a report of a sex difference is real is whether it is replicated (i.e., it reliably appears) in other experiments. Good researchers are aware of this test and plan replications of their own work before they publish sex differences results. A replication sample is a second or third sample of participants who are similar to those used in an original study. These participants receive essentially the same treatment (if there is one) and have the same measurements taken as those in the original sample. If sex differences are also found in the second or third sample, then we can accept the results with greater confidence than if they were found in only one sample. Although replication samples are always a good idea, they are especially important in research that doesn't use the random assignment of participants to conditions, because research of this sort provides weaker evidence than true experiments. Unfortunately, few reports of sex differences are based on research with replication samples. Later in this book, I describe in detail a research report by Harshman, Hampson, and Berenbaum (1983) that I consider to be pivotal in determining the involvement of biological variables. One of the strengths of their study is the use of three separate samples, which means that we can be more confident that the results were not due to chance factors than we would be if only one sample had been used.

Copyright Richard Cline (1985).

Measurement

Measurement is defined as the assignment of numbers according to rules. The way we measure or assign numbers directly influences the kinds of results we obtain. One of the major measurement issues with which sex differences researchers need to be concerned is how sex should be measured. This may seem like a surprising question if you are not familiar with the problem. Usually, sex is measured as a dichotomous (two-choice) variable with every participant being either male or female. However, there are many times when it is desirable to measure the degree of maleness or femaleness. For most of us, the usual indicators of sex are in agreement. Our chromosomes, hormones, genitals, gonads, sex of rearing, and self-definitions all agree that we are either male or female. However, this is not always true. Consider the anomalous case in which chromosomes may indicate maleness but genitals and sex of rearing are female. Is this person somehow "less male" and "less female" than the typical male and female?

Part of the measurement problem is that it is not always clear what researchers mean by *sex*. Although I have decided not to make this distinction, sometimes *sex* is used to refer to biological differences, with the term *gender* used to refer to the social construction of sex. The components of biological sex are usually, but not always, consistent, but gender identity, sexual preference, and gender role are often inconsistent with each other and with biological sex. These variations of sex make it difficult to think of sex as a single variable.

A more common dilemma with regard to dichotomous versus continuous measurement concerns sex role orientation. This concept refers to the extent to which an individual's behavior conforms to the female or male sex role as defined in a given society. That is, does one conform to sex-typed expectations or stereotypes? The question of whether sex role orientation should be dichotomous (i.e., men and women could be either masculine or feminine in sex role orientation) or discrete with three or four possibilities (masculine, feminine, androgynous, or undifferentiated) or continuous (more or less masculine or feminine) has been the subject of heated debate. Humphreys (1978) argued that masculinity–femininity requires continuous measurement, and Baucom and Welsh (1978) argued that dichotomous (extreme groups) level of measurement is appropriate. Continuous measurement generally provides more information and may be preferred when measuring other variables like handedness, in which one can be more or less right- or left-handed instead of dichotomously right- or left-handed. However, both types of measurement are useful in assessing sex differences. It may be that the extremely masculine individual is qualitatively, not just quantitatively, different from a feminine individual. It seems that both dichotomous and continuous measurement can be used depending on the nature of the question being asked. (For a lucid discussion of this topic, see Matlin, 1996.)

Date of Publication and Sex of Researcher

You may be wondering what the date of publication or sex of researcher has to do with understanding the results of research. The effects of these extraneous variables are indirect. Several experimenters have investigated the possibility that sex differences are diminishing over time. One way to do this is to find out if results that were published in the 1940s showed larger sex differences than those published in the 1950s and so on. Although it is logical to assume that researchers would report smaller and smaller sex differences over time if the size of the difference is diminishing, there is a major problem with this line of reasoning. There are many changes that occur with time. For example, if we were to measure reading ability among college freshmen over the past 50 years, we would have to consider the fact that the nature of college freshmen has changed in numerous ways. Fifty years ago, it was fairly unusual for females to enroll in college; those who made it into college were more likely from wealthy homes or were exceptionally intelligent or persistent. This is not true today. Over half of all first-year college students are female, so the group of females who are in college today is different in many ways from female college students 50 years ago. Research that has used date of publication to argue that sex differences are decreasing or increasing is considered in detail in chapter 3.

Sex of researcher is an even more subtle variable than date of publication. The reason that some people think that the sex of the researcher is important in understanding results is because there are numerous ways, both deliberate and unintentional, in which investigators bias the outcomes of their research. If we were to assume that more women are feminists than men, then we might expect that women researchers are more likely to provide results that are consistent with feminist philosophies than men who conduct similar research. We all interpret the world in terms of our own backgrounds and experiences. This does not mean that all research is biased or that we cannot keep an open mind and evaluate findings in a fair manner, only that we need to consider the ways in which personal beliefs can bias the outcomes of research. Hyde and Linn (1988), for example, found that female researchers were more likely to find evidence of female superiority in verbal abilities than male researchers. In an ideal world, sex of researcher would be an irrelevant variable.

Moderating and Situational Variables

We all are social creatures. The way we respond in any situation depends much more on environmental factors than individual factors. If you are sitting in a college classroom, shopping in a supermarket, or getting up in the morning, I can predict what you are doing with pretty good accuracy without knowing anything about you. Situational variables are extremely potent in determining behaviors. Researchers frequently study sex differences by controlling all variables other than sex of the participant. Suppose you wanted to study nurturing behavior to decide if females are more nurturant than males. Eagly (1987) pointed out that research conducted in carefully controlled laboratory settings often finds that there are no sex differences in nurturance. But, if the same researchers were to investigate nurturing behavior in more natural settings (caring for sick children, assisting the elderly), they would find that women occupy more of the nurturing roles in society. Thus, setting is a salient part of any research report.

It is important to keep in mind that all behavior occurs in a context. Almost everyone would agree that people often respond in different ways in different situations. This may be especially true of sex-related differences. Suppose, for example, that you are interested in sex differences in assertive behavior. Furthermore, you are aware that results obtained in laboratory settings may not generalize to the real world. So, you decide to examine assertiveness in a public place. In addition, suppose that you chose to study sex differences in assertiveness at the movies. You carefully note that in mixed-sex dyads (pairs in which one member is female and the other member is male), the male usually drives to the movies, purchases the movie tickets, hands them to the ticket taker, and yes, even makes the important popcorn decisions (buttered or unbuttered). On the basis of this naturalistic observation, you would conclude that males are more assertive than females. However, you would have failed to study other situations in which women tend to be assertive, such as dealing with a child's angry teacher, returning defective merchandise, handling an emergency at the office, or negotiating the sale of a residence as a real estate broker. You probably recognize each of these scenarios as stereotypically female; yet, you may never have realized that each requires assertiveness, a stereotypically male trait.

Experiments conducted in laboratory settings often involve artificial situations. Because so much of our behavior is situation-dependent, it is important to consider ways in which the experimental situation may bias the results. This is an important point in understanding sex-related cognitive differences. Men, for example, may not perform as well on tasks that are viewed in our society as feminine (e.g., embroidery) when they are being observed as they do when performing the same tasks in private. Sex of experimenter is an important situational variable that is often overlooked. Participants sometimes respond differently to same-sex versus other-sex experimenters.

It is easy to see how situational variables can influence the results we get. In Eagly's (1987) review of sex differences in helping behavior, she noted that most of the literature is limited to the extent to which participants helped strangers in potentially dangerous situations. Most of women's helping behavior occurs within the family or in the context of a long-term relationship. Not surprisingly, the research shows that men are more likely to offer help than women. Eagly concluded that this is not a valid conclusion because of the artificial and limited number of situations in most of the research.

Multivariate Indicators

An examination of sex-related differences in cognitive abilities requires that both sex and cognitive abilities be measured. In most research with normal populations, sex is measured by self-report. Virtually all people define themselves as either male or female. The measurement of cognitive abilities is more problematic. If you want to investigate spatial ability, for example, how can you measure it in a meaningful way?

A clear definition of what constitutes spatial ability is needed. There is often disagreement among researchers, each of whom tends to work with a somewhat different definition (Caplan, MacPherson, & Tobin, 1985). There is a wide variety of tasks that rely on spatial abilities—navigating in a forest without clear landmarks, navigating in a city with clear landmarks, using blueprints to visualize what a building will look like, and keeping a visual representation in memory to accomplish a task. These are all tasks that require spatial abilities, but do they all draw on a single underlying spatial skill, or are they separable, perhaps separate, dimensions? There are literally hundreds of tests that can be used to measure spatial ability, and as you can imagine, they do not all yield the same results. Some of the tests commonly used include the performance section of the Weschler Adult Intelligence Scale, finding simple figures that are embedded in larger ones, imagining how a figure will look if it is rotated in the depth plane, figuring out how the surfaces of a cube will fit together if a flat diagram is assembled, tracing a route on a real or imaginary map, and assembling a model from written instructions.

The problem for the researcher is to decide which of these tests will yield a true measure of spatial ability. It is usually possible to eliminate some tests on an a priori basis because they fail to meet certain criteria. Some of these tests may actually rely heavily on verbal skills or be inconsistent with working definitions of spatial abilities. There is probably no single ideal test. If a researcher wants to explore sex differences in spatial ability, then several tests of spatial abilities should be used in the same experiment.

Multiple indicators of cognitive abilities are desirable for several reasons. If sex differences in the same direction are consistently found on four different tests of spatial ability, then a more convincing claim that differences exist can be made than if differences are found on only one test. Furthermore, if sex differences are found on some tests of spatial ability but not others, the experimenter can examine ways in which these two types of tests differ, yielding a more fine-grained analysis of the nature of sex differences. A hypothetical example of the way several tests could be used to isolate the nature of the sex difference is the finding that the sexes differ on tests that require short-term memory of spatial information but not on other tests of spatial ability. These results would suggest that the locus of spatial ability differences is in spatial memory and not the ability to use spatial information per se.

Sometimes researchers use multiple indicators and then inappropriately use univariate data analytic techniques. For example, a researcher might use 10 different tests of spatial ability and then analyze each test separately to determine if sex differences exist. The use of multiple univariate analyses increases the probability that a researcher will find sex differences that are due to chance sampling differences. Multivariate statistical techniques (e.g., multivariate analysis of variance) are usually needed when multiple indicators are used.

STATISTICAL AND PRACTICAL SIGNIFICANCE

To understand research results, the reader must consider both the statistical and practical significance of any mean (average) difference between males and females. Let's begin with an example to clarify this point.

Suppose that a researcher wants to know if boys or girls watch more television. He carefully samples children within a given age range, socioeconomic status, and so forth, and then tallies the number of hours of television watched by each child in a week. He then computes the mean (average) number of hours of television watched by the boys and girls in the sample. Suppose that he finds that boys watch an average of 25 hours of television a week and girls watch an average of 25.4 hours of television a week. Obviously he can't simply look at these two mean values and conclude that the sexes differ with respect to average amount of television viewing. These differences could be due to chance factors (sampling error). Conclusions based on simply eyeballing the data are humorously called "binocular tests of significance." All serious researchers require a statistical test of significance.

Because research in sex differences always involves samples of people and because people are variable, there is always some chance or probability that conclusions based on the research are incorrect. There is very little in life, and especially in sex differences research, that is known with absolute certainty. It is important to keep in mind the probabilistic nature of research results. Suppose that 100 studies were conducted comparing the number of hours of television watched by boys and girls. If we set $p < .05$, then, by chance alone, even if boys and girls watch television the same number of hours each week, five of these studies would find sex differences. Furthermore, if only studies finding sex differences appear in the published literature, then it is easy to see how incorrect conclusions are reached. There is no simple remedy for the fact that sometimes researchers find sex differences just by chance. Tests of statistical significance constitute the backbone of research. They are essential in interpreting research results; however, they should be considered as a first step in making sense of the results.

When research results are statistically significant, it is correct to conclude that there probably are differences between the sexes, especially if the results can be interpreted in a theoretical framework and have been replicated with different samples. Given these results, a second question should be, "Is the difference large enough to have any practical significance?" In other words, are the results meaningful or useful? This is the most important question to ask about research results. Considering the current example, the researcher and the reader need to ask if the finding that girls watch, on average, 0.4 hours more television each week than boys has any practical significance. Clearly it would be incorrect to construe this difference as implying that girls are glued to television sets whereas boys are off doing other things. The obtained mean difference translates into an additional 24 minutes a week or 3.4 minutes a day! Even if such a result were statistically significant, it tells us very little of any practical importance about boy–girl differences in television watching.

Variability and Shapes of Distributions

To understand if a sex difference exists with respect to a particular variable, the investigator needs to be concerned with the distribution of scores for women and men because the relative number of each sex that obtains a particular score on a test has important implications for the way the data are interpreted. There are many ways distributions can differ. Consider the six hypothetical distributions of scores in Fig. 2.2.

The hypothetical distributions in Fig. 2.2 depict some possible outcomes for men and women on a test of musical ability. Figure 2.2A represents the case in which men and women obtain an identical distribution of scores, with most obtaining a score of 50 on this test (the mean or average), and a few obtaining scores as extreme as 0 or 100. The finding that both sexes have the same distribution of musical ability is seen by the overlapping identical curves. Both curves show the same peak (corresponding to the mean of the distribution in normal distributions) and the same bell-shaped curve (indicating that they have the same variability or "spread-outness" of scores).

Figure 2.2B shows a somewhat different distribution of scores for women and men. In this case, the sexes have the same mean score (the average for both women

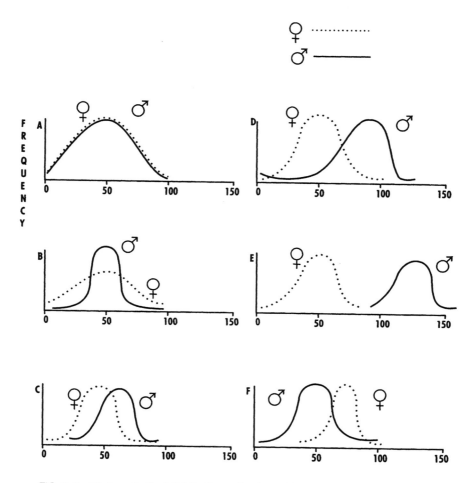

FIG. 2.2. Six hypothetical distributions of male and female scores on a test of musical ability.

and men is 50), but the sexes differ in variability. The scores for men are more closely clustered around the mean, indicating less variability for men than for women. Thus, any man selected at random would be expected to be near the mean value in musical ability, whereas any woman selected at random would be expected to be farther from the mean (either lower or higher) than her male counterpart.

Figures 2.2C, D, and E all depict situations in which the means between the sexes differ (in this case with males, on average, outperforming females) but the variability remains about the same. There is much overlap between the sexes in Fig. 2.2C, an intermediate amount of overlap in Fig. 2.2D, and virtually no overlap in Fig. 2.2E. Although each of these scenarios represents a case in which a researcher could legitimately conclude that males scored higher in musical ability than females, each figure tells a different story about the distribution of musical ability by sex. If Fig. 2.2E depicted the true results for males and females, then we would expect the most tone deaf males to have more musical ability than the most musically talented females. In contrast, if Fig. 2.2C represented the true distribution, then we would expect only slight differences in the percentages of women and men at every level of musical ability.

Figure 2.2F represents another possibility. In this figure, the female and male distributions have both different means and different variances. In this hypothetical example, females scored higher than males and showed less variability. If Fig. 2.2F were a true representation of these distributions, then we would expect more females to score well on this test and to score close to the female mean whereas men would be more variable, with some obtaining low scores and others high scores. It is important to consider the shape of the distribution of scores when exploring sex differences. Research reports of sex differences that don't provide information about the relative shapes and amount of overlap between distributions provide only a small part of the information needed to understand the data.

Mean Differences and Tail Ratios

Most of the research on sex differences reports mean group differences between women and men. Very few studies consider sex differences in the shape of the distribution of scores for the variable being measured and the extent to which they overlap. Percentiles of males and females at every ability level should also be provided. A report that women excel at verbal reasoning tasks is less meaningful than one that also indicates, for example, that 75% of women and 70% of men score at or beyond a given score on the test. The additional information presents a clearer picture of the distribution of this ability between the sexes and allows a more meaningful comparison.

A related issue is the way researchers report measures of central tendency. Most report group means (averages) as a single number summary of the scores obtained by each sex. Although this is useful, and probably essential, in understanding what the data represent, mean values should also be reported along with confidence intervals, which are a range of scores that probably contains the true population mean. It would be more meaningful to know that the population mean for women on a hypothetical aptitude test is probably between 85 and 115 while the comparable confidence interval for men is between 87 and 117 than it is to know that the sample mean for women is 100 and the sample mean for men is 102. (In a more statistical vein, confidence intervals are computed for selected confidence levels, such as 95%, and can be interpreted as meaning that if the experiment were repeated 100 times, 95% of the intervals computed would contain the true population mean.)

Sometimes, the differences between the means of two distributions (in this case, samples of females and males) are small, but the differences in the tails or extreme ends of the distributions are large. For this reason, several researchers (Feingold, 1996; Hedges & Nowell, 1995) suggested that, in addition to reporting "mean differences," all research concerned with sex comparisons should report "tail ratios." (Readers with a good background in mathematics should recognize tail ratios as one type of likelihood ratio.) To understand tail ratios, consider the upper (or lower) tail of a distribution—let's say the top 5% on a particular test of mechanical aptitude. If 1,000 people took this test, then 50 would score in the top 5%. (If we were concerned with the bottom 5%, there would also be 50 people in the lower tail, and the same logic would apply.) Suppose that of the 1,000 participants (or test takers in this example), 750 were male, and 250 were female. Among those scoring in the top 5%, 39 were male, and 11 were female. To calculate the upper tail ratio, you would compute

$$\frac{\dfrac{\#\,males\ in\ top\ 5\%}{\#\,males\ in\ sample} = \dfrac{39}{750} = .052}{\dfrac{\#\,females\ in\ top\ 5\%}{\#\,females\ in\ sample} = \dfrac{11}{250} = .044} = 1.18.$$

What this number means is that for every female in the top 5% on this hypothetical test, you would expect to find 1.18 males. Of course, males come in whole numbers only, but these are statistical averages. It is easier to think of these data as saying that for every 100 females who score in the top 5% of all test takers, there are 118 males. Tail ratios are especially important in understanding data when the tests are used for selection purposes. In these cases, only those who score above some cut score get selected (usually for employment or college admissions). Sometimes, tests are used to identify those who would benefit from a special program, and lower tail ratios are important in these cases. There are many data sets in which the mean differences between males and females are small but the differences in the tails of the distributions are large. If the purpose of the test is to select individuals who score above or below a particular score, then tail ratios need to be considered.

Meta-Analysis

The literature on sex differences is enormous. How can anyone sift through thousands, perhaps even tens of thousands, of research reports to determine which of the reported differences are real? No single experiment can ever provide the answer to sex differences questions. In an area as complex as this, researchers need to consider the preponderance of results before stating a conclusion. One of the best known and earliest attempts to synthesize the literature on sex differences was undertaken over 25 years ago by Maccoby and Jacklin (1974). They tallied all of the studies investigating sex differences that had been published in American journals during the 10-year period prior to 1974. They set a criterion that sex differences existed only when a large number of studies found sex differences in the same direction for a given variable. Although this was the first major attempt to synthesize the sex differences literature, their procedure has been criticized as the "voting method." (See Block, 1976, for a criticism of their methodology.)

A more sophisticated technique of integrating research findings is meta-analysis which, as its name implies, is the analysis of analyses, or an analysis of many individual research results. It provides a measure of the strength or importance of a relationship between two variables. The need for meta-analysis is obvious in a research area in which the size of the literature can be measured in linear yards or pounds of paper generated. Meaningful integrations of research findings are the best way to interpret the voluminous literature. The purpose of meta-analysis is to determine not only how many studies obtained sex differences results in the predicted direction but also how large the differences between women and men were.

The File Drawer Problem.   Meta-analysis allows us to take a broad overview in summarizing research results (Hyde & Linn, 1986). It is important that the individual studies that are analyzed with meta-analytic techniques be representative of the research in the field. A major problem is finding representative research. The most logical place to find research is in journals and books found in libraries; however, because of publication practices, there is a bias to publish only those studies that have found evidence of sex differences. Suppose that 100 researchers investigated sex differences in cognitive styles and that 90 of them found no differences. Furthermore, suppose that of the 10 that found differences, 2 found differences that favored men and 8 found differences that favored women. Given the current publication practices, it is more likely that the 10 studies that found sex differences would get published than the 90 studies that found no differences. In addition, suppose that a researcher who is eager to understand the nature of sex differences in this area attempts to perform a meta-analysis. She most likely would use only the published studies in her analysis. After all, how would she even know about the unpublished studies that could have been conducted in universities and other settings around the world? If the 8 studies supporting female superiority found even moderately large sex differences, meta-analytic statistics would support the conclusion that females have better cognitive styles than males, a conclusion that may be unwarranted in light of the 90 studies that found no sex differences.

Fortunately, there are a few sources that allow access to unpublished research reports. Doctoral dissertations are usually available through *Dissertation Abstracts International.* Education-related research that appeared as paper presentations at conferences or other unpublished presentations are available in ERIC (an educational information retrieval service). Anyone who is contemplating a meta-analytic review of an area should be sure to search these sources for research so that unpublished experiments are included. Although inclusion of these sources of data helps to ameliorate some of the bias associated with publication practices, it is also true that papers that report significant group differences are more likely to be accepted for presentation at a conference than research reports that fail to find differences. Doctoral dissertations presumably reflect a concerted effort to obtain statistically significant results. Thus, there is probably no truly unbiased data source.

Meta-analysis has been criticized for its use of unpublished research on the grounds that unpublished research tends to be poorer in quality than published research that has undergone the peer review process. As explained earlier in this chapter, there are many ways to obtain null results, including shoddy research. If the peer review process has any merit at all, then those studies that are published should, on average, be of a higher quality than those that are rejected for publication. Thus, a major criticism of meta-analysis is that it weighs good and poor research equally instead of somehow adjusting for the quality of the experiment.

The tendency to publish primarily statistically significant results has been declining in recent years, with more journal editors judging the quality of research apart from its results. It is, however, very difficult to judge the quality of research when the results are not statistically significant. Null results are almost impossible to make sense out of because it is not easy to determine why the researcher failed to find differences. Certainly, one possibility is that there are no differences between females and males with respect to the variable being studied. Although a single finding of null results doesn't mean much, numerous carefully conducted studies with large sample sizes, conducted by many different investigators at different laboratories, certainly provide evidence that if there are any sex differences, the differences are exceedingly small.

How can anyone summarize a large body of research when the studies that are available for scrutiny are biased toward those that report statistically significant differences? This question has come to be known as the "file drawer problem." The term *file drawer problem* refers to all of the studies that found null results and were never published. As the name implies, the underlying idea is that the results of these studies are languishing in file drawers in various laboratories. We can never know how many studies that are unavailable did not show evidence of sex differences. One way to handle this problem is to examine all of the available studies, and if the researcher concludes that there are sex differences with regard to some variable, then she would also calculate the number of null results that would be needed to change her conclusion. For example, suppose a researcher summarized 35 different studies on sex differences in cognitive styles and concluded that females have a more introspective cognitive style than males. (This is a fictitious example.) The researcher would then compute the number of studies with null results that would be needed to change her conclusion to "no sex differences." The actual number of null results that would change the conclusion depends on several variables, including the size of the difference, a topic that is discussed in detail later in this chapter. She would then add to her summary the finding that 20 (or whatever number is calculated) studies that found no between-sex differences would be needed to alter her conclusion. In this way, researchers can acknowledge the possibility that there are unpublished null results. The number of "file drawer" studies needed as counterevidence to a conclusion that a difference exists is a meaningful number. Suppose that a researcher determined that there would have to be 300 studies that found nonsignificance that were never published to change her conclusion that there are sex differences with regard to some ability. Because this number is so large, we could confidently conclude that there really are differences between men and women with regard to the ability that was assessed.

Effect Size Statistics

Three statistics that are used to determine the importance or size of the experimental effect are ω^2 (omega squared), d, and binomial effect size display. Each has a somewhat different meaning and use, although all three are used in understanding how much the sexes differ with respect to a given variable. Each of these measures is described separately and then compared so that readers can meaningfully grapple with the question, "When does an effect size become important?"

ω^2 *(Omega Squared).*   To understand the meaning of ω^2, we need to reconsider variance, which is a measure of the variability in a set of data. As previously described, variance is a measure of how dispersed or spread out the individual scores in a data set are. If the scores are very spread out, the variance for that sample is large, whereas if the scores are closely clustered, the variance for that sample is small. If everyone in a study had exactly the same score, there would be no variability, and variance would be equal to zero. ω^2 is a measure of the proportion of total variance in a data set that can be explained by a particular variable, in this case, sex of participant (Hays, 1981).

Consider the following hypothetical example. If we asked a sample of young and old women and young and old men to respond as quickly as possible to a set of stimuli, we'd usually find that the older participants took longer to respond than the younger ones. We might also find sex differences, depending on the type of stimuli we used. Suppose that in this hypothetical study we also found that men responded more quickly overall than women. The first test of the data would be to determine if the differences between age groups and sexes are likely to have occurred by chance when in fact there really are no differences between men and women in the general population. If we found that the results we obtained would have occurred by chance alone less than 5 times in 100, then we'd conclude that the results were unlikely to be due to chance; therefore, real differences probably exist between the age groups and sexes. This type of test is a test of statistical significance. Virtually every research report includes a test of significance. Finding statistically significant results should constitute the first step, not the final step, in data analysis.

In the hypothetical example being considered, some of the variability is due to the fact that two age groups of participants were used. If the differences in the age groups account for most of the variability in the data, then the proportion of total variability due to age would be large. Conversely, if there were large differences in the scores obtained by women and men, then ω^2 would be large for the sex variable. If ω^2 for sex was large, then if we knew an individual's sex, we could use this knowledge to predict his or her ability to perform the task. If ω^2 for sex was small, then knowing an individual's sex would yield poor predictions about her or his ability on the task. When two or more variables are investigated in the same experiment, the ω^2 associated with each variable can be compared to determine, for example, whether sex or age is more important with respect to the ability being investigated.

In a meta-analysis, ω^2 is computed for each of several experiments investigating the same ability. An average (median) ω^2 is computed from the values obtained in each of the studies. In this way, research results from many experiments on the same topic can be summarized with a single measure of the average effect size.

Despite the fact that effect size statistics have been available in the literature for decades and virtually every statistician advocates their use (e.g., Hays, 1963), it is still unusual to find them reported. This failure to report effect size statistics is probably due to the fact that they are often small, indicating that the variable being investigated is not an important determinant of the ability being measured. Effect size statistics are extremely important in understanding the extent to which sex plays a role in cognitive abilities.

A major limitation in interpreting ω^2 or any proportion of explained variance statistic is that the value obtained depends on the other variables investigated in the experiment. ω^2 for sex in an experiment that investigated sex and age variables would not be comparable to the ω^2 for sex in an experiment that investigated sex and socioeconomic variables. Because ω^2 depends on the other variables in the experiment, across-experiment comparisons can be made only when the same set of variables is investigated in different studies.

   d.   Another statistic that is used to index the size of an effect is d. It is a measure of the magnitude of the difference between two groups. d is a standard mode of expressing the difference between two group means on the basis of "standard deviation units," which means that you need to understand the concept of "standard deviation" to understand a measurement standard that is based on it. d is computed by calculating the difference between means on a given variable for men and women and then dividing by the standard deviation. When variables are normally distributed (i.e., they show a regular bell-shaped curve), approximately 32% of all scores fall between the mean and one standard deviation above (or below) the mean, 16% of all scores fall between one and two standard deviations from the mean, and 2% of all scores fall more than two standard deviations above (or below) the mean. A standard deviation is a measure of variability. It is equal to the square root of the variance. Mathematically,

$$d = \frac{M \text{ males} - M \text{ females}}{\text{Standard Deviation}}$$

One problem in using d is that the standard deviations for women and men are assumed to be equal when computing its value. As discussed earlier, equal variability cannot always be assumed; thus, the actual value of d may be somewhat off, although this is not likely to be a major concern.

The value of d is large when the difference between means is large and the variability within each group is small; it is small when the difference between means is small and the variability within each group is large. Unlike ω^2, d provides a measure of the direction of an effect. Thus, if we compare d from several different studies, a positive value indicates that males scored higher than females, and a negative value indicates that females scored higher than males as long as the female mean is always subtracted from the male mean. Both ω^2 and d allow for comparisons of results across studies. In general, large values indicate large sex differences, and small values indicate small sex differences. For a more advanced discussion of meta-analysis, see Orwin and Cordray (1985) and Hyde and Linn (1986).

Effect sizes are given in standard deviation units because different studies often use different scales of measurement. For example, SAT scores range from 200 to 800 on each test, whereas intelligence test scores average approximately 100 (with the lowest scores in the 30s and the highest scores just above 200). By using d, it is possible to compare female and male scores on both of these tests. In thinking about effect sizes, it is useful to consider a graph of the differences or some other visual display that can make this abstract idea more concrete. Unfortunately, the way the graph is drawn can make the same size effect appear large or small, and it is important for readers to understand the way they can be misled by graphical displays.

Consider a hypothetical test of honesty in which the mean is 100 and the standard deviation is 15. Now suppose that the average score for girls on this test is 107.5 and the average score for boys is 100. If we use the formula for d, this is expressed as

$$\frac{100 - 107.5}{15} = -.5$$

This indicates that the means for the girls and boys are 0.5 standard deviation units apart. The negative sign means that the girls scored higher on this test. Cohen (1977) suggested that effects sizes of 0.2 be considered small, 0.5 medium, and 0.8 large. Although this is a simple guideline, it is a misleading interpretation of effect size because sometimes a "small" effect can be very important. For example, an effect size of 0.2 in medical research can mean the difference in hundreds or hundreds of thousands of lives being saved or lost, depending on what is being studied and how many people are affected. As Eagly (1996) argued, seemingly small effects can have great practical importance.

Meta-analysis also allows tests of homogeneity of effect sizes from several studies. If, for example, half of the studies in a particular area showed large effect sizes favoring males (positive values for d) and half showed large effect sizes favoring females (negative values for d), it would not be logical to conclude that, on average, there are no sex differences with regard to the variable being studied. When a homogeneity of effect size test shows that the results are not homogeneous, then the reviewer is not sampling from a single population. In other words, moderator variables are causing the differences, and the studies should be subdivided into homogeneous subcategories. To clarify this concept, let's consider another example. Hyde (1986) conducted a meta-analytic review of sex differences in aggression. Because her test for homogeneity showed that aggression is not a homogeneous (uniform) concept, she subdivided the studies into meaningful categories. Hyde used "age of subject" as one of her subdivisions and found that "gender differences are larger with younger subjects" (p. 63). (In case you're wondering, she found that there were "no types or measures of aggression on which females are more aggressive than males" [p. 63].) I return to the concept of homogeneous types of studies in the next chapter when I examine the empirical evidence for sex differences in cognition.

Binomial Effect Size Display.   Because both ω^2 and d are somewhat advanced statistical concepts, Rosenthal and Rubin (1982) suggested that the size of a difference between any two groups is best understood with a "binomial effect size display," which is the percentage of each sex that is above the average response in the combined group of females and males. These values are readily comprehensible and do not require any statistical training to be understood. Binomial effect size displays are similar to tail ratios because they index the proportion of females and males in the tails of the distributions, except that they are probably easier to understand. Unfortunately, few researchers have used this statistic in their reports of their research.

In a thoughtful discussion of the effect of small differences in real-world outcomes, Martell, Lane, and Emrich (1996) used a computer simulation to show the cumulative effect of seemingly small effect sizes. They asked readers to consider a hypothetical situation in which women's work is evaluated less favorably than men's work even when it is objectively the same. They hypothesized that the devaluation of women's work is relatively slight, so that it accounts for only 1% to 5% of the variance in the data. They also considered the pyramid structure of most organizations in which promotion is accomplished in "tournament style," with early ratings influencing the likelihood of reaching top management positions. For their simulation, they set up a model with 500 incumbents at the bottom of the organization, 10 at the top, and 8 levels of promotions. The highest scorer at each level got the promotion. They found that with sex bias accounting for "only" 5% of the variance overall, only 29% of all top workers would be female compared with 58% of the bottom-level workers. If the size of the sex bias effect was 1% of all of the variance, then there would be only 35% of the top-level managers who were female. The point is that relatively small sex effects in performance ratings can cause substantially reduced promotion rates and disproportionately fewer women at the highest levels of organizations. In this example, they used binomial effect size statistics to communicate the cumulative effect of small effect sizes. Because of the intuitive nature of these statistics, I think that they make a strong point about the importance of effect sizes.

When Is an Effect Size Large?   Even if a researcher computes the value of ω^2 and d, the reader is still left with the task of deciding if the value reflects a "large" or a "small" effect, or, more accurately, whether the obtained effect size is large enough to be important. This is not an easy decision to make because it involves a value judgment about how large an effect (difference between groups) has to be to be considered meaningful or important. As I explained in chapter 1, the answer to this question is the same answer that I give to all difficult questions in life: "It all depends." The trick is deciding what it depends on. In medical research, an extremely small effect size can have enormous importance. If someone were to discover a drug that allows a small number of people with acquired immune deficiency syndrome to recover from this dreaded disease, everyone would agree that it was an extremely important drug. If you were one of the people who recovered from this disease, you would not care if the effect size was extremely small.

Comparing Effect Size Indicators.   To decide if an effect size is large enough to be meaningful, you have to understand what the numbers mean. Unfortunately, these values are not intuitive. In the next chapter, I give the values obtained by females and males on the SATs. These are numbers that are readily meaningful to most college students because they were required to take these tests. Other numbers, like average differences in reaction time tests (which are given in milliseconds or thousandths of a second) or number correct on a finger-tapping task (this is explained later), are much more abstract. When you read about research, you have to consider if the results are statistically significant; whether the effect size is large enough to be theoretically important; and even if both of these conditions are met, whether the effect is large enough to be practically important.

Eagly (1987) compared effect size indicators for several differences in social behavior. Let's consider differences in aggressive behavior. She reported that sex differences account for only 2% of the variance in aggressive behavior. (This is ω^2.) This certainly sounds like a very small effect. The corresponding d is 0.29, or slightly less than one third of a standard deviation. This is conceptually a "small" effect according to the guidelines suggested by Cohen (1969). However, when we examine the binomial effect size display, the effect size seems much larger—43% of the females and 57% of the males scored above average on the measures of aggression. These three indicators of effect size all apply to the same set of data. The value of ω^2 seems quite small, whereas the binomial effect size display seems quite large, even when they are describing the same set of data.

Eagly (1987) also computed three different effect size indicators for Hall's (1985) report of sex differences in social smiling. Sex of participant accounted for 9% of the variability in social smiling. The corresponding value for d was 0.63. By comparison, the binomial effect size display showed that 63% of the females and 35% of the males scored above the average for social smiling. The point that I want to make by comparing these three different indicators of effect size is that even when sex differences account for a small percentage of the variability in the data, the binomial effect size display can be quite large.

A study of sex differences in activity level provides another example for comparing effect size indicators. Eaton and Enns (1986) concluded that males have a higher activity level than females. The size of the sex difference in standard deviation units was $d = 0.49$ (almost one half of a standard deviation). This difference accounted for approximately 5% of the variability in activity level. Eaton and Enns calculated that there would have to be thousands of unpublished studies showing null results (the file drawer problem) to render this result nonsignificant.

According to Rosenthal and Rubin (1982), an effect that accounts for only 4% of the variance is associated with a difference of 60% versus 40% of a group's performance above average. If there were a test such that an individual must score at least average in order to qualify for employment, then 60% of one group and 40% of the other group would qualify. When considered in this way, it is easy to see how 4% of the variance can translate into huge between-sex differences that are of practical importance. Try to keep this in mind when evaluating research results.

The Interaction of Variables

One of the main themes of this book is that finding answers to sex differences questions is not easy, nor are the answers simple. The cognitive abilities that women and men develop depend on many variables. It seems likely that our abilities are influenced by age, birth order, cultural background, socioeconomic status, sex role orientation, learning histories, and so forth, in addition to the simple fact that we were born either female or male. In reality, these variables work together in their effect on cognitive abilities. It is possible, for example, that wealthy females who are firstborn tend to develop excellent verbal ability, whereas lower-middle-class females who are second- or thirdborn don't tend to develop these same excellent abilities (perhaps because firstborn wealthy females are talked to and read to more often). In this example, the influence of sex depends on the levels of other variables. A host of sociodemographic (e.g., age, place of residence), psychological (e.g., motivation), biological (e.g., health status), and life history (e.g., level of education) variables operate in conjunction with sex to determine the level of each cognitive ability that an individual obtains. The term *interaction* is used to denote the fact that the effect of sex differs depending on the value of other variables (e.g., low, middle, or high socioeconomic status). Recall also that many variables mutually affect each other. For example, a stressful environment can cause an increase in the body's output of some hormones, the increase in hormones can cause certain reactions that change behavior, which in turn increases hormone levels, and so on.

It is important to consider any research on sex differences in light of other variables that could be influencing the results. Understanding the manner in which sex interacts with other variables provides a richer and more meaningful interpretation of the way maleness and femaleness influence cognitive development than merely considering the main effect of sex alone.

DEVELOPMENTAL ISSUES

Cognitive abilities, like physical abilities, do not remain static across the life span. Different activities follow their own developmental course, reflecting the influences of age-dependent biological and sociological changes. Sex differences may appear and disappear depending on the age of the participant. The welter of contradictory evidence in the literature makes it clear that there can be no useful answer about sex differences in any cognitive ability without reference to the ages of the participants.

Cross-Sectional Versus Longitudinal Studies

If cognitive abilities wax and wane across the life span, developmental studies are needed to understand the phenomena involved. Developmental studies are usually either cross-sectional (sampling at random from different participants in several age groups) or longitudinal (repeatedly measuring the same individuals at several ages as they mature). Sometimes combinations of these techniques are used when, for example, several age groups are measured repeatedly over periods of 5 or more years.

A major problem with cross-sectional studies is the cohort or peer group effect. The *cohort effect* refers to the fact that people who are the same age also had similar age-dependent experiences. Consider, for example, the following problem: A researcher wants to know about age-dependent changes in the ability to read maps (a spatial skill). Using cross-sectional samples, she tests men and women in their early 20s, mid-40s, and late 60s. Suppose she finds that there are no sex differences in the young group, small differences favoring males in the middle-aged group, and large differences favoring males in the oldest group. Could she conclude that sex differences favoring males develop throughout the adult years? She couldn't make this conclusion, because experiences with reading maps of the oldest women are probably different from those of the middle-aged women, who in turn have different experiences than the young women. It seems likely that the oldest women have fewer years of driving experience—an activity that often requires map reading—whereas many of the middle-aged women and virtually all of the young women drive on a regular basis. By contrast, virtually all of the men in all three age groups drive regularly, thus having similar experiences with maps. The age-dependent sex difference in map reading is more likely due to cohort or generational experiences than it is to life span changes in abilities. It may be that the young women will maintain their map reading skills into old age, so that when they are in their late 60s, they will perform in a manner comparable to their male counterparts.

Cohort effects, which are always possible in cross-sectional developmental research, are especially likely to contaminate developmental data in sex differences. Women's roles are changing rapidly, and it is therefore difficult to control experiential factors across generations. Generational differences in the experiences of women and men make any determination of why the differences exist very difficult.

Longitudinal research also has drawbacks associated with it. When participants are measured repeatedly throughout their life span, it is always possible that earlier testing experiences influence later ones. There is also the problem of loss of participants due to death, moving out of the area, refusal to continue, or other reasons. It is likely that the lost participants differ from those who continue in subtle ways (e.g., they may be less able). Finally, longitudinal research takes years to provide answers. If you want to study changes that occur from birth into old age, your children or grandchildren will have to collect the last of the data because the study would extend beyond a single lifetime.

SELF-FULFILLING PROPHECIES

It would be naive to believe that researchers approach their work without any bias or prejudice about the expected outcome. Researchers are committed, in varying degrees, to either proving or disproving the notion that females and males have comparable cognitive abilities.

A large body of literature exists to document the finding that experimenter expectancies often influence research results. One of the pioneers in this area was Robert Rosenthal, who is famous for his work in the area of self-fulfilling prophecies. This term refers to the concept that experimenters and others often act in ways that influence results so that the outcome is in accord with their beliefs. In a classic study (Rosenthal, 1966), elementary school teachers were told that some of their pupils had obtained high scores on a special test designed to measure intellectual development. Intelligence tests given later in the school year showed that the "bloomers" had made greater gains in IQ points than the "nonbloomers." The teachers reported that the bloomers were more interested, more curious, and happier than the other children. What is remarkable about these results is the fact that the children identified as "bloomers" had been picked at random and, therefore, did not differ from the other children. Somehow, the teachers had communicated their expectations to the children, who in turn responded to these expectations.

Sex differences research is particularly vulnerable to experimenter and participant expectations. If an experimenter believes that females will outperform males on a particular test, he or she may unknowingly act friendlier toward the females or provide them with a little more encouragement or allow them a little extra time in completing the test. Participant expectations also influence results. If, for example, girls believe that mathematical ability is unfeminine, it is likely that they will reflect this belief in their performance. The girls could give up easily on more difficult problems because they don't believe that they can solve them, or even deliberately select wrong answers in order to maintain a feminine self-concept.

In reading research reports, it is difficult to detect ways that either experimenter or participant expectancies may have biased the results. One way to circumvent this problem is by having the data collected by researchers who are blind to or uninformed about the hypothesis being investigated. Participants should also be unaware of the fact that sex differences are being examined. Experiments in which the sex of the participant is unknown to the experimenter also eliminate the effects of sex-related experimenter expectancies. This is possible, however, only in research with young children and in research that doesn't require face-to-face interaction between the researcher and the participant. (Young children could dress in standard smocks or jeans that don't provide the experimenter with clues as to the their sex.)

Research in the area of sex differences is particularly vulnerable to self-fulfilling prophecies. In Fausto-Sterling's (1985) discussion of the way beliefs can bias research, she asked that every researcher understand that, by definition, no one can see his or her own blind spots. For this reason, every research report should provide enough information so that readers can identify possible biases in research.

It is not necessarily true that simply because someone maintains a philosophical position (e.g., feminist, misogynist, defender of status quo), he or she is unable to conduct research or formulate conclusions in a fair manner. Readers, regardless of their personal beliefs about the issues discussed in the following chapters, are asked to maintain an open mind and to consider the evidence on all sides of the issues.

EVALUATING RESEARCH CLAIMS

The purpose of this chapter has been to raise issues that are important in evaluating research claims about sex differences. In evaluating conflicting claims or strong statements, keep in mind the following issues:

1. Who were the participants and how were they selected? Is the sample size appropriate for the question being examined (keeping in mind that large samples virtually ensure significant differences and small samples yield unstable estimates of population parameters)? Are results from abnormal populations or other species being generalized to all women and men?
2. Are studies that used neither random assignment of participants to conditions nor manipulation of any variables inferring causal information?
3. Is the measurement appropriate? Have multiple indicators of abilities been used, and if so, were the data analyzed with multivariate statistical techniques?
4. Are the results both statistically significant and practically significant? How large is the effect size? Do the results fit into an established theoretical framework? If not, why not? Were the hypotheses clearly stated before the data were collected? Have critical studies been conducted that would allow the proposed theory to be found false?
5. Has detailed information about the distribution of scores within each sex been provided? Are the results logical and understandable?

6. Has the way sex interacts with other variables in determining the results been investigated? What alternative explanations are plausible?
7. How might the results vary across the life span? Have cohort effects been included as a possible explanation of the results?
8. Are the results reported consistent with the prior literature and/or theory of sex differences? If not, why not?
9. How could the results have been influenced by experimenter and participant expectations?

The literature on sex differences has been proliferating in recent years. Although much of it is thoughtful and high in quality, some of it is not. The goal of finding answers to the broad, complex, and socially and politically sensitive questions of sex differences is of profound importance. The informed reader has to evaluate the research with an open mind and an awareness of what constitutes good research.

3 Empirical Evidence For Cognitive Sex Differences

CONTENTS

3

INTELLIGENCE

Are men smarter than women? The answer to the above burning question is:
No, they are not. Data are now being laid on the table that show that,
on average, men and women are equal in mental ability.
—Seligman (1998, p. 72)

The first question that most people ask about sex-related cognitive differences is which is the smarter sex—males or females? Although this question has a long history, in the past few years, it once again has made its way into the popular press as a handful of researchers hotly debate the answer (Seligman, 1998). There are several ways to find answers to this question. One logical way is to obtain large random samples of women and men, give them a psychometrically sound intelligence test (one with good statistical properties), and compare the scores for women and men. The sex with the higher average score would be the smarter sex. Although this may seem like a logical, straightforward approach to answering the question of sex differences in intelligence, it won't work. Intelligence tests are carefully written so that there will be no average overall difference between men and women (Brody, 1992). During the construction of intelligence tests, any question that tends to be answered differently by males and females is either discarded or balanced with a question that favors the other sex. Therefore, average scores on intelligence tests cannot provide an answer to the sex differences question because of the way the tests are constructed.

A second way to decide whether men or women are, on average, smarter might be to look at who performs the more intelligent jobs in society. Of course, one would have to decide which jobs require greater intelligence. Suppose that we could agree in principle that jobs like government leader, architect, lawyer, physician, professor, mathematician, physicist, and engineer all require a high degree of intelligence. An examination of who performs these jobs would reveal that the overwhelming majority of these jobs are held by men. Does this mean that men are, in general, more intelligent? Looking at the types of jobs typically performed by women and men in society cannot provide an answer to the intelligence question because of differential sex roles for women and men. Many professions were formally or informally closed to women until recent years. Similarly, there are few male nurses, secretaries, and child-care workers because of the constraints imposed by the male sex role. There are still considerable differences between the sexes in background experiences, types of encouragement, amount and type of education, and social expectations for success. We cannot know if the differences in the numbers of men and women in the various job classifications are related to overall intelligence differences, differential socialization practices, or some combination of the two. This issue is discussed in greater depth in the chapters on psychosocial hypotheses (chaps. 6 and 7).

A third way of answering the intelligence question is to look at school achievement. Which sex, on average, gets better grades in school? It seems clear that females get better grades than males in school in every subject area (Adelman, 1991; Willingham & Cole, 1997). Paradoxically, girls get better grades than boys even in traditionally male content areas, such as mathematics and physics, in which boys score higher on ability tests (Kimball, 1989; Wentzel, 1988). Once again, however, this does not prove that there is a smarter sex because alternative explanations are possible. Being a good student is more consistent with the female sex role than it is with the male sex role. Schools tend to reward quiet, neat students who do as they are told. These are characteristics that are seen as more appropriate for girls than for boys in our society. Thus, school achievement cannot provide the answer to the question of whether males or females are smarter.

There Are Data and There Are Interpretations of Data

Lynn (1994) addressed the question of which is the smarter sex. He reanalyzed samples of IQ scores (scores on tests of intelligence) and concluded that, on average, males score 3–4 points higher than females on the Wechsler intelligence tests (one of the most popular tests for assessing intelligence). Lynn coupled these re-

Hagar the Horrible cartoon. Reprinted with special permission of King Features Syndicate.

sults with data showing that males, on average, also have significantly larger brains (approximately 8% larger) than females to advocate the position that males are more intelligent than females and that the difference in brain size is the reason for males' superior intelligence. (Brain size and weight hypotheses are discussed in chap. 4.) This latest pronouncement that men really are smarter than women has set off an explosion of acrimonious name-calling (actually, it is called debate, but it is closer to an intellectual brawl) among researchers in the field of intelligence.

First, there are logical problems with Lynn's (1994) line of reasoning. One cannot use a test that was deliberately constructed and tested with a large standardization sample to ensure that there would be no overall sex differences to then support the conclusion that there are sex differences. Second, the conclusion that males are smarter than females ignores the many other sorts of mental measures on which females score higher than males, such as grades in school, writing tests, and many types of memory. Which is the better measure of intelligence—a single score on a test that is given at one point in time or the cumulative judgment of dozens of teachers over many years? In a later article, Lynn (1996) claimed that females achieve higher grades in school because they work harder than males, not because they are smarter in school settings. However, there are mental ability tests, reviewed in later sections in this chapter, that show an overall female superiority. These tests were ignored by Lynn in his conclusion that females are less intelligent than males. In addition, the brain size–intelligence link is dubious at best. There are many statistical methods that can be used to adjust brain size for body size (males have larger overall body size than females), and these various adjustments do not yield the same conclusions. In addition, cognitive functions rely on specialized neural subsystems and cannot be assessed with a measure as gross as overall brain size.

Flynn (1998, 1999) criticized Lynn's (1994, 1996) reasoning on several different grounds and provided data that contradict Lynn's conclusions. Flynn examined intelligence tests that had been administered by the Israeli military, a sample that he chose because it represents one of the most extensive testing programs of an entire population that is available anywhere. One criticism of Lynn's work is that he selected participants in a biased way. Flynn found that overall the mean difference in intelligence test scores between females and males was a fraction of an IQ point—a value so small that it has no meaningful usefulness.

Recently, Jensen (1998) joined the debate. Jensen is no stranger to heated controversies about intelligence. In a 1969 article, he asserted that African-Americans are, on average, less intelligent than European-Americans. As a means of addressing the question of male–female differences in intelligence, Jensen (1998) analyzed tests that "load heavily on *g*." *g* is the generally accepted term for general intelligence. In his analysis, Jensen used only tests that had not been deliberately written to eliminate sex differences, thus making it more likely that he would find evidence for sex differences in intelligence, if they existed. Jensen was highly critical of the arbitrary way in which Lynn (1994) selected tests for his study. By contrast, Jensen (1998) used five different test batteries for which he had large representative samples that encompassed the full range of ability in the general population. Jensen (1998) concluded, "No evidence was found for sex differences in the mean level of g or in the variability of g .... Males, on average, excel on some factors; females on others" (pp. 531–532). Jensen also disparaged Lynn's (1994) use of brain size data to support his conclusion that males are the more intelligent sex. Jensen's cogent analysis of the relationship between brain size and intelligence is presented in chapter 4. His conclusion that there are no overall sex differences in intelligence has been supported by Stumpf and Stanley (1996) in their analysis of scores on the achievement tests and advanced-placement tests taken by college-bound high school seniors. Although they found sex differences on individual tests, overall the sex differences on these tests canceled each other.

Perhaps the most important lesson to be learned from this debate is that researchers, like the rest of the population, maintain a particular worldview that they use in interpreting research findings. This point became clear to me during a recent discussion of these issues that I had with a developmental psychologist. After I explained to him that females get higher grades in school and males get higher scores on (some) tests of cognitive abilities, his face brightened. He filtered this information according to his own worldview and exclaimed, "That proves that schools are biased against boys!" "Perhaps," I responded. "But it could just as easily be used to 'prove' that the tests are biased against girls." This is a good example of two contradictory explanations of the same findings—each of us making the leap from data to our interpretations of the data by our privately held worldviews. It also demonstrates the reality that everyone has a particular point of view, which influences what we see and how we make sense of our worldview.

The problem with questions like "Which is the smarter sex?" is that they contain the assumption that there is a smarter sex. The research reviewed in this book suggests several areas in which sex differences are consistently found and other cognitive areas in which sex differences are not found, but in no way does this mean that one sex is the "winner" and the other the "loser" or that one sex is smarter and the other is dumber. The more meaningful questions are when, where, and why are cognitive sex differences found. Modern society is complex and diverse. There is no single best set of intellectual abilities for all of society's tasks. It is important that we come to think of differences apart from value judgments about who or what is better. If society consistently values the abilities that are more frequently associated with one sex, then the problem lies in the way differences are valued, not in the fact that they exist.

A more fruitful approach to the cognitive sex differences question is to examine specific abilities, especially in light of the fact that intelligence is not a unitary concept. It is theoretically more useful to think of multiple intelligences than to consider intelligence as a single homogeneous mental ability. The question then becomes, "What are the sex differences in cognitive abilities?" Although intelligence tests are constructed so that there will be no overall sex difference in intelligence, the tests do differ in the pattern of intellectual abilities for the two sexes. Surprisingly, in an area as controversial as this one, there is little disagreement about which of the cognitive abilities differ by sex. As you will see, the most heated debates revolve around whether the differences are large enough to be important and why these differences exist.

THE WHEN, WHERE, WHO, AND HOW OF DIFFERENCES

Although there are no practical differences in intelligence between males and females, sex-related cognitive differences are found consistently on tests of some cognitive abilities. Between-sex differences show an uneven pattern of results that often depend on the portion of the ability curve being sampled (e.g., gifted individuals, mentally retarded individuals, or individuals in the average ability range), the age of the sample (infancy, preschool, middle childhood, adolescence, adulthood, or old age), the response format of the test (multiple-choice, essay, or diagram), and probably many other variables as well. What this means is that simple answers that apply to all females and all males are impossible. In addition, the size of the between-sex difference depends on other moderating variables, such as education, culture, and socioeconomic status.

Tales of Distributions

An example from an area outside of cognition may help in demonstrating how important all of these variables are in understanding sex differences. Virtually all social scientists believe that males, on the average, are more aggressive than females. What does a conclusion like this really mean? No one believes that the meekest male is more aggressive than the brashest female. There must be considerable overlap between the female and male distributions for aggression. As you will see in this example, the kind of conclusion that we draw depends on the portion of the distribution that we study. Let's consider the extremes of aggression, that is, people who are exceptionally high and people that are exceptionally low on aggression.

If we considered only the most aggressive individuals in society, we would have to conclude that there are huge sex differences with respect to aggression. The overwhelming majority of violent crimes (sadistic murders, rape, mutilation, serial killings, slasher crimes) are committed by males (U.S. Bureau of the Census, 1998). Thus, by sampling the upper end or the upper "tail" of the aggression distribution, we would conclude that sex differences are enormous. Similarly, we could consider the lower end of the aggression distribution and see if substantially more females are found among those who are classified as low on aggression. I don't know of any study that has actually examined the low end of the aggression distribution (in fact, I'm not sure what it would mean or how we would identify the least aggressive individuals in society), but if we found that there were significantly more females among those who are least aggressive, this finding would support the conclusion that males are more aggressive than females. But what about the vast majority of people who fall in the middle portion of the distribution? Between-sex differences for the middle portions of distributions are much smaller than those found in the tails. Thus, there is much less difference in female and male aggression for "average" people than there is for criminals. The kind of answer we are likely to get depends on the portion of the distribution from which the researcher samples.

When we turn our attention to cognitive abilities, researchers regularly (but not always) report that males are more variable than females. In other words, there are more males than females at the very high end and at the very low end in scales of cognitive abilities and correspondingly fewer males than females in the range of average abilities (Hedges & Nowell, 1995; Jensen, 1998; Willingham & Cole, 1997). Thus, we would find males to be overrepresented in both the top and bottom percentiles (e.g., more males in the top and bottom 10% on some tests) with smaller between-sex differences for those in the average range.

Developmental Perspectives

Conclusions about cognitive sex differences also depend on the age of the participants used in the sample. I use aggression again as a noncognitive example. Developmental psychologists have identified adolescence as a time of great change. If we looked at adolescent delinquency rates to assess sex differences in aggression, we would find that sex ratios for adolescents who are arrested are approximately 4:1, with the higher value representing the male rate (Kimmel & Weiner, 1985). If we examined sex ratios for those adults in U.S. prisons, the figure is closer to 8:1 or 9:1 (U.S. Bureau of the Census, 1998). Suppose, instead, the focus of the research was senior citizens sampled from homes for the aged population. Very few, if any, sex-related differences in aggression would be found among seniors (in part because there are so few men in the oldest age groups). It is easy to see how the age of the sample influences the data we get and the conclusions we can make on the basis of the data.

Age is also a critical variable in understanding cognitive sex differences. For example, in a massive study of the performance of millions of people on 400 different tests administered by the Educational Testing Service, Willingham and Cole (1997) found that females increased their advantage over males in language from Grades 4 to 8 whereas males increased their advantage over females in understanding mathematical concepts and science from Grades 8 to 12. Other developmental researchers (Kaufman, Kaufman-Packer, McLean, & Reynolds, 1991) found that verbal intelligence continues to increase in adulthood through the 60s and then shows little change into the mid-70s for both sexes, but performance factors (largely spatial skills) peak around age 22 and decrease across the adult life span. Thus, age is a critical variable in understanding cognitive sex differences.

Measurement Variables

How can we best measure amorphous concepts like aggression and intelligence? This is a difficult question to answer. The way we choose to measure these psychological constructs also affects results. This point is clearly seen in studies of aggression in which context can determine the nature of the results (Bettencourt &

Miller, 1996). Hyde (1986) found that studies in naturalistic environments (e.g., playgrounds) yielded larger sex differences in aggression than those conducted in laboratories and that differences were somewhat larger with measures of physical aggression than with measures of verbal aggression. Thus, the way we measure aggression also determines the results we get. Measurement is an important determinant of the conclusions that we obtain regarding cognitive sex differences as well. For example, Bridgeman and Moran (1996) found that women tend to score higher on written measures than on multiple-choice questions, with the reverse finding for males. In 1996, the U.S. Department of Education arrived at a court-mediated agreement with the College Board concerning the Preliminary Scholastic Assessment Test (PSAT), a precollege achievement test that is taken by 1.2 million students annually (Arenson, 1998). The PSAT is used as the sole criterion for determining semifinalist status for the award of the prestigious National Merit Scholarships for college. In the past, a disproportional number of these scholarships were awarded to males because they obtained higher average scores on the PSAT. Under the terms of the agreement, the PSAT now includes a writing component—one area in which girls usually excel. The addition of the writing component has resulted in a larger number of scholarship awards won by females. Although the exact numbers are not available, an article in *The Chronicle of Higher Education* estimated that "about 350 more female students will be awarded National Merit Scholarships" (Hughes, 1999, p. A42) in the first year that the writing sample was added compared with previous years. The academic areas tested on the PSAT remain the same, and, of course, the addition of a writing component did not alter the average abilities of girls or boys; the only change is in the way their cognitive abilities are assessed. As expected, girls are now outscoring boys on the test of writing, a fact that balances the fact that boys outscore girls on the mathematics portion of this exam. As you can see from this example, measurement issues are critically important to how we understand sex differences in cognitive abilities. They also have important social consequences, as can be seen in this example from the PSAT.

PERCEPTUAL AND MOTOR SKILLS

Better that a girl has beauty than brains because boys
see better than they think.
—Author Unknown (cited in Byrne, 1988, p. 115)

All of our information about the world around us comes from our sensory systems. The cognitive or thinking process begins with the ability to sense changes in the environment and to make meaning out of the bewildering array of sensory stimuli constantly impinging on us. The first steps in the cognitive process are perception and attention. Sex differences in perception and attention are of particular interest for two reasons: (a) If there are sex differences at the earliest stages of information processing, this provides a theoretical basis for positing sex-related differences in later stages, and (b) perception and attention are two areas in which there are no sex role stereotypes because we have little conscious awareness of the way in which the sensory and attentional systems function.

Baker (1987a, 1987b) reviewed a variety of sex-related differences in perception and attention; interested readers are referred to her excellent book on this topic. She documented numerous sex differences in each of the sensory systems. In hearing, for example, females are better at detecting pure tones (tones of one frequency) during childhood and most of adulthood. There are also sexually distinct patterns of hearing loss in middle age, with males beginning to lose the ability to detect high tones at about age 32 and females beginning to lose this ability at about age 37. These results were confirmed by Rebok (1987), Schaie (1987), and Morrell, Gordon-Salant, Pearson, Brant, and Fozard (1996). Other researchers (Bromley & Doty, 1995; Lehrner, 1993; Schab, 1991) investigated sex differences in odor perception. They found many studies that showed that females are better than males in their ability to categorize, identify, and perceive odors. Females also have better memory for odors than their male counterparts. The female advantage in odor identification extends across the entire life span, with females performing better than males on odor identification tasks from ages 5 to 99 years (Doty et al., 1984).

Vision is a critically important sensory system for humans. In general, males younger than 40 years of age have better dynamic visual acuity (ability to detect small movements in the visual field) than females. Age-related loss of far vision occurs earlier for females (between ages 35 and 44) than for males (between ages 45 and 54). Baker (1987b) also documented sex differences in taste perception (e.g., females have lower thresholds for detecting sweet, sour, salty, and bitter substances) and in touch sensitivity (e.g., females are more sensitive to touch on 19 of 20 tested body parts—the only exception was a touch on the nose). She documented a wide array of sex differences in perception, ranging from binaural beats (a somewhat abstruse auditory phenomenon) to visual acuity (the need for eyeglasses). It is unlikely that differences of this sort can be attributed to sex-differentiated socialization practices.

Many of these sex-related differences in perceptual thresholds are detectable soon after birth, suggesting that they do not reflect learning, response biases, or postnatal environmental factors. For example, Reinisch and Sanders (1992) reported that newborn girls are more sensitive to touch than newborn boys. They found evidence of sex differences in the functional development of the central nervous system as early as 3 months of age. These are important findings in our quest to understand sex differences in cognition because these early perceptual differences could create behavioral dispositions that vary as a function of sex. Slight behavioral predispositions could then be exaggerated, reduced, eliminated, or ignored, depending on the way in which cultures respond to male–female differences. These findings do not mean that sex differences in cognition are inevitable or unalterable, only that they probably have an early physiological basis.

There are also sizable sex differences in temporal cognition, that is, our knowledge of and judgments about the passage of time. Interestingly, the nature of the differences in temporal judgments depends on how they are measured. When the task involves saying how long an interval lasted, that is, a verbal response, women give longer estimates than men, but when the response requires producing a time interval (e.g., depress a buzzer for 12 seconds), women produce intervals that are shorter than those produced by men (Hancock, Arthur, Chrysler, & Lee, 1994; Zakay & Block, 1997). It has been hypothesized that these differences are caused by differences in body temperatures between females and males (Hancock, Vercruyssen, & Rodenburg, 1992). Females have higher resting body temperatures than males, which may affect the way in which each sex estimates time intervals. In an extensive review of sex differences in time perception, Block, Hancock, and Zakay (1999) concluded that there are small but reliable differences in the way women and men judge the passage of time, but these differences are moderated by many variables, including age and the way in which time judgments are assessed.

Sex differences favoring females have also reliably been found on speeded perceptual tests and some perceptual-motor tasks. There are several tests that tap these abilities, each somewhat different in what it measures. Tests of perceptual speed and perceptual motor skills may require the rapid matching of stimuli, such as novel shapes, the "Finding *A*'s Task," which requires scanning long columns of words and crossing those that contain the letter *A*, and copying simple forms from one line to another (Gouchie & Kimura, 1991). These tasks usually require rapid, fine motor movements, another area in which females excel. Jensen (1998) found a very large female advantage on tests of perceptual speed, with the effect size (d) as large as 0.86 among 12th-grade students. This is a very large difference between the boys and the girls on these tests.

Numerous studies have shown that females are usually superior at tasks that require fine motor manipulations. Kimura (1993) defined *motor dexterity* as "quick and effective use of the hands in the manipulation of small objects" (p. 1107). Nicholson and Kimura (1996) determined that women were faster than men when the task involved rapid repetitions of a sequence of movements; O'Boyle and Hoff (1987) and O'Boyle, Hoff, and Gill (1995) confirmed this conclusion with tasks that involved mirror-reversed spatial tasks. These tests are sometimes labeled *clerical skills tests* and have been used to argue that females are naturally suited for clerical tasks like typing. I note here that fine motor skills also are needed in a variety of other professions such as brain surgery and the repair of small engines. One could just as easily use these experimental results to argue that females are naturally better suited for these other professions as well. Once again, I stress the distinction between research findings and the interpretation of these findings.

Findings of female superiority on fine motor tasks were questioned by Peters and Campagnaro (1996), who hypothesized that female superiority on fine motor tasks is an artifact of sex differences in finger size. To test this possibility, they had males and females perform a task that required the participants to rapidly move pegs in a peg board. They used both thick and thin pegs and had the participants perform the task with and without tweezers as a way of controlling for finger size. They found that the female advantage on this task disappeared when the participants had to use tweezers, a result that they interpreted as support for their hypothesis. Even if the results were caused by differences in average finger size, it does not negate the finding that, on average, females perform fine motor tasks faster and with greater precision than males, showing once again that answers to questions about sex differences depend on a host of variables.

In contrast, motor tasks that involve throwing a projectile or otherwise aiming at a moving or stationary target show large advantages for males (Hall & Kimura, 1995; Watson & Kimura, 1991). This conclusion is based on studies that required throwing darts at a dartboard or balls at a target and computer games that required participants to "hit" a moving target on the screen, a task formally known as *projectile interception*. This is an important finding in the literature because of its implications for evolutionary theories. Recall from chapter 1 that males were the hunters in hunter–gatherer societies and would need these skills to kill prey and human and animal enemies. Of course, starting at an early age, males in Western societies have more practice throwing balls and other objects, so it is also possible that these differences in throwing accuracy result from differential life experiences and are not a legacy from our evolutionary past.

The ability to attend to stimuli and to switch attention is both a precursor to and a consequence of the thinking process. There are huge sex discrepancies in attention disorders. Sex ratios for attention deficit disorder (a psychiatric diagnostic category that often includes hyperactivity) range from 3:1 to 9:1, with the higher value corresponding to the proportion of males (American Psychiatric Association, 1994; Rebok, 1987). Thus, sex differences are found in both perception and attention—the earliest stages of information processing—and in some fine and gross motor skills.

Even though there is considerable evidence for some sex differences in perception and attention, it is difficult to translate findings like differential touch sensitivity and hearing thresholds into predictions about cognitive performance. A conservative conclusion is that although there seem to be perceptual and attentional differences between women and men, we can only speculate about their influence on cognitive abilities, especially for males and females in the middle range of intellectual ability—the portion of the abilities distributions in which most people (by definition) belong.

A COGNITIVE ABILITIES APPROACH

As stated earlier, there are no practical differences in the scores obtained by males and females on intelligence tests. However, sex differences are found in the subscores on intelligence tests. Intelligence tests consist of several subscores, each presumably reflecting a separate cognitive component. One of the most widely used intelligence tests was devised by David Wechsler. The adult version is known as the Wechsler Adult Intelligence Scale (WAIS, 1981), and the children's version is the Wechsler Intelligence Scale for Children (WISC, 1991). The newest version of the WAIS is designated as WAIS–III. The WISC and the WAIS yield three scores of intelligence: an overall IQ score, which does not show sex differences, a verbal subscore composed of scores on verbal subtests, and a performance subscore composed of scores on performance or spatial subtests (Brody, 1992).

There are theoretical reasons for separating mental abilities into separate categories. One line of research has focused on the memory systems that are used for performing different cognitive tasks. Logie (1995) and Shah and Miyake (1996) presented data and theories that support the idea that there are separable cognitive processes that operate (somewhat) independently from each other. Shah and Miyake separated working memory into verbal and visual–spatial processes. Visual–spatial working memory is the type of memory that is used for simultaneously processing and maintaining spatial information and other types of information that may involve sequencing or interconnectedness. It is used for creating mental representations, such as imaging what a figure would look like in another orientation or performing mental arithmetic, and for storing information about the beginning and intermediate steps in these processes. Logie as well as Shah and Miyake presented an array of experimental results showing that these separate systems can operate simultaneously with little interference from each other. Spatial thinking and language comprehension have long been identified as separable components of cognition. It is a useful distinction for studying sex differences in cognitive abilities. It is interesting to note that sex differences in memory also are found with nonhuman primates (Bachevalier & Hagger, 1991).

In 1974, Maccoby and Jacklin published a text that has become a classic in psychology. In their text, they reviewed more than 1,000 research reports on sex differences that had been published before 1974. Although their synthesis and review of the literature is now more than 25 years old and has been severely criticized on methodological grounds, it provided a foundation for much of the research that has followed. They identified three cognitive abilities and one personality variable in which sex differences are "fairly well established" (Maccoby & Jacklin, 1974, p. 351). The sex differences literature has burgeoned in the years since 1974 and, in general, has confirmed and extended their conclusions. The three cognitive abilities that have been identified as the loci of sex differences are verbal, quantitative, and visual–spatial abilities. Each of these abilities is discussed in turn below. Aggression was identified as the personality variable that differs by sex. The possibility that aggression may mediate or influence cognitive abilities is discussed in chapters 4 and 5. It is important to keep in mind that although the preponderance of the data supports these conclusions, there is also conflicting evidence in each of these areas, and no single sex difference is unanimously supported in the literature.

In tackling the vast literature on cognitive sex differences, it is difficult to know how to organize research findings and their theoretical implications. Keep in mind that the categories that scientists create to conceptualize research findings and to guide future research also constrain the results. It is possible that a different system of categorizing cognitive abilities would show a different pattern of sex differences. By discussing differences in verbal, quantitative, and visual–spatial abilities, the organizing schema is the type of material—words, numerical information, or spatial arrays—that is being learned, retrieved, and used. But there are also multiple cognitive processes that could serve as the organizing framework. We could just as easily examine differences in working memory (the type of memory used when we are actively working on a task such as recalling a string of numbers, imagining what a figure would look like if it were rotated in space, or calculating the answer to a lengthy problem). Working memory could be subdivided into rote recall, transformations of visual–spatial information, and so forth. In the following sections, I not only follow the usual organization of tasks into verbal, quantitative, and visual–spatial, with a separate section on memory, but I also show how these tasks can be organized according to their underlying cognitive process, an organizational framework that may be more useful in understanding the way in which a multiplicity of factors influences cognitive abilities.

MEMORY

There are many varieties of memory, which means that cognitive psychologists do not think of memory as a unitary construct. Because there are many different types of memory, no single test can correspond to memory in general, and any conclusions about sex differences in memory have to be modified to make them more specific to the task used to assess memory and what we believe to be true about the underlying cognitive processes. In an examination of sex differences in memory, Stumpf and Jackson (1994) analyzed a battery of tests that each assess different aspects of memory. Their participants were medical school applicants in Germany during a 9-year period. They found that women were substantially better on these tests of memory than were men ($d = 0.56$, more than one half of a standard deviation unit). Stumpf (1995) explained that memory is usually not studied in the context of sex differences because it is not a single concept (in the jargon of cognitive psychology, it is not a pure factor), a fact that makes it difficult to obtain consistent findings among studies. He believes that the size of the female advantage on memory tasks has been underestimated because the tasks that researchers use are unreliable and memory is a multidimensional construct. Stumpf and Jackson's use of a test battery corrected for some of these problems. In a later study, Stumpf and Eliot (1995) examined academically talented students in middle school and high school in the United States. In that study, they also found an advantage for females on tests of visual memory. Recall from an earlier discussion in this chapter that females also have better memory than males for odors.

In a study of healthy adolescents between 16 and 18 years of age, Geffen, Moar, O'Hanlon, Clark, and Geffen (1990) found that girls recalled significantly more words from word lists than boys did. An extensive review of multiple tests by Jensen (1998) showed that females scored higher on tests of short-term memory (memories that were approximately 1–2 minutes old), with an effect size between 0.20 and 0.30 depending on the nature of the test. These results also have been found with a sample of Chinese high school students in which the girls had larger word spans (short-term memory for words, $d = .54$) and larger working memories

($d = 0.35$; Huang, 1993). These differences in some types of memory can be found throughout the life span. Larrabee and Crook (1993) reported that among older adults, women perform better than men on several different verbal-learning–remembering tasks, name–face associations, the grocery-list selective-reminding task (which is exactly what its name implies), and first–last-name associates learning (also exactly what its name implies).

Females also may have better memories for spatial locations. This is the conclusion from studies by Eals and Silverman (1994), who believe these data reflect evolutionary origins from hunter–gatherer societies in which females needed good memory for the locations of plants in their role as the gatherers. Birenbaum, Kelly, and Levi-Keren (1994) reported that females excel at associative memory tasks, once again confirming that, overall, females have better memories than males. Another way of conceptualizing differences in types of memory is to divide memories into episodic—memory for events in one's own life—and semantic—general memory for facts, such as the multiplication tables, historical events that were not experienced personally (e.g., the life of George Washington), and general word knowledge. Herlitz, Nilsson, and Baeckman (1997) found that females have better episodic memory than males. In interpreting this finding, it is useful to consider that Herlitz et al. used only verbal tasks, so it may be that the advantage they found for females in episodic memory pertains only to verbal memories or the language skills used in reporting them. We now know that this advantage extends into old age, with older women showing the same advantage as their younger counterparts (Luszcz, Bryan, & Kent, 1997).

The female advantage in memory is found across a variety of tasks and ages. Females have better recognition memory than males throughout childhood and through their adult years (McGivern et al., 1997). In a very different approach to the question of sex differences in memory, Mullen (1994) found that females report their earliest memories as occurring at an earlier age than males do. The mean age for females' first memory is 37.8 months, whereas the mean age for males' first memory is 43 months. Mullen concluded that "whenever differences are found, it is females that have the earlier memories" (p. 63).

VERBAL ABILITIES

Women appeared to perform relatively well with a format
that requires written responses.
—Bridgeman and McHale (1996, p. 16)

Evidence from a variety of sources supports the finding that, on average, females have better verbal abilities than males. Like the other cognitive abilities, verbal abilities are not a unitary concept. The term applies to all components of language usage: word fluency, which is the ability to generate words (both in isolation and in a meaningful context); grammar; spelling; reading; writing; verbal analogies; vocabulary; and oral comprehension. There is also strong neurological evidence that separate brain subsystems are involved in generating language, comprehending language, using grammatical rules, and producing and decoding speech sounds (Gazzaniga, Ivry, & Mangun, 1998). The size and the reliability of the sex difference depend on which of these aspects of language usage are being assessed. Consider the various verbal questions that are shown in Fig. 3.1. As you can see, they tap related but somewhat different abilities. Much of the confusion in the literature comes from the failure to distinguish between language tasks, some of which show no sex differences whereas others show large sex differences. When sex differences in verbal abilities are found, they vinrtually always show female superiority.

TESTS OF VERBAL ABILITIES

1. Name as many words as you can that start with the letter "k."

2. Select the word that is most nearly the same in meaning:

     VIVACIOUS   A) HONEST

                       B) MEDIOCRE

                       C) LIVELY

                       D) BRAT

3. IGLOO : INDIAN :: TEPEE :

     A) ICE   B) CANVAS   C) ESKIMO   D) HOME

4. Answer the questions based on the information provided in this passage.

The literature with regard to sex differences in verbal abilities has been mixed with some researchers reporting large differences and others reporting no statistically significant differences. It seems that the controversy can be resolved by looking at the types of verbal tasks in which differences are found and determining how they differ from tasks in which differences are not found. It may be that tasks like solving verbal analogies are more similar to mathematical problem solving than to some of the other verbal tasks.

a) What is the "controversy" that is referred to in the second sentence?

b) Why does the author suggest that verbal analogies are similar to mathematical problems?

5. Which is correct?

a) Give the money to Bob and I.

b) Give the money to Bob and me.

6. Recall the words in a word list (e.g., book, sign, worry, sleep, justice, railroad, money, diamond, child, hospital, movie, lamp) or recall the objects in a room you were in recently.

7. Write a story about growing up as an immigrant in a foreign country.

Figure 3.1. Tests of Verbal Abilities. Each of these tests may be tapping a qualitatively different type of verbal ability.

There are numerous indicators of sex differences in verbal abilities when we consider the low end of the verbal abilities distribution. Boys are classified as learning disabled at approximately twice the rate of girls and as emotionally disturbed at four times the rate of girls, two factors that are probably related (Henning-Stout & Close-Conoley, 1992). Stuttering, a disability in the production of fluent speech, is overwhelmingly a male problem. Approximately 4% to 5% of the population are considered stutterers. Of this large number, there are three to four times more male stutterers than female stutterers (Skinner & Shelton, 1985). Other experts have estimated sex ratios in stuttering to be as high as 10:1 (Starkweather, 1987). When Andrews, Morris-Yates, Howie, and Martin (1991) tallied those people who reported that they "ever stuttered," sex ratios reduced to 2.7:1. Thus, the exact ratio of males to females depends on how stuttering is operationalized, but all measures clearly show that stuttering is overwhelmingly a male disorder. Dyslexia, a severe reading disability found in individuals whose other cognitive abilities are within normal ranges, is also predominantly a male problem (Vandenberg, 1987). Although approximately 2% of the school population is dyslexic, mild dyslexia is 5 times more likely to occur in males than in females, and severe dyslexia is 10 times more likely to appear in males than in females (Bannatyne, 1976; Gordon, 1980; Sutaria, 1985). Recently, researchers have suspected that boys are more likely to be identified as dyslexic because of behavior problems and that the actual sex ratios are not as extreme as there figures suggest (American Psychiatric Association, 1994). James (1992) addressed the question of a possible referral bias that causes more boys than girls to be diagnosed as dyslexic but concluded that there is a biological propensity that make boys more susceptible to dyslexia. The same conclusion has been reached by other researchers (DeFries & Gillis, 1993). Stein (1994) estimated that four to five times as many boys as girls are dyslexic, a figure that is comparable with sex ratios in other common neurological disorders. Even young boys who don't fall into the extreme low-ability end of the distribution are more likely to stutter when producing speech and are more likely to have difficulty in learning to read (Corballis & Beale, 1983); however, it is important to note that differences are much smaller when we consider the majority of the population that falls within the "normal" range of verbal abilities.

There are also sex differences in the ability to regain language after strokes and brain surgery, with males having more language impairment and recovering language ability more slowly than females (Witelson, 1976). Thus, the research evidence from a variety of sources favors female superiority on verbal tasks. Despite the finding that females score higher on many tests of verbal ability, the overwhelming majority of critically acclaimed writers are male. Other careers and prestigious professions that require advanced verbal abilities, careers like lawyer, politician, and journalist, are also predominantly male. Adelman (1991), in a report for the U.S. Department of Education, called this the "paradox of achievement" and lamented the economic loss to the United States created by the underdevelopment of women's intellectual potential. In his own words, "The paradox of this story—that women's educational achievements were superior to those of men, but that their rewards in the labor market were thin by comparison—is set in the context of national economic development" (Adelman, 1991, p. v). There are several possible reasons for the discrepancy between women's abilities and their achievement. It is possible that women are not using their talents as frequently as men, the tests are not measuring high-level creative ability, or differential criteria are being used to judge women's and men's writing. Another likely reason for the lack of critically acclaimed female writers is the fact that until recently women were not educated to the same extent as men and, even when educated, had little time to write. It is interesting to note that several outstanding female writers, such as Dickinson and the Brontes, were single women with other means of support. If ability is only a small part of eminence, then the lack of eminent female writers is not surprising.

Age Trends in Verbal Abilities

Of all the cognitive sex differences, differences in verbal ability are among the first to appear developmentally. Girls between 1 and 5 years of age are more proficient in language skills than their male counterparts (McGuiness, 1976; Smolak, 1986). There is also some evidence that girls may talk about 1 month earlier than boys and produce longer utterances than boys (e.g., Gazzaniga et al., 1998; Moore, 1967; Shucard, Shucard, & Thomas, 1987). There are significant sex differences in the rate of vocabulary growth during the toddler years. On average, there is a 13-word difference in vocabulary size between girls and boys at 16 months of age, which grows to a 51-word difference at 20 months and a 115-word difference at 24 months (Huttenlocher, Haight, Bryk, Seltzer, & Lyons, 1991). These researchers found that the differential rate in vocabulary growth was unrelated to how much mothers spoke to their children—mothers spoke as much to their infant sons as to their infant daughters. They concluded that "gender differences in early vocabulary growth seem to reflect early capacity differences" (Huttenlocher et al., 1991, p. 245).

In one of the most detailed investigations of language development among children aged 2½ to 4 years old, Horgan (1975) examined the mean length of utterances for girls and boys. She argued that mean length of utterances is a good indicator of linguistic maturity for preschool children who are learning their first language. Horgan reported that before a mean length of utterances of four words, boys and girls perform equally well; however, sex differences favoring girls occur beyond mean length of utterances of four words (i.e., girls use longer utterances at younger ages than boys). Horgan also analyzed other indicators of linguistic maturity, including use of the passive voice (e.g., "The lamp was broken."), use of truncated passive voice (e.g., "The window's broken."), and use of participles (verbs used as adjectives; e.g., "The moving truck crashed."). Girls spontaneously generated all of these advanced linguistic forms at an earlier age than boys; furthermore, they made fewer errors in language usage overall. Horgan (1975) concluded, "Girls produce longer utterances at younger ages, they produce more varied constructions, and they make fewer errors" (p. 48). It also seems that girls between 20 and 30 months of age spontaneously produce language more often than boys of the same age (Morisset, Barnard, & Booth, 1995) Of course, not every study shows exactly the same findings. Wolf and Gow (1985), for example, found that among 5- and 6-year-olds, girls were better in language and reading processes but boys showed an advantage in vocabulary knowledge. No sex differences were found in spontaneous language use among a sample of "high-social-risk" infants (Morisset et al., 1995). In general, the majority of the evidence tends to support the idea that females are more verbally precocious than males, but the effects are small and probably of little practical significance.

There is also evidence that girls maintain their superiority in verbal skills throughout elementary school (e.g., Butler, 1984). From approximately age 5 and older, girls have an advantage on verbal learning tasks (Kramer, Delis, Kaplan, O'Donnell, & Prifitera, 1997). Martin and Hoover (1987) conducted a large-scale longitudinal study in which they examined children's scores on the Iowa Test of Basic Skills in each grade from Grades 3 to 8 for 4,875 girls and 4,497 boys. They reported that girls scored higher on tests of spelling, capitalization, punctuation, language usage, reference materials, and reading comprehension. It is important to note here that the between-sex differences were quite large. In Grade 8, for example, two thirds of the highest scoring students on the language tests were female. Results from the Differential Aptitude Test of Spelling also show a significant female advantage ($d = 0.38$ to 0.50; Stanley, Benbow, Brody, Dauber, & Lupkowski, 1992). As psychologists learn more about the nature of verbal abilities, new tests have been devised that show very large sex differences. Hines (1990) found very large differences on tests of associational fluency (which is a fancy term for generating synonyms). Her results showed a huge female advantage, with an effect size of 1.2! Similarly high values have been reported on a consonant–vowel matching test, with a female advantage effect size of 1.3 (Block, Arnott, Quigley, & Lynch, 1989). These are enormous effect sizes—so large that tests of statistical significant are not even needed.

Female superiority on verbal tasks may seem reminiscent of the stereotype that females talk more than males, but it is important to keep in mind that it is the quality of the speech produced and the ability to comprehend or decode language that is being assessed, not merely the quantity. Studies in naturalistic mixed-sex settings show that males talk more and interrupt more than females (Bilous & Krauss, 1988).

Effect Sizes for Verbal Abilities

In an extensive meta-analytic review of the literature on sex differences in verbal ability, Hyde and Linn (1988) divided experiments on the basis of the age of the participants and the type of verbal ability assessed—all tests, vocabulary tests, and tests of reading comprehension. Differences were found in the "all tests" category for children 5 years and younger ($d = 0.13$) and for adults older than 26 years ($d = 0.20$), both favoring females. There were no notable differences as a function of sex for ages 6 through 25. The developmental pattern of vocabulary proficiency is difficult to comprehend. They reported a male advantage in the 6- to 10-year-old age range ($d = -0.26$) and a female advantage in the 19- to 25-year-old age range ($d = 0.23$), with essentially no differences in the other age categories. The largest differences were in reading comprehension for children 5 years of age and younger, with girls reading more proficiently than boys ($d = 0.31$). Hyde and Lynn's meta-analytic review is now more than a dozen years old and may have underestimated the size of the female advantage on a variety of verbal tasks, at least when compared with more recent studies, probably because of the types of verbal ability tests they reviewed.

Females appear to have a clear advantage on writing tasks, a fact that led to the inclusion of a writing component on such high-stakes tests as the PSAT as a means of increasing gender equity on this test. Skillful writing is a generative activity that includes good organization of ideas, grammatically correct constructions, and accurate use of words. The conclusion that females excel in writing was bolstered by data released by the U.S. Department of Education on writing proficiency tests given at Grades 4, 8, and 11 in 1984, 1988, and 1990. These data are graphically presented in Fig. 3.2. Take a careful look at Fig. 3.2. The graph shows that girls in these grades were writing better than same-age boys and that the female advantage was stable during the developmental period from Grades 4 to 11 and during the 6-year period from 1984 to 1990.

When we examine sex differences in verbal abilities in old age, the picture becomes less clear. In a meta-analytic review of 25 studies of older adults, Meinz and Salthouse (1998) did not find the expected female advantage in verbal abilities. As the authors noted, they did not have measures of those verbal areas in which women show the largest advantage, for example, reading comprehension and writing. It is possible that they would have reached a different conclusion if tests of these key verbal ability areas had been included. We really do not know if women retain their overall advantage on these complex verbal tasks into old age.

VISUAL–SPATIAL ABILITIES

Too many jokes to recount here are made about the spatial skills of women versus men. While once good-humored, they now take on a social significance that becomes lost in current social values.
—Gazzaniga et al. (1998, p. 507)

The term *visual–spatial abilities* may not convey much meaning to people who are not cognitive psychologists. In fact, it is not an easy term to define because it is not a unitary concept. Linn and Petersen (1985) provided this definition: "*Spatial ability* generally refers to skill in representing transforming, generating, and recalling symbolic, nonlinguistic information" (p. 1482). Generally, it refers to the ability to imagine what an irregular figure would look like if it were rotated in space or the ability to discern the relationship between shapes and objects. The ability to use spatial relationships is an important aspect of human thought. Visual–spatial skills

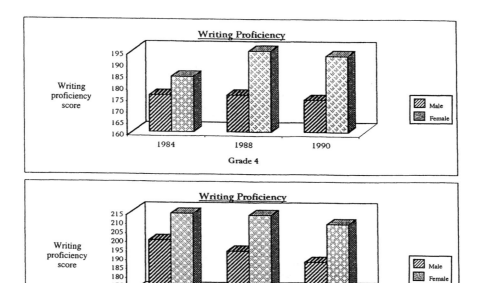

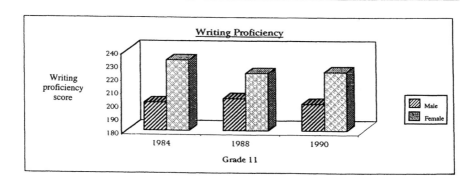

FIG. 3.2.   Comparisons of girls' and boys' scores on a writing proficiency test administered in 1984, 1988, and 1990 at Grades 4, 8, and 11. (Source: U.S. Department of Education, National Center for Education Statistics, National Assessment of Educational Progress, Trends in Academic Progress, prepared by Educational Testing Service, Indicator 32: Writing Proficiency, 1998).

are used extensively in engineering, architecture, chemistry, the building trades, and aircrew selection (Lohman, 1988). Tests of visual–spatial ability have been used to predict success in 1st-year engineering courses (Poole & Stanley, 1972). After reviewing the literature on visual–spatial ability, Cooper and Mumaw (1985) concluded, "The spatial aptitude literature is quite clear in showing that a broadly defined spatial factor exists independently of verbal and quantitative factors and that this spatial factor is more effective than other measures of intelligence in predicting success in certain academic and industrial areas" (p. 71). Early factor-analytic studies that sought to delineate the structure of intelligence found that verbal tests and visual–spatial ability tests formed two distinct factors. The distinction between verbal and visual–spatial abilities as separate components of intelligence has been replicated many times.

Part of the difficulty in understanding the literature on visual–spatial ability is due to the fact that, like all of the other broad cognitive categories, it is not a unitary concept. In 1983, Nyborg summarized the literature to date by noting that males usually scored higher than females on numerous tests of spatial ability including Porteus Mazes, Money's Road Map Test, Piaget's Perspectives, Water-Level Tasks, Geometric Forms, House Plans Task, Rod and Frame Test, Embedded Figures Test, Tilting Room/Tilting Chair, Mental Rotation, and WAIS Analytic Triad. In 1986, Linn and Petersen factor analyzed tests of visual–spatial abilities, and three separate factors emerged. Although numerous new tests of visual–spatial ability have been used since then, and hundreds of different tests have been identified as measures of visual–spatial abilities (Stumpf & Eliot, 1995), the three categories that they identified plus two others—one that involves movement through space and another that involves the generation and maintenance of visual images—are a good organizing framework for understanding the literature in this area. If you wonder what "generation and maintenance of visual images" means, try this demonstration: Think about a lowercase letter *B*. Is the round portion of the *B* to the left or to the right of the vertical line that forms the other portion of the letter? To answer this question, you have to generate a visual image of a lowercase *b* and then maintain that image in memory while answering questions about its appearance. This is an example of generating and maintaining a visual image.

I have included memory for visual–spatial information on this list of visual–spatial tasks, even though it was discussed in the section on sex differences in memory. All of these tasks involve several types of memory, so they fit into more than one cognitive category. It seems that there are at least five qualitatively different types of visual–spatial ability:

1. *Spatial perception,* which requires participants to locate the horizontal or the vertical in a stationary display while ignoring distracting information. Examples are the Rod and Frame Test, which requires participants to position a rod within a tilted frame so that it is either vertical or horizontal, and the Piaget Water-Level Task, which requires participants to draw in the water level of a tilted glass that is half filled with water.

2. *Mental rotation,* which includes the ability to imagine how objects will appear when they are rotated in two- or three-dimensional space. There are timed and untimed versions of these tests. Several researchers believe that mental rotation is a measure of a general spatial reasoning ability (Casey, Nuttall, Pezaris, & Benbow, 1995).
3. *Spatial visualization,* which refers to complex, analytic, multistep processing of spatial information. Tests that tap spatial visualization are the Embedded Figures Test, paper folding, hidden figures, and Spatial Relations Test.
4. *Spatiotemporal ability,* which involves judgments about and responses to dynamic (i.e., moving) visual displays. There are several different tasks that involve information that is moving, such as having participants press a key when a target is coincident with a stationary line (Smith & McPhee, 1987) and making "time of arrival" judgments about a moving object (Schiff & Oldak, 1990). Investigators have concluded that the ability to reason about dynamic visual displays is correlated with, but different from, the abilities used in reasoning about static displays (Hunt, Pellegrino, Frick, Farr, & Alderton, 1988).
5. *Generation and maintenance of a spatial image,* which requires participants to generate an image (either from long-term or short-term memory) and then use the information in the image to perform a task.

Figure 3.3 depicts test items similar to the kinds used to measure spatial perception, mental rotation, spatial visualization, spatiotemporal abilities, and the generation and maintenance of visual–spatial images.

Given the large variety of tests that have been used to measure visual–spatial ability, it is not surprising that sex differences depend on the type of test used. Not coincidentally, this is an area replete with contradictory findings because of the multidimensional complexity of visual–spatial abilities. Caplan et al. (1985) questioned the legitimacy of the assumption that the construct "spatial abilities" exists. They believe that the entire notion suffers from a "definitional dilemma." As noted in Halpern's (1986) response to Caplan et al., much of the confusion in this area is attributable to the types of spatial ability tests used. Although some researchers have failed to find sex differences (e.g., Fennema & Sherman, 1978, using the Spatial Relations Test), sex differences that favor males are consistently found with two of the three factors that entail static displays—spatial perception and mental rotation tasks (Linn & Petersen, 1986)—and with spatiotemporal tasks (Schiff & Oldak, 1990; Smith & McPhee, 1987). Tasks involving the generation and maintenance of a visual–spatial image also seem to show male superiority in speed of processing with no differences in accuracy. McGee's (1979) summary of the literature is apparently still valid—male superiority on tasks requiring spatial abilities is among the most persistent of individual differences in all the abilities literature. This conclusion was echoed by Schiff and Oldak (1990): "There is strong converging evidence for gender-related differences in accuracy of judging time of arrival" (p. 315).

Spatial Perception

A Schematic Diagram of the Rod and Frame Test
Align a rod within these frames so that the rod is vertical.

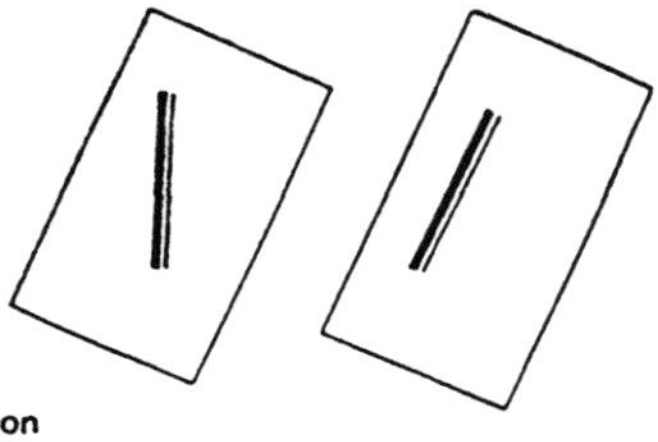

Mental Rotation

Are these pairs of figures the same except for their orientation? (reaction times and accuracy measured)

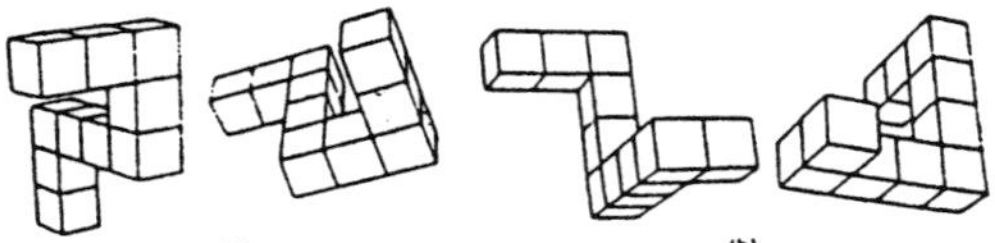

(a)   (b)

Spatial Visualization

Is Figure (a) part of Figure (b)?

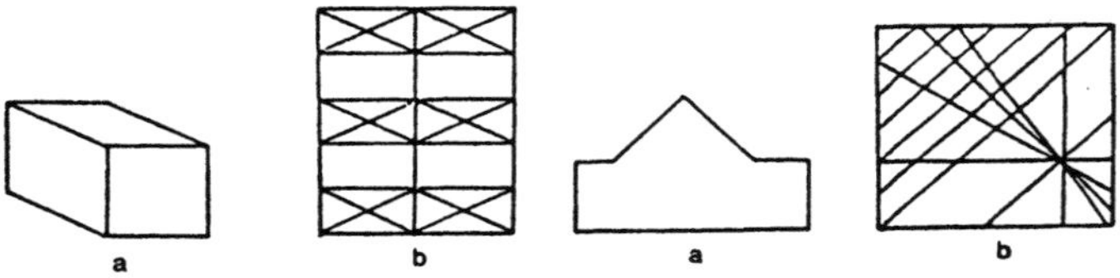

a   b   a   b

Spatiotemporal Abilities

A moving ball is obscured by the solid area on a computer screen.
Press computer key when you expect it to be visible on other side of
solid area. (Reaction times measured)

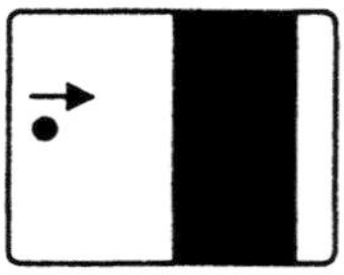

Generation and Maintenance of a Visual Image

(1) Image a capital   (2)   (3) Does the capital
    letter "b" on the   letter "b" cover
    grid at right.   the solid square?

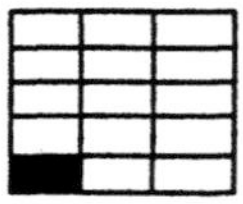

(4) Press one computer key for "yes" and a different one for "no".
    (Reaction times measured)

FIG. 3.3.   Examples of tests used to measure spatial perception, mental rotation, spatial visualization, spatiotemporal abilities, and generation and maintenance of a visual image. In the Rod and Frame Test, participants are required to position a rod to the vertical position within a tilted rectangular frame. The rod is incorrectly positioned in the right-hand figure.

Robust sex differences favoring males are found when the task involves move-ment-related judgments, such as judging velocity (Law, Pellegrino, & Hunt, 1993). Although it is difficult to isolate any single factor that may be responsible for these results, judgments concerning dynamic visual displays must involve time estimation (i.e., when will the moving object reach a destination). Recall that there are sex differences in time perception, with females overestimating time intervals relative to males when the task requires a verbal response and females underesti-mating time intervals relative to males when the task involves producing a re-sponse. Because the perception of movement involves judgments about both time and space, it may be that some portion of the sex-related differences found with dy-namic displays may be due to differences in time perception. A more likely or per-haps larger contribution to these differences is the differential experience with games involving balls and other activities that develop eye–hand coordination. These possible explanations are considered in later chapters in this book in which the theory and the research that bear on these findings are discussed.

Visual–spatial imagery was recently investigated by Loring-Meier and Halpern (1999) with a set of four tasks. In one of the tasks, participants had to generate an image of a capital letter and then decide if the letter would cover a portion of a rect-angular frame. A second task required participants to image a geometric figure that had just been displayed (i.e., without retrieval from long-term memory) and then make a similar spatial judgment. A third task required participants to scan an im-age that they retrieved from long-term memory, and a fourth task required the men-tal rotation of an image. These tasks were developed by Dror and Kosslyn (1994) for use in a study on age-related differences in visual imagery. In all four tasks, the male participants were significantly faster than the female participants, with no differences in accuracy (all $ds = 0.63$ to 0.77). The faster response times for the males could reflect an actual difference in the time it took to perform the cognitive tasks, but they also could reflect greater confidence on this task. There are cogni-tive tasks on which females generally show faster responding, so these results are not simply a matter of motor speed needed to respond or a general reflection of confidence or cautiousness. Readers are asked to keep all of these possible expla-nations in mind as they review the theories and the research presented in later chap-ters in this book.

Males are more likely than females to use imagery when solving problems, es-pecially problems that involve moving objects (Richardson, 1991). Perhaps the male advantage on spatiotemporal tasks can be partially explained by the use of vi-sual imagery in these tasks. Converging support for this idea comes from a study of gifted students who were in either the top 20% in spatial ability or the top 20% in verbal ability. For both females and males, twice the number of students who were majoring in the physical sciences were in the group with high spatial ability (Humphreys, Lubinski, & Yao, 1993). Given the importance of visual–spatial abil-ity to success in the physical sciences and many other professions (e.g., dentistry, carpentry, fashion design), the authors of this study argued for the addition of vi-sual–spatial tests to the math and verbal test batteries that are used for admission to colleges and graduate schools. Other evidence for the importance of visual imagery in solving two- and three-dimensional problems comes from a study of *mental animation*—the ability to infer movement in a static diagram (Hegarty & Sims, 1994). The researchers found that 47% of the test questions on the Differential Aptitudes Test of Mechanical Reasoning (Psychological Corporation, 1990) and 38% of the test questions on the Bennett Mechanical Comprehension Test (Bennett, 1969) involve inferring motion from a static display. For example, examine Fig. 3.4, which depicts a pulley system. Diagrams like this one are familiar to anyone who has ever taken a course in physics. To understand the concept of pulleys, and many other physical concepts, the reader must be able to visualize the system in motion only on the basis of the diagram shown. Performance on these test items was compared for students who were either high or low on spatial ability. As the researchers predicted, students in the low-spatial-ability group made significantly more errors on these problems than students in the high-spatial-ability group. Although this study did not address sex differences in these tasks, I note here that mechanical reasoning tests show large sex differences favoring males ($d = 0.66$ to 0.89; Stumpf, 1995).

Caplan et al. (1985) noted that the types of tasks that are used to assess spatial ability are fairly abstract and that a much more valid test would involve finding one's way in a real-world environment. This is certainly a sensible suggestion,

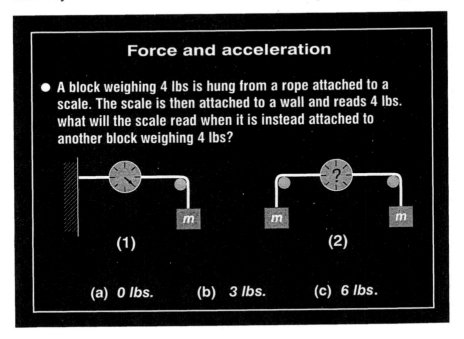

FIG. 3.4.   In this diagram of a pulley system, the reader needs to be able to imagine the simultaneous movement of multiple pulleys to understand the underlying physics principles.

even though spatial ability tests that are conducted outside of the laboratory are more difficult to administer. There is always the problem that some participants will have greater knowledge of a given geographical area. Furthermore, participants could rely quite well on verbal strategies when they have to maneuver through a real-world space (e.g., turn at the green house). The few studies that have investigated route knowledge and "way finding" tend to support laboratory findings. In general, men learned a route from a two-dimensional map in fewer trials and with fewer errors than a matched group of women (Galea & Kimura, 1993). This conclusion has been supported by research with other species. Even male rats excel in most maze learning tasks, a spatial task (Williams & Meck, 1991). Holding and Holding (1989) found that when college students made judgments about traveled distances (with route information provided on slides), male students were much more accurate than female students. Recent studies with computer-simulated mazes have shown "a large and reliable sex difference" (Astur, Ortiz, & Sutherland, 1998, p. 185), with males performing more accurately and more quickly on these mazes. Possible reasons for these differences are considered in later chapters in this book, so readers are urged to consider a variety of possible explanations that could include differential practice with computer games.

Data from the National Geography Bee tell a very compelling story. Liben (1995) estimated that 6 million school children in the United States participate in this competition. She described "a shocking gender disparity among winners at every level" (Liben, 1995, p. 8). In 1993, of the 18,000 school winners, approximately 14,000 were boys; of the 57 state winners (including U.S. territories), 55 were boys; and in most years, all 10 finalists were boys, despite the fact that girls and boys participate at almost equal rates. Liben found that geography is not a stereotypically male domain (unlike other fields like "being a plumber" or "fixing cars"). She reported that the boys were more interested in geography and liked it more than the girls did. Furthermore, these huge sex ratios are not a fluke that is unique to samples from the United States. They are similar to those found with the International Assessment of Education Progress that samples students from many countries.

There is not enough research at this time to conclude that there are any differences in how males and females actually find their way around in the world, which is different from, but related to, knowledge of geography. Thus, we do not have an answer for what may be the most practically significant spatial task. Nor are there any data to support the notion that females are less able drivers than males. In fact, all of the data suggest that the opposite is true—women have far fewer automobile accidents and auto citations than men, who are involved in 63% of all reported auto accidents (*Time,* 1990). Of course, it is possible that the female superiority in driving—fewer accidents and citations—is due to personality or sex role variables that are manifested in a more cautious response style and not spatial ability.

Unlike the other visual–spatial tasks, memory for location shows a female advantage (Biernbaum et al., 1994; Eals & Silverman, 1994; Silverman & Eals, 1992). These results are supported by studies that have found that females recall more landmarks when they are learning and using routes (Galea & Kimura, 1993) and they recall more objects in real-life locations (Hill et al., 1995), although recent studies have raised the question of whether females are really better at remembering objects, even when they are moved to a different location, or whether they are better at remembering the locations of objects (James & Kimura, 1997). In one test of the hypothesis that women have superior memory for location, Kimura (1996) presented participants with an array of objects in different locations and gave them 1 minute to study the array. She then showed them a second array in which half of the objects had been moved from their original location. Females were better than males at recalling which objects had been moved, an advantage that held up when Kimura repeated the study using unfamiliar objects that would not be easily labeled. It may be that the ability to remember the location of objects involved two separate processes—object memory and spatial memory, with females showing better object memory and males showing better memory for location (Postma, Izendoorn, & De Hoan, 1998; Postma, Winkel, Tuiten, & van Honk, 1999).

Most major reviews of the literature have concluded that males are more variable in their visual–spatial performance than females (e.g., see Willingham & Cole, 1997, for a review of hundreds of tests, many with spatial ability components). Hedges and Nowell (1995) conducted a meta-analysis of many types of tests and also concluded that males are more variable than females in their spatial ability. The finding of greater variability in male performance on spatial tasks is theoretically important because one hypothesis about the cause of the sex difference is that many females do not use a spatial-imagery strategy to solve problems that are spatial (e.g., geometry problems). Perhaps some try to visualize an answer, and others try to use verbal labels. If the sex difference in spatial ability were caused by the fact that more women than men use inappropriate strategies, then the females should show more variable performance than the males. Given the opposite finding, it seems unlikely that females use a greater variety of strategies with these tasks.

Age Trends in Visual–Spatial Abilities

The male advantage in spatial abilities is evident throughou the life span.
—Meinz and Salthouse (1998, p. 56)

Many of the differences in visual–spatial abilities appear early in life. The male advantage in transforming information in visual–spatial working memory is seen as early as it can be tested—perhaps at 3 years of age (Robinson, Abbott, Berninger, & Busse, 1996). The developmental pattern is probably somewhat different for each of the types of visual–spatial ability. In a meta-analysis of static spatial ability tasks, Linn and Petersen (1986) concluded that sex differences in mental rotation tasks appear as soon as they can be measured reliably (around age 10 or 11 years). The developmental pattern for spatial perception tasks is more complicated. In general, differences favoring males can first be detected around age 7; they accelerate to adult levels around age 11 but only reach statistical significance by age 18. The developmental question was also examined in a large-scale study of 1,800 students in Grades kindergarten through 12 (Johnson & Meade, 1987). The authors of this study compared performance on seven spatial tests by sex at each grade level. They concluded that a male advantage in spatial ability exists at least as early as 4th grade (age 10) over a wide range of paper-and-pencil measures and remains stable through age 18. The developmental pattern of sex differences in spatiotem- poral ability (e.g., time-of-arrival judgments about a moving display) is unknown at this time, although they are reliably found in college populations.

In addition to sex differences, there are age-related differences in both verbal and visual–spatial abilities. It is well established that both males and females maintain their verbal abilities into old age whereas visual–spatial abilities (especially when measured with speeded performance tests) begin to decline considerably earlier. The decline in old age of visual–spatial abilities is so well established that it is often referred to as "the classic aging pattern" (Winograd & Simon, 1980). For example, Dollinger (1995) reported that performance on mental rotation tasks and the Performance subtest of the WAIS declines significantly in aging populations. In applied research on this question, Halpern (1984) found that older drivers took significantly longer to respond to common symbolic or pictograph traffic signs (e.g., a red slash through an arrow pointing to the right) than to their verbal analogues (e.g., the words "No Right Turn") whereas young adult drivers were equally fast at responding to both types of traffic signs.

A common experimental paradigm for assessing visual–spatial abilities is the mental rotation task devised by Shepard and Metzler (1971). In this paradigm, participants are required to make a comparison between a rotated figure and its standard form and to decide whether the rotated figure is the same as its standard or the mirror image. An experiment by Clarkson-Smith and Halpern (1983) found that both the time to respond and the number of errors in a mental rotation task increased as a function of age; however, when their participants, all of whom were women, were encouraged to use verbal strategies in this task, errors decreased significantly for the oldest group. It seems that verbal mediation strategies can attenuate the sex and age-related deficits in visual–spatial abilities.

Meinz and Salthouse (1998) recently posed a question that is of great interest in an aging society, "Is age kinder to females than to males?" They examined data from 25 separate studies that compared men's and women's cognitive abilities in old age with those of younger adults. For the older group, they found the same overall pattern of cognitive sex differences that has been reported with younger age groups: Older women were faster than older men on speeded perceptual tests and were slightly (in this study, it was nonsignificantly) better on verbal fluency tasks; older men scored considerably better than older women on spatial tasks and somewhat better on working memory tasks (which may have been caused by the type of memory tasks they used). It is comforting to know that although the older adults declined in most cognitive abilities, especially spatial ability, they showed increases in knowledge into old age and no change in verbal fluency. There were also few sex by age interactions, but when they were found, it seems that males fared slightly better into old age. This means that for most cognitive measures, aging males and females declined at the same rate, with some evidence that males declined more slowly on some tasks. In answer to the question they posed, women did not maintain cognitive abilities into old age better than men. When considering cognitive abilities, age is not kinder to women than to men.

Water-Level Test

One test that is sensitive to sex differences is the Water-Level Test originally devised by Piaget and Inhelder (1956). In one version of this test, the participant is shown a bottle partially filled with water and is told to notice the way the water fills the bottle. The participant is then asked to predict where the water will be when the bottle is tipped. Piaget and Inhelder believed that the knowledge that water level remains horizontal would be attained at an average age of 12 years. It seems that girls demonstrate this principle at a later age than boys. In fact, it has been estimated that 50% of college women don't know the principle that water level remains horizontal. This is a surprising result that has been replicated many times (Thomas, Jamison, & Hummel, 1973; Wittig & Allen, 1984). Robert and Chaperon (1989), for example, reported that 32% of college women and 15% of college men failed the water-level task. Sex differences in the Water-Level Test have been confirmed with a sample from Bombay, India (DeLisi, Parameswaran, & McGillicuddy-DeLisi, 1989). It is difficult to understand why this is such a formidable task for college women. One possible version of the Water-Level Test is shown in Fig. 3.5.

Results from the Water-Level Test are strange. Why do women (in many samples college women were used as participants) perform less well on a test of whether water remains horizontal in a tilted glass? As discussed in chapter 6, at least part of the sex differences we find with spatial tasks can be attributed to differential learning experiences, with boys typically engaging in more spatial activities. Sex differences in the Water-Level Test are not amenable to this sort of explanation because no one believes that boys have more experiences than girls with glasses of water. In one study, Hecht and Proffitt (1995) hypothesized that experience with liquid surfaces would be associated with poorer performance on the

FIG. 3.5.   One version of the Water-Level Test. Assume that these glasses are half filled with water. Draw a line across each glass to indicate the top of the water line.

Water-Level Test because people who work frequently with liquids in containers may have adopted a perspective that was relative to the tilt of the container. In a test of the hypothesis that more experience would lead to poorer performance on the water-level task, Vasta, Rosenberg, Knott, and Gaze (1997) found the reverse results, that is, those participants with more experience performed better than those with less experience. Thus, the poorer performance of females on this test remains unexplained.

Kalichman (1989) investigated the possibility that the results reflect some idiosyncracy of the test, rather than sex differences in either the knowledge that water remains horizontal or the ability to draw an approximately horizontal line. Kalichman devised a more "ecologically valid" (i.e., more like the real world) test in which the tilted glass was held in a human hand. An example of his stimuli is shown in Fig. 3.6.

Kalichman (1989) found that significantly fewer college women than college men drew an approximately horizontal line to indicate the water level in both the standard test format and the human context format. He concluded that "sex differences on the water-level task remain robust regardless of task context" (Kalichman, 1989, p. 138). Many psychologists have studied sex differences on

FIG. 3.6.   The Water-Level Test embedded in an ecologically valid (i.e., real-world) context. This glass is half filled with water. Draw a line across the glass to indicate the top of the water line. Reprinted with permission from Kalichman (1989).

the water-level task, perhaps because it is surprising. Correct performance on this task requires that participants understand that the surface level of water remains horizontal regardless of the tilt of the glass. There have been numerous attempts to find strategies that would eliminate the sex difference on this task. Participants have performed this task both sitting and standing as a way of manipulating upright references and by statistically controlling for level of performance on the Rod and Frame Test (Robert & Ohlmann, 1994) and with and without practice (Vasta, Knott, & Gaze, 1996), without eliminating the sex difference on this task. As Vasta and Liben (1996) concluded in their review of this task, the puzzle is far from solved.

Cognitive Styles

There has been considerable interest in recent years in the notion that males and females may have different cognitive styles. The term *cognitive styles* does not have an intuitive meaning. In general, it refers to individual differences in modes of perceiving, remembering, and thinking (Kogan, 1973). It is used by some psychologists in conjunction with the concept of psychological differentiation (Witkin, Dyk, Faterson, Goodenough, Karp, & 1962). An individual who is highly differentiated can separate himself or herself from the environment and can separate items from each other in the environment. According to the theory of psychological differentiation, we all differ in terms of how well we can separate items in the environment. There are several dimensions or aspects of psychological differentiation. One dimension along which the sexes are said to differ is in field articulation, or "field dependence and independence." These terms were coined by Witkin et al. and have been used to characterize the degree to which participants are influenced by objects in their visual field.

One way of assessing field dependence and independence is with the Rod and Frame Test. In this test, participants are seated in a darkened room and are presented with a luminous rectangle (the frame) that has a luminous rod positioned inside of it. The rectangle is rotated to different orientations by the experimenter. The task for the participants is to position the rod so that it is vertical. Figure 3.3 shows a schematic drawing of some rod and frame combinations with which participants could be presented. Some participants' judgments of true vertical for the rod are influenced by the tilt of the frame surrounding the rod. They are labeled *field-dependent*. Other participants' judgments of true vertical for the rod are not influenced by the tilt of the frame surrounding the rod. They are labeled *field-independent*. In general, sex and age differences are found with the Rod and Frame Test (although differences are not unanimously reported). The usual findings are that children are more field-dependent than adults and that females are more field-dependent than males.

Measures of field dependence and independence obtained with the Rod and Frame Test are highly correlated with measures obtained with a test known as the Embedded Figures Test. In the Embedded Figures Test, participants are shown a simple geometric form and then must maintain it in memory and pick it out from a more complex form. Sample items similar to those found in the Embedded Figures Test are also shown in Fig. 3.3.

Both the Embedded Figures Test and the Rod and Frame Test require participants to segregate a geometric form from its context (the form is either an embedded multisided figure or the rod), and in both tests, females are more influenced by the context than males. Field dependence has been hypothesized to reflect personalities that are conforming, submissive to authority, into comfortable ruts, and passive (Elliot, 1961). Women's field dependence has been described as "accepting the field more passively than men" (Sherman, 1967, p. 290). On the basis of these test results, women's cognitive style has been described as "global," "conforming," and "child-like." According to Witkin et al. (1962), it is similar to the undifferentiated thought processes found in "primitive" cultures. The field independence associated with male performance has been described, by contrast, as reflecting a cognitive style that is "analytic" and "self-reliant." (The value-laden bias in these descriptive terms is too obvious to require comment.) Witkin et al. (1962) believed that because women are unable to maintain a "sense of separate identity" (p. 218), they are less skilled at certain types of problem solving, more likely to conform to group pressure, and more concerned with the facial expressions of others. Thus, different cognitive styles have been ascribed to men and women on the basis of their performance on these two tests. Purported differences in men's and women's cognitive styles have been used to explain the low participation rate of women in the physical sciences (Bar-Haim & Wilkes, 1989).

It would appear, however, that spatial tests of field dependence and independence are not indicative of cognitive styles, that is, they are unrelated to passivity or submissiveness, notwithstanding the claims of Witkin (1950; Witkin et al., 1954) and others, but merely reflect sex differences in visual–spatial abilities. Several researchers have argued that sex differences in field independence are an artifact of sex differences in visual–spatial ability because both the Rod and Frame Test and the Embedded Figures Test have a strong spatial component (Sherman, 1967). This is yet another example of the important distinction between experimental results and the explanations that we "invent" for them. Somehow a test of spatial ability came to be used as an indicator of personality traits and the inferiority of women.

Effect Sizes for Visual–Spatial Abilities

First of all, we have specified a number of tests that show highly significant sex differences that are stable across age, at least
after puberty and have not decreased in recent years.
—Voyer, Voyer, and Bryden (1995, p. 264)

As stated earlier, findings of sex differences in visual–spatial ability are the most robust (found consistently) of the cognitive sex differences, but the size of the effect varies depending on which visual–spatial task is being assessed. It also appears that the largest sex differences are found here. Earlier studies may have underestimated the size of this effect, probably because many different tests of visual–spatial ability were lumped together in the earlier studies. In thinking about sex differences in visual–spatial abilities, keep in mind the fact that we are really dealing with at least five separate abilities and the size of the sex difference is not the same across all of them. In a meta-analytic review of 286 studies, Voyer et al. (1995) concluded that spatial abilities are not a unitary concept and that, overall, of the ability factors, the mean effect size favoring males is 0.37. The authors calculated a "fail-safe" value for these findings. Recall from chapter 2 that the fail-safe value is the number of nonsignificant findings that would need to exist (unpublished and therefore unavailable) to nullify their conclusion. The fail-safe value for sex differences in visual–spatial abilities is 178,205. In plain English, there would need to be 178,205 studies that showed no significant sex differences and never were published to offset the available studies that found sex differences in visual–spatial abilities.

Voyer et al. (1995) concluded that there is a nonsignificant difference between males and females on spatial visualization tasks, but the effect size for spatial perception tasks is 0.44 and for mental rotation tasks is 0.56. By comparison, in a review of mental rotation studies, Masters and Sanders (1993) showed the effect size to be 0.90, and Resnick (1993) estimated the effect size to be in the range of 0.74 to 0.80. Differences in these exact values are not important (exact values also vary depending on whether the tests are timed or untimed, whether they include corrections for guessing, and the way responses are scored), but what is important is that the size of the sex difference in spatial abilities depends on the type of test, with some types of tests showing no sex differences and the largest differences found on mental rotation tests.

Another way of understanding the size of the sex-related differences is to compare the percentages of females and males exceeding a given score on a test. This is the binomial effect size display that was discussed in chapter 2. To underscore the size of the sex difference on a mental rotation test, Bouchard and McGee (1977) reported that only 20% of the females in the 200 families they tested scored above the median (50%) for males. A number of other researchers found similar male–female disparities (Harris, 1978). In fact, the Differential Aptitudes Tests are separately normed for each sex because of these differences. At Grade 12, for example, a girl who scores at the 80th percentile has a test score that is equal to that of a boy at the 70th percentile.

QUANTITATIVE ABILITIES

The underrepresentation of women in mathematics related careers, long an issue of equity and justice, has serious economic implications
as the United States faces a shortage of scientists, engineers,
and mathematically trained workers.
—Dunham (1998, www.ed.gov/databases/ERIC_digests/ed324195.html)

Plake, Loyd, and Hoover (1981) summarized findings of sex-related differences in quantitative (mathematical) ability this way: "There is little doubt that females score differently from males on mathematical tests" (p. 780). As you can probably guess, "differently" is a euphemism for poorer, but does this necessarily mean that males have more quantitative ability?

It seems that quantitative abilities, like spatial and verbal abilities, are a heterogeneous concept. There are several different aspects of quantitative abilities, and there is good evidence that sex differences are manifested in only some of them. Examples of the types of tasks that are used to assess quantitative ability are shown in Fig. 3.7.

Stones, Beckmann, and Stephens (1982) examined the question of sex differences in quantification abilities with students at 10 different colleges. The students, who obviously are not representative of all females and males because they had already met college admissions requirements, were given tests in 10 different mathematical categories. No significant overall sex differences were found using multivariate procedures that allowed the experimenters to consider all 10 test scores at once. Sex differences were found, however, on the individual subtests. Females scored significantly higher than males on the tests of mathematical sentences and mathematical reasoning, perhaps reflecting the use of verbal strategies in solving these problems. Males scored significantly higher than females in geometry, measurement, probability, and statistics, perhaps reflecting the use of visual–spatial strategies in these areas.

The finding of sex differences in some tests of quantitative or mathematical ability is robust. Consistent sex differences have been found in many large-scale studies. The largest differences favor males, who tend to outscore females on the quantitative portion (M) of the SAT (SAT–M). The male advantage on this highly standardized test that is administered nationally to college-bound high school seniors in the United States is approximately 40 points (College Entrance Examination Board, 1997). Because the SAT permits comparisons of scores across multiple years and with large samples, it is considered in a separate section in this chapter.

Quantitative skills are a prerequisite for entry into jobs requiring scientific and technical skills. Sells (1980) described mathematics as a "critical filter" that allows only some to pass into the higher paying prestigious jobs. One major problem with reports of sex differences in quantitative abilities is the failure to take into account the fact that the sexes are disproportionately represented in advanced mathematics courses. The single best predictor of scores on tests of mathematics is the number of mathematics courses an individual has taken (Jones, 1984). Meece, Eccles-Parsons, Kaczala, Goff, and Futterman (1982) reported that when the data are adjusted to take into account the number of prior mathematics courses, sex differences are substantially reduced, but not eliminated. Thus, a major portion of the difference can be attributed to mathematical background, but not all of it.

Like all of the cognitive areas, results are highly dependent on the portion of the distribution that is being studied. Large sex differences have been reported among mathematically gifted boys and girls. Johns Hopkins University has been involved in a nationwide talent search to identify boys and girls who are exceptionally talented in mathematics (Benbow, 1988; Benbow & Stanley, 1980, 1981, 1983). One

SAMPLE QUESTIONS USED TO ASSESS QUANTITATIVE ABILITIES

(1)   276
         x 18

(2)   If Fred can paint the room in two hours and Sally can paint it in three hours, how long will it take them if they work together?

(3) $\displaystyle \iint_s \int f = \int_0^{\pi/2} \int_{\pi/A}^{\text{arctan } 2} \int_0^{\sqrt{6}} \frac{1}{\rho} \, \rho^2$

(4) $\displaystyle \hat{\sigma} = \sqrt{\frac{1}{n} \sum_{i=1}^{n} [y_i - (\hat{\alpha} + \hat{\beta} x_i)]^2}$

(5)

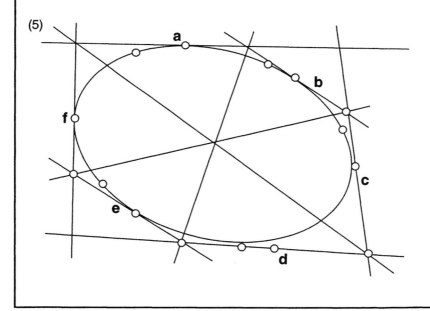

FIG. 3.7.   Sample questions used to assess quantitative ability.

finding is that there are substantial sex differences in the number of girls and boys identified as "mathematically precocious." They reported that among seventh and eigth grade students identified as mathematically talented, the male-to-female ratios on the College Board's SAT–M were as follows: 2:1 at greater than 500, 5:1 at greater than 600, and 17:1 at greater than 700 (Stanley & Benbow, 1982). Furthermore, Benbow (1988) reported that this ratio has remained stable for more than 15 years. This is a considerable sex difference that has generated heated controversy and has received extensive coverage in the popular press and nonprint media. The fact that these differences emerged from very large samples and have been replicated numerous times lends credibility to these results. Do these differences reflect actual ability differences, or are they artifacts of the way the students were identified? Benbow and Stanley (1981) believe that students were selected in an unbiased manner and that the large sex differences are attributable, at least in part, to biological mechanisms, whereas their detractors argue that girls will always be underrepresented in fields that are defined by society as masculine (e.g., Halpern, 1988). These two possibilities are considered in the following chapters in this book.

Stanley (1990) documented the absence of females from the highest levels of mathematical achievement with the following statistics: In the U.S.A. Mathematical Olympiad contest for high school students, there have been 144 winners since 1972. Of these, only 2 were female. Comparisons with the International Mathematical Olympiad show an equally unbalanced representation by sex. There have been no female participants from the United States since 1975. In the 1988 International Mathematical Olympiad (the only year with detailed data), there were only 4 female participants from 3 of the 49 countries that sent delegates. Interestingly, for the 4 years that China has competed in the International Mathematical Olympiad, there was a female on their team each time. These four Chinese females won three silver medals and one gold medal. What can we learn from these astounding statistics? First, females are seriously underrepresented in the highest achieving mathematical groups, and, second, although their absence is also found in other countries, the extremely low participation rate of females is not universally true; the Chinese have managed to produce extremely high-achieving females in mathematics.

Rossi (1983) believes that even if these numbers reflect genuine sex differences at the upper end of ability, the way they are presented is misleading. He has argued that by reporting sex differences in terms of ratios instead of an effect size statistic such as d or ω^2, the actual group differences are exaggerated. (See chap. 2 for a discussion of these statistics.) Only 5% of Stanley and Benbow's (1992) sample scored higher than 599 on the mathematics portion of the SAT. For the other 95%, the actual sex differences were only moderately large ($d = 0.44$). Although these distinctions may seem highly technical to a reader without an extensive background in statistics, they are important in understanding the size and nature of sex differences in mathematical ability. In summary, the differences seem large when considering only the most highly gifted youth and much smaller when considering moderately gifted youth.

Age Trends in Quantitative Abilities

The overrepresentation of boys among the most gifted in mathematics can be detected at very young ages. In a study of mathematically precocious young children, Robinson et al. (1996) found that more young boys were referred for giftedness in mathematical reasoning than young girls, despite special attempts to include girls. They administered a test battery to 143 preschool girls, 167 preschool boys, 201 girls in kindergarten, and 248 boys in kindergarten who were identified as possibly having the potential for mathematical giftedness. In this select group, they found sex differences favoring the boys in tests of number knowledge, number series, numeration, problem solving, calculation, word problems, counting span, an arithmetic screening test, and a test of visual–spatial span. These children also were administered three different verbal tests. Although the sex differences on the three verbal tests were not statistically significant, for all six comparisons (two age groups on three verbal tests), the girls scored higher than the boys. Robinson et al. reported sex differences in every analysis—more boys were nominated for the mathematically gifted program, a greater proportion of the boys qualified for admission to the program, and the boys scored higher than the girls on 8 of the 11 subtests. It is important to note here that sex differences usually are found more in highly select groups, so these conclusions are not generalizable to young children of average intelligence.

The developmental nature of quantitative sex differences through adolescence was examined in a study of more than 5,000 students aged 13 and 17. No sex differences were found for the 13-year-olds, whereas by age 17, the males were significantly outperforming the females with an average of 5% more correct answers (Jones, 1984). There is also evidence that sex differences in quantitative abilities emerge earlier for boys and girls pursuing an academic curriculum than for students in a nonacademic course of study. A longitudinal study conducted by the Educational Testing Service found that sex differences emerged in 7th grade for a group of college-bound students but did not appear until 11th grade for their peers who were not college-bound (Hilton & Berglund, 1974).

Effect Sizes for Quantitative Abilities

In a meta-analytic review of 100 studies, Hyde, Fennema, and Lamon (1990) found that there was a slight female superiority in elementary and middle school, a small to moderate male superiority in high school ($d = 0.29$), and larger male advantages in college ($d = 0.41$) and later adulthood ($d = 0.59$). However, these age trends were modified by type of task, with female superiority in computation in elementary and middle school and no difference with respect to computation in later years. There were essentially no sex differences in understanding mathematical concepts at any age. The most dramatic age trends were found on tests of mathematical problem solving, favoring females slightly in elementary and middle school, with a moderate effect favoring males in high school and college. Hyde, Fennema, and Lamon's conclusions are the most reliable because of the large number of studies in their meta-analysis and the care that they used to divide the data into homogeneous categories.

Aiken (1986–1987), in his review of the area, also concluded that the largest differences occur in mathematical problem solving, with males answering more questions correctly than females. Marshall and Smith (1987) confirmed these results with their study showing that third grade girls surpass boys in computation, an advantage that they retain through sixth grade, whereas boys show superiority in solving word problems and on geometry and measurement problems.

More recent attempts to understand the size of sex differences on quantitative tasks compared females and males who had been matched on the number and types of mathematics courses they had taken. Bridgeman and Wendler (1991) found that the magnitude of the male–female gap on the SAT–M was reduced, but not eliminated, when the males and females were equated for course-taking patterns in math. For example, the initial difference between males and females of 0.48 standard deviation units was reduced to 0.42 for students in algebra classes, 0.36 for students in precalculus classes, and 0.32 for students in calculus classes. These results need to be interpreted in light of the usual finding that females get higher grades in most courses, including advanced mathematical courses. Similar results were obtained with the Graduate Record Examination (GRE; a test used for admission to graduate school). The size of the between-sex difference on the GRE for all test takers is 0.65 standard deviation units, a value that is reduced, but not eliminated, when course-taking patterns are equated.

A more recent and sophisticated way of understanding the size of sex differences on quantitative tests was conducted by Gallagher (1998), who coded quantitative test items from the GRE along a variety of dimensions such as whether the item required the use of visual imagery, retrieval of a formula or a known solution from memory, and type of response. She found that effect sizes varied along several dimensions that were unrelated to the area of mathematics being tested (e.g., algebra vs. calculus). In a follow-up study that categorized mathematical test questions by the strategies used to solve them, Gallagher et al. (1999) found that sex differences favoring males were largest on those items that required test takers to construct and mentally transform a mental representation. The differentiation of tasks into their cognitive processes is an exciting line of research that could help investigators understand the underlying cognitive processes that are used on these tests.

RELATIONSHIP BETWEEN VISUAL–SPATIAL ABILITIES AND QUANTITATIVE ABILITIES

Several researchers have suggested that sex differences in quantitative abilities, like those in field dependence and independence, are a secondary consequence of differences in visual–spatial ability. There are a number of logical and empirical reasons to support this causal link. If you think for a minute about the nature of advanced topics in mathematics—geometry, topology, trigonometry, and calculus—you'll realize that they all require spatial skills. In addition, a National Science Foundation study of female mathematicians found that they were more likely to select algebra and statistics as an area of specialization than other mathematical specialties in which spatial perception is central (Luchins, 1979). More direct empirical evidence for this relationship comes from a variety of studies. In Anderson's (1990) review of cognitive abilities, he concluded that "psychometrically, measures of mathematical ability tend to be strongly correlated with spatial ability" (p. 449).

A factor-analytic study of skills conducted with college undergraduates also supports the relationship between visual–spatial and mathematical skills. Hunt (1985) found that three distinct ability factors or dimensions emerged when his participants were given a variety of cognitive tests. The first factor was a verbal ability factor composed of reading comprehension, grammar, and vocabulary tests. The second factor was a quantitative–spatial factor made up of tests of visual–spatial ability and mathematical tests. The third factor was identified as "mechanical reasoning." The fact that quantitative and spatial skills loaded on one factor suggests that there is a single underlying dimension that is responsible for performance on both types of tasks.

In one of the most careful studies to date on the relationship between visual–spatial abilities and quantitative abilities, Casey, Nuttall, et al. (1995) administered a paper-and-pencil test of mental rotation (Vandenberg Mental Rotation Test) to 760 males and females for whom they also had scores on the SAT–Verbal (SAT–V) and the SAT–M. They expected to find that the relationship between visual–spatial and quantitative abilities would depend on the nature of the sample—that is, whether it was a high-ability sample, an average-ability sample, or a low-ability sample. As noted in several places thus far in this book, results often depend on the portion of the abilities curve that is being sampled, with the largest sex differences found in the tails of the ability distributions—the very brightest and the least bright—and with smaller sex differences found in the average-ability midrange. These researchers had four different samples of young adults: (a) mathematically precocious youth (average age around 13 years old), (b) a general college sample, (c) college-bound seniors of high ability, and (d) college-bound seniors of low ability. The sex differences on the SAT–M and the mental rotation test (in this order) for these four groups were $d = 0.70$ and 0.79 for the precocious youth, $d = 0.42$ and 0.61 for the high-ability high school seniors, $d = 0.29$ and 10.01 for the college students, and $d = 0.11$ and 0.07 for the low-ability high school seniors. Thus, the largest between-sex differences were found for the most intellectually gifted males and females on both the SAT–M and the Mental Rotation Test. For all the females in all the ability groups, scores on the Mental Rotation Test predicted SAT–M scores, even when controlling for scores on the SAT–V. In plain English, spatial ability, as measured with the Mental Rotation Test, was an important factor in the SAT–M scores for all samples except the low-ability high school sample. Also, as might be expected, the largest male advantage on the SAT–M was found for geometry and word problems, both of which depend on the ability to generate and manipulate the information in a mental representation.

In a review of numerous studies, Friedman (1995) found that, in general, scores on tests of mathematics usually correlate more highly with verbal test scores than with spatial test scores, but for highly select samples, correlations between mathematical tests and spatial tests are especially high for girls. A relationship between visual–spatial and quantitative abilities was also found in the study of mathematically precocious preschoolers and kindergarteners: Among this group of extremely gifted young children, the correlation between spatial and quantitative factors was stronger for the boys than for the girls (Robinson et al., 1996).

Like almost every other hypothesis concerning ability differences, data relating spatial ability to mathematical ability have been mixed. It seems most likely that there is a spatial component to some, but not all, mathematical tasks. For example, computation is not a spatial task, and females excel in computation during the early grades. Similarly, the ability to solve word problems must depend, to some extent, on overall reading ability, especially when the problem is complex, so reading comprehension should also be important when word problems are complex. Thus, it seems that the use of spatial skills in solving mathematical problems is task-specific and most likely to be important for those who score among the highest on mathematical tests.

THINKING ABOUT THE MAGNITUDE OF THE DIFFERENCES

Test performance may have real, quantifiable educational and social implications.
Small mean differences combined with modest
differences in variance can have a great effect on the number of individuals who excel.
—Beller and Gafni (1996, p. 375)

Although the preponderance of the experimental evidence points to some sex differences in verbal, visual–spatial, and quantitative abilities, the question of the size or magnitude of these differences has not been easy to resolve. Are the differences trivial and of no practical significance, or do they represent meaningful ability differences between the sexes? Even if we were to conclude that there are large between-sex differences with respect to cognitive ability, it is very important to remember that most research analyzes group average results that cannot be applied to any individual.

All of the cognitive sex differences have been replicated numerous times and are statistically significant, which means that they are unlikely to have occurred by chance, but are they of any practical significance? Can they be used to explain why we have so few female mathematicians or engineers? Can they help us predict a male's or a female's ability to perform a task? Can they be used to justify discrimination? Are they merely curiosities whose only value is to keep psychologists (and publishers) busy? Answers to these questions are hotly debated and have important implications for modern society.

On an intuitive level, effect size is a quantification of the size of the average between-sex difference on a particular test or set of tests. Unfortunately, the numbers we use to express effect size are not intuitive. Differences like the finding that men tend to outscore women by an average of 40 points on the SAT–M have an immediate meaning to anyone who is familiar with the scoring system for the SAT. Unfortunately, sex differences in abilities are measured with many different tests, and a common measure of the average difference is needed to make comparisons across many studies. The effect size statistic is used to convey the size of the differences when many different tests are used. (Readers for whom this is a new concept are referred back to chap. 2 in which statistical concepts are discussed in more depth. It is also possible to follow the gist of the following discussion without understanding the fine points of some of the statistical concepts that are discussed.)

There are few guidelines for determining if the size of a sex difference with respect to a cognitive ability is large enough to be important. Cohen (1969) provided an arbitrary statistical definition of small, medium, and large effect sizes using standard deviation units (0.20 SD is small, 0.50 SD is medium, and 0.80 SD is large). There is, however, no good reason to accept his effect size markers except for the fact that they provide a common ruler for comparing differences. It is important to realize that effect size should not be confused with importance. A small effect could still be important, depending on how importance is defined and who defines it. Percentage of explained variance statistics (e.g., ω^2, R^2, h^2) are useful in this regard, but they still leave us with the question of how much explained variance is large enough to be important. If sex explained 5% of the variance in the data, is this a large or small number? In another context, like medicine, 5% of explained variance attributable to a treatment could mean many lives would be saved. Thus, the question of whether 1%, 5%, or 50% of explained variance is important depends on both the context and value judgments. Value judgments never lend themselves to statistical analysis, and thus, precise answers to the question of how large does a difference have to be to be important will remain debatable.

Williams (1983) and others (Gelman et al., 1981; Hyde, 1981) have concluded that looking at the ways in which large numbers of women and men differ, on average, is misleading because the magnitude of the differences is quite small. "This means that when we look at measures of such behavior we invariably find that differences within a sex category, for example, differences *among* women, are greater than differences *between* women and men" (Williams, 1983, p. 115). Although this statement focuses on the finding that there is considerable variability among women, it does not necessarily imply that the between-sex differences are small or unimportant. Readers are asked to keep all of these admonitions in mind when considering whether the effects are large enough to be meaningful. Recall, also, that sex differences are largest in the tails, or extreme ends, of the distributions and that there are few or no studies that have included the extremely low end of the abilities scales.

Some researchers assumed a broader view and studied the effect size for several cognitive abilities in the same study. Backman (1979), for example, studied the relationship among ethnicity, socioeconomic status, and sex and their joint influence on mental abilities. She administered tests of verbal knowledge, English language, grammar, mathematics, reasoning with spatial forms, perceptual speech, and memory to more than 2,000 twelfth-grade students. She accounted for more than 90% of the total variance with the main effects and interactions of her variables, but the relative importance of these variables was surprising. "Differences between the patterns of mental abilities of males and females were more marked than were differences among the patterns of ethnic or SES [socioeconomic status] groups. Sex accounted for 69% of the total variance, ethnicity 9% and SES 1%" (Backman, 1979, p. 264). It is difficult to know how to interpret the extremely large effect of sex in this study, given that it accounted for a much smaller percentage of explained variance in the other studies of individual abilities. It seems that sex was a very important determinant of how well the students performed on these tests. It also seems that sex as a variable can explain a much greater percentage of the total variance when several sex-related cognitive abilities are considered simultaneously in a single experiment than when individual abilities are being studied.

In one of the most lucid discussions on how to interpret effect sizes, Rosenthal and Rubin (1982) attempted to shed light on the question of how large an effect size must be to be of practical importance. Using a statistical test known as the binomial effect size display, they calculated that when sex explains only 4% of the variance in test scores, this translates into distributions in which 60% of the higher scoring sex is above the median and only 40% of the lower scoring sex is above the median. They argued that outcome rates of 60% versus 40% are important because they can be used to predict performance on ability tests in these areas. They also looked at the consistencies among effect sizes across 12 studies of verbal ability, 7 studies of visual–spatial ability, 7 studies of quantitative ability, and 14 studies of field articulation (field independence and dependence). They concluded that effect sizes differed from study to study, supporting the idea that the magnitude of the sex difference in any area depends on the type of test used.

CROSS-CULTURAL COMPARISONS

We have observed reliable, cross-culturally replicable sex differences.
—Mann, Sasanuma, Sakuma, and Masaki, (1990, p. 1074)

In earlier editions of this book, I lamented the lack of cross-cultural data. Data from a variety of countries with different customs and educational practices are an important piece of the puzzle in understanding the *why* of cognitive sex differences. In the many years since the first edition of this book, cross-cultural data on cognitive sex differences have been published at a brisk rate. Despite the burgeoning research literature, simple and direct transnational comparisons are still difficult because the studies vary on multiple dimensions: the nature of the test or task used, the age or educational background of the participants, and the portion of the abilities distribution from which the sample was selected. Suppose, for example, that we have studies of spatial abilities from Mexico and South Africa, but one of these countries used a mental rotation test with gifted college seniors and the other used a rod and frame test with a community sample of older adults. Although both may claim to have examined sex differences in spatial abilities, these two hypothetical studies would not be directly comparable. Despite all of the difficulties in making cross-cultural comparisons, the conclusions about cognitive sex differences hold up remarkably well around the world.

Consider, for example, the results of the International Assessment of Educational Progress (Beller & Gafni, 1996). Tests of mathematics, science, and geography were administered to children in 20 different countries. Across the countries, there were eight different tests given to two age groups (9-year-olds in 14 of the countries and 13-year-olds in all 20 countries). For these 16 comparisons (eight tests at two ages), boys scored higher on 15 of them. The only test that favored girls was a test of data analysis at age 9. In general, the effect sizes were not large, ranging from close to 0 ($d = 0.03$) for tests of "nature of science" at both ages to $d = 0.34$ for uses of science at age 13. Beller and Gafni argued that these results cannot be due to differential course taking because boys and girls take the same academic curriculum through age 13. The many possible explanations for these consistent transnational findings are discussed in later chapters in this book.

Other international findings support the conclusions reached with samples from the Unites States. Mann et al. (1990) compared junior high school students in Japan with those in the United States using English language and Japanese versions of the same tests. The girls in both countries scored higher than the boys on an immediate and delayed test of memory (story recall), a digit-symbol test (perceptual-motor skill), and a test of word fluency (produce as many words as possible that begin with the same letter in a limited time). The boys in both countries outscored the girls on a test of mental rotation. The researchers found that the results were independent of culture. Similar conclusions can be made from studies of older adults in Finland (females scored higher on recall for words and objects and a digit-symbol test and males scored higher on a block design and a spatial test called "trail making"; Portin, Saarijärvi, Joukamaa, & Salokangas, 1995).

Although there are many differences among various cross-cultural studies in terms of the tests they used and the ages and ability levels sampled, the majority of the findings show amazing cross-cultural consistency when comparing males and females on cognitive tests. This conclusion is based on studies conducted in Colombia (Ardila & Rosselli, 1994), Germany (Stumpf & Jackson, 1994), China (Huang, 1993), Israel (Birenbaum et al., 1994; Cahan & Ganor, 1995), Italy (Zappalà et al., 1995), South Africa (Owen & Lynn, 1993), Ireland (Lynn, 1996), Serbia (Jovanovic & Lerner, 1994), and Japan and Canada (Silverman, Phillips, & Silverman, 1996). After reviewing data from a Finnish sample, Portin et al. (1995) noted, "Gender-related differences were remarkable" (p. 1295). Despite the stability of the sex differences, there are some large between-country differences that cut across both sexes. As the International Mathematics and Science Studies have shown, among the 45 countries participating in the study, 8th grade students in the United States ranked 28th in mathematics and 17th in science (Colvin, 1996), a result that is disturbing to anyone concerned with the future economic and social development of the United States and one that calls for enhanced efforts to produce girls and boys with higher levels of achievement in science and mathematics.

UNDERLYING COGNITIVE PROCESSES

Examining sex differences for cognitive abilities is only one way of conceptualizing how females and males may differ in their intellectual processes. The division of abilities into verbal, visual–spatial, and quantitative has been useful, and as discussed in chapters 4 and 5, each of these abilities has distinct biological correlates. But there are other ways of investigating the thinking process. One such way is to consider what the participant does when he or she is engaged in a particular task. This alternate approach can be thought of as examining the underlying cognitive processes.

Look carefully at Table 3.1. I have listed the types of tasks on which females tend to excel and the types of tasks on which males tend to excel. One approach is to consider these two types of tasks as representing different underlying cognitive processes. The tasks at which females excel include language production; synonym generation; word fluency; memory for words, objects, and locations; anagrams; and computation. Skilled performance on all of these tasks requires rapid access to and retrieval of information that is stored in memory. In contrast, consider those tasks at which males tend to excel: mathematical problem solving, verbal analogies, mental rotation, spatial perception, and tasks the require using information in dynamic visual displays (spatiotemporal tasks) and visual images. These sorts of tasks require the ability to maintain and manipulate mental representations. Thus, it may prove meaningful to differentiate cognitive tasks on the basis of the type of cognitive process that each requires. When we adopt this framework, we can account for sex differences that do not divide neatly under the tripartite cognitive abilities rubric (verbal, mathematical, and visual–spatial), such as female superiority on some verbal tasks and computation tasks and male superiority on some verbal tasks.

A summary of research findings about sex differences in cognitive abilities is shown in Table 3.2. The research presented in each category is only a sampling of this huge literature.

ARE SEX DIFFERENCES DECREASING?

Contrary to the findings of small scale studies, these average differences do not appear to be decreasing but are relatively stable across the 32-year period investigated.
—Hedges and Nowell (1995, p. 45)

Chapters 4–7 describe theories that have been proposed to explain why sex differences are sometimes found. If these differences were created by sex-differentiated

---

Table 3.1
Possible Sex Differences In Underlying Cognitive Processes

Tasks at which females excel:

- Generating Synonyms (Associational Fluency)
- Language Production and Word Fluency
- Computation
- Anagrams
- Memory for words, objects, personal experiences, and locations
- Reading comprehension and writing

Underlying Cognitive Processes: Rapid Access to and Retrieval of Information in Memory

Tasks at which males excel:

- Verbal Analogies
- Mathematical Problem Solving
- Mental Rotation and Spatial Perception
- Spatiotemporal Tasks (dynamic visual displays)
- Generating and using information in visual images
- Mechanical reasoning and some science-related topics

Underlying Cognitive Processes: Maintaining and Manipulating a Mental Representation in Visual–Spatial Working Memory

---

psychosocial variables like sex roles and different rewards for males and females, then we would expect to see some decline in the magnitude of the differences as the impact of sex roles diminishes. Thus, the question of whether sex differences in cognitive abilities are decreasing is important. To conclude that sex differences are decreasing, we need to have comparable samples of participants who have taken the same cognitive abilities tests in different time periods. There are few samples that meet these stringent requirements.

Several experimenters have examined effect sizes as a function of the date when the study was published. The underlying rationale for investigating results as a function of their date of publication is that, in general, more recent studies should show smaller sex differences than studies published many years ago, if sex differences really have been decreasing. The problem with this approach is that many other variables also have changed during the intervening years. In response to concerns that publication practices tend to be biased toward studies that report significant differences, many more journal articles and paper presentations now report

TABLE 3.2

Cognitive Tests and Tasks That Usually Show Sex Differences

Type of test/task	Example
Tasks and tests on which women obtain higher average scores	
Tasks that require rapid access to and use of phonological, semantic, and other information in long-term memory	Verbal fluency—phonological retrieval (Hines, 1990) Synonym generation—meaning retrieval (Halpern & Wright, 1996) Associative memory (Birenbaum, Kelly, Levi-Keren, 1994) Memory battery—multiple tests (Stumpf & Jackson, 1994) Spelling and anagrams (Hyde, Fennema, & Lamon, 1990) Memory for spatial location (Eals & Silverman, 1994) Memory for odors (Lehrner, 1993)
Knowledge areas	Literature (Stanley, 1993) Foreign languages (Stanley, 1993)
Production and comprehension of complex prose	Reading comprehension (Hedges & Nowell, 1995; Mullis et al., 1993) Writing (U.S. Department of Education, 1997
Fine motor tasks	Mirror tracing—novel, complex figures (O'Boyle & Hoff, 1987) Pegboard tasks (Hall & Kimura, 1995) Matching and coding tasks (Gouchie & Kimura, 1991)
Perceptual speed	Multiple speeded tasks (Born, Bleichrodt, & van def Flier, 1987) "Finding As"—an embedded-letters test (Kimura & Hampson, 1994)
Decoding nonverbal communication	(Hall, 1985)
Perceptual thresholds (Large, varied literature with multiple modalities)	Touch—lower thresholds (Ippolitov, 1973; Wolff, 1969) Taste—lower thresholds (Nisbett & Gurwitz, 1970) Hearing—males have greater hearing loss with age (Schaie, 1987) Odor—lower thresholds (Koelega & Koster, 1974)
Higher grades in school (all or most subjects)	(Stricker, Rock, & Burton, 1993)
Speech articulation	Tongue twisters (Kimura & Hampson, 1994)
Tasks and tests on which men obtain higher average scores	
Tasks that require transformations in visual working memory	Mental rotation (Halpern & Wright, 1996; Voyer, Voyer, & Bryden, 1995) Piaget Water Level Test (Robert & Ohlmann, 1994; Vasta, Knott, & Gaze, 1996)

continued on next page

Tasks that involve moving objects	Dynamic spatiotemporal tasks (Law, Pelligrino, & Hunt, 1993)
Motor tasks that involve aiming	Accuracy in throwing balls or darts (Hall & Kimura, 1995)
Knowledge areas	General knowledge (Feingold, 1993; Wechsler Adult Intelligence Scale [Wechsler, 1981]), Geography knowledge (Beller & Gafni, 1996), Math and science knowledge (Stanley, 1993; U.S. Department of Education, 1996)
Tests of fluid reasoning (especially in math and science domain)	Proportional reasoning tasks (Meehan, 1984), Scholastic Assessment Test–Mathematics Graduate Record Examination–Quantitative (Willingham & Cole, 1997), Mechanical Reasoning (Stanley et al., 1992), Verbal analogies (Lim, 1994), Scientific reasoning (Hedges & Nowell, 1995)

Males are also overrepresented at the low-ability end of many distributions, including the following examples: mental retardation (some types; Vandenberg, 1987), majority of attention deficit disorders (American Psychiatric Association, 1994), delayed speech (Hier, Atkins, & Perlo, 1980), dyslexia (even allowing for possible referral bias; DeFries & Gillis, 1993), stuttering (Yairi & Ambrose, 1992), and learning disabilities and emotional disturbances (Henning-Stout & Close-Conoley, 1992). In addition, males are generally more variable (Hedges & Nowell, 1995). References provided are examples of relevant research. The literature is too large to attempt a complete reference list in this article. Table adapted from Halpern (1997).

nonsignificant results, thus changing the nature of the studies that can be included in meta-analyses. (In other words, a study that failed to find significant differences is now more likely to be published than in the past.) The more recent tendency to publish nonsignificant results would cause effect sizes to decrease as a function of publication date.

The nature of samples also has changed with time. Two to three decades ago, college enrollments were overwhelmingly male. Now, women make up more than 50% of college enrollments in the United States (U.S. Bureau of the Census, 1998). Because a larger percentage of all females are now attending college than the percentage of males, a more select group of college men is probably being sampled than college women. The nature of many of the tests also has changed (Halpern, 1989). The Educational Testing Service, which authors the SAT, has come under severe criticism for the disparities in female and male scores. Accordingly, it has responded in the past few years by scrutinizing every test question for sex-related bias in content or use of pronouns. The Educational Testing Service now trains all of its test committees on ways to avoid bias in the questions that are used on its examinations. Many of the other tests that show the greatest sex differences have been developed in the past few years (e.g., paper-and-pencil mental rotation tests, word fluency, and consonant–vowel matching tests) and therefore cannot be compared with comparable older studies to see if the effect sizes are diminishing.

Hyde and Linn (1988) reported that for studies published before 1974, the effect size (d) for verbal abilities was 0.23 and for those studies published after 1974 the effect size was 0.10. Although this difference suggests that sex differences are decreasing (and are presently so small as to be considered nonexistent), a very different conclusion emerges if we exclude nonsignificant results from the summary analysis. On the basis of studies that show statistically significant results, the pre-1974 median effect size is $d = 0.32$; the post-1974 median effect size is $d = 0.33$ (favoring females). These results don't support the idea that effect sizes in verbal ability are decreasing. Instead, they support the idea that more studies with nonsignificant results have been published since 1974.

Hyde, Fennema, and Lamon (1990) also concluded that sex differences in mathematics are decreasing. They found that $d = 0.31$ for studies published before 1974 and $d = 0.14$ for those studies published after 1974 (favoring males). Unfortunately, they did not present their data in a way that allows the separation of statistically significant and nonsignificant studies. Although these values suggest that sex differences may be declining, the decline in effect size could be caused by changes in publication practices, the composition of the samples of participants, the type of test used, or numerous other confounding variables.

Several meta-analyses of spatial abilities have examined the question of whether effect sizes are decreasing. Feingold (1988) argued that sex differences in spatial abilities are decreasing, but his conclusion was based on scores on the Space Relations subtest on the Differential Aptitudes Test. As described in the section on visual–spatial abilities, this test assesses spatial visualization—the only visual–spatial ability that does not show reliable sex differences. Thus, we can make no conclusion about whether sex differences in visual–spatial abilities are changing on the basis of these data.

The SAT

Sex differences in verbal ability are commonly found on the SAT, used for college admissions, but the differences are not easy to interpret. Male and female scores on the SAT–V and SAT–M are shown in Fig. 3.8 and Fig. 3.9. Both show fairly consistent sex differences during the past quarter of the 20th century.

Given that many of the verbal abilities discussed in this chapter favor females, readers may be surprised to find that males consistently obtain higher average scores than females on the SAT–V. We can only speculate why SAT–V results are discrepant with the other studies. Possible reasons include: (a) low-ability males do not take the SAT because they have a significantly higher dropout rate from high school (Halpern, 1989); (b) SAT–V items are biased in some way, perhaps drawing more vocabulary terms and more reading examples from scientific or other male-biased domains; (c) the males who take the SAT are more advantaged in terms of socioeconomic status (Ramist & Arbeiter, 1986); (d) the verbal areas that show the largest female advantage are not included on the SAT–V (e.g., word fluency and writing); (e) the low-ability end of the verbal distribution (e.g., dyslexic individuals, mentally retarded individuals) does not take the SAT, and therefore the verbal advantage of females is underestimated; and (f) the only verbal ability in which males exceed females on other verbal ability measures is solving analogies. The SAT–V is heavily weighted with analogies, thus giving undue weight to the one verbal ability area in which males outscore females. It seems likely that the abilities used in solving verbal analogies are similar to those used in mathematical problem solving, which also shows a large male advantage. Future research is needed to determine which, if any, of these possibilities is responsible for the anomalous results with the SAT–V.

SAT–M scores do not reveal time trends. The correlation between size of the sex difference (in SAT–M points) and year of publication is not statistically significant. As shown in Fig. 3.9, the female and male curves appear almost parallel.

All meta-analyses conducted during the past 5 years or so support the idea that there have been few, if any, changes in the size of sex differences in cognitive abilities. In an extensive review of reading, writing, mathematics, and science, Hedges and Nowell (1995) concluded that sex differences have not changed during the 32-year period that they investigated. Voyer et al. (1995) reached the same conclusion from a study of tests of visual–spatial abilities. They found that effect sizes for mental rotation tests have increased over time whereas effect sizes for some of the other visual–spatial tests have decreased. Overall, there was no change in effect size for tests of visual–spatial abilities over time. Masters and Sanders (1993) and Stumpf and Stanley (1996, 1998) reached the same conclusion from their analyses of between-sex differences on numerous tests of cognition (with a few possible exceptions, such as the possibility that sex differences favoring males on the Advanced Placement Test of Computer Science are narrowing).

SIMILARITIES

Although the focus of this chapter has been the identification of cognitive abilities that show sex differences, the flip side of this issue is at least as important—those areas of cognition in which similarities are found. I have focused on differences because the logic of hypothesis testing allows conclusions only about differences. Despite this limitation, it is important to note that the number of areas in which sex differences are even moderate in size is small. Males and females are overwhelmingly alike in their cognitive abilities. It is important not to lose sight of this fact as we consider theories that have been posited to explain the differences and similarities in cognitive sex differences. Also, please keep in mind that even in the relatively few areas in which differences are found, these conclusions are based on data gathered from a large number of participants. They cannot be applied to any single individual because the within-sex variability is so large.

CHAPTER SUMMARY

Although sex differences have not been found in general intelligence, there are some types of cognitive abilities that vary, on average, as a function of sex. There are some sex-related differences in the earliest stages of information process-

SCHOLASTIC ASSESSMENT TEST-VERBAL

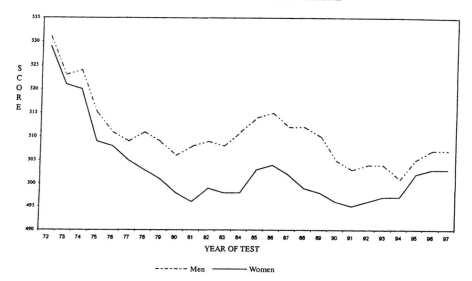

FIG. 3.8.   Scholastic Assessment Test–Verbal scores for college-bound seniors from 1972 to 1997. Data are from College Entrance Examination Board (1997).

SCHOLASTIC ASSESSMENT TEST-MATHEMATICAL

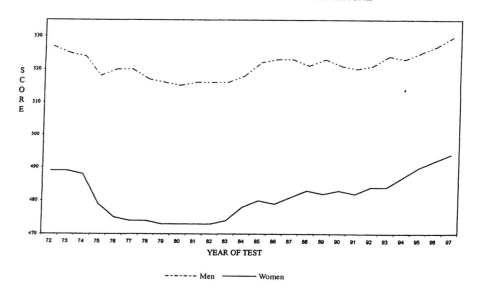

FIG. 3.9.   Scholastic Assessment Test–Mathematics scores for college-bound seniors from 1972 to 1997. Data are from College Entrance Examination Board (1997).

ing—perception and attention—but the effect of these early stage differences on later cognitive processes is unknown. Males comprise a disproportionate share of the extremely low-ability end of the verbal abilities distribution, with males overwhelmingly categorized as stutterers, dyslexics, and mentally retarded. The only type of verbal ability that shows a male advantage is solving verbal analogies. By contrast, females excel at anagrams; general and mixed verbal ability tests; speech production; writing; memory for words, objects, and locations; perceptual-motor skills; and associational fluency. These differences appear as soon as speech and language usage begin. Females excel in computation during elementary school, with males showing superiority in mathematical problem solving. The highest ability end of the mathematical ability distribution is disproportionately male. There are at least five types of visual–spatial ability that have been identified: visual perception, mental rotation, spatial visualization, spatiotemporal ability, and generation and maintenance of visual images. Sex differences favoring males are found on all of them except spatial visualization, which does not show sex differences. The effect size for mental rotation is among the largest found in the literature and can be found developmentally by the early elementary school years. An analysis of the underlying cognitive processes was proposed, with males performing especially well on tasks that involve maintaining and manipulating mental representations and females performing especially well on tasks that require rapid access to and retrieval of information from memory. It is important to keep in mind that the list of cognitive differences is relatively small and that cognitive similarities between the sexes are greater than the differences.

4 Biological Hypotheses Part I: Genes and Hormones

CONTENTS

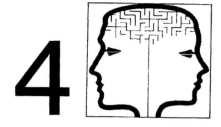

4

BIOLOGICAL HYPOTHESES PART I: GENES AND HORMONES

After sexism is stripped away, there will still be something different—something grounded in biology.
—Konner (1988, p. 35)

Perhaps this chapter and the next chapter should come with a warning similar to the ones found on cigarette advertisements:

> **WARNING: Some of the research and theories described in this chapter may be disturbing to your basic belief systems.**

I have taught this material many times, and there always have been students who are profoundly disturbed by the possibility that even a small portion of the sex differences in cognitive abilities may be attributable to biological factors. When reading this chapter and the following one devoted to sex-related brain differences, it is important to keep in mind that even if we were to conclude that biological variables are partial determinants of sex differences in cognitive abilities, the importance of psychosocial factors is not necessarily diminished. Biological and psychosocial variables interact in their influence on the development of individuals, and although biological and psychosocial hypotheses are presented in separate chapters, this organization is not meant to imply that they are diametrically opposed or independent concepts. As you read the chapters that focus on biological and environmental factors, keep in mind the psychobiosocial model that was presented in chapter 1 of this book—it is an integral conceptualization of nature and nurture. To understand broad topics, like the variables that create and influence human cognition, we have to break them down into smaller units, but they also have to be put back together again, a feat that is accomplished in the last chapter in this book.

THE NOTION OF BIOLOGICAL DETERMINATION

More and more, our society looks to genes to explain ...
even complex social behaviors.
—McGoodwin (1998, p. B8)

The concept of *biological determination* can take a strong or a weak form. A proponent of the strong form was Sigmund Freud, who is well known for his oft-quoted aphorism, "Biology is destiny." This quote represents the strong form of biological determination or determinism because it implies that, for each of us, our destiny is unavoidably preplanned by biological forces beyond our control. A proponent of the weaker form of biological determinism would maintain that although biology may underlie some tendencies or make certain experiences more probable, we are not inevitably the products of the biological systems that make up our bodies. Biology imposes certain limitations on our abilities, but environment determines the extent to which we develop our abilities. An analogy from health science may help to explain this point. Some people may be born with a biological tendency to become fat; however, with proper exercise and diet, they can avoid or postpone this destiny. Similarly, a weak form of biological determinism allows for the possibility that females and males may, by self-determination or some other means, overcome or avoid sex-related, biologically based predilections or tendencies to develop certain cognitive abilities; the weak form of biological determinism considers the impact of environmental influences on male and female human existence.

Of course, there are numerous and obvious biological differences between women and men, but many of these differences are much less pronounced in humans than in any other vertebrates. If we were concerned with sex differences in reproduction instead of cognition, there would be little or no controversy. The different roles that men and women normally play in reproduction are incontrovertible, although new technological possibilities in reproduction, such as cloning, could change even this most basic difference between the sexes. When the issue is cognition, the questions and answers become more difficult. Are the sex-related differences in cognitive ability inherent in the biology of femaleness and maleness? Or are the biological factors that make us male or female unrelated to the types of cognitive abilities that we develop? Or perhaps a better way to ask this question is "To what extent are sex-related differences in cognitive abilities tied to the biology that makes us male or female?"

The Zeitgeist for John/Joan

Nature is a political strategy of those committed
to the status quo of sex differences.
—Money (1987, p. 14)

Look carefully at the three questions posed at the end of the preceeding paragraph. Each question presupposes a different type of answer: The first is framed (or phrased) to suggest that biological variables are critically important, the second suggests an answer that is more heavily weighted toward environmental variables, and the third implies a "how much of each" type answer. Psychological scientists want answers that are supported with strong empirical data and a well-reasoned set of assumptions and beliefs. But we are not equally open to all sorts of information. There have been different historical periods and social–political contexts in which some types of answers were more readily acceptable than others. A *Zeitgeist* is a philosophical tenor of the times, a bias in the type of information that the members in a society find acceptable. For example, when I was a student, an influential book on the psychobiology of femaleness and maleness was published in 1972. It was aptly titled *Man & Woman, Boy & Girl*. It was written by two leading sex researchers, John Money and Anke Ehrhardt, who described various case studies from the Psychohormonal Instititute at Johns Hopkins University. There was one case study that was particularly intriguing. They told of a pair of identical twin boys, one of whom suffered severe injury to his penis during a routine surgery. The anguished parents took him to the Psychohormonal Institute for assistance. At that time, penile reconstructive surgery was extremely crude, so after considerable deliberation, they decided to have their son's genitals reconstructed to appear like those of a female. Hormone therapy was planned for this child during his adolescence so that he would have the general physical appearance of a girl. In this way, overnight, John became Joan. Of course, their new daughter would not menstruate or be able to have children because she lacked the internal organs of a female, but she would appear female, and it was hoped that she would develop into a normal female in all other respects. At the time the book was published, Joan (not her real name) was described as dressing in frilly dresses and "granny" nightgowns and playing with dolls and was reported to be adjusting well. Perhaps the most intriguing aspect of this case history was the willingness of the academic and medical community to accept the premise that it would be easy to change a normal, healthy baby boy into a girl with surgery on his genitals, hormones administered at puberty, and girl-type environmental experiences. The idea that one's sexual identity (belief that one is either a boy or a girl) and sex role adjustment (conformity to societal expectations about behaviors that are desirable for boys or girls) depended primarily on social learning and appropriate hormones administered at puberty was consistent with the Zeitgeist in the United States in the late 1960s and early 1970s.

It is interesting to note that John Money, the first author in the 1970s account of his success in changing John to Joan, introduced the use of the word *gender* to refer to nonanatomical differences between men and women (LeVay, 1996). It is to Money's credit that he popularized the idea that there are many differences between females and males that are unrelated to their anatomy, but unfortunately, he also helped to create the "mind-set" that sex-typical societal roles are exclusively the product of one's environment.

However, there were some sex researchers and others who doubted that any male could so easily be transformed into a female. Milton Diamond and H. Keith Sigmundson, two researchers who had long believed that the public had been misled with this story, obtained permission to interview John/Joan 30 years later (described in Hamer & Copeland, 1998). As they suspected, John/Joan had had a very difficult life. She never adjusted to her status as a girl. In childhood, the other children taunted her with cries of "caveman" because of her gawky way of walking, awkwardness, and propensity for rough play. As planned, she began estrogen therapy at age 12 to develop breasts and other female characteristics, a fact that seemed to increase her misery and discomfort with her body. At age 14 and in complete despair, she threatened suicide. Only then did her parents tell her the truth about her medical background. You will be pleased to know that this story has a happy ending. As a young adult, she had her breasts surgically removed, surgically added a penis (which is now possible), and is taking male hormones. Joan once again became John and is now married with adopted children. By all accounts, John is a fairly well-adjusted heterosexual male, just like his identical twin brother who did not undergo the same ordeal that he did.

It is difficult to know what message to take away from this intriguing story. Of course, it represents the experience of just one person, and we cannot safely generalize from a single individual. The most salient message is that so many people were willing to accept the original John/Joan story because it supported the view that we all are born sex-neutral and with secondary sex characteristics induced by hormones that were administered at puberty and sex-typical rearing experiences, a male could easily become a female or vice versa. The present Zeitgeist, at the turn of the 21st century, is far more biologically oriented. I urge all readers to remain open to the information presented in all of the chapters in this book and to consider the way their worldview or the larger societal Zeitgeist is influencing their willingness to accept or reject experimental findings.

Are Biological Theories Sexist?

Woman is a pair of ovaries with a human being attached, whereas man is a human being furnished with a pair of testes.
—Virchow (cited in Fausto-Sterling, 1985, p. 90)

There are numerous sex-related inequalities in contemporary society. As noted in the first chapter, women earn much less than men, spend more time on housework, and comprise the majority of persons living in poverty. Men, in contrast, often find it difficult to obtain custody of their children following divorce and have been effectively closed out of female-dominated professions such as secretarial work and nursing. Suppose that researchers conclude that there are biologically determined sex differences in cognition. Could this conclusion be used to justify the social inequality that exists between women and men?

The possibility that biological theories could be used to justify discrimination is chilling. One tacit assumption that is inherent in this line of reasoning is that, if the truth were known, females would be found to be "less"—less smart, less able, less strong, or less of whatever society values. I return to this assumption later in this chapter when I consider the question of monthly fluctuations in sex hormones and cognitive abilities. The data do not support the tacit assumption that women might be found to be "deficient," if biological data were examined. As you will see from the data reported here, the results of biological research do not favor either sex. Although differences are reported, they are exactly that. A point that is made in several places throughout this book is that differences are not deficiencies. If we find that society values the traits and skills that are associated with being male and devalues the traits and skills that are associated with being female, then it is time to rethink societal values instead of denying the existence of biologically based male–female differences.

As you read about biological research on cognitive sex differences, recall the discussion about the distinction between research results and the interpretation of research results that appeared in chapter 3. As Reinisch et al. (1987) noted, correlations between biological and behavioral differences may be bidirectional (behaviors affect biology and biology affects behaviors), imperfect within and between people (both biology and behavior vary), and inconsistent across species (there are critical differences between nonhuman and human mammals). Even if we find biologically based differences, we are a long way from understanding how they are manifested in an environmental context that provides different rewards for its females and males.

Researchers have identified three interrelated biological systems that could be responsible for cognitive sex differences: (a) chromosomal or genetic determinants of sex; (b) differences in the sex hormones secreted from the endocrine glands and other structures; and (c) neuroanatomical differences in the structure, organization, and function of the brain. Theories and research on the biological determinants of sex-related cognitive differences have centered on these three biological systems. Like any division in biology, these are not separate systems; genes and hormones presumably operate on behavior through some neurological mechanism, and differences in sex hormones are dependent on genetically coded information. In keeping with the psychosocial framework introduced in the first chapter, keep in mind the environmental context in which the biology of maleness and femaleness expresses itself. There are many environmental variables that affect brain structures and the type and quantity of hormones that are excreted into the bloodstream, thus blurring the distinction between biological and environmental variables.

One of the major difficulties in understanding the contribution of each of these biological systems is that in normal individuals they are confounded. Chromosomes determine the type of sex hormones that are secreted, and these hormones influence brain development. Sex hormones also direct the development of the internal reproductive organs and external genitals. Thus, for most people, all of the biological indications of sex are congruent and interdependent. Although these three systems exert influences on each other, one way to comprehend these intricately enmeshed biological systems is by separately examining each system and then putting them back together to understand how they work in concert. Possible genetic and hormonal influences are presented in this chapter. Brain mechanisms and links among these three systems are presented in chapter 5. The question for research psychologists is whether any or all of these biological sex differences underlie cognitive sex differences and, if so, how much and in what ways.

BEHAVIORAL GENETICS

Genes are like musical instruments. Genes don't determine exactly what music is played—or how well—but they do determine the range of what is possible.
—Hamer and Copeland (1998, p. 12)

Like many other fields of study, "psychology is feeling the repercussions of the explosion of new finds and methods in genetics" (Plomin, 1997, p. 58). Investigators in the field of behavior genetics look for evidence of linkages between genetic information and complex human behaviors. Genetic material is the basic building block of life. Fetal development proceeds under the direction of the genetic information coded in the genes. Whether you were born male or female with black or white skin and blue or brown eyes was determined by the chromosomes and genes that are responsible for your very existence. Every trait, which you have inherited from your ancestors, was transmitted by your genes. Genetic information constitutes the "genotype" of an individual, whereas traits that are expressed are called the "phenotype." Phenotype is what we see in terms of either physical appearance or behavior. Phenotype depends on the interaction of genes with environmental influences. The term *gene–environment transaction* is sometimes used to emphasize the fact that most behavioral traits that are expressed depend on the mutual effect of genetic and environmental influences.

Researchers use observable characteristics (phenotypes) to infer genetic information (genotypes). There are four research strategies commonly used to study the influence of genetic information on cognition (adapted from Eliot & Fralley, 1976):

1. Examine a large number of people to determine, for example, the proportion of women and men who exhibit good spatial or verbal abilities.
2. Look at the heritability pattern of abilities across generations to determine the "pedigree" of cognitive abilities. Researchers using this approach might examine siblings or parents and children to ascertain whether good mathematical or verbal ability tends to run in families.
3. Utilize individuals with genetic abnormalities to infer the effect of genetic information in normal individuals. An example of this approach would be to discover if individuals who are genetically male, but appear female, show typical "male" patterns of cognitive abilities.

4. Examine monozygotic (identical) and dizygotic (fraternal) twins to determine the extent to which cognitive abilities are under genetic control. If monozygotic twins are more similar than dizygotic twins, then these results would provide some support for genetic influences on cognitive abilities. (This is especially true when researchers are able to compare cognitive abilities for identical twins who were reared apart. In this case, the twins share a common heredity but have experienced a different environment.)

All of these research strategies have been used to understand the role of sex-related genetic factors in the development of cognitive abilities.

An example from twin data is seen in the study of reaction time measures of intelligence. One controversial measure of intelligence is speed of processing. The underlying idea in measuring speed of processing is that differences in intelligence can best be understood by determining the time that it takes to complete simple cognitive tasks. Such measures are called "reaction times," and they are commonly used in cognitive research. Sex differences are more likely to be found with timed than untimed tasks, although, as noted in chapter 3, sex differences also are found with untimed tasks (Masters, 1998). For example, the large sex differences in mental rotation are often based on the time that it takes to mentally rotate a complex figure to determine if it is identical to another figure (Loring-Meier & Halpern, 1999). According to this view, a fast speed of processing is indicative of a high level of spatial ability.

Researchers have examined speed of processing as one way to measure genetic contributions to cognitive abilities. (You can think of it as a measure of thinking speed, which is measured in milliseconds—thousandths of a second.) For example, in one study, the investigators measured speed of information processing in infants on the basis of the reasoning that information-processing speed in infants is largely a function of heredity (Rose & Feldman, 1995). They used these measures to successfully predict scores on intelligence tests when the children were 11 years old. Speed of processing is a pervasive factor that underlies many aspects of cognition. Vernon (1987) presented evidence that reaction time measures and other measures of intelligence are "highly correlated" (p. 2). In his review of this area of research, Vernon concluded that sex differences in mental abilities—specifically verbal, spatial, and quantitative—may be related to differences in the speed with which women and men perform specific cognitive operations. In support of his conclusion that speed of processing is an inherited trait, he cited studies that reported that there is greater similarity among monozygotic twins (identical twins) than among dizygotic twins (fraternal twins). Vernon made a case for using reaction time data as an index of the "hardware" or underlying neural structure of intelligence and suggested that sex differences in reaction times can be viewed as part of one's genetic inheritance.

Are Females and Males Affected Equally by Heredity?

The pendulum in the eternal debate about nature versus nurture
is swinging back toward nurture.
—de Waal (1996, p. B1)

To explain sex differences in cognitive abilities with appeals to heredity, it would be necessary to show that heredity varies, in some way, as a function of one's sex or to establish some other link between one's sex and the heritability of cognition. Merely knowing that cognition is, in part, inherited does not help in understanding why females and males, on average, show different patterns of cognitive abilities. One possible explanation for sex differences in cognitive abilities is that females and males differ in the extent to which they inherit cognitive abilities. This possibility was investigated by Baker, Ho, and Reynolds (1994). They compared the cognitive abilities of adopted and nonadopted children at ages 1, 2, 4, and 7 years with those of their biological parents, adoptive parents (where applicable), and control parents. As reported by numerous other researchers, they found no overall sex differences in intelligence and no support for the hypothesis that boys and girls are differentially affected by heredity or environment in the heritability of cognitive abilities. The results from this study suggest that we cannot look to differences in the extent to which genetics determine cognitive abilities for each sex as a means of understanding cognitive sex differences. However, the young age of their participants means that we cannot make strong conclusions from this study because sex differences in cognition are small in childhood, and it remains possible that larger differences may emerge as the children grow older.

Some researchers have examined the possibility that the chromosomes that carry information about the sex of a developing fetus also carry information that influences cognitive abilities. Studies of this sort distinguish between sex-linked and sex-limited traits. A promising area of investigation is the possibility of *imprinting,* which in this context means that the way genetic material is expressed depends on whether it is maternally or paternally supplied (e.g., Skuse et al., 1997). This is a relatively new line of research that I expect will become more popular in the coming decade. So far, it is too early for summary statements.

Sex-Linked Versus Sex-Limited

Environmental transmission from parent to offspring has little effect
on later cognitive development.
—Plomin, Fulker, Corley, and DeFries (1997, p. 447)

One of the major differences between males and females is the pair of sex chromosomes that differ markedly from each other in size and shape. Females have two X chromosomes—one is contributed by the biological father and the other by the biological mother during fertilization. The male sex chromosome pair is designated XY. The X is contributed by the biological mother and the Y is contributed by the biological father. The Y chromosome is very small and contains little genetic information except for determining sex (Carter, 1972). In contrast, the X chromosome is relatively large and contains a great deal of genetic information. Characteristics (like whether an individual develops ovaries or testes and certain types of red–green color blindness) that are determined by information coded in the genes on the sex chromosomes are called "sex-linked characteristics." Such characteristics are tied to the fact that we are born either male or female because they are carried on the chromosomes that determine sex.

In addition to the pair of sex chromosomes, humans have 22 pairs of other chromosomes known as autosomes. Sometimes a characteristic that is coded on an autosome appears predominantly in one sex or the other. Such characteristics are called "sex-limited" and appear predominantly in one sex because of a multiplicity of genetic influences. The genetic basis for sex-limited traits is the same for both sexes (Jensen, 1998). Pattern baldness, for example, occurs primarily in men and is inherited through genetic information on an autosomal pair of chromosomes. Even though this type of baldness occurs most frequently in men, the genetic information that causes it is not coded on the sex chromosomes. Thus, not all traits that occur only or mostly in one sex are coded on the sex chromosomes. Such characteristics are less intimately tied to genetic determinants of sex than are sex-linked characteristics.

Studies have shown that males are more biologically vulnerable from the moment of conception. Researchers have estimated that at conception there are 140 males conceived (called "46, XY" to denote the fact that there are 46 chromosomes with the sex chromosome pair XY) to every 100 females conceived (46, XX). The ratio of male:female live births is 105 males born for every 100 females. By age 65, the male:female ratio is 70:100 (Money, 1986). These numbers reflect the fact that fewer male embryos ever make it to birth and after birth males die an average of 7 years earlier than females (Coren & Halpern, 1993; Halpern & Coren, 1988, 1990).

Genetic research is progressing at a rapid rate as biomedical sleuths unravel the mystery of the DNA molecule. It is only within the past 15 to 20 years that researchers have located the gene that acts as a switch for maleness, "transforming a growing human fetus that otherwise would become a girl into a boy." The gene for maleness is located on the Y chromosome. It becomes operative during the 7th week of pregnancy, "setting off a complex biological cascade that turns the fetus's immature sex organs into testes" (Braun, cited in Angier, 1990, p. 3). If this gene is missing (as it is in normal females), the developing organism will be a female. This fact has led some researchers to note that the basic human blueprint is female, although it is probably more accurate to think of female and male genitals as two variations of a common theme. During embryonic development, the internal and external structures go through an "indifferent" stage from which either male or female versions develop.

Molarity or Modularity?

Psychologists who study human cognition often disagree about whether intelligence is best considered as a single, unitary process—a sort of general intelligence that operates across a variety of cognitive tasks. This unitary view of intelligence is called "molarity." By contrast, when we break general intelligence into different types of abilities, such as verbal or visual–spatial ability, this multipart view of intelligence is called "modularity." This is the same distinction that was made in the first chapter of this book in which the idea of separate cognitive abilities was discussed. In the context of behavioral genetics, the question is whether general intelligence is inherited—the molar view—or whether separate cognitive abilities are each inherited—the modular view. Look carefully at Fig. 4.1, which is adapted from an article by Petrill (1997).

Figure 4.1 shows general intelligence and four separate cognitive abilities—verbal, spatial, speed of processing, and memory. Each of the four cognitive abilities is measured with at least two different tests. This is shown in Fig. 4.1 by two arrows pointing from each cognitive ability to boxes labeled *test*. As Petrill (1997) concluded in his article on the heritability of cognitive abilities, there is evidence that both general intelligence and the separate cognitive abilities are inherited. Although most of the genetic effects for intelligence are general, there are also some independent genetic influences on each of the four cognitive abilities depicted in Fig. 4.1 (verbal, spatial, speed of processing, and memory). Thus, behavioral genetics provides evidence for both a general factor for intelligence (molarity) and separate cognitive abilities (modularity).

Heritability of Cognitive Abilities

The importance of genetics for various aspects of human behavior hardly is a matter of discussion any longer.
—Boomsma, Anokhin, and de Geus (1997, p. 106)

There has been considerable interest in the hypothesis that spatial ability is inherited. Vandenberg (1969), for example, administered a test of spatial abilities to a sample of twins, reasoning that the greater the percentage of genes shared by two people, the greater the similarity that would be expected in their ability scores if the ability is inherited. The test included measures of the ability to visualize and mentally rotate figures in space. High correlations between twin pairs led Vandenberg to conclude that these abilities are partially determined by heredity factors. However, as explained in a prior section in this chapter, simply knowing that some cognitive abilities may be inherited doesn't explain sex differences in these abilities.

In general, more recent research has yielded higher heritability values than studies published in the 1960s and 1970s, probably because researchers have be-

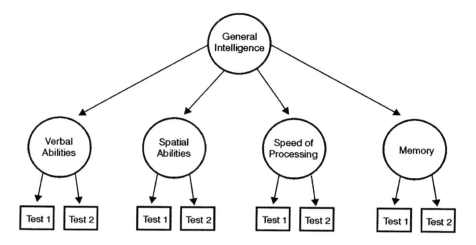

FIG. 4.1.   Molarity versus modularity. Schematic depiction of general intelligence (molarity) and four separate cognitive abilities (modularity)—verbal ability, spatial ability, speed of processing, and memory. The two arrows pointing away from the abilities indicate that each ability is measured with two separate tests. Petrill (1997) found evidence for heritability for both general intelligence and these four separate cognitive abilities. Figure adapted from Petrill (1997).

come more sophisticated in their measurements and research designs. For example, a 20-year study with 245 adopted children and the same number of nonadopted children estimated heritabilities of .56 for general cognitive ability, .54 for verbal ability, .39 for spatial ability, .26 for speed of processing, and .26 for memory (Plomin et al., 1997). Another study with identical (monozygotic) and fraternal (dizygotic) twins reported similar estimates of heritability (McClearn et al., 1997). The exact values are not important because they are estimates, but what is important is the idea that heritability contributes to cognition and other variables are also important in determining cognitive abilities. The same conclusion is obtained whether we compare identical and fraternal twins or adopted and nonadopted children. Interestingly, it seems that genetic contributions increase throughout the life span, even into old age (Gottesman, 1997).

More behavioral genetic data have been obtained for measures of intelligence than for any other trait (Plomin, 1990). The whole question of the extent to which intelligence is inherited has been hotly debated throughout the history of psychology and seems no closer to being resolved today than it was more than a century ago. The heated controversies generated by the publication of *The Bell Curve* (Herrnstein & Murray, 1994) and the firestorm of vitriolic responses show that this topic is as contested at the start of the 21st century as it was more than 100 years ago. Despite the lack of agreement on the question of how much intelligence is inherited, even staunch environmentalists agree that it is at least partially inherited. In Petrill's (1997) review of the literature, he concluded that genetic heritability accounts for 50% of the variability in the cognitive abilities that comprise intelligence, a figure that most researchers in the field find acceptable. It is fair to conclude that both environmental and genetic factors are important in intelligence.

Sex-Linked Recessive Gene Theory

Genetics is a profound idea. It is an idea that poses disturbing questions and yields disturbing implications.
—Begley (1999, p. 68)

Any genetic explanation of sex differences in visual–spatial ability would need to posit an inheritance mechanism that is differentiated by sex. A major genetic theory of cognitive sex differences is based on the assumption that high spatial ability is a sex-linked recessive trait that is carried on the X chromosome. (A recessive trait is one that will be expressed, that is, it will appear in a person's phenotype, only if both chromosomes carry the gene for the recessive trait.) If this theory were correct, then females would have a double dose of the genes that determine spatial ability because they have two X chromosomes, whereas males would have only one dose and that one would always come from the mother, who contributes the X chromosome to her son. For males, their other sex chromosome is the very small Y chromosome, which does not carry any genetic information about spatial ability. According to this theory, the "high spatial ability" gene is recessive; therefore, this trait will occur more frequently in males than in females because males have no other gene to mask the effects of the recessive gene. Given that females would have to have the "high spatial ability" gene on both X chromosomes and males would need to have it only on one, males would therefore be more likely to demonstrate good spatial ability. Table 4.1 depicts which individuals would be predicted to demonstrate good spatial ability as a function of their genotype if the sex-linked recessive theory were true.

The beauty of this theory is the explicit quantitative nature of the predictions derived from it. One of the predictions generated from the sex-linked recessive gene theory concerns the total proportion of men and women who would be expected to show good spatial ability. Bock and Kolakowski (1973) estimated that a recessive spatial ability gene should appear among American Caucasians with a frequency of approximately 50%. (Estimates for other racial groups were not given.) If this were true, then approximately 50% of all Caucasian men and approximately 25% of all Caucasian women would be expected to show this trait phenotypically. This prediction can be seen in the male genetic configurations shown in Table 4.1. There are two equally likely male genetic patterns, one of which would be associated with good spatial ability. The 25% prediction for females also can be seen in

TABLE 4.1

Predictions Derived From the X-Linked Recessive Gene Theory of Spatial Ability

Good spatial ability would be found in:

1. Hemizygous recessive males (Gene for good spatial ability is carried on the X chromosome)	♂	X^r Y
2. Homozygous recessive females (Gene for good spatial ability is carried on both X chromosomes)	♀	X^r X^r

Good spatial ability would not be found in:

1. Hemizygous dominant males (Gene for poor spatial ability is carried on the X chromosome)	♂	X^D Y
2. Heterozygous females (Gene for poor spatial ability is carried on one X chromosome; gene for good spatial ability is carried on the other X chromosome)	♀ or ♀	X^D X^r or X^r X^D
3. Homozygous recessive females (Gene for poor spatial ability is carried on both X chromosomes)	♀	X^D X^D

Note. r = recessive; D = dominant.

Table 4.1. There are four equally probable female configurations, only one of which would be associated with good spatial ability. The data, however, do not conform to these proportions. The prediction that one half of all males and one fourth of all females would show this trait phenotypically has not been supported (DeFries, Vandenberg, & McClearn, 1976).

Another prediction derived from the sex-linked theory of spatial ability is an explicit pattern of relationships among parents, children, and siblings (Boles, 1980). One of the hypothesized relationships is that sons' spatial abilities should resemble their mothers' more than their fathers'. The reasoning behind this hypothesis is that males have a single X chromosome that they inherited from their mothers. If a spatial ability gene is carried on this chromosome, then, on average, sons should be more similar to their mothers in spatial ability than to their fathers. Daughters, in contrast, should tend to be more similar to their fathers in terms of their spatial ability than to their mothers. The reasoning behind this relationship is somewhat more complex. Mother–daughter pairs have a total of four X chromosomes, two each from the mother and the daughter. Two of these four are held in common because the daughter receives one of her X chromosomes from her mother. Daughter–father pairs have a total of three X chromosomes, two of which are jointly held because daughters receive one of their X chromosomes from their fathers. According to this logic, daughters share a larger proportion of their total daughter–parent

X chromosome pool with their fathers than with their mothers. The prediction that sons' spatial abilities should resemble their mothers' more than their fathers' and that daughters' spatial abilities should resemble their fathers' more than their mothers' is opposite from any predictions made from psychosocial theories, which would posit some sort of same-sex modeling. Thus, if this pattern of relationships were empirically supported, it would constitute strong support for genetic determination.

Early studies with small samples provided weak support for this hypothesis. Stafford (1961, 1963) found the pattern of relationships between daughters and fathers, daughters and mothers, sons and mothers, and sons and fathers in the order predicted by this theory, but only for 1 of the 10 tests he used to measure spatial abilities and even that 1 failed to reach statistical significance. Later studies with larger samples failed to replicate this pattern (Bouchard & McGee, 1977; Loehlin, Sharan, & Jacoby, 1978).

Despite early support for the sex-linked recessive hypothesis, it now seems clear that its validity is unfounded. Recent research has not supported the X-linked recessive gene theory of spatial ability (Gittler & Vitouch, 1994). Perhaps one of the biggest problems is with the notion that a complex multidimensional variable like visual–spatial ability would have a single genetic determinant. As described in chapter 3, spatial ability consists of at least five distinct components (mental rotation, spatial perception, visualization, image generation, and spatiotemporal processing). These components are not necessarily related. Genetic theories that fail to make distinctions among these components of spatial ability will never be able to adequately describe the phenomenon. All of the sex-differentiated cognitive abilities are composed of multiple components, and it is unlikely that there is a single gene that controls the expression of any of these abilities. In addition, visual–spatial ability is a characteristic that we all exhibit to some degree, a fact that cannot be explained with a single gene.

In Vandenberg's (1968) study of the verbal and spatial abilities of twins, he made two conclusions: (a) Both abilities have heritability components, and (b) verbal abilities are more influenced by environmental events than are spatial abilities. Vandenberg's conclusions were based on the similarity between twins on verbal tests. Monozygotic or identical twins, who share 100% of their genetic makeup, were more similar than dizygotic or fraternal twins. Nontwin siblings showed the least similarity. A major problem in inferring the heritability of any cognitive ability from twins' data results from the fact that twins are also more likely to be similar to each other than are other pairs of nontwin siblings in terms of their social and learning histories. It is just as likely that the similarity in environmental factors could be responsible for the similarity in their scores as the hypothesis that the degree of genetic information that they share is responsible.

An X-linked recessive trait theory for verbal ability, similar to that proposed for visual–spatial ability, was proposed by Lehrke (1974). Lehrke's hypothesis was based on the inheritance pattern or pedigree of certain mental deficiencies involving verbal abilities. Although some mental deficiencies are transmitted by

X-linked recessive genes, there is no evidence for an X-linked gene for verbal ability among individuals in the normal range of intelligence.

Stafford (1972) offered a pattern of family intercorrelational data in support of the notion that mathematical skills are inherited through the now familiar X-linked recessive gene. Sherman (1978) provided a cogent criticism of these data, which not only failed to fit the proposed model but were substantially divergent from those predicted by the model. There is no support for a sex-differentiated mode for the inheritance of mathematical skills.

Arguing From Abnormalities

In normal individuals, genetic information and concentrations of sex hormones are confounded. Individuals whose sex chromosomes are XX also appear female, are raised as females, and secrete sex hormones associated with being female. Of course, the reverse is true for males with XY sex chromosome pairs. The problem is isolating the effect of any one of these variables on the cognitive abilities that are differentiated by sex. To decide if the finding that men and women tend to excel in different types of intellectual tasks is due to genetic programming, the influence of genetic information needs to be disentangled from that of hormones and the large number of life experiences that vary with sex. One way of examining genetic effects is to study people with genetic abnormalities such that the sex hormones, the external genitals, or both are not consistent with genetic sex.

There have been several studies of people with genetic abnormalities on their sex chromosomes. Rovet and Netley (1979), for example, studied five females with a genetic anomaly known as Turner's syndrome. Instead of the usual pair of X chromosomes, females with Turner's syndrome have a single X chromosome. This syndrome is designated as 45XO to indicate the fact that these individuals have 45 chromosomes instead of the usual 46 and only 1 intact X chromosome. The 2nd X chromosome is either missing or seriously defective. Individuals with Turner's syndrome are clearly female in appearance. Perhaps their major distinguishing feature is that they tend to be short and usually require treatment with female hormones in order to exhibit female secondary sex characteristics at puberty. According to the X-linked recessive gene theory, females with Turner's syndrome should display the male pattern of cognitive abilities, that is, on average, they should score higher on visual–spatial performance tests than on verbal tests. The reasoning behind this prediction is straightforward. Like men, they have a single X chromosome and thus should be more likely to show a recessive X-linked characteristic because there is no other gene to carry the dominant trait. Rovet and Netley found results opposite to those predicted from this theory. All five of the females they tested had higher verbal scores than visual–spatial performance scores, which were substantially lower than the scores obtained by 46XX (genetically normal) females.

In the same study, Rovet and Netley (1979) also tested three individuals who were phenotypically male (appeared to be male) with a 46XX genotype (female gene pattern). If the sex-linked recessive gene pattern were correct, then these males should show a female pattern of cognitive abilities, with higher verbal skills than visual–spatial skills. The reasoning behind this prediction is that if the sex chromosomes are direct determinants of cognitive ability, then any group of individuals with female sex chromosomes should, on average, tend to show the pattern of abilities associated with being female. Again, this theory was not confirmed. Contrary to predictions, all three of the phenotypical males scored higher on the visual–spatial performance tests than on the verbal tests. Although this study used only a small number of participants, these results are compelling and have been confirmed by other researchers and in several other samples of females with Turner's syndrome (e.g., Money & Ehrhardt, 1972; Murphy et al., 1994; Temple & Carney, 1993). It seems clear from these studies that cognitive abilities conform to phenotypic rather than genotypic sex and that genetic information can act in ways that are unrelated to hormonal levels, at least in abnormal populations. Currently, there is little support for the notion that sex differences in cognitive abilities are due to inherent differences in male and female genetic makeup per se.

The reason that I added "per se" to the last sentence is that genes underlie the development of every living organism. Every individual's genetic makeup contributes to brain development and, by extension, brain functioning. Females with Turner's syndrome perform poorly on tasks requiring visual–spatial and numerical skills and often perform below average on tests of verbal abilities as well (Temple & Marriott, 1998). Modern imaging techniques also have shown the influence of 45XO on brain structures, thus providing a linkage between brain structures and cognitive deficits (Reiss, Mazzocco, Greenlaw, Freund, & Ross, 1995). Later in this chapter, I return to the finding that females with Turner's syndrome tend to be only somewhat deficient in their verbal abilities but more seriously deficient in their spatial ability. This lopsided pattern of cognitive development has provided support for the hypothesis that prenatal hormones (which are under the direction of genes) affect brain development in sexually differentiated ways.

The Genetics of the Environment

In some instances, the environment reflects rather than affects characteristics of the individual.
—Saudino (1997, p. 86)

The goal of behavioral genetics is to understand the links between genes and behaviors. This is no small task given that psychologists estimate the number of genes to be approximately 100,000 and the number of potentially related behaviors is virtually limitless (Hamer, 1997). In attempting to separate various influences on behavior, psychologists often compare identical twins, who are genetically identical, with fraternal twins and nontwin siblings (both are intermediate in their shared genetic inheritance), adopted siblings (dissimilar in genetics but similar in environment), and twins and siblings who are reared separately from a young age (dissimilar in environment). One consistent and surprising outcome from these various comparisons is that growing up in the same home often makes people more different. In other words, the environment is important but not in the way that most people would predict. Many measures of the environment show genetic influences! Even though two children may have been raised in the same home, each child, to some extent, created her or his own environment on the basis of individual predilections, needs, and desires. This idea may seem paradoxical; after all, the environment doesn't have DNA (the building blocks of genes), so how can it be affected by genetic factors? It seems that we each select different aspects from the environment. For example, a child with excellent reading abilities might select books from among a large collection of possible play objects (e.g., a television, a ball, a building set) and thereby create an environment that reflects the child's genetic predispositions. When twins grow up in the same household, they may tend to select different activities as a means of differentiating themselves, but when they grow up in different households, they may tend to select more similar activities, ones that are consistent with their biological propensities. According to this point of view, genetic effects can be found in the environment.

The field of behavioral genetics has changed the way we think about the environment, so that it not only reflects genetic influences but also operates prenatally. In an article on the importance of environmental variables, Phelps, Davis, and Schartz (1997) reminded researchers that during gestation, the developing fetus is subject to a prenatal environment that can be as critical to development as the genetic program that is orchestrating the creation of a new human. Thus, researchers may attribute an effect to genetics when it is primarily influenced by the prenatal hormonal environment. The membrane that surrounds the developing fetus is called the chorion. Some monozygotic (identical) twins share a single chorion; others develop separate chorions. Twins who develop in a single chorion have a more similar prenatal environment than those who develop in separate chorions. Recent studies have shown that single-chorion twins are more similar in intelligence and cognitive abilities than twins with separate chorions (Phelps et al., 1997). Thus, the shared prenatal environment is an important contributor to the trait being measured. The chorion produces hormones (estrogen, progesterone, and others), and thus its action is probably through the effect of these hormones on the developing fetus.

The burgeoning field of behavioral genetics also has created a renewed emphasis on the environment with the use of co-twin experimental controls. Consider the classic notion of examining identical twins who are reared separately. These individuals share 100% of their genetic makeup and none of their environment, so any measures of similarity are assumed to be "pure" measures of the genetic contribution to the trait being measured. But systematic studies of environmental effects also have shown the importance of environmental variables. Identical twins who are reared apart may have created similar environments for themselves, thus making it impossible to separate environmental and genetic effects.

SEX HORMONES

One fact must be kept in mind. ... Humans are biological creatures.
—Doyle (1995, p. 45)

A person's gender, however, is an arbitrary, ever-changing
socially constructed set of attributes that are culture specific and culturally generated,
beginning with the appearance of the external
genitals at birth.
—Bleier (1991, p. 66)

Mention sex differences with respect to almost any ability and someone is sure to say, "It's all in the hormones." Clearly, one of the major biological differences between females and males is the relative concentration of the "female" sex hormones, estrogen and progesterone, and the "male" sex hormones or androgens, most notably testosterone. Sex hormones are powerful chemical messengers secreted by the ovaries in women, by the testes in men, and by the adrenal glands in both sexes. Because they circulate freely throughout the bloodstream, sex hormones are able to affect distant target organs, including the brain, muscles, skeleton, and sensory organs.

Despite common misconceptions, it is not true that women have only female hormones and men have only male hormones. Both sexes have measurable quantities of estrogen, progesterone, and testosterone. The relative concentrations of each of these hormones vary by sex and throughout the life cycle. Hormonal actions on the human brain are exceedingly complex. Not only do all normal humans have measurable amounts of all of the hormones that we tend to think of as female or male hormones, but the body converts these hormones from one chemical configuration to another. Most of the time, before the cells of the brain can use testosterone, it needs to be converted into estradiol, a form of estrogen, which is chiefly a hormonal secretion of the ovaries. More rarely, the brain can directly use androgens—either testosterone or a different form of androgen, dihydrotestosterone—without the conversion to estradiol (Collaer & Hines, 1995). Not only do masculine hormones occur in different forms (metabolites), but the different forms have different effects on development. In addition, there are different critical periods when hormones have their greatest effect on development, so the development of the genitals in either a female or a male direction has a different critical period than the development of different portions of the brain and behavioral traits (e.g., preference for rough-and-tumble play). Thus, it is very difficult to discern the effects of what we typically think of as female or male hormones because these two types of hormones can be chemically transmuted from one to the other, and variations in hormone concentrations at different times during prenatal development lead to different effects. This means that the differentiation of the genitals in one sex-specific form (e.g., penis for males) does not guarantee that all sex-differentiated aspects will take the same (e.g., male) form.

Theories Relating Sex Hormones to Cognitive Abilities

Two theories about the relationship between hormone levels and cognition have spurred much of the research on these questions. It is useful to review the theory proposed by Geschwind and his colleagues (Geschwind & Galaburda, 1987) and the theory proposed by Nyborg (1990) before we examine the data because these theoretical perspectives will help readers understand the background and rationales for the studies.

Geschwind's Theory of Prenatal Hormonal Effects.

An influential theory proposed by Geschwind and his colleagues (e.g., Geschwind, 1983, 1984; Geschwind & Galaburda, 1987) is based on the belief that prenatal hormones have a pervasive effect on cognition. This theory is based on the assumption that the prenatal sex hormones that both direct and reflect the sexual differentiation of the fetus also exert powerful influences on the central nervous system of developing organisms. In humans, the right hemisphere (half of the brain) normally develops at a faster rate than the left hemisphere. Because of this differential rate of development, the left hemisphere is at risk for a longer period of time than the right hemisphere, and therefore is more likely to be affected by an adverse intrauterine environment. Proponents of this theory assert that high levels of testosterone slow the growth of neurons in the left hemisphere. The result is right-hemisphere dominance, which means that the right hemisphere has greater control than the left hemisphere.

One index of which hemisphere is dominant is handedness, that is, whether an individual is right-handed or left-handed. Because the right hemisphere coordinates movement for the left half of the body and the left hemisphere coordinates movement for the right half of the body, a right-hander is (usually) left-hemisphere dominant, and a left-hander is (often) right-hemisphere dominant. (People with mixed hand use, performing some tasks with the right hand and other tasks with the left hand, are usually considered to be left-handers.) If high levels of prenatal androgen slow neuronal growth in the left hemisphere, as proposed, the result would be right-hemisphere dominance, which is manifested in left-handedness. (For an extensive review of the literature on left-handedness, see Coren, 1990.)

There are three sources of prenatal testosterone: (a) maternally produced testosterone, which comes from the maternal ovaries, adrenals, and other structures such as fat; (b) adrenal glands in both female and male fetuses; and, (c) for male fetuses, testosterone produced by their own developing testes. Thus, normal males are exposed to higher levels of prenatal testosterone than normal females. As would be predicted by this theory, numerous studies have found a higher proportion of left-handedness in males than in females (Bryden, 1977; Halpern, Haviland, & Killian, 1998; Hardyck, Goldman, & Petrinovich, 1975; Stellman, Wynder, DeRose, & Muscat, 1997). It is interesting to note that women who are exposed to abnormally high levels of prenatal androgens because of adrenal abnormalities also show higher proportions of left-handedness than other females, as predicted from this theory (Resnick, Berenbaum, Gottesman, & Bouchard, 1986).

An important corollary of the sex hormone hypothesis is that other susceptible organs in the developing fetus are also affected by high testosterone levels. One such organ is the thymus gland, which is an essential component of the developing immune system. The simultaneous effect of testosterone on the development of the left hemisphere, the thymus gland, and other organs results in the prediction that there would be a greater incidence of immune disorders among left-handed individuals. The first evidence for this relationship came from Geschwind and Behan (1982, 1984). They showed that autoimmune diseases (especially those involving the intestinal tract and the thyroid gland) and atopic diseases (allergies, asthma, eczema, and hay fever) are 2.5 times as frequent in strong left-handers as in strong right-handers. These results have been essentially confirmed in several subsequent studies. (See Bryden, McManus, & Bulman-Fleming, 1994, for a critique and review of this theory.)

If, as this theory predicts, left-handedness is sometimes the result of exposure to higher than average amounts of prenatal testosterone, then we would expect a positive association among being male, being left-handed, having immune disorders, and demonstrating patterns of cognitive abilities that are known to be lateralized (or specialized) in the right or the left hemisphere. There are at least two possibilities: (a) overall poorer performance by males on cognitive tasks that are usually associated with the left hemisphere and (b) overall higher performance by males on cognitive tasks that are believed to be primarily under right-hemisphere control.

As you know from chapter 3, males tend to excel at some spatial tasks and some mathematical reasoning tasks, most notably tasks that require mental manipulations of spatial information and the SAT–M. These tasks are associated with right-hemisphere functioning. Males also have a majority of the language production and reading problems, thus confirming, in a general way, some of the theoretical predictions. Geschwind and Galaburda's (1987) theory is summarized in Table 4.2.

TABLE 4.2
Summary of Geschwind and Galaburda's Theory

Relationship among:	Sex, handedness, immune disorders, and cognitive abilities
Theory:	High levels of prenatal testosterone slow neuronal growth in the left hemisphere and diminish the size of the developing thymus gland
Predictions:	Positive associations among: Being male Being left-handed Immune disorders (e.g., allergies) Anomalous right-hemisphere cognitive abilities (e.g., mathematical giftedness, some types of retardation)

Nyborg's Theory of Optimal Level of Estradiol

A second theory that relates sex hormones to cognitive abilities was proposed by Nyborg (1984, 1988, 1990). Nyborg's model is called the general trait covariance—androgen/estrogen balance model. (Quite a mouthful! I don't know why they can't give these models simple names like "Fred.") Nyborg's model is based on two important assumptions. The first is that spatial ability is inversely related to certain verbal abilities. To support this assumption, Nyborg cited a study by Lynn (1987) that showed a negative correlation between spatial ability and verbal ability (after controlling for general level of intelligence). The second assumption is that there is a range of hormone levels that yields optimal expression of spatial ability. Unlike some of the other hormone-based theories, Nyborg targeted estradiol as the critical hormone.

Recall that androgens can be chemically converted (the correct term for this is *aromatized*) to estradiol for use by the brain. According to Nyborg (1984, 1988), it is estradiol, a hormone that is stereotypically thought of as a female hormone (but we know better—it is found in both males and females), that is consequential in the expression of spatial abilities. Nyborg's model is depicted in Fig. 4.2.

Look carefully at Fig. 4.2. As you can see, the central portion of the inverted U-shaped curve represents the optimal concentration of estradiol for spatial ability. In general, females have greater amounts of estradiol (more than the optimal amount), and males will tend to have smaller amounts of estradiol (less than the optimal amount). According to this theory, males who are more "feminized" and females who are more "masculinized" will have better spatial skills. If you look closely at Fig. 4.2, you will see that the left-hand portion of the curves represents low levels of estradiol. When the concentration of estradiol is raised in women who had extremely low levels of prenatal hormones (e.g., females with Turner's syndrome, the genetic abnormality noted as 45XO), they move closer to the middle portion of the curve (Nyborg, 1983).

There has been some support for Nyborg's (1983) general notion of an inverted U-shaped relationship between estradiol or its precursor testosterone and spatial ability, but the data are still open to alternative interpretations. Tan and Tan (1998) found a curvilinear relationship between testosterone (measured in blood samples) and performance on a spatial test of intelligence known as the Catell Culture Fair Intelligence Test. As reported elsewhere, there were no overall sex differences on this measure of intelligence. Of course, there were large differences between the women and the men in the total amount of testosterone found in their blood, but the same inverted U function applied for both sexes. Data on the use of estrogen replacement for older women provide results that are also supportive of Nyborg's (1983) model. Older women, who presumably have very low levels of estradiol, improve in their cognitive abilities when their estrogen levels are raised, but the beneficial effects for older women on cognitive tasks include improved verbal memory as well, so the effect is not limited to spatial ability (Resnick, Maki, Golski, Kraut, & Zonderman, 1998).

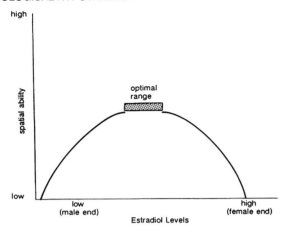

FIG. 4.2.   Graphic depiction of Nyborg's (1990) model, which posits that there is an optimal range of estradiol that is needed for the expression of spatial abilities. Note that most males are relatively low on estradiol and most females are relatively high on estradiol. According to this theory, increasing estradiol for most males and decreasing estradiol for most females will improve their spatial abilities.

According to Nyborg (1983), prenatal hormones determine each individual's sensitivity to the sex hormones that are secreted at puberty. Prenatal hormones permanently alter the body's sensitivity to puberty sex hormones. Nyborg's (1983) theory targets both prenatal and pubertal hormones as important determinants of spatial ability. However, this theory also allows for learning and environmental effects on the development of spatial ability.

A Life-Span Developmental Approach

Because of dramatic age-dependent fluctuations in hormone levels, it seems likely that the influence of these hormones also would vary with age. The age-dependent nature of hormone effects are examined in separate sections for each developmental stage, beginning with prenatal influences and ending with adulthood and old age.

Prenatal and Early Postnatal Hormones

Research on the importance of experience during prenatal life has documented the ability of fetuses to respond to changes in the intrauterine environment, to learn by association of stimuli, and to retain prenatal experiences into postnatal life.
—Smotherman and Robinson (1990, p. 97)

Prenatal hormones are critically important determinants of whether a developing fetus will grow into a male or a female infant. The genetic configuration of the sex chromosomes (XX for female, XY for male) determines whether the undifferentiated developing gonads (sex glands) will become ovaries or testes. If they are developing according to a male program, they will begin to differentiate approximately 7 weeks after conception. The newly formed testes will secrete male hormones (primarily testosterone), which, in turn, direct the development of the internal male reproductive organs and external genitals. If, in contrast, the genetic program is XX, the gonads will develop into ovaries, and in the absence of male hormones, internal female reproductive organs and external female genitals will develop. It is important to note that it is the absence of male hormones, not the presence of female hormones, that directs the growth of female organs because in the absence of hormones, or usable hormones, the sexual differentiation of the fetus will be female. It is also important to keep in mind the fact that the determination of one's sex is composed of a mosaic of factors. Regardless of the genetic sex of a fetus, it can develop the genitals, brain structures, and behaviors of either a male or a female (Collaer & Hines, 1995; Hines & Collaer, 1993).

A schematic diagram of prenatal development is presented in Fig. 4.3. It charts the development of females and males from conception until birth. If you read the first edition of this book, you may notice that this figure looks different from its earlier version. Data presented in chapter 5 now show that female prenatal hormones play a role in the differentiation of the brain but (probably) not in the differentiation of the genitals (e.g., Berrebi et al., 1988; Fitch & Denenberg, 1998; McEwen, Alves, Bulloch, & Weiland, 1997). It was formerly believed that these hormones were not important during prenatal development.

There is good reason to believe that the presence or absence of particular sex hormones during critical stages of prenatal development also plays a role in the sexual differentiation of the developing brain. Hormones are elevated for the first 6–12 months after birth, and scientists are not sure whether specific brain effects can be traced to prenatal hormones or postnatal hormones within the 1st year of life (Brown & Dixson, 1999). Thus, it is likely that the hormones that are secreted by the newly formed testes in males or the absence of these hormones in females affect the appearance of the genitals, but hormones secreted by the testes (in males), ovaries (in females), and adrenal glands (in both males and females) direct the development of neural pathways in the newly forming brain.

Approximately 7 weeks after conception, which is when the testes begin secreting androgens, the first fully developed neurons (basic brain cells) begin to form a rudimentary brain. If ovaries are formed, they will develop at approximately 12 weeks, a timing difference that may be important in early brain development. At 28 weeks after conception, "interneurons" form, which are essential to the higher level cognitive activities that we consider distinctly human. Brain development continues at a rapid pace during infancy and thus is probably influenced by the high levels of gonadal hormones that are secreted in the 1st year of life. The brain continues to develop throughout the entire life span (Patlak, 1990).

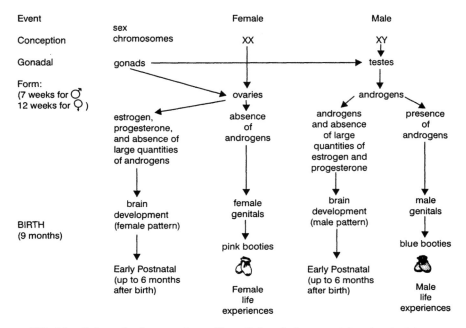

FIG. 4.3.   Schematic diagram of sex differentiation during prenatal and perinatal development.

Organizational and Activational Effects.

Because prenatal and perinatal (around the time of birth) hormones act by directing the formation of the developing brain, some researchers have called these "organizational effects." By contrast, hormonal effects that occur later in life are sometimes called "activational effects" because they activate neural events but do not change the structure or organization of the brain or other portions of the central nervous system. Organizational effects were thought to be more long-lasting, whereas hormonal effects later in life were considered more transient, lasting only as long as the hormone was present in the body. Like any dichotomy, it seems that the division of hormonal effects into organizational versus activational is not absolute. We now know that brains are far more plastic throughout life than earlier researchers had believed and that hormones and environmental events can permanently alter brain structures even into very old age (Fitch & Denenberg, 1998). Thus, the distinction between organizational and activational effects is blurred and may soon disappear from the literature as we learn more about the ways that hormones influence the brain.

Much of the experimental research in this area has been performed on nonhuman mammals, especially rats (e.g., Daniel, Fader, Spencer, & Dohanich, 1997). Although there are numerous biological similarities between nonhuman mammals and humans, one of the major differences is the extent to which hormones direct and control behavior. Hormones are less important in determining behavior for humans than for nonhuman mammals. Thus, although results obtained with rats or other mammals may be suggestive of possible relationships for humans, they are not directly applicable. Extrapolation from animal data to humans can lead to erroneous conclusions and, for this reason, must be made very carefully.

For most people, the configuration of their sex chromosomes, prenatal and postnatal sex hormones, reproductive organs, genitals, sex role pressures, and sex of identification are the same. To understand the role that hormones play in shaping the other biological and psychological indexes of sex, it is necessary to isolate experimentally and manipulate sex hormones independent of the other covariates of sex. Two general approaches are used to understand the effect of sex hormones. The quantity and type of sex hormone are manipulated in nonhuman mammals under careful laboratory conditions, and naturally occurring or drug-induced abnormalities in humans are studied. We consider here some of the most relevant research with nonhuman mammals and with humans with hormonal abnormalities. There are strengths and weaknesses associated with each of these approaches.

Laboratory Investigations With Nonhuman Mammals.   The majority of the work in this area has been conducted with rats, although other mammals and primates have been used. Prenatal hormones are manipulated by either castrating a developing male rat or giving antiandrogens to block androgenic effects, thereby depriving him of the testosterone secreted by the testes; removing the ovaries of a developing female rat, thereby depriving her of the hormones secreted by her ovaries; administering androgens to developing females or administering ovarian hormones to developing males; or administering any hormone of interest to a pregnant mother, who will pass the hormone onto the developing fetus. Timing of these manipulations is important because there appears to be a critical developmental period for brain differentiation. Research using these techniques with rodents has mapped hormone-sensitive cells in the brain that respond to prenatal sex hormones (McEwen, 1981). In an early review of the literature, MacLusky and Naftolin (1981) cited a number of sex differences in brain morphology that depend on prenatal hormone exposure, including volume differences in certain cell groups and differences in synaptic and dendrite organization. Diamond (cited in Kimura, 1985) found that testosterone can have asymmetrical effects on the developing brains of prenatal female and male rats. When additional testosterone was supplied, male rats showed increases in the thickness of their right hemisphere, whereas female rats showed increases in the thickness of their left hemisphere. I return to the possibility that female and male humans differ in the way their hemispheres are specialized for different tasks in the next chapter, in which I discuss sex differences in brain structure and function.

One well-established effect of prenatal hormones is in the function and development of a tiny brain structure known as the hypothalamus. The hypothalamus influences reproductive behavior and controls the release of reproductive hormones from the pituitary gland. There is no reason to believe that the hypothalamus and the pituitary gland are involved in the higher level cognitive abilities that vary by sex; however, other brain structures may also be affected by prenatal and perinatal hormones. Clear-cut findings in lower mammals have led researchers to conclude that prenatal and perinatal hormones influence a wide variety of behaviors and cognitive abilities. In general, if androgens are administered, typical male behavior results, and if androgens are removed, typical female behavior results. As explained earlier, we know much less about the role of prenatal and perinatal ovarian hormones than we know about the role of prenatal and perinatal hormones secreted by the testes. Researchers have recently made a strong case for the importance of ovarian hormones in early life for some normal female behaviors, but our knowledge of their effects is still sketchy and incomplete (Fitch & Denenberg, 1998).

One area of the brain that figures prominently in theories about female–male differences in the brain is the corpus callosum. The corpus callosum is a thick band of neural fibers that connects the two halves of the brain. Again, we know more about the corpus callosum of the rat brain than the human brain because scientists are able to conduct research with rats that would be unethical with humans. Although sex differences and similarities in brain structures are discussed more fully in chapter 5, readers need to understand that brain differences develop under the influence of early hormones. The rat's corpus callosum is sexually dimorphic. This means that, on average, there are some differences that vary as a function of sex. For rats, the male's corpus callosum is larger than the female's even after adjusting for brain size and body weight. In a careful series of studies, Denenberg and his colleagues (Berrebi et al., 1988; Denenberg, Berrebi, & Fitch, 1988) administered testosterone to newborn female rats and castrated newborn male rats. (Yes, I know what you're thinking. The quest for knowledge can lead to bizarre experiments.) The administration of testosterone masculinized the corpus callosum of the female rats, but castration had only a minor effect on the size of the corpus callosum of the male rats. They also found that prenatal female hormones affected the size of the corpus callosum, debunking the long-held myth that prenatal ovarian hormones do not influence brain development. This set of experiments provides strong evidence that sex differences in the corpus callosum are created by prenatal and perinatal (around the time of birth) sex hormones.

Research with rodents, other nonhuman mammals, and humans clearly shows that prenatal and early postnatal hormones influence a wide variety of sex-typed behaviors, including activity levels, aggression, roughness of juvenile play, sexual behaviors, maze performance (a spatial skill), and visual discrimination learning (e.g., Grisham, Kerchner, & Ward, 1991; Hines & Sandberg, 1996; Williams & Meck, 1991). It is through research with rodents that investigators learned that estradiol, a hormone that is normally secreted by the ovaries, has a masculizing effect on behavior. For example, when estradiol is administered to rodents, maze performance improves. To understand how this occurs in normal rodents, recall that testosterone, secreted in large quantities from the testes, is converted into estradiol, which then activates neural estrogen receptors in the brain to induce masculine-type development. This series of events is depicted in Fig. 4.4.

The finding that sex differences in rodent and primate brains and cognitive, sexual, and aggressive behaviors are mediated by prenatal and postnatal hormones is interesting in its own right, but there is ample reason to believe that for humans, cognitive, sexual, and aggressive behaviors are also shaped, to a great extent, by social learning and other life experiences. (Evidence in support of this claim is presented in chaps. 6 and 7). Of course, such manipulations are unethical for human participants. The closest we can come to examining hormone effects in humans is to examine "human accidents" or hormone abnormalities.

Prenatal Sex Hormone Abnormalities   There are many clinical syndromes in humans that result from abnormalities in the prenatal hormone environment. These "accidents of nature" allow us to examine the way in which different hormones act prenatally for humans. As you will see, in general, findings from experiments with nonhuman mammals and with people with abnormal prenatal hormones corroborate each other and extend what we are able to learn from people with normal hormone levels.

Fetal Androgenization.   What are the effects of high levels of male hormones on a developing fetus? This question has been answered with two different groups of people who were exposed to abnormally high levels of androgens during fetal development.

Since the early 1950s, millions of pregnant women have been treated with synthetic sex hormones to prevent miscarriage. Although a variety of hormones have been used in varying doses, depending on the individual situation and current medical practice, most have some androgenic or masculinizing effect. Research with nonhuman mammals has shown that aggressive behavior is hormonally mediated. Reinisch (1981) reasoned that if prenatal hormones have similar effects in hu-

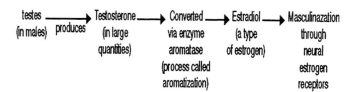

The Prenatal / Early Postnatal
Masculinization of Development

FIG. 4.4.   How estradiol (an estrogen) masculinizes behavior. Testosterone, which is secreted in large quantities in males by their testes, is converted (the technical term is *aromatized*) into estradiol by an enzyme so that it can be used by the brain. It is estradiol, converted from testosterone, that underlies many male-typical behaviors.

mans, then individuals who had been exposed to high levels of masculinizing hormones before birth should also demonstrate an increased potential for aggressive behavior. She studied 17 female and 8 male participants who had been exposed to synthetic hormones before birth. The measurement of aggression in humans poses a research problem because most people demonstrate aggressive impulses only under limited and threatening circumstances. For this reason, Reinisch used a paper-and-pencil measure of aggression (fantasies about aggression). She used same-sex unexposed siblings as the control group in the belief that siblings offer a control for environmental and genetic influences. Both the participants and their siblings had a mean age of 11 years at the time of testing.

As expected from all of the sex differences literature, Reinisch (1981) found that males had higher aggression scores than females. She also found that the participants who had been exposed to synthetic hormones before birth reported higher physical aggression than their unexposed same-sex siblings. She interpreted these results as providing strong support for prenatal hormone mediation of human aggressive behavior. The implication of this research is that because under normal conditions males are exposed to more androgens before birth than females, sex differences in aggression are due to sex differences in prenatal hormonal milieu. Other researchers have provided corroborative evidence that prenatal hormones contribute to aggression, general energy level, or both (Ehrhardt & Meyer-Bahlburg, 1979). Although it is reasonable to conclude that, at least under abnormally high concentrations, prenatal hormones affect human aggressive potential, what about their role in sex-differentiated human cognitive abilities?

Once researchers suspected that synthetic hormones were having a negative effect on prenatal development, these hormones were no longer routinely prescribed for pregnant women; thus, there are no well-controlled studies with enough participants to make strong conclusions about the effect of prenatal synthetic hormones on cognition. Dalton (1976) studied English children whose mothers had been given extremely high doses of sex hormones during pregnancy. Dalton reported that these children had significantly better "number ability," a result that would be predicted if these hormones also influence quantitative ability. However, Dalton's studies have been criticized on a number of statistical and methodological grounds, including her failure to use a control group when evaluating number ability, thus considerably weakening the impact of these findings. Meyer-Bahlburg and Ehrhardt (1977) attempted to replicate these results using better controls and more rigorous research methods. They did not find any relationship between prenatal hormone exposure and number ability, although the synthetic hormone taken by participants' mothers in Meyer-Bahlburg and Ehrhardt's study was less potent than the one investigated by Dalton. A more recent study of the effect of DES on cognition concluded that when it was administered to pregnant women, it had little or no effect on the cognitive abilities of the offspring, although the authors believe that other hormones administered during the early months of pregnancy might show the sex-typed cognitive effects that they were looking for (Hines & Sandberg, 1996). It is reasonable to conclude that DES and other synthetic hormones might affect cognition in developing fetuses, but the research was not well controlled, so we cannot make a definitive conclusion (Berenbaum, Korman, & Leveroni, 1995).

A second condition that exposes developing fetuses to extremely high levels of androgens is congenital adrenal hyperplasia (CAH; also known as androgenital syndrome). CAH is a genetic recessive disorder in which the adrenal glands produce abnormally high amounts of androgens beginning in the 3rd month of fetal life (Nyborg, 1983). When the genetic pattern for the developing organism is female (XX), she is exposed to abnormally high levels of prenatal androgen; when the genetic pattern is male (XY), he is exposed to elevated levels of prenatal androgen (Newcombe & Baenninger, 1989).

Do high levels of androgens during fetal life influence the cognitive abilities of the developing organisms? In an attempt to answer this question, researchers examined 17 females and 8 males with CAH (Resnick et al., 1986). The CAH girls scored significantly higher than their unaffected relatives on three different tests of spatial ability (out of five), thus providing evidence that, for females, prenatal androgen is associated with higher spatial ability. The researchers also found that the CAH girls were more likely to engage in "aggressive play," which provides more evidence for a causal link between prenatal hormones and behavior in later life (at least for females exposed to very high levels of prenatal androgen). These conclusions have been supported in a study of 22 CAH women who showed a verbal disadvantage relative to a control group (Helleday, Bartfai, Ritzen, & Forsman, 1994). The authors of this study concluded that CAH women develop a more masculine cognitive pattern (better spatial abilities than verbal abilities) because of the high level of prenatal androgen to which they were exposed. It is interesting to note that the CAH boys did not differ from their unaffected relatives on any of the cognitive or behavioral measures. The additional androgen had little or no effect on male prenatal development, perhaps because the levels were only slightly elevated. It is also interesting to note that the CAH girls showed other sorts of masculinized behaviors. For example, CAH girls showed a preference for "typical boys' toys"—trucks, blocks, and other building toys (Berenbaum & Hines, 1992). This is a good example of the concept that there is a genetic contribution to the environment: Individuals are born with certain personality and activity-level predispositions, which in turn influence the experiences that they select from the environment or create for themselves. CAH girls are more prone to rough-and-tumble play than matched controls. Their higher activity level may have made them more likely to select action toys to play with than to select sedentary toys, like books. As reviewed in Collaer and Hines (1995), CAH girls are more likely to prefer to play with boys and more likely to be either bisexual or homosexual than a control group of girls who did not experience high levels of prenatal androgen.

Androgen Insensitivity and Turner's Syndrome.   All of the studies discussed in the preceding section examined the effect of high levels of prenatal masculinizing hormones. Another pseudoexperimental approach is to examine the effect of extremely low levels of masculinizing hormones. Do such individuals develop cognitive abilities and personality traits usually associated with being female?

Androgen insensitivity is the term used to describe genetic males whose bodies are unable to respond to male hormones. (This disorder is also known as *testicular feminization.*) During fetal development these males' testes produce the appropriate male hormones, but for reasons not fully understood, their tissues are insensitive to these hormones, and development proceeds as though no male hormones are present (Christiansen & Knussmann, 1987). These genetic males develop female genitals, are generally identified as girls at birth, and usually are raised as girls. Ehrhardt and Meyer-Bahlburg (1979) reported "a significant, but modest, tendency toward verbal rather than spaceform abilities" (p. 422) in genetic males with androgen insensitivity. Even if these males were much better at verbal tasks than spatial ones, we would not know if this pattern of results was due to prenatal hormone effects, postnatal hormone effects, or the fact that they were identified and raised as girls. Thus, these results can be used to support either hormonal or environmental effects on cognition.

Another possible population for investigating prenatal hormone effects is women with Turner's syndrome. Recall that these women have a genetic abnormality such that their 2nd sex chromosome is missing or deformed. They are genetically denoted as 45XO to signify that they have a total of 45 chromosomes and only a single intact X sex chromosome. (The "o" signifies that one X chromosome is either damaged or missing.) They usually have underdeveloped ovaries and very low levels of available hormones. Hines (1982) reported that although women with Turner's syndrome have normal-range IQs and verbal abilities, they tend to have specific deficits in visual–spatial functioning. Could these specific deficiencies be due to extremely low levels of hormones? McCauley, Kay, Ito, and Treder (1987) think so. These researchers were interested in understanding why women with Turner's syndrome also tend to have social problems. They hypothesized that specific cognitive deficits were, in part, responsible for the social problems. To test this possibility, they had 9- to 17-year-old girls with Turner's syndrome judge the emotions being expressed in pictures of several faces. They found that these girls were less accurate at judging emotions than matched control participants. (The control participants were similar to the girls with Turner's syndrome with respect to height, socioeconomic status, age, and verbal intelligence scores.) The researchers believe that females with Turner's syndrome have social difficulties because they are poor at interpreting facial expressions. Extracting information from a face is, in part, a spatial task. The researchers found that these same girls also performed more poorly than the controls on tests of arithmetic, digit span (a short-term memory task), picture completion, and object assembly. It seems likely that there is a mutual relationship between cognitive and social skills. The relatedness between cognition and socialization makes it difficult to ever determine whether the poor spatial skills caused poor social skills or vice versa.

All of the multiple studies with girls and women with Turner's syndrome show quite clearly that they do not differ significantly from normal controls (usually other female relatives who do not have Turner's syndrome) on some verbal ability measures, but their visual–spatial skills are significantly lower than normal (Murphy et al., 1994; Rovet, Szekely, & Hockenberry, 1994; Temple & Carney, 1993, 1996). In studies that also examined mathematical ability, women with Turner's syndrome showed particularly poor performance (Rovet et al., 1994). These women also have certain physical characteristics that could be mediating these results. They tend to be short with a relatively unfeminine body type (small breasts, thick necks). If they respond to these external manifestations of their genotype, it is possible that they exaggerate female tendencies, including poorer visual–spatial abilities, thus allowing for the possibility that these cognitive results also have an environmental component.

Taken together, research on the influence of prenatal and perinatal sex hormones on cognitive abilities suggests that the early hormone environment is important in determining the development of one's cognitive potential, although the data do not yet permit any definitive conclusions. In general, high levels of androgens during prenatal development are associated with higher than average levels of spatial ability for girls, but not for boys, probably because their androgen levels do not differ markedly from that of normal males. Low levels of androgens (or an inability to respond to androgen) are associated with poorer than average spatial ability. Data from females with Turner's syndrome, in which the primary deficit (relative to normal females) is the lack of estrogen and progesterone, suggest a general depression of intelligence, with spatial and mathematical abilities being particularly low. (Females with Turner's syndrome do have some androgens, which are produced by their adrenal glands.) But remember, even in those instances in which positive effects have been reported, it is very difficult to tease out the contributions of genetic influences, postnatal hormones, and life experiences. Furthermore, abnormal hormone levels could produce results that are not associated with normal levels of the same hormones.

Prenatal Hormone Effects on Normal Development

Hormones do not exert their actions simultaneously or directly,
but rather they exert their influence in concert with many other biological events in a
variety of different systems. There appears to be
a running conversation in the CNS among hormones, neurotransmitters,
neuromodulators, and probably other, as yet unknown,
elements of CNS function.
—Brush and Levine (1989, p. xiii)

You may be wondering whether concentrations of prenatal hormones that are within normal levels affect cognitive development. It is possible that results obtained with abnormal levels of hormones are not directly relevant to the way that cognitive abilities develop under normal hormonal levels.

In an attempt to answer the important question of whether normal prenatal hormone levels have effects on human cognition, Grimshaw, Sitarenios, and Finegan

(1995) measured testosterone levels in the amniotic fluid of normally developing fetuses in the 14th through 20th weeks of gestation. The same individuals were then tested with a mental rotation task when they were 7 years old. Girls with higher levels of prenatal testosterone were faster at the mental rotation task than girls with low levels of prenatal testosterone. The reverse effect was found for boys. (The data for the boys were not as strong as the data for the girls.) The authors concluded that "these findings are consistent with the hypothesis that testosterone acts on the fetal brain to influence the development of spatial ability" (Grimshaw et al., 1995, p. 85). This is one of very few studies that actually measured prenatal hormones and correlated these values with cognitive performance later in life.

Additional evidence for the effect of prenatal sex hormones on normal cognitive development was reported by Jacklin, Wilcox, and Maccoby (1988). These investigators obtained blood samples from the umbilical cords of newborn babies. The concentration of androgens found in these samples is a direct measure of the level of androgens that was present in a narrow window of time at the end of the prenatal environment. Of course, it is possible that the stress of labor altered hormone levels from prenatal levels before labor, a fact that may have obscured a significant relationship for the boys in this study or led to the wrong conclusion for the girls. Jacklin et al. correlated prenatal androgen levels with spatial ability displayed by normal girls and boys 6 years after birth. They found that girls with higher levels of testosterone in their blood at birth had lower scores on tests of spatial ability at age 6. Thus, they found an inverse relationship between prenatal testosterone levels and spatial performance for girls at age 6, but no relationship for boys.

Three relationships are suggested by these findings. First, prenatal sex hormones appear to affect cognitive development later in life. Second, when prenatal hormones are at abnormally high levels, spatial performance is probably enhanced for girls. At abnormally low levels, spatial performance is probably decreased for both girls and boys. Other sex-typed behaviors such as childhood play may be affected to a greater extent than cognition. All of these statements are "hedged"; that is, they are modified with words like *probably* and *maybe* because the research results do not warrant more definite conclusions at this time. Third, when prenatal hormones are within normal levels, conclusions are even more uncertain. It may be that higher levels of prenatal testosterone are associated with good spatial ability for girls with the reverse effect for boys. Very few studies, thus far, have measured prenatal hormones at different critical periods and then related these measures to cognitive performance later in life. Much more research is needed before we can understand how, when, and why prenatal hormones exert their influence.

Childhood and Puberty

Throughout infancy and childhood, both girls and boys have very low levels of all sex hormones. In fact, in those instances in which, for some medical reason, sex reassignment surgery is needed (e.g., ambiguous or deformed genitals as in the case of John/Joan), there is usually no need to begin hormone therapy until adolescence. The body shapes of young boys and girls are so similar that it is difficult to tell girls and boys apart unless they wear sex-typed clothing or hairstyles. Sex hormones, however, become extremely important at puberty because they are necessary for the development of secondary sex characteristics in both sexes and the timing of menarche (first menstruation) in girls. Several researchers have investigated the possibility that hormone events at puberty also are implicated in the development of cognitive sex differences.

There are few studies that examined sex hormone levels in children and attempted to relate these measures to cognitive abilities, probably because there are no good theoretical reasons to expect them to be related. In one correlational study of 6-year-old boys and girls who had been identified as "gifted" or "nongifted," the researchers examined testosterone levels and performance on a test of spatial reasoning (Ostatnikova, Laznibatova, & Dohnanyiova, 1996). As expected, the gifted children outperformed the control group of nongifted children on the test of spatial reasoning. Testosterone levels were measured (with saliva samples) in both groups of children, with the samples taken at the same time the spatial reasoning test was administered. The researchers found a negative correlation between testosterone and scores on the spatial reasoning test, with significantly lower levels of testosterone for the gifted children. Thus, low levels of (salivary) testosterone were associated with good spatial performance, and high levels of (salivary) testosterone were associated with poor spatial performance. It is difficult to interpret results such as these, especially because there are very few studies with which to compare these results. Because the effect was strongest for the boys in this study, at least the data from the boys are consistent with the optimal level theory that posits better spatial performance for boys with lower levels of estradiol (which is presumably being converted from the testosterone).

Recall that sex hormones (also known as sex steroids) are secreted from the gonads—ovaries in females and testes in males—and from the adrenal glands in both sexes. The average age at which the ovaries mature is 12; the average age at which the testes mature is 14. But, for both sexes, the adrenal glands mature between the ages of 6 and 11, with increasing quantities of sex hormones secreted by the adrenal glands throughout middle childhood (McClintock & Herdt, 1996). Dehydroepiandrosterone (DHEA) is a sex hormone secreted by the adrenal glands. DHEA metabolizes into both testosterone and estradiol. It is only in the past few years that researchers have focused on the fact that sex hormones from the adrenal glands may also be important in influencing sex-typed behaviors and characteristics. McClintock and Herdt, for example, hypothesized that DHEA plays an important role in the development of feelings of sexual attraction, in part because many homosexual males report that they felt sexual attraction to other males in childhood—years before the onset of puberty. If DHEA is an important component of the feminization or masculinization of sexual orientation, it is possible that it also plays a role in the development of sex-typical cognitive patterns. It is likely that there will be much more research on this question in the future, but at this time, the role of DHEA in cognition is not known.

You may have seen hyped advertisements in so-called health food stores for DHEA. There is no scientific basis for most of the claims that are made about DHEA or, for that matter, about many of the other hyped products that promise to improve memory or heighten sexuality (whatever that means). It is also possible that some of the hormone-like supplements that are available for purchase can be harmful. If the claims about the beneficial effects of DHEA were true, they would be on the front page of major newspapers, not on dusty store shelves. Always seek unbiased, reliable information that is backed up with solid evidence before taking any hormonal supplement.

Maturation Rate Hypotheses.   Two different theories of cognitive sex differences are based on the well-established fact that girls physically mature at a faster rate than boys, reaching puberty, on average, 2 years earlier. At birth, girls are more mature physiologically, and they continue to mature more quickly than boys through puberty (Smolak, 1986). One of these theories is concerned with the general rate of maturation; the other is specific to maturation processes at puberty. Each of these theories is reviewed.

Do Early Maturers Have an Intelligence Advantage?   In the 1960s, Tanner (1962) suggested the possibility that growth spurts in physical height are associated with spurts in mental ability. If this were true, then there would be an intelligence advantage for children who mature at a young age because they would have enhanced intellectual capabilities at a younger age than their peers. Newcombe and Dubas (1987) conducted a meta-analytic review of the literature that pertained to this question. They found a small but reliable advantage in IQ for early maturers before, during, and after puberty. The extended line of reasoning is that because girls mature earlier than boys, girls have a "maturation advantage" that could explain the finding that girls outperform boys in early language-related skills. The major problem with this hypothesis is that the underlying cognitive mechanisms that vary as a function of

Calvin and Hobbes   by Bill Watterson

CALVIN AND HOBBES © 1990 Watterson. Reprinted with permission of Universal Press Syndicate. All rights reserved.

maturation are unspecified, making this a weak theory. It also requires two assumptions: (a) verbal abilities rely on different biological mechanisms than spatial abilities, and (b) only verbal abilities primarily benefit from early maturation.

Age at Puberty.   A second hypothesis that links sex-related cognitive patterns to rate of maturation posits that sex-differentiated cognitive patterns are a by-product of sex differences in maturation rate at puberty. Waber (1976, 1977), a proponent of this theory, found that later maturing adolescents, regardless of sex, exhibited better spatial skills than earlier maturing adolescents of the same age. (Waber measured maturation by the development of secondary sex characteristics during a well-child physical examination conducted in a nurse's office. There are numerous problems with such a subjective measure.) Thus, in general, late maturers have higher spatial skills than verbal skills, and early maturers have higher verbal skills than spatial skills. The fact that girls generally attain physical maturation earlier than boys could explain cognitive sex differences. Thus, according to this view, the same hormonal events that are responsible for the timing of puberty are also responsible for sex-differentiated patterns of cognitive differences. The idea that cognition could be predicted by the age at which an individual experiences puberty was appealing for several reasons. Most important, Waber linked this theory to developmental differences in brain organization (a topic discussed in chap. 5), which gave this theory a solid grounding in biology. In support of this theory, Petersen and Crockett (1985) also found that late-maturing adolescents performed better than their early maturing peers on the Embedded Figures Test.

Sanders and Soares (1986) investigated the age-at-puberty hypothesis with a sample of college students. The students responded to a series of questions about the timing of puberty events. The students used a 5-point scale on which they indicated, relative to others of the same sex, when they experienced several milestones of puberty, such as menstruation (for females), nocturnal emission (for males), underarm hair growth, and so forth. They found that college students' scores on a mental rotation test were significantly related to their reports of when they reached puberty. As predicted by Waber's (1976, 1977) age-at-puberty hypothesis, late maturers of both sexes had higher scores on a mental rotation test than early maturers.

Despite its appeal and early support, more recent research has shown that age at puberty has limited validity in our quest to explicate the biological bases of cognitive sex differences. Two different literature reviews (Newcombe & Dubas, 1987; Signorella & Jamison, 1986) concluded that the association between spatial ability and age at puberty is small; others concluded that there is no association between spatial ability and timing of puberty (Geary, 1988). As you will read in chapter 6, there are good reasons to believe that psychosocial events that occur at puberty (e.g., choice of preteen activities) play a more important role in the development of spatial skills. Furthermore, it is difficult to tease apart hormonal and genetic influences. The timing of puberty is under genetic control. It begins as a brain event with the release of a hormone (gonadotrophin-releasing hormone) from the hypothalamus. Thus, genes, hormones, and brain activity work in concert to make us the unique beings that we are.

Two other theories have been proposed to explain the relationship between sex hormones and cognitive abilities. Like Waber's (1976, 1977) theory, these other two also point to puberty as a critically important time in one's life for the development of these abilities.

Minimal Level of Androgens at Puberty.   Hier and Crowley (1982) proposed that the amount of androgens available at puberty can be a determinant of visual–spatial ability. They studied 19 men with androgen deficiencies at puberty. Compared with normal male adolescents, the androgen-deficient males showed impaired spatial abilities. There were no differences between the groups with regard to verbal ability. Furthermore, they found a direct relationship between the severity of the androgen deficiency and the severity of the spatial impairment. That is, the men with the lowest amounts of androgen were also the poorest at spatial tasks, and those whose androgen levels were closer to normal showed the least impairment. Hier and Crowley believe that puberty is a critical period for the development of spatial skills and once spatial skills are established by sufficient levels of androgens at puberty, these skills are viable for a lifetime, even if androgen levels fall later in life. Conversely, if spatial abilities fail to develop in puberty because of low levels of androgens, this disability cannot be corrected later in life. They supported their argument by noting that both females with Turner's syndrome and genetic males with androgen insensitivity have poor spatial ability and both groups have abnormally low levels of androgen (or, in the case of androgen insensitivity, usable androgen) at puberty and throughout life.

Hier and Crowley (1982) admitted that they don't understand the mechanism by which male hormones mediate the development of spatial ability. They hypothesized that testosterone, the major male hormone, has transient effects on the central nervous system. Their own conclusion was that "our results suggest that androgenization (presumably mediated by testosterone or one of its metabolites) is essential to the full development of spatial ability" (Hier & Crowley, 1982, p. 1204). It is important to keep in mind the fact that Hier and Crowley used a small sample of abnormal males to arrive at their conclusion. Even if it were true that a minimal level of male hormones is needed for the development of spatial ability, we have no idea what that minimal level is or whether the effect occurs at puberty or during the prenatal–perinatal period. Females have measurable quantities of male hormones in their bloodstream, most of it produced by their adrenal glands with a smaller quantity produced by their ovaries (Bleier, 1984).

Optimal Level of Estradiol.   As described earlier, Nyborg's theory of optimal level of estradiol (1983) was based on the idea that prenatal and later life hormone levels are important determinants of cognitive abilities. This theory is best supported for spatial abilities, where Nyborg believes that there is an optimal level of estrdiol for good spatial abilities. There is a considerable body of data to support this theory. For example, Petersen (1976) inferred the quantity of sex hormones available from the development of secondary sex characteristics in a sample of normal females and males at 13, 16, and 18 years of age. She found that for males, high levels of male hormones were associated with low spatial ability whereas the reverse was true for females. For females, high levels of male hormones were associated with high spatial ability. In other words, superior spatial ability was associated with more male hormones for females and less male hormones for males. Taken together, these sex-differentiated results point to an optimal balance of female and male hormones. Support for this position was provided by Maccoby (1966), who reported that boys with high-spatial-ability test scores were rated as less masculine by their peers than boys with low-spatial-ability test scores. Using the theoretical framework provided by Petersen's theory, Maccoby's results can be understood by reasoning that the boys who appeared less masculine probably had lower levels of androgens, a condition that Petersen believes is correlated with high spatial ability in males. Unfortunately, the specific effects of estrogens and testosterone are difficult to tease apart because testosterone can be converted to estradiol (an estrogen) for use by the brain.

In summary, four theories have been proposed to explain the effect of sex hormones available during puberty on the development of cognitive abilities. I have summarized these theories in Table 4.3 for review and ease of comparison.

When considering the role of sex hormones in the development of cognition, it is important to remember the social and environmental effects that come into play at every stage of development. Although there is some evidence that adolescence is the time in the life cycle when sex-related cognitive differences most clearly emerge, as well as the time when dramatic changes in sex hormone levels begin, the coincidence of these two events may be secondary to other salient life changes that occur at the same time, such as the adoption of adult sex roles and different expectations of adolescents with mature bodies. This topic is considered more extensively in chapter 6.

One problem with theories that focus on the biology of adolescence is that they cannot explain the sex differences that are found in childhood. Although cognitive differences are found more reliably in adolescence, multiple studies reported in chapter 3 found sex differences emerging in preschool, most notably for verbal skills and select tests of spatial ability (mental rotation and the Water-Level Test). The nature and validity of cognitive sex differences in childhood is likely to be an active area of research during the next several years. If future researchers can document childhood and toddler differences, then theories that focus on adolescence as the critical period for the development of these cognitive abilities will have to be revised.

Adulthood

Sex hormones throughout adulthood and old age follow very different patterns for women and men. For women, the female hormones follow a monthly (approximately) cycle in which they ebb and flow whereas the concentrations of male hormones remain relatively constant. At menopause, the amount of the female hormones diminishes substantially, with little change in the levels of male hor-

TABLE 4.3

Summary of Theories Designed to Explain the Effect of Sex Hormones at Puberty on Cognitive Abilities

1. Rate of physical maturation

Early physical maturation is associated with enhanced verbal abilities—girls, in general, mature earlier than boys.
Current status: Some support for this theory, although the effect is probably small.

2. Age at puberty:

A later age at puberty is associated with enhanced spatial skills (because of the effect of sex hormones on the organization of the brain)—boys, in general, experience puberty 2 years later than girls.
Current status: Little or no support for idea that the timing of the biological events that occur at puberty influence spatial abilities (although social events may be important).

3. Androgens at puberty:

A minimal concentration of androgens is needed at puberty for spatial ability to develop; puberty is a critical period for the development of spatial skills.
Current status: Only confirmed with abnormal populations and therefore may reflect prenatal and perinatal hormones (e.g., early organizational effects).

4. Optimal hormone concentration:

There is an optimal concentration of some hormones (possibly estradiol) that is needed fro expression of spatial ability.
Current status: Recent research shows some support that more "feminine" men and more "masculine" women have better spatial skills, but much more research is needed.

---

mones. For men, the concentrations of sex hormones remain fairly constant throughout the adult years, with various cyclical variations that correspond to daily and seasonal cycles and a gradual decline into old age.

A hormone-based theory devised to explain cognitive sex differences was proposed by Broverman, Klaiber, Kobayashi, and Vogel (1968). They began with the premise that sex hormones activate the central nervous system in a manner that facilitates the performance of simple, overlearned, repetitive tasks and interferes with tasks that require inhibition of an initial response. Their second supposition was that female hormones are more "powerful" than male hormones, with the result that women are superior on "simple, overlearned, perceptual motor tasks" such as those found on "clerical aptitude tests." Males, in contrast, are naturally better at "more complex tasks requiring inhibition of immediate responses." Broverman et al.'s theory has been criticized on a number of grounds (Singer & Montgomery, 1969). One major problem concerns the way in which they classified their tasks. Verbal skills, including language comprehension and usage, are neither simple nor overlearned, yet these are the tasks at which females usually excel. Their initial assumptions about the effects of estrogens and androgens on the central nervous system are incorrect on physiological grounds. There is little supporting evidence and considerable contradictory evidence for the hypothesis of Broverman et al. that neural processes respond in the ways that they proposed.

By contrast, there are many studies in which low testosterone for males and high testosterone for females are associated with better performance on several different spatial tests, with the reverse pattern occurring for verbal and articulatory tests. Thus, the effects of sex hormones on adult cognitive functioning are specific (not global) and depend on the amount that is in the bloodstream and the sex of the individual (Sherwin, 1994). For example, in a sample of healthy young men, high estradiol was associated with two different measures of visual memory (Kampen & Sherwin, 1996). In fact, an inverted U-shaped relationship between testosterone and performance on a variety of cognitive tests was even found with a sample of !Kung San Bushmen in Africa (Christiansen, 1993). For these men, there was a positive relationship between testosterone and spatial ability and a negative relationship between testosterone and verbal ability. Although there are numerous differences among studies, numerous researchers have reported reciprocal relationships of this sort (e.g., Christiansen & Knussmann, 1987).

Do Cognitive Abilities Vary Over the Menstrual Cycle?

Monthly fluctuations in sex hormones affect women's cognitive skills.
—Kimura (1989, p.83)

Tests to study sex differences don't relate to anything in real life.
—Benderly (1989, p. 68)

Given that the major female hormones vary in a cyclical fashion throughout the month in adult women, it would seem that cognitive abilities also should vary in a similar cycle, if these hormones mediate cognitive processes. For most healthy adult women, both estrogen and progesterone, the major female hormones, are available in only small quantities during the premenstrual, menstrual, and immediately postmenstrual portion of their cycle. Both hormones increase to a peak quantity at approximately midcycle (estrogen peaks slightly before midcycle and progesterone peaks soon after midcycle) and then decline to premenstrual levels. Monthly variations in progesterone and estrogen are shown in Fig. 4.5.

Is there any evidence that women's cognitive or intellectual abilities vary during the menstrual cycle? In response to this question, Tiger (1970) wrote, "An American girl writing her Graduate Record Examinations over a two-day period or a weeklong set of finals during the premenstruum begins with a disadvantage which almost certainly condemns her to no higher than a second class grade. A whole career in the educational system can be unfairly jeopardized because of this phenomenon."

In the first edition of this book, which was published in 1986, I wrote, "Research on this question has clearly shown that Tiger is wrong" (p. 101). More re-

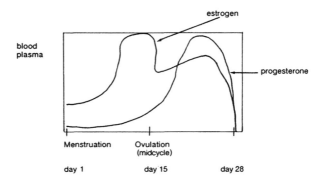

FIG. 4.5.   Ovarian hormone levels as they vary over the menstrual cycle. Note that both estrogen and progesterone are available in very low levels immediately before and during menstruation and at high levels midcycle.

cent research has shown that some cognitive abilities may vary during the menstrual cycle; however, Tiger (1970) is still wrong. Before I consider the research that has addressed this controversial question, think about Tiger's comments. Even if we had solid evidence that monthly hormone fluctuations affect cognition, it would not follow that women are inferior to men either at some portion or during the entire monthly cycle. The unstated assumption in Tiger's statement and those of many others is that women are (or will be shown to be) intellectually inferior to men, at least during some portions of their menstrual cycle. The finding that women and men differ does not imply that whatever traits are associated with being male are better than those associated with being female. Similarly, the mere fact that women's cognition may vary during the menstrual cycle doesn't mean that they are more or less intellectually able than men.

"The Women Have Less" Fallacy.   Before you read the following section, stop for a few minutes and think about the possibility that monthly hormone fluctuations affect the cognitive skills of women. Do you find this to be a repugnant idea? If so, why? Are you afraid that the results will be used to discriminate against women? If you answered "yes" to this question, then you are also demonstrating what I call "the women have less" fallacy. It is the fallacious (erroneous) belief that the biological bases of cognition will reveal that women have less ability than men. Society decides which skills and abilities it values. If female skills and abilities are devalued, the fault lies in the society that we have created, not in the biology that has created us.

Cognition and Cyclical Fluctuations in Hormones.   One of the first scientific investigations of whether there are differences in women's cognitive functioning during the menstrual cycle was conducted by Golub (1976). Her results with 13 different cognitive tests administered to 50 women between the ages of 30 and 45 showed no significant menstrual cycle effect. Even though some women reported mood changes between the premenstrual and menstrual phases of their cycle, apparently these changes were not large enough to affect their ability to perform cognitive tasks.

However, more recent research has suggested that there is evidence to support the notion that women's cognitive abilities fluctuate in a cyclical fashion. This research received a great deal of coverage in the popular press, with front-page stories in *The Los Angeles Times* and *The New York Times* and articles in weekly news magazines (e.g., *Newsweek*). This research received such widespread coverage because it is an emotionally explosive issue. Unfortunately, the coverage tended to be more sensationalistic than scientific and may have created a false impression about the nature and findings of the research. Because it is "cutting-edge" research and because so much has been written and said about it, I go into some detail about what was and wasn't found.

First, the idea that cognitive abilities may vary during the menstrual cycle is not viewed as heresy by anyone who has studied sensation and perception. As noted in chapter 3, there are some differences between men and women in their ability to sense and perceive certain stimuli and in their attentional ability. It is well documented that for women, sensation and perception change at adolescence and also vary over the monthly cycle. Consider, for example, the ability to detect small concentrations of a chemical called androstenone. Androstenone is a scent that is known to influence the sexual responsiveness of female pigs. (Odorants that impel behavior are called pheromones.) It is found in the urine, sweat, saliva, fatty tissues, and blood plasma of all human males. It is also present in much lower concentrations in females. Researchers have found a decline in the ability to detect androstenone during adolescence, with approximately 28% of males unable to detect the odor and 42% of females unable to detect the odor (Dorries, Schmidt, Beauchamp, & Wysocki, 1989). The experimenters believe that the sex hormones that flood the body during adolescence are responsible for the sex differences in the ability to detect this scent.

The ability to perceive pain is another example of a sensory–perceptual system that shows periodic fluctuation. It has been shown that women are more sensitive to painful stimuli during the middle portion of the cycle (when hormone levels are highest) than at menstruation (Goolkasian, 1980, 1985). The change in sensitivity to painful stimuli was found only for menstruating women. Women who did not menstruate (e.g., had undergone surgical removal of the ovaries) did not show the change in pain sensitivity. Goolkasian (1985) concluded from a carefully executed series of studies, "It is apparent that a woman's ability to discriminate the presence of painful stimuli varies as a function of menstrual phase" (p. 25). Other sensory–perceptual effects that are known to vary periodically are the ability to detect a pure tone and the ability to discriminate between two closely spaced touches (Baker, 1987b).

Although I have mentioned the differences in the concentrations of sex hormones across the menstrual cycle, it might be useful to consider exactly how much the hormones fluctuate. The level of estrogens in adults varies monthly from 3 times as much in women as in men during the portion of the cycle following menstruation to 50 times as much at ovulation. Levels of progestins (e.g., progesterone) vary from equal to that in men following menstruation to 17 times as high. Conversely, men average about 17 times more androgens than women (Kimmel & Weiner, 1985). Thus, fluctuations of the sex hormones in women across the month and between the sexes are so large that it seems unlikely that they would have little or no effect on men and women.

Hampson and Kimura (1988; Hampson, 1990a, 1990b) examined whether women's cognitive abilities vary as a function of the monthly ebb and flow of estrogen and progesterone. One possibility is that midcycle, when both of these hormones are abundant, women would excel on those tasks that tend to favor women and show a decrement in those tasks that typically favor men. Conversely, at menstruation, when both of these hormones are at low levels, women would show improved performance on those tasks that favor men and decreased performance on those tasks that favor women. As you know from chapter 3, women tend to excel in speech articulation. There is also evidence that women are better, on average, than men at fine muscle movements (e.g., those that are needed in surgery, machine repair, and, yes, also typing and needlepoint). By contrast, men tend to score higher on some spatial tasks (e.g., mental rotation, rod and spatiotemporal tasks). Hampson and Kimura selected those tasks that vary most dramatically as a function of sex and examined the way they vary over the menstrual cycle. They found that women performed significantly better on speech articulation (speed of reciting a tongue twister), a test of manual dexterity, and verbal fluency in the high-hormone or midleutal phase than during the menstruation portion when hormones are low. By contrast, performance on spatial tasks (e.g., size of errors on the Rod and Frame Test) was better during the low-hormone phase of the cycle than the midleutal phase. Control groups included nonmenstruating women who were receiving hormone replacement therapy (they showed the same variations) and nonmenstruating women who were not receiving hormone replacement therapy (they did not show the variations). Heister, Landis, Regard, and Schroeder-Heister (1989) and many others obtained results that confirmed those of Hampson and Kimura. They found that women were faster and more accurate on nonverbal tasks during the midcycle phase than the menstrual phase. Heister et al. believe that the periodic fluctuations seen in women's cognitive performance can explain the variability often found in experimental results. The theory of periodic fluctuations across the menstrual cycle is summarized in Table 4.4.

In a more recent test of the hypothesis that women's cognitive abilities vary over the menstrual cycle, Phillips and Silverman (1997) compared female performance on two-dimensional and three-dimensional versions of the mental rotation task. In the two-dimensional version, participants have to mentally rotate a figure in the picture plane; in the three-dimensional version, the mental rotation needs to

TABLE 4.4
Do Women's Cognitive Abilities Vary Across the Menstrual Cycle?

Portion of Cycle	Estrogen	Progesterone	Prediction
Menstruation	Low ↓	Low ↓	Better performances on maps, mazes, and spatial tasks (cognitive tasks on which males typically excel)
Midcycle	High ↑	High ↑	Better performance on speech articulation, manual dexterity, and verbal fluency (tasks on which females typically excel)

include the depth plane. They found a menstrual phase effect (better performance around the time of menstruation than midcycle) only for the three-dimensional task. The researchers interpreted these results as being consistent with their preferred hypothesis—that these results reflect the evolutionary basis of behavior. The argument they made goes like this: In the hunter–gatherer societies from which we evolved, movement through three-dimensional space was a critically important spatial skill, and thus three-dimensional rotation tasks are more ecologically valid than two-dimensional ones. Once again, I caution readers to distinguish between research findings and the way in which they are interpreted. As you can probably guess, I find the interpretation of these results highly dubious.

What do these results mean? It is easier to report research findings than it is to interpret them. Although I find this research fascinating, I do not believe that it has much immediate application. What are the implications of being able to say tongue twisters several seconds faster during one portion of the month? We have no idea if this differential ability has more extensive consequences. The real finding is the reciprocity of spatial and verbal abilities such that when one is high, the other is low. These results tell us little about sex differences because only women menstruate, so they cannot be used for between-sex comparisons.

Nyborg (1990) used these results as support for his theory that spatial ability depends on an optimal level of estradiol (which is secreted by the ovaries and converted from testosterone). Because women tend to have more estradiol than men, their spatial skills improve when estrogen levels are low around the time of menstruation (bringing them closer to the optimal range), and their spatial skills decrease when estrogen levels are high around midcycle (bringing them farther from the optimal range).

Although studies about monthly variations in the cognitive skills of women were covered by all of the news services, there has been very little interest by the news media in the more recent findings that male hormone and cognitive skill levels also fluctuate. Males show cyclical patterns of hormone concentrations and the correlated rise and fall of specific cognitive abilities, although the cycle is both daily and seasonal, not monthly. The spatial skills performance of normal males fluctuates with daily variations in testosterone. Males have higher testosterone levels in early morning than later in the day; spatial skills decline for men when their testosterone levels are high and improve when they are low (Moffat & Hampson, 1996). Men also show seasonal variations. In North America, testosterone levels are higher in autumn than in spring, spatial skills for North American men are correspondingly lower in autumn and higher in spring (Kimura & Hampson, 1994). Thus, hormone-related cyclical variations in cognitive abilities are found for both adult females and adult males.

As you consider this line of research, keep in mind that fluctuations in hormone levels have very little effect on the day-to-day lives of normal women and men. Certainly, there is nothing in this research that could be used to support the notion that women or men are better fit for any type of job. Monthly fluctuations in menstruating women and daily or seasonal fluctuations in men tell us nothing about their absolute level of ability.

Old Age

Evidence is growing that estrogen affects cognitive function.
—Luine, Richards, Wu, and Beck (1998, p. 149)

Research on the roles of sex hormones in older adults has burgeoned in recent years. Large numbers of postmenopausal women are now taking estrogen replacement therapy to prevent osteoporosis and heart disease. For women, the level of circulating estrogen drops sharply during menopause. When the estrogen is replaced, with pills, patches, or other external methods, healthy older women show a variety of positive effects in cognitive abilities. The number of studies of estrogen replacement therapy and cognition is large, so only a sample of the research findings is presented here. When compared with control groups of women who did not receive estrogen replacement therapy, women with replaced estrogen made fewer errors on tests of short-term visual memory, visual perception, and construction and showed stable performance over time, while the control group declined in their performance (Resnick, Metter, & Zonderman, 1997). Estrogen replacement therapy also reduced the incidence of Alzheimer's disease by approximately 50% and markedly reduced the symptoms of Alzheimer's disease in women with mild to moderate dementia (Jacobs et al., 1998; Ohkura et al., 1995; Paganini-Hill, Buckwalter, Logan, & Henderson, 1993; Tierney & Luine, 1998).

Animal studies and human autopsies have shown that estrogen replacement has observable effects on the brain. It spurs neuronal growth and increases the speed of communication among the brain's neurons (Simpkins, Singh, & Bishop, 1994). The hippocampus is one of the brain regions that mediates the effect of estrogen on memory (Packard, 1998). It is clear that ovarian hormones have many effects on the brain throughout the life span, including very old age (McEwen et al., 1997).

Men also have estrogen receptors in their brains, with much of the estradiol used by men's brains converted from testosterone. Unfortunately, we know very little about the use of estrogen replacement in older men. The concern that external estrogen supplied in a pill, a patch, or another form will feminize the male body has made this a difficult area to study. Men also suffer less than women from Alzheimer's disease, both in terms of the percentage who get the disease (perhaps because they do not live as long) and in the severity of the dementia, although there are many men with Alzheimer's disease (Buckwalter, Sobel, Dunn, & Diz, 1993). At the present time, we do not know if estrogen replacement therapy will reduce the incidence or the severity of Alzheimer's disease in men. Selective effects on memory were found for a small sample ($N = 29$) of male-to-female transsexuals who received estrogen treatments in advance of sex-change surgery (Miles, Green, Sanders, & Hines, 1998). When compared with a group of male-to-female transsexuals waiting to begin estrogen treatment, the transsexuals who had been taking estrogen showed enhanced performance on some verbal memory tasks but no differences on mental rotation. Thus, there is some indication that estrogen may play a role in maintaining some cognitive abilities in adult men, but much more research is needed with a broader range of participants before even tentative conclusions can be made.

Research on testosterone replacement is also many years behind research on estrogen replacement, but it is now being conducted at a rapid rate. When normal aging men were given testosterone to enhance sexual functioning, they also showed improved performance on visual–spatial tests, with no changes in other cognitive tests (Janowsky, Oviatt, & Orwoll, 1994). In addition, when female-to-male transsexuals were given high doses of testosterone in preparation for sex-change surgery, their visual–spatial skills improved dramatically, and their verbal fluency skills declined dramatically within 3 months (Van Goozen, Cohen-Kettenis, Gooren, Frijda, & Van De Poll, 1995).

Sex Hormones, Sexual Orientation, and Cognition

Unless you are familiar with the theories in this area, you are probably surprised to learn that some theorists have suggested a link among sex hormones, sexual orientation (gay, lesbian, bisexual, heterosexual), and cognitive abilities. Research with nonhuman animals (rats, hamsters, ferrets, pigs, zebra finches, and dogs) has shown that prenatal sex hormones contribute to variations in sexual orientation. In reviews of the literature relating the effect of prenatal sex hormones on sexual orientation, Adkins-Regan (1988) and James (1989) concluded that early castration of males or early testosterone administration to females can change sexual orientation in nonhuman mammals. Of course, it is always "risky" to assert anything about sexual orientation in nonhuman animals because all we can observe is sexual behavior. Sexual orientation in humans is far more complex, involving relational and affectional components. (For an overview of the research literature, see Halpern & Crothers, 1997.)

Recall that Geschwind and Galaburda (1987) hypothesized that high levels of prenatal testosterone alter the innate human bias toward left cerebral hemisphere dominance by slowing its development in early life. As predicted by this theory, left-handedness (a correlate of right-hemisphere dominance) is more frequently found in males (who, of course, are exposed to higher levels of prenatal testosterone) than females (Halpern & Coren, 1991). Extrapolating from Geschwind and Galaburda's theory, it also seems possible that the amount of prenatal testosterone available to a developing fetus will influence the sexual differentiation of the brain (a topic considered in more depth in chap. 5) as well as the sexual orientation of the developing fetus when it obtains maturity. Thus, there might be a link among hand preference (right-handed, left-handed, or mixed hand use, a correlate of cerebral dominance), sexual orientation, and cognition. Studies of gay males show considerable evidence that left-handedness is more prevalent in homosexual males than in heterosexual males (e.g., Annette, 1988). Lindesay (1987), for example, found significantly more left-handedness in a sample of gay males at a venerology clinic than in a sample of heterosexual males at the same clinic. He concluded that male sexual orientation is related to biological mechanisms that underlie the distribution of hand preference and cerebral dominance. (I should also note that Rosenstein and Bigler, 1987, and others failed to find a relationship between hand preference and sexual orientation. Most of these studies, however, used an extremely small number of participants, which virtually ensured that they would not detect group differences. This is a good example of why we cannot argue from null results.) An increased incidence of left-handedness in homosexual men has been confirmed in at least seven separate studies (e.g., Becker et al., 1992; Gotestam, Coates, & Ekstrand, 1992; Halpern & Cass, 1994; Holtzen, 1994; Lindesay, 1987; McCormick, Witelson, & Kingstone, 1990; Stellman et al., 1997).

Sanders and Ross-Fields (1986) reasoned that sexual orientation in males might be affected by the same prenatal hormones that are involved in cognitive sex differences. Using several different tests of spatial ability, they found that a sample of gay males demonstrated a level of spatial ability that was similar to that of a sample of females (whose sexual orientations were unknown). Both the gay males and the females scored significantly lower in visual–spatial ability than the male heterosexuals. Sanders and Ross-Fields replicated this finding in three different experiments. They concluded that "the results are interpreted as support for a common biological determinant of cognitive ability and male sexual orientation" (Sanders & Ross-Fields, 1986, p. 280). They maintained that there is a link among sexual orientation, cognitive abilities (specifically, visual–spatial), brain organization and the level of prenatal testosterone. These results have been replicated by other researchers. In a carefully controlled study in which participants were matched for age, education, and vocational interests, Gladue, Beatty, Larson, and Staton (1990) found that "male homosexuals performed more poorly than male heterosexuals on a version of the water jar test and on the Mental Rotation Test" (p. 101). On the basis of a review of several studies, Gladue (1994) proposed that homosexual males perform somewhere between heterosexual males and heterosexual females on cognitive tasks that typically yield sex differences. Kimura (1996) found exactly this pattern of results using a "throw to target" task in which participants aimed a Velcro-covered ball at a target using both underhand and overhand throwing. In two separate studies, heterosexual males were more accurate than homosexual males, who in turn were more accurate than heterosexual females. Similar results with homosexual males intermediate in skill between heterosexual males and heterosexual females were found with the Purdue Pegboard, a task that measures manual dexterity (Hall & Kimura, 1995). (Females excel on peg board tasks.) Because there are no differences in adult hormone levels as a function of one's sexual orientation, Kimura and others have posited prenatal hormones as the critical factor in changing cognitive patterns and sexual orientation.

You may be wondering if there has been any similar research with lesbians. Gladue et al. (1990) found that lesbians performed more poorly than heterosexual women on the Water-Level Test of spatial ability. Given these results, Gladue et al. concluded that simple hypotheses like lesbians are cognitively more similar to males than to females are certainly wrong. In fact, we still know very little about lesbianism and whether there is a relationship with cognitive abilities. It is likely that different mechanisms are involved in determining female homosexuality than in determining male homosexuality. Lesbianism may be more closely tied to life experiences, given that it often appears later in life than male homosexuality (LeVay, 1993).

It seems likely that sexual orientation is influenced by a host of factors that may include the effect of prenatal and perinatal hormones on the developing nervous system. Thus far, researchers have not found any social or experiential variables that could predict sexual orientation. Of course, much more research is needed on this question before we can make any meaningful conclusions. If prenatal hormones are an important factor, then sexual orientation is just another one of the myriad of ways in which humans differ. This is all part of natural human variation and does not support any bias that one sexual orientation is better or worse than another.

It is presumed that both genes and hormones operate through their influence on the brain—that marvelous organ that is responsible for our every thought and action. The question of sex differences in the structure and function of the brain is discussed in chapter 5. General statements about the limitations of biological theories and the way in which biology interacts with psychosocial variables are also made in chapter 5. So, stay tuned for Biological Hypotheses Part II: The Brain, coming soon in a textbook near you.

CHAPTER SUMMARY

Although many people are disturbed by biological theories that have been used to explain cognitive sex differences, such theories are not necessarily sexist. Experimental studies show different patterns of cognitive abilities, on average, for men and women. There are no data to suggest that there is a smarter or better sex. Biology always operates in an environmental context, and it is the influence of biology within an environment that permits or prohibits the development and expression of cognition. Females and males are biological organisms, so it should not be surprising to find biological data that are predictive of cognitive abilities.

Research in behavioral genetics has been progressing at a rapid rate in recent years. New conceptualizations now include the idea that individuals influence their environment in ways that make separation of heredity and environment impossible. There is also a new emphasis on the prenatal environment and perinatal hormones as important contributors to developing organisms. Genetic theories have been proposed to explain cognitive sex differences. It seems that females and males are equally affected by heredity and that both general intelligence and separate cognitive abilities are, in part, inherited. The genetic theory that has received the most attention as an explanation of cognitive sex differences is the sex-linked recessive gene theory. According to this theory, spatial ability is determined by a genetic code on the X chromosome. Predictions from this theory (e.g., the proportion of women and men that would be expected to show good spatial ability) have not been supported. There is no good evidence for a sex-differentiated link between heredity and cognition. Studies of individuals with genetic abnormalities have permitted a partial separation of genetic influences from other sorts of variables that affect development. In cases of genetic abnormalities, prenatal hormone levels are more directly involved in development than gene action per se. Of course, with normal development, genetic and prenatal hormones are consistent, so their effects are not separable.

Sex hormones—mainly estrogen, progesterone, and testosterone—have been identified as possible causes of sex differences in cognition. Sex hormones are secreted from the gonads (ovaries for females and testes for males) and from the adrenal glands for both sexes, and they are converted from one to the other by chemical processes in the brain. Prenatal and perinatal hormones play a critical role in brain development and subsequent sex-typical cognition and behavioral traits. Research with abnormal populations (e.g., females with Turner's syndrome, individuals with CAH) and nonhuman mammals provides strong evidence that prenatal hormones have a major influence on the development of intellectual abilities. Two theories of hormone action that have some support are (a) high levels of prenatal testosterone may slow the growth of the right hemisphere of the brain and (b) there exists an optimal range of estradiol for the expression of some spatial abilities. Recent research has shown that women's cognitive abilities vary in a reciprocal fashion over the menstrual cycle, with verbal skills and manual dexterity best at midcycle when estrogen and progesterone levels are high and worst during menstruation when estrogen and progesterone levels are low. Spatial ability varies in an inverse fashion. Similarly, men show daily and seasonal variations in hormone levels and cognitive abilities.

Estrogen replacement therapy can reverse intellectual decline in older women and can prevent and improve the symptoms of Alzheimer's disease. Less is known about the use of testosterone replacement in old age, but it seems to selectively improve spatial skills in older men. Research on the cognitive effects of sex hormones in old age is being conducted at a rapid rate.

Because sexual attraction to the opposite sex is a type of sex-typical behavior, it is likely influenced by some of the same variables that are responsible for sex-typical patterns of cognition, right- and left-handedness, aggression, and type of childhood play. Much more research is needed in this area before definitive conclusions can be reached.

5

Biological Hypotheses Part II: Brains, Evolutionary Pressures, and Brain–Behavior Relationships

CONTENTS

5

A BRIEF INTRODUCTION TO THE BRAIN

Men's and women's brains are to a significant extent wired differently from the start.
—Kimura (1996, p. 259)

Every thought you've ever had, every movement you've ever made, and every emotion you've ever felt were brought to you by that amazing mass that sits within your skull. If you could examine your own brain, you would, no doubt, be surprised to find that it looks like a giant (approximately 3-pound) mushy walnut with the consistency of a soft-boiled egg. The brain and the spinal cord that it sits on top of make up the central nervous system.

Not surprisingly, researchers have considered the possibility that sex differences in cognitive abilities may, in part, reflect sex differences in the underlying neural structure or organization of the brain. All intellectual activity results from patterns of neural activation by large groups of neurons. I begin with a brief introduction to the brain so that you can follow the logic of the research that has investigated sex-related brain differences.

Look carefully at the picture of a human brain in Fig. 5.1. Like many other organs, the brain appears bilaterally symmetrical. Each half of the brain is called a hemisphere. The two hemispheres are connected by a thick band of neural fibers called the corpus callosum. There are spaces in the brain that are filled with cerebrospinal fluid—a fluid that serves two purposes. It helps to cushion the brain against injury and carries hormones and nutrients (glucose and oxygen) to different parts of the brain (Smock, 1999).

The cerebral cortex is the outer portion of the brain. In humans, the cortex is the largest and most complex part of the brain. Its highly convoluted (wrinkled) appearance is the distinguishing feature between human brains and those of other animals. We know that different parts of the cortex are specialized for different functions and that different aspects of the same cognitive function can have differ-

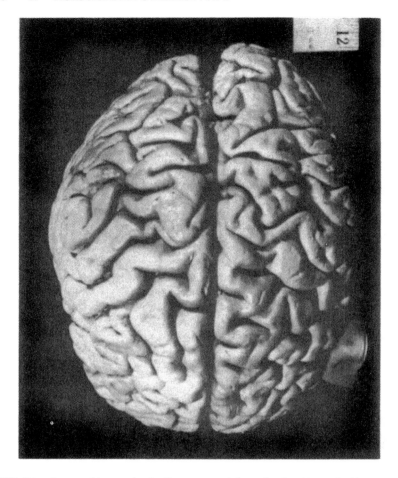

FIG. 5.1.   A normal human brain. Can we ever fully understand how all of human experience is processed and stored in this complex web of neurons and chemical neurotransmitters?

ent locations in the brain. For example, one part of the brain that is known as Wernicke's area is primarily responsible for comprehension of speech, whereas a different area known as Broca's area is primarily responsible for the production of speech. For most people, both of these verbal-related areas are found in the left half of the brain. Similarly, there are different cortical areas for recognizing what an object is and for knowing where an object is in space (Courtney, Ungerleider, Keil, & Haxby, 1996). These two types of spatial processing are primarily accomplished in the central portion of the cortex known as the parietal lobe.

Neuroscientists use the term *gray matter* when they refer to clusters of cell bodies and their nearby synaptic connections in the central nervous system. One example of gray matter, the cortex, has a gray appearance because large numbers of cells are packed together there. White matter refers to axon tracts, the bundles of spidery extensions that project from the cell bodies and send their output to other neurons. The axons are often covered with a fatty sheath (myelin) that gives them a whitish appearance. The cortex covers other brain structures that lie deeper within the hemispheres. It is the interconnections (synapses) among neurons that underlie complex cognitive abilities. Neurons "connect" or "communicate" through the release of neurotransmitters, which are chemicals that are released into the microscopic spaces between the axon terminals of the neuron "sending" the chemical message and the dendrite (receiving portion) of the neuron "receiving" the chemical message. (There are several excellent texts that explain these processes. See, e.g., Gazzaniga, Ivry, & Mangun, 1998.)

Although the brain appears symmetric, extensive research has shown that each side of the brain controls different functions. The left half of the cortex receives sensory information about the right half of the world, and it controls the motor responses on the right side of the body. Sensory information and motor control for the left half of the world are under the control of the right hemisphere. Thus, brain mechanisms for sensory input and motor output are under contralateral (or opposite side) control.

You may have read or heard some pop psychology that makes a distinction between people who are "right-brained" and "left-brained." As you probably have guessed by now, the picture of brain functioning that is emerging is more complicated than a simple division of functions by right or left hemisphere. Because a major theory of sex differences in brain organization concerns the possibility that female and male brains differ in the way that the two hemispheres are specialized for different tasks, this is a focal topic in sex differences research. The brain is divided into regions, which are relatively more important for certain tasks and relatively less important for other tasks. In general, and especially for most right-handed people, the language areas of the brain are found in the left hemisphere, which tends to be more involved in symbolic and analytic thought processes. For most people, the right hemisphere is involved more in perceptual and spatial processing. Research on the specialization of the two hemispheres (e.g., Banich & Heller, 1998) suggests that the difference between verbal (sequential) processing and spatial (analog) processing is a "fundamental dichotomy in human cognition" (Lohman, 1988, p. 182), with different brain regions involved in the sequential analytic processing best suited for verbal tasks and the simultaneous holistic processing best suited for spatial information tasks.

Hormonal Influences on the Brain: A Developmental Perspective

As explained in chapter 4, brain development begins during the same prenatal period in which the genitals are forming, and both the newly forming brain and sexual differentiation of the genitals depend on the type and quantity of sex hormones that are available. There are very large differences in prenatal hormones for female and male fetuses. For humans from 34 to 41 weeks gestational age—a time interval when the brain is undergoing major developmental changes—testosterone levels are 10 times higher in males than in females (Swaab, Zhou, Fodor, & Hofman, 1996). In addition to those periods in the life span when hormonal effects on the brain are especially critical, there is a lifelong relationship between brain development and functioning and concentrations of sex hormones. Thus, brain development is best conceptualized as a developmental process lasting from the beginning period of prenatal life until very old age that varies for different neural regions at different times in the life span, affecting different behaviors (Collaer & Hines, 1995; Hines & Collaer, 1993).

Prenatal Period and Infancy

With all due consideration for the contribution of social–cultural factors, it seems probable that these sex differences [in cognition] also reflect underlying differences in brain organization, presumably induced by different prenatal hormonal environments.
—Van Strien and Boumsa (1995, p. 137)

As explained in chapter 4, many brain regions convert testosterone to estradiol (a form of estrogen), which then masculinizes the brains of normal males. It seems ironic that estradiol, a variant of what is usually considered a female hormone, is the predominant hormone in the development of male brains. Although most of the research in this area has focused on the way that testosterone affects brain development, we now know that ovarian hormones are also important in the sexual differentiation of the female brain (Fitch & Denenberg, 1998). According to earlier accounts of brain development, the female brain was the "default" template or prototype that developed in the absence of testicular hormones—just add (usable) testosterone to make a male brain, or omit it during the prenatal period and you would get a female brain. We now know that this theory of brain development is wrong. There is abundant evidence that ovarian and testicular hormones are both critical determinants of whether a brain will develop in a female or a male direction. Recent research also has shown that brain portions that underlie some of the sensory systems also respond to early life hormones and thus could be underlying sex differences in some of the sensory systems (Horvath & Wikler, 1999). The presence, absence, and proportional mix of these hormones affect the neuroanatomy of the brain, the sexual behavior of the organism, and the extent to which sex-typical cognitive abilities develop in later life. Fitch and Denenberg (1998) summarized this important finding in a cleverly worded pun, "Default is not in the female, but in the theory" (p. 341).

The first 2 years of life are also critically important in brain development. Hormone levels are particularly high in the first 6 months of life for both girls and boys and then drop to low levels and remain stable at these low levels until age 10 or 11

(Doyle, 1995). The rate of brain development parallels the ebb and flow of sex hormones throughout childhood. Beginning soon after birth, the brain forms new synapses (microscopic connections among neurons) at a high rate of speed. The brains of most 2-year-olds contain twice as many synapses as the brains of normal adults (Nash, 1997). The number of synapses remains relatively stable between age 2 and age 10 or 11, when the connections are selectively pared or pruned. Thus, it seems that the intellectual gains associated with puberty are correlated with (selective) neuronal death, a process that presumably eliminates redundant connections and allows for increased efficiency in those that remain.

Functional asymmetry—the specialization of each hemisphere for some types of cognitive processing—begins before birth and may be fairly complete by age 5 or 6 (Martin, 1998). Different parts of the brain mature at different rates, with the frontal lobes maturing later than most other areas of the brain, and maturation proceeding from left to right and from anterior to posterior.

Puberty and Adulthood

By the time individuals reach puberty, their brains are functioning at a sophisticated level, owing to the complex interplay of experience and physical maturation. At around the time of birth, the average human brain weighs approximately 350 grams; by age 2, it has reached about 75% of its adult weight (Martin, 1998). The next time you have an opportunity to spend some time with toddlers, notice how large their heads are relatively to their body size, reflecting the early development of the brain. The process of myelination, which is the development of the fatty covering on the axons, continues into adulthood, perhaps up to age 60 or later. It has generally been believed that younger individuals recover from brain damage better than older individuals because younger brains are more "plastic," or able to transfer cognitive functions from one area of the brain to another. Studies reviewed by Martin show that, as a general principle, this adage may be true.

The most conspicuous sex difference in the human brain is found at puberty. The sexually dimorphic nucleus (SDN) of the preoptic area (POA) becomes so much larger in males than in females that the size difference is visible with the naked eye. (Readers with a good background in this area will want to distinguish between SDN-POA, which is used when referring to rats, and INAH-3-POA, which is used when referring to humans.) These findings were reported a quarter of a century ago with rats and only within the past decade with humans (Gorski, Gordon, Shryne, & Southam, 1978). The sexually dimorphic nucleus of the POA may seem like a long name for a small brain part, but in this case, the question of size is important. When LeVay (1991) reported that this part of the POA is smaller in gay men than in heterosexual men, scientists, politicians, religious leaders, and the rest of the population were forced to struggle with the question of whether sexual orientation is a conscious choice or a biologically based disposition. I return to this question later in this chapter. This small brain part with the long name may change how we think about human nature.

The Aging Brain

The brains of men aged faster or earlier than those of women.
—Cowell et al. (1994, p. 4748)

By age 70, brain volume is reduced by approximately 6%, with the greatest loss seen in the frontal cortex (Cowell et al., 1994; West, 1996). New methods of imaging the brains of healthy humans, coupled with huge increases in the number of elderly individuals, have created a flurry of research on the aging brain. The decline in some intellectual abilities with increasing age for healthy older adults and the increased incidence of many types of dementia as a function of increasing age have naturally led to the question of whether the neural changes in the aging brain can be linked to the age-related changes in cognition.

Recent studies have found sex differences in the way the brain ages. For example, older men experience greater loss in the frontal and temporal lobes (front and side portions of the brain) than older women (Cowell et al., 1994). Males also begin the decline in brain volume while in their 50s, whereas women do not begin to lose brain volume until they are in their 60s (Kaye, DeCarli, Luxenberg, & Rappoport, 1992). Numerous other examples of the differential aging effects on the brains of men and women were summarized by Meinz and Salthouse (1998).

The brain contains receptors for androgens and estrogens, which are distributed in varying concentrations in different portions of the brain. The uneven distribution of these receptors provides a theoretical basis for finding that different regions of the brain decline at different rates for women and men. One possibility is that female sex hormones protect female brains from age-related atrophy (Gur et al., 1991). Recent research has shown that estrogen influences the morphology (structure) of the glial cells in the brain, suggesting ways in which male and female brains differ that depend on the availability of hormones (Mong, Kurzweil, Davis, Rocca, & McCarthy, 1996). It is interesting to note that recent research also shows sex differences in aging with respect to the two halves of the brain. Gur et al. found that the left hemisphere showed the greatest effects of atrophy in aging men, with more symmetrical effects found in the aging brains of women. These authors concluded that "women are less vulnerable to age-related changes in mental abilities; whereas men are particularly susceptible to aging effects on left hemisphere functions" (Gur et al., 1991, p. 2845).

The Activation–Organization Continuum

New knowledge is changing the way we think about the organ with which we think. Until recently, it was common to differentiate between organizational and activational effects of hormones on the brain. Hormone effects that occurred relatively early in development, causing morphological changes (changes in cell structures) and permanent changes in behavior, were called "organizational" to denote their effect on the way the brain was organized. By contrast, hormone effects that occurred later in life and were more transient were called "activational" to denote the activation of a brain process of structure that already existed. Experiments by Fitch and Denenberg (1998) and others showed that the dichotomy of lifelong and transient effects needs to be replaced with a more continuous view of hormone action. We now know that brains are far more plastic throughout life than earlier researchers believed, a fact that has created renewed interest in the way experience and other environmental conditions alter brain structures.

Environmental Influences on the Brain

Experience is the chief architect of the brain.
—Perry (cited in Nash, 1997, p. 55)

In understanding sex-related differences and similarities in the human brain, it is important to keep in mind the fact that there are many variables that affect brain structures. Neural structures change in response to environmental events. In fact, it is often difficult or impossible to classify a variable as primarily biological or primarily environmental. Structural and functional differences in the anatomy of the brain result from different environmental experiences and cause individuals to select different experiences from the environment. In an influential study, Greenough, Black, and Wallace (1987) showed that intellectually enriching environments caused neural growth in the brain and created new connections among neurons.

More recently, Ungerleider (1995) used brain imaging techniques to show changes in cortical representations that occurred after specific experiences. What people learn influences brain structures such as dendritic branching and cell size; brain architecture, in turn, predisposes individuals to seek additional experiences (Halpern, 1997). Hormone secretions, already identified as important in brain development, are also affected by a host of environmental stimuli, such as prolonged stress, drug use, and starvation.

In thinking about environmental influences on the brain, consider these examples, excerpted from Mascie-Taylor (1993): home environment, obstetric complications, maternal smoking, occupational level, family and school moves, geographical region, myopia, nutrition, and lead exposure. The list of environmental variables that affect brain development is virtually endless, and the number of possible combinations is beyond comprehension. Consider the long-term consequences of being born to a mother who smokes, a behavior that is usually considered to be relatively benign. Babies born to mothers who smoke have, on average, lower birth weights, which also means smaller brains. Children born to mothers who smoke are more likely to be left-handed, probably reflecting hypoxia (Bakan, 1990). Low-birth-weight children have specific visual–motor and spatial skills problems (Brooks-Gunn, Klebanov, & Liaw, 1992). But it is not just environmental influences early in life, like being born to a mother who smokes, that have demonstrable effects on the brain. Unfamiliar tasks may utilize different neural substrates than well-learned ones, even in adults. Voyer (1995) found that the left hemisphere is more active during the early learning stages of a new task but the right hemisphere takes over as the task becomes well learned, with sex differences in the way the hemispheres shift in representation as a function of practice. Musicians who began their training at a young age have larger corpus callosa than matched controls (Schlaug, Jancke, Huang, Staiger, & Steinmetz, 1995). The authors of this study believe that the corpus callosum is larger in musicians because of their early musical training, especially extended practice with the use of both hands in producing music.

Experimental data with rodents clearly show that the amount they are handled affects brain development, with measurable differences for several brain structures (e.g., Juraska, 1991). In a review article on the way in which the brain responds to environmental enrichment, Diamond (1999) explained how experimental studies with rats have profound implications for humans. When rats are given "toys" to play with and other enriching experiences, their cortices become thicker, and several other areas of the brain show neuronal changes. Relative to control rats that do not receive the enrichment, these lucky rats run mazes better, utilize less brain glucose, and produce rat pups who weigh more and have thicker cortices than the rat pups of the controls. Diamond also documented sex differences in the way in which the brain responds to enrichment. Furthermore, the brain effects of enriched environments can be found into very old age. Thus, new knowledge of the psychobiology of the brain has brought the environment inside the skull, a change that may finally erase the false dichotomy of nature and nurture (Nelson, 1999).

COGNITIVE NEUROSCIENCE: BRAIN–BEHAVIOR RELATIONSHIPS

Cognitive neuroscience walks a thin line. It must be exacting and build its foundation on the best and most stringent of observations about
the mysteries of nature. On the other hand, it has to explore, in an intelligent and probing and verifiable way, how primary data speak
to the issues of how brain enables mind.
—Gazzaniga (1995, p. xiii)

Cognitive neuroscience is a new interdisciplinary field of knowledge that combines cognitive psychology with the study of its neural substrate (underlying neural structures). It is an exciting field in which new techniques for imaging the brain are rapidly advancing our knowledge. Cognitive neuroscientists study the relationship between the brain and behavior. Simply knowing that there are sex-typical patterns of performance on cognitive tests and seeing how male and female brains differ don't permit the conclusion that the brain differences are the cause of the cognitive differences or vice versa. To infer a brain–behavior relationship, we need (a) evidence that links those portions of the brain that differ by sex to sex-typical differences on cognitive tasks and (b) a good theory (one that can be falsified) that predicts or explains the relationship. There are many studies that are bridging the gap between brain and behavior, providing both the data and the theory. Here are some examples.

Shaywitz et al. (1995) were interested in understanding the brain mechanisms that are responsible for sex differences in several different types of verbal tasks. They used magnetic resonance imaging, which is one of several techniques that allows researchers to see what is happening in the brain while participants are engaged in different types of cognitive tasks. They gave participants a letter recognition task ("orthographic" task), a rhyming task ("phonological" task), and a semantic task ("category" task) and examined which areas of the brain were active during each of these tasks. They found the clearest sex differences for the phonological task: Males showed activation that was lateralized to the left hemisphere (frontal gyrus region), but females showed more diffuse activation involving both the right and left hemispheres (also frontal gyrus regions). By using different types of verbal tasks while viewing brain activity, the researchers were able to isolate the specific components of language that are used in reading, map verbal tasks onto regions of the brain, and see how male and female brains respond in different places to the same task.

Another example of the way in which cognitive tasks are linked to brain structures and functions is seen in a study of normal women (Hines, Chiu, McAdams, Bentler, & Lipcamon, 1992). These researchers assessed verbal fluency in the participants and measured the size of brain regions that they believed were involved in the generation of words. They found that verbal fluency correlated positively with the area of the splenium, a subregion of the corpus callosum, and correlated negatively with the extent to which language was lateralized to one side of the brain. As in the prior example, the researchers made predictions from a theory of brain–behavior relationships and then collected data to determine if the data would support the hypothesized relationship. Studies like these link cognitive processes to underlying brain structures in an attempt to understand the cognitive architecture of the brain.

THE SEXUALLY DIMORPHIC BRAIN

Just, therefore, as higher civilization is heralded, or at least evidenced, by increasing bulk of brain; ... so we must naturally expect that man, surpassing woman in volume of brain, must surpass her in at least
a proportionate degree in intellectual power.
—*Popular Science Monthly* (1878–1879, cited in Russett, 1989, p. 16)

Many cognitive neuroscientists have been concerned with the question of whether there are differences in male and female brains and, if so, whether these differences can be used to explain sex-related cognitive differences. Recall from chapter 4 that the term *sexually dimorphic* refers to two different structures that vary as a function of sex. In an influential article on this topic, Kimura (1987) asked, "Are men's and women's brains really different?" (p. 133). Her simple answer is "yes, of course," but the real question is how and how much.

If we were to examine brains taken from females and males, there would be no gross differences that could be used to identify the sex of their owner. Microscopic examinations of the structure of the nerve cells and nerve tissues that comprise the brain would show that the cells are morphologically identical except for visible X chromosomes (known as Barr bodies) in many of the nerve cells in women's brains and Y chromosomes in the men's nerve cells (Gersh & Gersh, 1981).

Although there are no gross anatomical differences in female and male brains, it is clear that there are some sex-related brain differences. Menstruation, for example, begins as a brain event with a hormonal feedback loop involving the pituitary gland and the hypothalamus, which are brain structures. Certain between-sex synaptic differences are visible microscopically in the hypothalamus, which could be a reflection of some or all of the many between-sex differences in reproduction, including the fact that women menstruate and men don't.

The picture becomes somewhat more complicated when we also consider that there are cortical neurotransmitters that function as sex hormones, indicating some between-sex cortical hormone differences (Keeton, 1967). Despite these well-documented differences in female and male brains, the brain structures and systems involved in reproductive functions are not thought to be important in influencing intellectual abilities. There is no reason to believe that the portions of the brain that regulate menstruation in females and sexual behavior in males and females are also involved in the higher cognitive functions we have been considering. As you read about sex differences in the human brain, keep in mind the fact that male and female brains are more similar than they are different. Bishop and Wahlsten (1997) objected to the use of the term *sexually dimorphic* as a description of brains because it implies that there are "two distinct forms" of brains—one for males and one for females—which is certainly not true. There are some important differences, but they are all subtle, and our knowledge of sex differences in the brain is still in its own perinatal period.

Size, Weight, and Complexity

The assumption that "bigger is better" as it applies to individuals
of the same species has not survived the test of scientific examination. ... It may even
be the case that paradoxically, less is better.
—Smock (1999, p. 187)

Early reports of differences between female and male brains parallel findings of Black and White racial differences. According to earlier theorizing, the supposedly inferior race and the supposedly inferior sex had similar brain deficiencies. Nineteenth-century physicians warned that the female nervous system was delicate and not well suited for intellectual work. According to Burnham (1977), these physicians claimed that both women and Blacks had "smaller brains with less capacity" (p. 10). One of the arguments for denying women and Blacks the right to vote was their purportedly inferior biology. Presumably, their smaller and less complex brains couldn't handle the complex decisions required of informed voters. The "theory" went even further in suggesting that intellectual endeavors would be bad for women's health because the increased blood flow to the brain would drain the blood normally needed for menstruation.

In fact, women's brains are somewhat smaller than men's brains; male brains at birth are approximately 12% heavier and 2% larger in circumference that female brains (Janowsky, 1989). But this finding does not support the prejudicial position that females are inferior. I raised the question of brain size in chapter 3 when I introduced the concept of science in service to politics. Although the basic reasoning that "bigger must be better" when the topic is brains may seem simple-minded, it is important to think through the underlying assumptions, the data, and the implications of the brain size question because it has been used for centuries as a means of justifying some group's superiority over another group.

Brain size and weight are positively correlated with body size. Because men, on average, tend to be larger than women, they also tend to have larger brains. In the first and second editions of this book, I concluded that when brain size was ad-

Copyright © 1991, Distributed by the Los Angeles Times Syndicate. Reprinted by permission.

justed for differences in body size, the differences disappeared. Not surprisingly, whether the differences disappear when body size is used depends on how the adjustment is made. (The arguments over the "correct" way to adjust for body size are technical and not relevant to the discussion.) Although there is still considerable disagreement on this point, I now think that small differences in brain sizes result, even after body size is used to make the values more comparable (e.g., Gur & Gur, 1990). But there is no evidence that larger brains are, in any way, better than smaller brains (within normal limits). If this hypothesis were true, then people with the largest hat sizes (reflecting greater brain sizes) would be the smartest, a "prediction" that is obviously untrue. (I have had students with large heads argue with me about this one. In fact, I once debated this point in front of a large audience of scientists, and my opponent, a very large man, concluded by noting that his head was much bigger than mine, thereby proving his point. Naturally, it seemed to me that he had just shown that his hypothesis had been falsified.)

There are many ways to interpret the brain size issue. Females and males score identically on IQ tests (with some studies showing small advantages for males, some showing small advantages for females, and others showing no differences, as reviewed in chap. 3), and an independent analysis of tests that were written without concern for sex differences showed no overall difference in female–male intelligence (Jensen, 1998). Given that both sexes are equally intelligent, one could just as logically argue that female brains are superior because the smaller female brain has the same "IQ power" as the larger male brain. It would be like finding more intelligence per brain unit (or something like that). These sorts of arguments are like asking, "Which sex has the better genitals?" Jensen argued that the sex difference in brain size is best explained by the fact that neurons are packed more densely in female brains than male brains, resulting in a configuration that allows the same number of neurons in male and female brains despite differences in overall size. When we think about intelligence and the brain, we conceptualize the underlying "hardware" of intelligence as a complex web of interconnected neurons. Thus, it is not brain size but the number and way in which neurons interconnect that are a primary determinant of cognitive ability.

Analyses of the evolution of the brain suggest that both body size and brain size are shrinking, with brain size shrinking faster than body size, at least over the past 25,000 years or so (Ruff, Trinkhaus, & Holliday, 1997). It may be that the shrinkage in brain size represents an efficient fine-tuning after a long period of rapid and, perhaps, crude increase in size. I liken this to the change in computers, which used to have very large central processing units—the "brain" part—and now have gotten much more powerful and much smaller. Regardless of the reason, Gee (1997) concluded that "brain size alone is not a particularly good measure of intelligence."

Regional Cerebral Blood Flow

Another way of measuring what is happening in the brain when individuals perform cognitive tasks is to monitor the rate of cerebral blood flow in different regions of the brain, a measure known as regional cerebral blood flow. The brain needs a constant supply of oxygenated blood to function. The Gurs and their colleagues (R. C. Gur et al., 1982, 1995; R. E. Gur & Gur, 1990) used regional cerebral blood flow measures in a series of experiments examining sex differences in cognition. A clear pattern of results emerged from these studies—women have a faster rate of blood flow per unit of brain weight than men when they are performing the same cognitive tasks. Gur and Gur (1990) believe that the higher regional cerebral blood flow in women compensates for their smaller brain volume. Thus, brain size is not meaningful unless it is considered in the context of other brain measures of brain functioning.

Key Structures

Gender is a major moderating variable in brain-function.
—Gur and Gur (1990, p. 247)

Because overall gross measures like the size or the weight of the brain cannot be used to understand the brain basis of cognitive sex differences, we turn to key structures in the brain that are known to be involved in those cognitive tasks that differ, on average, by sex.

Hippocampus

Numerous studies with humans and other mammals have shown that the hippocampus is a brain structure that is crucial in many types of memory tasks, especially spatial memory. In a classic book by O'Keefe and Nadel (1978), entitled *The Hippocampus as a Cognitive Map,* the authors made the case that the hippocampus builds cognitive maps that contain information about spatial relations. Its role in the formation of long-term memories is known to virtually everyone who has had an introductory course in psychology, in which the story of H.M. is (almost) always told. H.M., the initials of one of psychology's best known case studies, had severe epilepsy. In an attempt to stop the debilitating seizures, he underwent brain surgery in which portions of his hippocampi and related brain structures were lesioned. The surgery worked in that the seizures stopped, but he was left with the unfortunate and unexpected (the surgery was done in the 1950s) side effect of being unable to create certain types of new long-term memories (Keane, Gabrieli, Mapstone, Johnson, & Corkin, 1995). The story is compelling because of the insights it provides into the way the brain stores memories and in the compassion for H.M. that it elicits from readers. I expect that many readers recall the story of H.M. from an introductory psychology course.

The hippocampus plays a role in estrogen feedback loops in women and also is influenced by testosterone concentrations (Juraska, 1991). It is a sexually dimorphic brain structure, which, as explained earlier, means that it differs in structure as a function of sex. In studies with two species of voles (types of rodents) and two species of kangaroo rats, researchers found that in the species in which males travel long distances, either to find food or a mate, they had larger hippocampi than males in the species that did not travel long distances (Gaulin & Fitzgerald, 1989; Jacobs, Gaulin, Sherry, & Hoffman, 1990). Other researchers have argued that sex differences in the rat's hippocampus may explain why male and female rats use different strategies to solve spatial navigation problems (McEwen et al., 1997). Because of ethical considerations, it always is more difficult to obtain definitive studies with humans, but recent research using magnetic resonance imaging with people who have undergone brain surgery has shown that removal of the right hippocampus is associated with a decline in visual memory (which is also spatial in nature) for women but not for men. The authors used these data to conclude that the hippocampus functions differently in women and men (Trenerry, Jack, Cascino, Sharbrough, & Ivnik, 1996).

Hypothalamus

The hypothalamus is an important brain structure in the regulation of many biological and psychological functions. Many hormones or releasing factors for hormones are produced by the hypothalamus, which plays a primary role in the endocrine system. Structures in the hypothalamus secrete hormones that regulate menstruation in women through a cyclical pattern of hormone release, so it is obviously one brain structure that differs for men and women (Kalat, 1998). The hypothalamus is an important component in the regulation of emotion. Neurons project from the hypothalamus into many other brain regions, including the frontal cortex, so it is likely that it is also important in some cognitive tasks. As mentioned earlier in this chapter, there is a dramatic sex difference in one portion of the hypothalamus. One cell group in this area is involved in masculine behavior. (It has been studied in rats, humans, and other mammals.) In humans, this cell group (INAH-3) is smaller in homosexual men than in heterosexual men (LeVay, 1991). Later in this chapter, I turn to the question of whether sexual orientation also correlates with performance on sex-typical cognitive tasks. It may be that size differences in the hypothalamus correlate with sex-typical behaviors but do not directly cause them. This is an active area of research because there are still too many unknowns to permit strong conclusions.

Corpus Callosum

The past 15 years have witnessed an explosion of research on sexual dimorphism in the human corpus collosum.
—Hampson (1998, p. 331)

The corpus collosum, composed of 200 to 800 million nerve fibers that transfer information between the right and the left hemisphere, is the primary pathway for communication between the two halves of the brain (Banich & Heller, 1998; Innocenti, 1994). It is the largest fiber track in the brain, and it is made up, almost exclusively, of axons. There is a voluminous research literature examining the question of whether this large band of neural fibers differs in shape, size, or some other significant way between females and males. The reason for all of the interest in the corpus callosum is that a major theory of sex differences in cognitive abilities maintains that the sexes differ in the way that the two hemispheres are specialized for cognitive tasks. If this theory is correct in positing sex differences in hemispheric specialization, then it is logical to expect that the corpus callosum, which is the main communication route between the two hemispheres, also differs between the sexes.

The corpus callosum is a difficult structure to study because of its irregular shape. Until recently, data on the corpus callosum came from autopsies. Now that magnetic resonance imaging is more routinely available, we can study this important brain structure in normal healthy people. There is much interest in the question of whether different hormones, prenatally or at other periods in the life span, can be related to the size or the shape of the corpus callosum. Of course, it is unethical to deliberately manipulate hormone levels in humans, so the types of experimental studies that permit causal statements (e.g., hormone levels and types cause size differences in the corpus callosum) necessarily rely on research with nonhuman mammals. Correlational data from humans (e.g., correlations between the size of a particular area of the corpus callosum and scores on tests of spatial ability) provide corroborating evidence.

One experimental approach is to vary hormone levels in developing organisms and then determine if the hormones that were manipulated had an effect on the corpus callosum. Using this approach, investigators have found that if they administer testosterone to newborn female rats, the corpus callosum becomes larger—a typical brain finding in male rats—and when pregnant female rats are given an antiandrogen, the size of the corpus callosum of their male offspring becomes smaller—a typical brain finding in female rats (Denenberg et al., 1988; Fitch & Denenberg, 1998). These researchers also found that ovarian hormones are important in determining the overall size of the corpus callosum, a result that shows that ovarian hormones are important in brain development. It seems clear that for rats, the corpus callosum is larger in the male and that the size difference is caused by prenatal sex hormones. This research is particularly important because it provides causal evidence that ovarian hormones play an active role in organizing the fetal brain in a female direction.

Of course, studies of rodent brains are not directly generalizable to human brains, and although we would expect the general principle that sex hormones affect brain development to be similar, the exact effects of hormones may not be the same. Research with humans has generally shown that there are sex differences in the shape and probably the volume of selected portions of the corpus callosum (e.g., the splenium), with females generally having a larger and more bulbous structure (Allen, Richey, Chai, & Gorski, 1991; Steinmetz, Staiger, Schluag, Huang, & Jancke, 1995), a result that was first reported by de Lacoste-Utamsing and Holloway (1982). In a recent study on sex differences in the corpus callosum, the researchers concluded that "women (have) larger corpus callosi relative to cranial capacity than men" (Bigler et al., 1997, p. 11). These authors criticized studies that did not find differences as having too few subjects or failing to control for overall head size. This is an important conclusion because it supports the idea that females may have better connectivity between their cerebral hemispheres (Innocenti, 1994) or may transfer information at a higher rate of speed (Jancke & Steinmetz, 1994). In an extensive review of 13 empirical studies pertaining to sex differences in the size of the corpus callosum, Hines (1990) concluded that most of the studies found that a particular region of the corpus callosum is larger (relative to brain weight) in female humans than in male humans. She believes that a larger corpus callosum is associated with better interhemispheric transfer of information, which contributes to verbal fluency. In other words, females, in general, are better than males, in general, in verbal fluency because females have a larger and more efficient corpus callosum.

It is probably difficult for most readers to understand how much controversy has been generated over the question of whether the corpus callosum differs between men and women. In an earlier article on this question, I wrote, "The debate over sex differences in the corpus callosum is more often acrimonious than scholarly" (Halpern, 1998, p. 330). This summary of the field should suggest that there are researchers who do not agree with my conclusion about the corpus callosum. Interested readers will enjoy a section of the journal *Behavioral and Brain Sciences* (1998, Vol. 21) in which scientists fought about (oops, I mean debated) this question. Here is one example of the controversy: Two researchers, Bishop and Wahlsten (1997), conducted a meta-analysis in which they combined results from many different studies and concluded that there are no sex differences in the corpus callosum. Holloway (1998) criticized their research because they included poor studies in their meta-analysis, which are more likely to obtain null results (no significant differences) than strong studies. Descriptive terms like *pseudostatistics* and *smoke screens* were used by some of the researchers as a type of "high-brow name-calling." After reading some of the exchanges between the scientists who work in this area, you will understand why I described the study of sex differences in cognitive abilities as a hot area of research.

What does the finding that there are sex differences in the corpus callosum, the large tract of axons connecting the two halves of the brain, tell us about brain functioning? It suggests that male and female brains may differ, on average, in the extent to which different tasks are specialized in each hemisphere. We now consider theories that posit that the main difference between female and male brains is in the way in which the cerebral hemispheres are organized for different cognitive tasks.

SEXUAL DIMORPHISM IN HEMISPHERIC SPECIALIZATION

If there is one unifying theme ... it is that the direction for future research in lateralization of function lies in exploring how the hemispheres act as complementary processing systems and integrate their activities.
—Banich and Heller (1998, p. 1)

All of the major theories of sex differences in cerebral organization begin with a simple analogy. Given that the types of abilities that differ by hemisphere of specialization are the same ones that differ by sex, it seems to many psychologists only a short leap to suggest that the sexes differ in the way their hemispheres specialize these abilities. The logic behind this reasoning is that because sex differences are primarily found with verbal and visual–spatial tasks and because hemispheric specialization differs with respect to these two abilities, then it is plausible that there are sex differences in cerebral lateralization. The following question is being posed here: "Are female and male brains different in the way the hemispheres are lateralized (or specialized) for cognitive tasks?"

A large body of research has revealed that the two hemispheres or halves of the brain are, to some extent, lateralized or dominant for different cognitive functions. But what does it mean to say that one hemisphere is dominant with respect to a cognitive ability? According to Geschwind (1974), "one hemisphere may be said to be dominant for a given function when it is more important for the performance of that function than the other hemisphere" (p. 9). Hemisphere dominance does not mean an either/or division of tasks. It means instead that one half of the brain is more or less specialized or proficient in its ability to process certain types of stimuli.

Our latest understanding of lateralization of function suggests that the component tasks that underlie complex cognitive feats, like understanding or producing language, are handled with different degrees of speed and ease by each hemisphere. For example, left hemispheric processing is "sharp" at categorization tasks and selection of plausible interpretations of language by using context cues, whereas the right hemisphere allows for multiple interpretations of language and has been described as "coarse" in its ability to decode language (Beeman & Chiarello, 1998). In describing the way that each hemisphere specializes for the encoding of spatial information, similar distinctions are made. The left hemisphere is more adept at categorizing spatial relations (e.g., above, below, inside), and the right hemisphere is more adept at maintaining coordinate relations, which utilize information about distance and more exact locations in space (Chabris & Kosslyn, 1998). Interestingly, it also seems that the right hemisphere is more specialized for processing emotional information (Heller, Nitschke, & Miller, 1998). It probably will not surprise many readers to learn that researchers have found that, overall, men are less sensitive to emotional expressions in faces than women are (Erwin et al., 1992). This brief overview of lateralization parallels findings by sex, but how well does the premise that males and females differ in cerebral lateralization explain the massive research literature?

Laterality and Handedness Groups

Although this book is concerned with sex differences in cognition, there are other groups that show some consistent cognitive differences. People differ in many ways besides sex. One of the differences that has been of interest to psychologists is the difference between right- and left-handers. Hand differences are of particular interest when we consider brain organization because preferred hand use (right or left) is an indirect index of lateralization or brain dominance. Recall that the right hemisphere controls the movements of the left side of the body and the left hemisphere controls the movements of the right side of the body. Thus, most right-handers have dominant motor control in their left hemisphere, and most left-handers have dominant motor control in their right hemisphere. (This has led some left-handers to conclude that they are the only ones in their right mind.) Of course, many people are not consistently right- or left-handed; handedness is a continuous variable, with each of us more or less right- or left-handed. However, to simplify the following discussion, I refer to right- and left-handedness as though there were only these two categories. (For many purposes, people who use their right hand for some tasks, such as writing, and their left hand for other tasks, such as throwing a ball or drawing, are classified along with the left-handers in a group that is commonly called "non-right-handed.")

We are not only right- or left-handed but also right- or left-footed (Which foot do you use to step on a bug?), right- or left-eared (Which ear do you use to listen to a faint conversation that is on the other side of a wall?), and right- or left-eyed (Which eye do you use when looking into a microscope?). Preferred eye, ear, foot, and even nostril are also measures of laterality. Although these other measures can be useful, most research in laterality has used preferred hand, so we think of hand group (right- or left-handed) as a measure of brain lateralization. In general, preferred hand and preferred foot are the same.

Although there had been social pressure placed on natural left-handers to write or eat with their right hand, research has shown that such pressures are usually not successful, and even when they are, the change in hand use is limited only to writing or eating (Porac & Coren, 1981). There are no social pressures to change foot preference, and because foot preference is usually in agreement with hand preference, researchers believe that hand preference is a biologically determined index of cerebral organization. The functional asymmetry of the hemispheres (different cognitive functions specialized in different hemispheres) is present at birth, so it is not due to experience (Witelson, 1989). Additional evidence to support this view can be found in Davidson and Hugdahl (1995) and Hellige (1993).

The research literature on handedness groups must be at least as large as the literature on sex differences. We know that there are higher proportions of left-handers among architects, engineers, university mathematics teachers and mathematics students, artists, astronauts, chess masters, championship "Go" players, and performing musicians than in the general population (Deutsch, 1980; Mebert & Michel, 1980; O'Boyle & Benbow, 1990) and a higher proportion of left-handers among those medical school applicants who are accepted than among those who are not accepted (Halpern et al., 1998). There is also an excess of left-handers at both tails of the abilities distributions, for example, among dyslexic individuals (Boliek & Obrzut, 1995; Richardson, 1994) and among highly precocious youth (Benbow & Lubinski, 1993; O'Boyle, Gill, Benbow, & Alexander, 1994).

Approximately 95% of all right-handed people maintain speech and language control in their left hemisphere. Actual percentage estimates vary somewhat for the proportion of left-handed people who maintain the same lateralization pattern as right-handed people. Levy and Reid (1978) estimated that among the left-handed population, 60% maintain language functions in the left hemisphere, with the remaining 40% having the reverse pattern. Springer and Deutsch (1998) estimated that among left-handers, 70% have speech and language control in their left hemisphere, with approximately 15% maintaining verbal control in their right hemisphere, and the remaining 15% with control in both hemispheres. In Moffat and Hampson's (1996) review of the literature, they estimated the percentage of left-handers with speech and other language function in the left hemisphere to be approximately 70%. These small variations in these estimates are of no practical concern for the purposes of this review; however, the fact that a much larger proportion of left-handers than right-handers have right-hemisphere language specialization is important in understanding hypotheses about the relationship between sex and cerebral lateralization.

There is a large research literature documenting the finding that left-handers differ from right-handers on some cognitive abilities. For example, research has shown that left-handers are inferior to right-handers on certain verbal tasks (Bradshaw & Bradshaw, 1988). Many researchers have concluded that left-handers are superior on cognitive tasks that are mediated by the right hemisphere, such as spatial abilities (Lewis & Harris, 1990; Moffat & Hampson, 1996). It also seems that left-handers are more likely to have some of their language functions specialized in their dominant right hemisphere (Harshman & Hampson, 1987; Hines, 1990). In a study of applicants to medical school, left-handers were overrepresented among the highest scorers on a test of verbal reasoning, probably reflecting the processes used in these cognitive tests and not the fact that the task was verbal (Halpern et al., 1998). If you're thinking that these results are similar to some of the findings in the sex differences literature, you're right. In fact, there are many parallels between the findings of researchers who study cognitive sex differences and researchers who study cognitive handedness differences.

Given that the pattern of cognitive results are the same for males and left-handers and for females and right-handers, you may be wondering if more males are left-handed (and, by inference, more females are right-handed). Estimates of the percentage of each sex that is left-handed vary considerably depending on how handedness is measured, the group that is selected as participants, and the age of the participants (Coren & Halpern, 1991). Virtually all studies find that a greater proportion of males are left-handed than females (e.g., Annett, 1994; Coren, 1990; Halpern et al., 1998). A higher proportion of left-handedness among men than women also has been found in a sample from India (Singh & Bryden, 1994). Thus, because left-handedness is statistically associated with being male and right-handedness with being female, the similarity in cognitive patterns is not surprising. In accord with this conclusion, Hines and Sandberg (1996) reported that women who were exposed to DES, a masculinizing hormone, when they were fetuses showed a decreased incidence of right-handedness and an increase in brain lateralization for language tasks. Both of these are behavioral–neuroanatomical traits that are associated with being male, suggesting that handedness and language lateralization are, in part, determined by prenatal hormonal environments.

In an interesting investigation of the link between handedness and the action of sex hormones, Nikolova, Stoyanová, and Negrev (1994) collected data about age at menarche from 1,695 women between 16 and 25 years of age. They found that, on average, the left-handed girls began menstruation at a younger age (mean age = 12.07 years) than the right-handed girls (mean age = 13.32 years). They explained this finding by reminding readers that both handedness and age at menarche have hormonal antecedents, both tied to the hypothalamic–pituitary–gonadal axis. They posited a relationship between functional brain asymmetry and menarche because both are affected by gonadal hormones.

Sex by handedness interactions, that is, subgroup effects for right-handed females, left-handed females, right-handed males, and left-handed males, are complex and seem to depend, not surprisingly, on the nature of the cognitive task, the age of the sample, and the part of the abilities distribution (i.e., very smart, average, or low end) being studied.

Assessing Brain Laterality

Handedness provides only an indirect measure of brain laterality. There are numerous other methods for determining which hemisphere is more specialized for select cognitive tasks and whether males and females differ on both the measure of laterality and the task.

Hand Posture

One index of cerebral lateralization is writing hand posture. Recall that left-handers, as a group, are more variable than right-handers in their hemispheric specialization for language functions. Levy (1974) posited that left-handers who write with a "hooked" or an inverted hand posture have language specialization in their left hemisphere, whereas those who write with an "upright" hand posture have language specialization in their right hemisphere. Similarly, right-handers who write with a hooked hand posture have language specialization in their right hemisphere (very rare), and those who write with an upright hand posture have language specialization in their left hemisphere. These different hand postures are shown in Fig. 5.2.

Brain Lesions

Another way to determine the organization of the hemispheres for cognitive tasks is to study the way that individuals respond following brain surgery where some portion of the brain is lesioned (cut, damaged, or removed), which could be the re-

Left-handed writers   Right-handed writers

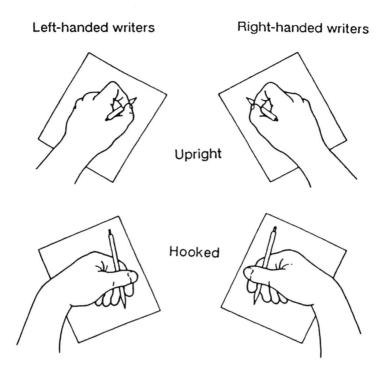

Upright

Hooked

FIG. 5.2.   Using writing hand posture to determine which hemisphere is lateralized for verbal abilities. According to Levy (1974), a "hooked" hand posture indicates ipsilateral (same-side) lateralization and an "upright" hand posture indicates opposite-side lateralization for verbal abilities. Thus, a left-hander with a hooked posture is dominant for verbal abilities in the left hemisphere, whereas a left-hander with an upright posture is dominant for verbal abilities in the right hemisphere.

sult of a stroke or head injury. Clinical populations have included people who have had their corpus callosum (the thick bundle of nerve fibers that connect the two halves of the brain) split to alleviate the symptoms of epilepsy, individuals with damage to one area of the brain, postmortem examinations of corpses, and patients undergoing laboratory tests such as direct electrical stimulation of selected brain regions. This is a fascinating area of study because it has allowed us to understand what happens when the two halves of the brain lose their ability to communicate with each other. Roger Sperry won a Nobel Prize in 1981 for his extraordinary work with split-brain patients. For split-brain patients, it is possible to present stimuli to only one hemisphere, which allowed researchers to determine the role of each hemisphere in information processing. It is largely due to Sperry's work that the general public became aware of the fact that the two hemispheres of the brain are each specialized for certain types of information.

Information about sex differences in the way the hemispheres are specialized came from a variety of sources—sometimes using normal healthy individuals as participants and other times using clinical samples. Unfortunately, large numbers of people suffer from strokes each year. Data from stroke patients clearly show that males and females are affected differently, even when these patients are matched on the location and severity of the brain damage caused by the stroke. For example, one study found sex differences in the location of language "zones" in the brain (Hier, Yoon, Mohr, Price, & Wolf, 1994), another study found that females are more impaired than males on visual–spatial tasks following a stroke (Desmond, Glenwick, Stern, & Tatemichi, 1994), and another study found that women are less impaired than men on verbal tasks following a stroke (Herring & Reitan, 1992). It is probably easiest to summarize the literature (Gazzaniga et al., 1998) on brain damage in a table format, which is presented in Table 5.1.

Indicators of Brain Activity

Researchers also want to know about sex differences in hemispheric specialization with normal healthy individuals, not just with clinical populations. There are many techniques that provide information about brain functioning in normal humans. One popular technique is to record electroencephalographic (EEG) activity and evoked potentials off the scalps (measures of the electrical activity in the brain) of people who are either sitting passively or performing a cognitive task. These are easy, noninvasive techniques that can be used even with infants. For example, in an examination of the early development of lateralization, Shucard et al. (1987) took electrophysiological recordings from the right and left hemispheres of infants who were processing both speech and musical stimuli. They concluded that the right hemisphere is more active in processing both speech and music for male infants than for female infants. They also found that female infants shift to the more usual adult pattern at an earlier age than male infants. (The usual adult pattern is greater left-hemisphere response to verbal stimuli and greater right-hemisphere response to musical stimuli.) Molfese (1990) also found a different pattern of brain activity

TABLE 5.1
The Effects of Unilateral Brain Damage

Sex	Hemisphere	Deficits	Type of Cognitive Test
Men	left	Yes	Verbal
	right	Yes	Spatial
Women	left	Yes	Verbal and spatial equally
	right	No	No deficits on either test

to known words for female and male infants. He was able to record different brain responses to known words than to unknown words in 16-month-old infants. Molfese found that different regions of the brain appear to be involved in female infants' comprehension of words than in male infants' comprehension of words.

As an example of EEG research, consider a recent study by Gill and O'Boyle (1997). They monitored certain brain waves, taking their EEG recordings from the right and left hemispheres while healthy participants manipulated arcs and circles (a spatial task). They found that the males were more accurate on this spatial task and had more frontal lobe activation in the right hemisphere than in the left hemisphere, whereas the females had more bilaterally symmetrical patterns of activation. Like many other researchers, but not all, they concluded that women and men have different functional organizations of their cerebral hemispheres for processing spatial tasks.

Sex differences in EEGs are frequently reported for adults, with higher activity rates reported for women in both resting states and some cognitive tasks (Erwin, Mawhinney-Hee, Gur, & Gur, 1989). In this particular study, the EEG data were corroborated with measures of regional cerebral blood flow, and these experimenters reported greater hemispheric asymmetry of cerebral blood flow for women when spatial and verbal tasks were compared. They believe that the EEG and regional cerebral blood flow data provide evidence for sex differences in the portions of the brain that are used by men and women when they perform verbal tasks (verbal analogies were used in this study) and spatial tasks (a line orientation task was used). In a more recent investigation, Gur et al. (1995) specified the brain regions in which sex differences are found. (For those readers with a good background in neuroscience, men had higher rates of metabolism in the temporal–limbic regions and cerebellum, and women had higher metabolism in the cingulate region. If these locations are not meaningful to you, just take away the message that there are different brain regions involved.) The authors of these studies made the clear conclusion that there are sex differences in hemispheric asymmetry in metabolic activity.

Interference Tasks

Another way of assessing hemispheric involvement in a particular task is to have participants perform some task with each hand (e.g., tapping rhythmically) while performing either a verbal or a spatial task. Consider the rationale for studying finger tapping. If you are tapping with your right hand, your left hemisphere is coordinating the movement. Suppose that while you are tapping, I have you perform some verbal tasks (e.g., anagrams) and then some spatial tasks (e.g., mental rotation). If the verbal tasks interfered more with the right-hand tapping than the spatial tasks did, I could conclude that you were primarily using your left hemisphere for the verbal tasks and not for the spatial tasks. The underlying idea is that two tasks interfere with each other more if they are performed by the same hemisphere than if they are performed by different hemispheres (Bowers & LaBarba, 1988; Kee & Cherry, 1990).

Dichotic Listening and Divided Visual Fields

Laboratory investigations of hemispheric dominance rely on the fact that most of the nerves from one side of the body connect to the contralateral (opposite) hemisphere. Consider audition (or hearing), for example. A majority of the nerves in the auditory track that connect to the right ear send their impulses to the left hemisphere, with the reverse innervation for the left ear. In a classic experimental paradigm, the researcher presents different stimuli to each ear simultaneously. The participant would be required to respond to the stimuli in some way such as classifying it as a letter or a word or responding with a key press as quickly as possible to certain types of stimuli. The usual finding is that right-handed participants respond more accurately to linguistic stimuli (letters or words) when they are presented to the right ear than when they are presented to the left ear (known as a right ear advantage), suggesting that for right-handers the left hemisphere is dominant or specialized for linguistic tasks. Stimuli that are difficult to verbalize (random sound sequences or noises that are not readily identifiable) are usually responded to better when they are presented to the left ear than the right, suggesting that the right hemisphere is specialized or dominant for nonlinguistic tasks for right-handed participants (Bryden, 1986).

The presentation of different stimuli to each ear is called "dichotic listening." You can get some idea of what this is like by having two friends stand next to you, one on each side, and having them read different passages at the same time. You will hear one message in your right ear and a different one in your left ear. In Bryden's (1988) review of sex differences in dichotic-listening research, he concluded that although not all studies found significant handedness effects, virtually all found at least a trend for left-handers to show a reduced laterality effect. This means that they showed less difference in how quickly or accurately they responded to stimuli presented to their right or left ear than the right-handers did. In his extensive review, Bryden concluded that 82% of right-handers and 64% of left-handers show a right ear advantage in dichotic listening, with similar percentages confirmed by Hugdahl (1995). When Bryden examined the same studies as a function of sex, he found that 81% of males and only 74% of females showed a right ear advantage, with no studies showing a greater proportion of right ear advantage in females. He used these data to conclude that, in general, females have a more bilateral organization of cognitive abilities than males.

Numerous reviewers (e.g., Hellige, 1993; Hines, 1990; Voyer, 1996) agree with Bryden's (1988) conclusion that the degree of left-hemisphere dominance is greater in males than females. Thus, according to this hypothesis, females have a more bilateral organization of brain function than males. A more bilateral organization means that the two hemispheres are more equal in the degree to which they underlie a specific type of cognitive task. The hypothesis that women's brains are more bilaterally organized (which also implies that men's brains are more laterally or one-sided organized) is hotly contested in the research literature.

Research similar to that described with hearing is also conducted with vision, although the pattern of innervation, or the way the neurons connect, is somewhat more

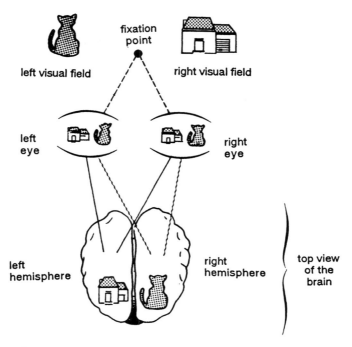

FIG. 5.3.   Schematic drawing of the images projected onto the right and the left half of each eye when a participant is looking at a fixation point that is straight ahead. Notice that the cat in the left visual field is projected onto the right half of the left eye and the right half of the right eye. Both of these portions of each eye connect to the right hemisphere. The opposite pattern occurs for the house shown in the right visual field.

complicated. Nerve fibers from the left half of each eye connect to the left hemisphere, and nerve fibers from the right half of each eye connect to the right hemisphere. Researchers can determine which hemisphere is receiving visual information by presenting visual stimuli very briefly (a fraction of a second) to the right or the left of a participant's fixation point. A fixation point is the point an individual is looking directly at when he or she is looking straight ahead. Any stimuli presented to the left of the fixation point, an area known as the left visual field, are initially represented in the right hemisphere. Similarly, any stimuli presented to the right of the fixation point, an area known as the right visual field, are initially represented in the left cerebral hemisphere (Kitterle & Kaye, 1985). A schematic diagram of this experimental paradigm is presented in Fig. 5.3. Results with visual stimuli support those found with audition: The right hemisphere is primarily important in visual–spatial skills (depth perception, detecting the orientation of a line, visual point location), and the left hemisphere is primarily important in verbal skills (naming concrete nouns and recognizing words and digits; Geschwind, 1974).

Research that displays stimuli to the right or left visual field is called divided visual field research. To conclude that men's brains are more lateralized than women's, we would need to find that there is a greater difference in how men respond to stimuli in their left and right visual fields than in how women respond to stimuli in their right and left visual fields. For example, suppose a researcher presents words to the right or left visual field. The task for the participant is to say the word as quickly as possible. The dependent measure in this example is reaction time, or the time between presenting the stimuli and the participant saying the word. If we had a large sample of women and men, we could compute the average difference in reaction time for stimuli presented to the left visual field and stimuli presented to the right visual field for each sex. If this difference were significantly larger for men than for women, this would be evidence that men's brains are more lateralized or specialized than women's brains.

Voyer (1996) reviewed the research literature that used divided visual fields and other techniques for assessing laterality. He conducted a meta-analysis, using 396 significance levels from a variety of studies that investigated the question of whether males and females differ in the degree to which each hemisphere is specialized for cognitive tasks. He arrived at the strong conclusion that males are more lateralized than females for both visual and auditory modalities, meaning that males are more likely to separate information processing, with each hemisphere working more independently. Women's brains are more bilaterally organized, that is, there is more communicating between the hemispheres. Recall from the chapter on research methods, chapter 3, that a fail-safe value can be calculated for meta-analyses. It is the number of studies that found no differences between males and females that would be needed to change the conclusion. Voyer calculated that for studies using the visual modality, the fail-safe number of unpublished studies of no differences that would be needed to alter the conclusion that women are more bilaterally organized and that men are more lateralized for cognitive functions is 1,155. He concluded that "the hypothesis that men and women differ in functional lateralities has been used to account for sex-related differences in verbal and spatial skills. ... The data indicated the presence of sex differences in favor of men in functional asymmetries" (Voyer, 1996, p. 51). Conclusions about sex differences in brain lateralization only make sense in the context of a strong theory (one that is falsifiable) that can explain them. Let's consider some of the prominent theories.

Theories of Sex Differences in Cerebral Organization

Cognitive Crowding Hypothesis

Levy (1976; Levy & Nagylaki, 1972; Levy, Agresti, & Sperry, 1968) hypothesized, at least in her earlier research, that spatial performance is optimized when spatial ability is strongly lateralized in one hemisphere. Thus, she began with the assumption that lateralization is the best neural organization for spatial tasks. According to Levy (1976), when verbal and spatial processes are confined to single and separate sides of the brain, the underlying neural connections are optimal for each of these functions. However, if lateralization is incomplete or weak, then the two hemispheres compete when an individual is performing a task. This aspect of her hypothesis has come to be known as the "cognitive crowding hypothesis" on the basis of the reasoning that if two (or more) cognitive abilities are primarily controlled by the same hemisphere, there will not be enough "neural space" for each to be developed optimally. Task performance is impaired under these conditions. Levy went on to suggest that because verbal skills are so important to the human species, spatial ability is more likely to suffer when verbal and spatial processes compete in the same hemisphere.

In explaining sex differences in cognitive abilities, Levy (1976) posited that females are less lateralized than males because of sex-related biological differences in the rate and pattern of development and, therefore, they are more likely to have bilateral representations of verbal abilities. Bilateral representations of verbal abilities are an advantage to verbal skills because more "cortical space" is devoted to language functions. In contrast, bilateral representations of verbal skills impair the ability to perform spatial tasks because there is less cortical space devoted to spatial function due to the "crowding out" of spatial representation by the bilateral cortical representation of language. In other words, females are more likely to involve both hemispheres when solving spatial tasks than are males. One implication of this brain organization is that females may use a verbal cognitive style when solving spatial problems, a point that I return to in the next chapter. Because bilateral representation is not an optimal neural organization for spatial tasks in which holistic approaches work best, women show impaired performance on these sorts of spatial tasks.

Levy (1976) has also suggested that women's patterns of cognitive abilities should be similar to those of left-handed men. Given that approximately 90%–95% of all right-handed people maintain language control primarily in their left hemisphere and spatial control in their right hemisphere and less than 70% of left-handed people have this pattern of neural organization, as a group left-handers of both sexes are more likely to have bilateral representation of language functions. According to Levy's hypothesis, women, as a group, are also more likely to maintain bilateral representation. Thus, left-handed men and women in general should have bilateral representation of verbal skills, which is a cerebral pattern that is detrimental to spatial skills. (Recall that left-handers are overrepresented on both the high and low ends of many ability distributions, so the general idea that left-handers would perform less well at complex spatial tasks has not been supported.) Both groups would be expected to have better verbal skills than spatial skills, if this theory were true. Later in this chapter, I return to the theme that cognitive abilities depend on both sex and handedness. A schematic diagram of the cognitive crowding hypothesis is shown in Fig. 5.4.

If the cognitive crowding hypothesis is correct and females rely more on both hemispheres in processing information than males, then we would expect a lower incidence of language disorders for females because they can rely on both hemi-

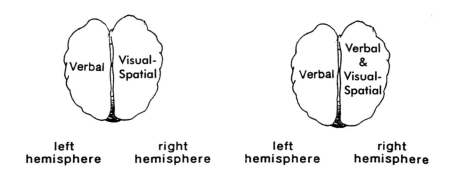

| left hemisphere | right hemisphere | left hemisphere | right hemisphere |

Hand: Right handers   Left handers

Sex: More male-typical   More female-typical

Predicted
Interactions: Left-handed males have cognitive patterns similar to that of
women (verbal skills better than spatial skills)

(Other sex by handedness interactions were not specified, but possibilities
include left-handed women are most likely to have higher verbal than spatial
skills and right-handed men are most likely to have higher spatial skills than
verbal skills)

FIG. 5.4.   A schematic representation of the cognitive crowding hypothesis. According to this hypothesis, women (in general) and left-handers (especially males)
have better verbal skills because language is bilaterally organized and poorer spatial skills because spatial ability is "crowded out" due to the fact that spatial abilities
share the neural architecture in the right hemisphere with the neural substrate for
verbal abilities.

spheres and would be less impaired by local brain injury or trauma. This is true. Females have fewer reading disabilities, including dyslexia; fewer speech disorders,
including aphasia, dysphasia, and stuttering; and a lower incidence of autism
(American Psychiatric Association, 1994; DeFries & Gillis, 1993; Yari &
Ambrose, 1992). Although there still are researchers who disagree with the conclusion that women maintain a more bilateral representation of cognitive functions than men, I believe that most have adopted this conclusion. (In earlier
editions of this book, I noted the intense disagreement about this position.) Despite
the fact that there are many researchers who have failed to find experimental results that would support the idea that the female brain is more symmetrically organized than the male brain, what is most compelling is that when hemisphere
differences are found, they are almost always in the same direction—females less
lateralized than males. If these were spurious findings, then we would expect the
results to go in either direction about equally often.

Jaeger et al. (1998) suggested that the reason why research on sex differences in lateralization has yielded conflicting results is because of differences in the task used to measure them. They believe that sex differences in lateralization are found when the linguistic demands of the task are difficult but not when the task is easy. In the (difficult) grammatical and (easy) reading tasks that they used, there were no sex differences in task performance, but the males were more lateralized with the (difficult) grammatical task than the females were, with no laterality differences with the (easy) reading task. These results support the general idea that women have a more bilateral brain organization than men and that this pattern is seen most clearly when difficult tasks are used. The best summary in the literature on the question of sex differences in lateralization comes from Voyer's (1996) meta-analysis of 396 separate comparisons. On the basis of this extensive review of the literature, he concluded that males are more lateralized for visual and auditory tasks.

The Effect of Prenatal Sex Hormones on Lateralization

In the last chapter, I discussed an influential theory by Geschwind and Galaburda (1987) that posited that prenatal sex hormones play a critical role in brain development. As you recall (note my optimism), the underlying idea is that during prenatal development, the left hemisphere is at greater risk than the right because the left hemisphere takes longer to develop than the right. According to this theory, high levels of prenatal testosterone slow neuronal growth in the left hemisphere. The result is right-hemisphere dominance, which is manifested in left-handedness. Because males are usually exposed to higher levels of testosterone during prenatal development (from their own developing testes, which secrete testosterone, in addition to the lower amounts that are supplied by their mothers), males are more likely to be right-hemisphere dominant. Research presented in this chapter showed that males are more likely to be left-handed. Recent studies reporting that gifted males showed more right-hemisphere activity during a spatial task (Benbow & Lubinski, 1993) and that left-handers of both sexes had lower salivary testosterone than right-handers (Moffat & Hampson, 1996) support predictions made by Geschwind and Galaburda. (As noted in chap. 4, Bryden, McManus, and Bulman-Fleming, 1994, presented a negative review of Geschwind and Galaburda's theory, noting several other predictions that have not been confirmed.)

Another way of investigating the relationship between prenatal hormones and brain lateralization is by examining the extent to which females with Turner's syndrome are lateralized for cognitive tasks. Recall that these women have particularly poor spatial skills. When Hines (1982) investigated this relationship, she found that women with Turner's syndrome had reduced laterality for cognitive tasks. Although this result is consistent with a brain organization that may be detrimental to spatial tasks, the cause of this organization is not entirely clear. Postnatal hormones could contribute by altering either hemispheric specialization or unrelated aspects of brain development given that females with Turner's syndrome have generally low levels of all gonadal hormones both prenatally and during early postnatal life.

Hypogonadal men, that is men with extremely low levels of testosterone, are another clinical population that has been used to study the relationship between sex hormones and cerebral lateralization. Do hypogonadal men show the male-typical pattern of greater cerebral asymmetry than women? When researchers tested this possibility, they found that hypogonadal men showed *less* asymmetry than normal men for some tasks (Wisniewski, Nguyen, Flannery, & Dobs, 1999). It seems that adult hormone levels influence cerebral lateralization. Men with extremely low levels of testosterone showed female-typical responses on some tasks used to assess laterality.

Maturation Rate Hypothesis

It is widely documented that girls begin puberty earlier than boys. Girls in sixth and seventh grade not only tend to be taller than their male classmates but also tend to exhibit secondary sex characteristics at an earlier age and develop reproductive capabilities earlier (Faust, 1977). One of the leading proponents of the maturation rate hypothesis is Waber (1976), who speculated that sex differences in lateralization are due to differences in maturation rate. As explained in chapter 4, Waber believes that early maturation is beneficial to verbal abilities and detrimental to spatial abilities. To test her hypothesis, she compared early and late maturers of both sexes ranging in age from 10 to 16 years old.

Early maturers of both sexes were better at the verbal tests than the spatial ones; late maturers of both sexes showed the reverse pattern of results. This difference in performance, however, was almost entirely due to the considerable superiority of the late maturers on the spatial tests. There were no statistically significant sex differences in the verbal and spatial tests when the sexes were equated for maturation rate. A final result was that the dichotic-listening task showed the strongest lateralization among the older participants who were late maturers, regardless of sex. Taken together, these results suggest that late maturation is associated with good spatial skills and strong lateralization for both sexes, and early physical maturation is favorable to the development of good verbal abilities and weaker lateralization. Because, in general, girls mature earlier than boys, they would be expected to show less lateralization, better verbal ability, and poorer spatial ability.

Partial confirmation of Waber's (1976) maturation rate hypothesis was provided by Ray, Newcombe, Semon, and Cole (1981). They found a positive correlation between age at puberty and performance on the Guilford–Zimmerman test of spatial orientation, with later maturing individuals correctly solving more problems than those who experienced puberty at an earlier age. Petersen and Crockett (1985) also found a timing of puberty effect in their study of 135 postpubertal adolescents. Late maturers out performed early maturers on the Embedded Figures Test. However, a timing of puberty effect was not found with a mental rotation test—a test that usually shows large sex differences prior to adolescence. Thus, the notion that the biological substrates that are responsible for the onset of puberty also affect spatial ability has been replicated but only with selected spatial ability tests.

There are, however, several problems with any theory that ties cognitive abilities to rate of maturation at puberty. The most obvious one is that sex differences are found in childhood (e.g., mental rotation), so puberty explanations come too late in development for these differences. Furthermore, the effect of timing of puberty on spatial ability is very small. As you will read in the next chapter, which discusses psychosocial explanations of sex differences, the finding that a later age at puberty is correlated weakly with better spatial skills does not necessarily support any biological hypothesis. Early and later maturers could adopt different strategies for solving different sorts of problems or could be reacting to sex-differentiated social pressures (e.g., Newcombe, Dubas, & Baenninger, 1989).

Sex, Lateralization, and Cognitive Abilities—A Sectional Summary

Lateralization is a fundamental property of brain organization
with widespread evolutionary significance.
—LaHoste, Mormede, Rivet, and LeMoal (1988, p. 296)

It would probably be useful at this point to recapitulate the main points in the theories concerning the relationship among sex, lateralization, and cognitive abilities:

1. Data from EEGs, regional cerebral blood flow, behavioral tasks such as dichotic listening and dichoptic visual presentations, handedness, strokes, and more all show evidence of sex differences in the way that the brain is functionally organized for men and women.
2. Women are more likely to have language functions represented in both hemispheres, although any simple dichotomy, whether by type of task, sex of participant, or hemisphere, is an oversimplification of a complex interplay of variables. This theory has come to be known as "cognitive crowding."
3. Sex differences in cerebral specialization are caused, at least in part, by the effect of prenatal hormones on the development of each hemisphere (Geschwind & Galaburda, 1987).
4. It seems that answers to all of the important questions in psychology require a qualifying "it depends" or "sometimes." The finding that there is a disproportionate number of left-handed males at both the high and low ends of many ability distributions shows that although we can talk about differences, we do not yet understand why these translate into both very high and very low ability.

SEX DIFFERENCES WITHIN EACH CEREBRAL HEMISPHERE

Brain researchers who are opposed to the notion that there are sex differences in cerebral lateralization posit other ways in which male and female brains differ that could explain cognitive sex differences. One concept that they all agree on is that the sexual differentiation of the brain is a more subtle and more complex process than the sexual differentiation of the genitals (Goy, Bercovitch, & McBrair, 1988).

Kimura (1987, 1999) conducted a fascinating series of studies over the past two decades that showed sex differences in each of the hemispheres that she believes can explain some of the usual cognitive results. She examined a large sample of patients selected from individuals with brain damage to only one hemisphere. She looked at the kind of disability that resulted and the area of the brain that was damaged. (I am greatly simplifying her research. This is engrossing research that I recommend to interested readers.) Kimura concluded that the language areas in the female brain are more focally organized in the left hemisphere (specifically, the anterior or frontal region) whereas the language areas in the male brain are more diffusely organized, also in the left hemisphere. Kimura cited corroborating research by other investigators working in other laboratories. She also found even sharper sex differences when she examined the brain areas responsible for manual dexterity. Recall from chapter 3 that most studies report that females are better on many tasks of manual dexterity than males. Kimura found that the area of female brains that seems especially important in manual dexterity is also more focal (less spread out) than the corresponding area in males. She concluded that there is "no evidence in the clinical findings of a more ... bilateral organization for speech and related praxic functions in women" (Kimura, 1987, p. 140). (*Praxia,* or *praxic,* is the formal word for what I am calling "manual dexterity.")

Kimura (1987) bolstered her argument by noting that the anterior regions of the left hemisphere are larger in female brains during the first 2 trimesters of prenatal development. Thus, she also tied her theory of sex differences in each hemisphere of the brain to prenatal development. Other researchers have identified the left central portion of the brain as critical in language. Research that has examined the brains of dyslexics using modern imaging methods (computerized axial tomography and magnetic resonance imaging) have shown that the brains of dyslexics are more symmetrical and smaller in these areas than the brains of normal readers (Hynd & Semrud-Clikeman, 1990). (For readers who have had a basic course in physiology or the neurosciences, the areas involved are regions in the left planum temporale and parieto-occipital cortex. These are the areas that are involved in phonological coding, language comprehension, and auditory perception. The names of the specific regions have little meaning unless you've already studied these brain areas in other course work.) Thus, this is a body of research that supports the concept that male and female brains differ in the way that cognitive functions are represented within each hemisphere and not in differences between the hemispheres. Other researchers also have noted that there are probably sex differences in the cortical organization of the anterior and posterior regions of the brain in each hemisphere (Levy & Heller, 1992).

TABLE 5.2

Summary of Theories of Sex Differences in the Organization and Structure of the Brain

1.Sex Differences in Lateralization

This is really a class of theories with the underlying premise that female brains are more symmetrically organized for cognitive functions (called a more bilateral organization) and male brains are more asymmetrically organized (called a more lateralized organization). A recent meta-analysis confirmed these sex differences in lateralization for visual and auditory modalities (Voyer, 1996).

Cognitive crowding is one theory of how male and female brains differ in lateralization. According to this theory, female brains are more likely to have verbal ability represented in both hemispheres, with visual-spatial ability sharing neural space with verbal abilities in the right hemisphere; male brains are more likely to have the left hemisphere devoted exclusively to verbal abilities and the right hemisphere devoted exclusively to visual-spatial abilities.

Prenatal and perinatal hormones have been suggested as the cause of sex differences in lateralization. According to this hypothesis, high levels of male prenatal or perinatal hormones slow neuronal growth in the left hemisphere. The result is a male-typical brain pattern with more right-hemisphere dominance among males than among females.

Maturation rates at puberty also have been suggested as the cause of sex differences in lateralization, with early maturers less lateralized than late maturers. (Girls tend to mature earlier than boys.) There is very little support for the maturation rate hypothesis, which cannot explain sex differences in cognition that are found in childhood (prior to puberty).

Although some researchers will not agree with my conclusion, I believe that the data are strong enough to warrant the conclusion that female brains are more bilaterally organized and male brains more lateralized for cognitive tasks.

2.Intrahemispheric Sex Differences

Sex differences in the organization of cognitive abilities within each hemisphere also have been proposed. There is good evidence that these functions are more focally organized in female brains and more diffusely organized in male brains.

3.Size of the Corpus Callosum

The corpus callosum, the thick band of neural fibers that connect the right and left hemispheres, also has been suggested as the site of sex differences in brain structures. The usual finding is that the posterior portion of the corpus callosum is larger and more bulbous in shape in human females than in human males. It seems that both prenatal and perinatal androgen and ovarian hormones are important in determining the size of the corpus callosum. This finding is consistent with the conclusion that female brains are better organized for the use of both hemispheres in cognition.

It is likely that both of these positions are correct and that sex differences can be found both within and across hemispheres.

I have summarized the three theories of cerebral sex differences in Table 5.2. It should be useful at this point to look over Table 5.2 and to consider how the theories differ.

The research reviewed in this chapter provides strong evidence for the conclusion that there are sex differences in the human brain that underlie cognition, although we are a long way from understanding the organ that is responsible for all we know and do.

EVOLUTIONARY PRESSURES

Cognitive traits and their neuroanatomical bases are likely targets
of sexual selection.
—Gaulin (1995, p. 1211)

According to the basic tenets of evolutionary theory, the human brain evolved into its present form as a result of pressures to adapt to the environment. Sex differences in brain structure and function can be understood as an evolutionary process. The most convincing evidence that sex-related brain differences can be traced to evolutionary pressures comes from studies with voles (rodents). As described earlier in this chapter, for species of voles in which the males have to travel long distances in search of a mate or food, the hippocampus of the male is significantly larger than that of the female, which has a smaller "home range." By comparison, for species of voles in which the males and the females have the same size home range, there are no differences in the size of their hippocampi (Gaulin, 1995). The hippocampus is the (primary) neuroanatomical basis for spatial ability, so its size reflects the extent to which it is developed for the task of finding one's way in space. There is an adaptive advantage (more food and more mates) for a species if the males develop brain structures that support their successful navigation.

Similar evolutionary-based arguments have been applied to humans. Most of human history has been spent in hunter–gatherer societies in which males roamed over large areas in their hunt for large animals that provided the protein for the society and females gathered crops and traveled shorter distances because much of their adult lives was spent in pregnancy, nursing, and child care. Thus, the neurocognitive systems of human males should have evolved in ways that support navigation in three-dimensional space, and although males no longer hunt for large animals to provide the main source of protein, the superiority in spatial navigation and related skill areas, such as aiming at a target, remains as a legacy of these earlier societies (Buss, 1995; Gazzaniga et al., 1998). Evolutionary theory has also been used to explain the female advantage on spatial tasks that require memory for location, based on the idea that this sort of skill would have been critical for gatherers who had to find wild food crops, whose locations would vary depending on the season of the year (Eals & Silverman, 1994; Silverman & Eals, 1992).

Geary (1995a, 1996d, 1998) refined the basic evolutionary explanation of cognitive sex differences by making a distinction between those skills that are primary, that is, they were shaped by evolutionary pressures and therefore would be found across cultures, and those that are secondary, that is, they are found only in technologically advanced societies (e.g., skills like reading and spelling that are important in school but would not have evolved for hunter–gatherer societies). Although I have no doubt that the human brain evolved in response to adaptation pressures, it is difficult to find direct links between the sex-differentiated tasks in hunter–gatherer societies and modern sex differences in human brains. As I noted in earlier chapters, virtually any finding can be explained by positing how it might have been advantageous to hunter–gatherers. There is also the tendency to ignore data that are inconsistent with evolutionary theories, such as the spatial nature of much of women's work in these early societies, including weaving baskets to hold the gathered food and traveling considerable distances to find food.

The What–Where System

One distinction that is consistent with the idea that our brains evolved in response to adaptive pressures is the separation of visual information about what an object is from where an object is located (Braddick, 1993; Brown & Kosslyn, 1995). These two types of information are handled by two kinds of neural encoding. As an example of how research into this distinction is conducted, consider two different cognitive tasks—one that requires memory for what an object is, regardless of where the object is located, and another that requires memory for the location of an object, regardless of the identity of the object. Using this research paradigm, Mecklinger and Müller (1996) recorded EEGs from different positions on the scalp and found that "object and spatial information ... are subserved by functionally and anatomically different subsystems" (p. 453). Evolutionary theory would predict sex differences in the functioning and neuroanatomy of the *what* and *where* systems because of the differential importance of *what* and *where* information for gatherers and hunters in early societies. As far as I know, this prediction has not yet been tested. Advances in brain recording and imaging are moving rapidly, and we are still new at using them to reveal the mysteries of the brain. The application of these techniques to questions of sex differences usually lags behind their primary use as a basic technique to study brain–behavior relationships. Perhaps by the time you are reading this text, experiments comparing males and females with regard to brain activity in *what–where* tasks will have been conducted. Thoughtful readers are invited to speculate on what the results of these yet to-be-conducted studies might show and how findings are likely to be interpreted.

SEXUAL ORIENTATION AND THE BRAIN

Differences related to sex and sexual orientation are important aspects of human diversity, well worth studying regardless of the supposed benefit or harm that such research will bring.
—LeVay (1996, p. 284)

In chapter 4, I provided a brief overview of research that found that gay males often perform midway between heterosexual males and females on cognitive tasks that typically show sex differences. As I explained, most of the reseacrh concerning sexual orientation and cognition has compared gay males, heterosexual males, and females, usually without regard to the sexual orientation of the females. Thus far, there are too few studies with lesbians to warrant any conclusions about their cognitive abilities relative to heterosexual females or gay and heterosexual males. There are several reasons why lesbians have not been systematically studied, including the probability that there are fewer lesbians than gay males, so they are more difficult to sample in an unbiased way, and they probably declare their homosexual orientation later in life than gay males. Interested readers can find a fuller explanation of the ways in which heterosexuals, gay males, and lesbians differ and are similar with regard to cognition in a book by LeVay (1996).

Here is a sampling of the large and rapidly growing body of research in this fascinating area: Gay men scored midway between heterosexual men and women on aiming tasks (Hall & Kimura, 1995; Sanders & Wright, 1993); had a higher verbal IQ than performance IQ, a pattern that is more typical of females than males, with scores on both measures midway between those of females and heterosexual males (Willmott & Brierley, 1984); obtained scores on three measures of spatial ability and one measure of verbal fluency that were midway between the scores of heterosexual males and females, with no significant differences from the female group (McCormick & Witelson, 1991); and performed less well than heterosexual males on mental rotation and other visual–spatial tasks (Gladue et al., 1990; Hall & Kimura, 1995; Sanders & Ross-Field, 1986). Of course, not all of the studies found exactly the same results because the different studies used different sorts of tasks and different measures and sampled from different groups. For example, Halpern and Crothers (1997) found that among college students, gay males outperformed heterosexual males and females on a mental rotation task and scored lower than both groups on a verbal fluency task (generating synonyms). If all of these findings were due to chance, then the expected pattern of results across many studies would average out, which is not the case. The question for this context is what can the atypical pattern of cognitive abilities for gay males tell us about the underlying brain mechanisms of sex differences in cognition?

Brain Correlates of Sexual Orientation

At least seven different studies, conducted in laboratories all over the world, have reported that homosexual men are more likely to be left-handed than heterosexual men (Becker et al., 1992; Gotestam et al., 1992; Halpern & Cass, 1994; Holtzen, 1994; Lindesay, 1987; McCormick et al., 1990; Stellman et al., 1997). Given that handedness is an indicator of cerebral dominance, homosexual men are more likely to be highly lateralized for cognitive tasks or, in other words, are more likely to be more specialized for different tasks in each hemisphere of their brain. On the basis of experimental research with nonhuman mammals, Kerchner and Ward (1992) hypothesized that prenatal hormones are important in the development of a wide range of sex-typical brain organizations and sex-typical behaviors, with strong evidence of their role in determining sexual orientation. Kerchner and Ward (and others) believe that prenatal stress attenuates the surge in testosterone that is critical for male development during the prenatal period. In addition to affecting sexual orientation, the attenuation of testosterone is hypothesized to negatively affect the left hemisphere, which matures more slowly than the right, which increases the incidence of left-handedness. The decrease in testosterone may also result in incomplete masculinization of the POA, the tiny brain structure found to be smaller in homosexual males than in heterosexual males.

Of course, brain structures may not directly cause any particular sexual orientation; they are correlates of sexual orientation that may reflect prenatal and early life hormones that interact with a lifetime of environmental experiences to make us the people that we are. The environmental effects are also complex. For example, Green, Roberts, Williams, Goodman, and Mixon (1987) found that a disproportionately high number of gay men engaged in female-typical play as children. More often than their heterosexual counterparts, gay men played with dolls, role played as females (e.g., dress up), and avoided male-typical rough-and-tumble play. Thus, on average, the gay men had many female-typical childhood experiences, presumably self-selected, that made up their childhood experiences. If you are reading these chapters in order, then you probably recall studies of females who received high levels of adrenal testosterone prenatally. These CAH females also engage in play activities that are more typical of male play behavior, so their early hormone environment affects many life choices and experiences (Berenbaum, 1999). Brain structures and functions vary as a result of experience, making it impossible to disentangle the totality of our biology and life experiences.

CRITIQUE OF BIOLOGICAL HYPOTHESES

Should society halt research that generates such knowledge?
—Hunt (1999, p. 347)

Why are so many people opposed to any biological theory of cognitive sex differences? Perhaps we can understand some of the intense emotions generated by biologically based theories by examining their weaknesses.

Biological and Environmental Interactions

Sex-related brain differences result from prenatal and postnatal hormone levels, and they are influenced by sex-differentiated patterns of socialization. Most of the biological theories discussed in this chapter either have failed to consider or have downplayed the fact that biology and the environment interact. For example, although it is possible that males are better at spatial skills because their cerebral organization is more lateralized than that of females, it also might be possible that because males excel at spatial skills or perform them more frequently, their hemispheres develop a more lateralized organization. Similarly, we know that young girls receive more verbal stimulation and are encouraged to read and speak correctly. (These data are described more fully in the next chapter.) Their early reliance on verbal skills could cause verbal skills to be developed at the expense of other types of abilities, such as spatial skills. Although the possibility that life experiences influence biological processes such as brain lateralization must be considered, it is also clear that biology influences the types of experiences to which people are exposed. For example, if boys are better than girls at spatial tasks for biological reasons, parents could differentially encourage this ability by buying them spatial toys (e.g., puzzles, erector sets), which in turn provide them with more experience with spatial manipulations than their sisters would receive. Numerous other examples are possible.

As an example of the difficulty in disentangling biological from environmental influences, consider the following problem that has come to be known as the "20th-century conundrum." Over the past two generations, girls have begun menstruating at an earlier age than their mothers, who experienced earlier menarche than their mothers (Frisch, 1983). Although no one is really sure why this has been happening, it is probably related to improved nutrition, sanitation, increased prevalence of pesticides in food and the environment that can act like hormones, and changes in work environments. According to Waber (1977), early menarche implies early physical maturation, which is related to bilateral cerebral organization. Taken to its logical conclusion, we would have to conclude that the improved living conditions of the 20th century have been detrimental to women's spatial ability! This is an unsatisfactory conclusion because it implies that conditions that are good for women's physical development are bad for their intellectual development. In addition, early menarche among 20th-century girls would also predict that the current generation of young women are less adept at spatial skills than their mothers, who in turn are less adept at spatial skills than their mothers. All of the evidence suggests the reverse—today's young women are better at spatial tasks than previous generations of women. Women have been entering traditional academic fields that require these skills at increasing rates over the past 20 years. Almost all engineering and architecture schools report that the proportions of women have increased substantially since the women's movement began in the 1960s. Even if these demographic data only reflect changes in societal expectations, they certainly are not consistent with the idea that females are becoming less adept at spatial tasks, as biological data might suggest. Biological explanations cannot account for this phenomenon.

In contrast, psychosocial variables cannot account for all of the sex differences data presented in chapters 4 and 5, which considered genes, hormones, and brains—all of which differ in important ways that would be expected to produce sex differences in a variety of behaviors. Some of the strongest data are the recent findings that the administration of sex hormones to healthy adults can improve some types of cognitive skills, depending on which hormone is administered, such as the finding that testosterone improves spatial, but not verbal, skills in males and the finding that estrogens can reverse or delay the ravages of Alzheimer's disease in older women (Buckwalter et al., 1993; Janowsky et al., 1994).

Quantitative Abilities

You may have been wondering why I haven't mentioned quantitative or mathematical abilities in this chapter. The reason is that there are no good theories of sex-related brain differences that can account for the finding that females excel on computation during early development and males score higher on some tests of mathematical reasoning abilities, such as the SAT–M. Gardner (1983) used the fact that there are idiot savants with exceptional mathematical skill as evidence that mathematics is a distinct, localizable intellectual ability, but mathematical ability is difficult to localize. Some mathematical problems are largely verbal in nature, such as some word problems, and others are clearly spatial in nature, such as some geometry problems.

A severe mathematics disability called acalculia is usually found when there is left-hemisphere damage, and dyscalculia, the mathematics analogue to dyslexia, frequently accompanies severe language disorders (Spiers, 1987). Damage to the right hemisphere frequently causes difficulties in developing spatial relations, a skill that is fundamental in mathematics. Thus, we can conclude that mathematics requires the use of both right and left hemispheres, so lateralization theories cannot be useful in understanding sex differences in mathematics. Mathematical abilities don't divide neatly into categories because there is so much variation in terms of the underlying cognitive processes.

The Notion of Optimal Cerebral Organization, Optimal Hormone Concentration, and Optimal Genetic Configuration

Complex cognitive tasks are multidimensional in nature, so there can be no single optimal cerebral organization, best hormone balance, or optimal genetic pattern. Consider the fact that male and female brains differ along several dimensions, with the smaller female brain composed of more densely packed neural units, a higher level of neural activity (as recorded on EEGs), and higher regional cerebral blood flow. Size cannot be considered without reference to all of the other systems and structures that reflect brain action. Single dimensions cannot be used in understanding systems in which multiple components interact.

It may even be that an optimal organization for males is not optimal for females. Perhaps bilateral organization is best when the hormone concentrations are female, and lateralized cerebral organization is best when the hormone concentrations are male. The finding that males tend to be more lateralized and better at spatial tasks does not mean that they are better at spatial tasks because they are more lateralized. They could be better at spatial tasks for environmental reasons and more lateralized for unrelated biological reasons. It does not necessarily follow that lateralization is the optimal brain organization for spatial ability because it is found more frequently in the sex that tends to have better spatial ability.

Intervening Variables

It is also possible that biology affects the development of cognitive skills in indirect ways that are generally not considered by proponents of the biological theories. Evidence was provided in the last chapter for the position that aggressive behavior is, at least in part, under hormonal control. Research with lower animals has clearly shown a link between prenatal hormones and later aggressive behavior and energy levels. Although the research reviewed with humans is less clear, there is still good reason to believe that prenatal and possibly postnatal hormones play a role in human aggression and activity levels. Suppose that males tend to be more active because of higher levels of prenatal hormones. Individuals who are more active would be expected to develop better spatial skills because they move around the environment more often, roam farther at an earlier age, and interact with more objects. Thus, there could be biological reasons for sex differences in cognitive abilities, but they could be different from those being investigated.

A second intervening variable that could mediate between biology and environment is body type. Consider the notion that early maturing adolescents have poorer spatial skills than late-maturing adolescents (Waber, 1976, 1977). As Waber pointed out, early maturing adolescents not only may have different patterns of cerebral lateralization but also may have different social environments. Shapely seventh-grade girls and tall, muscular seventh-grade boys are responded to differently than their less developed peers. This could cause them to consider their math and science classes less seriously and create or increase differences in these areas that correlate with maturation rate. Support for these hypotheses is examined in the following chapter.

Body type is also a likely intervening variable for individuals with genetic or hormonal abnormalities. Much of the research in this area has used women with Turner's syndrome to support or refute biological arguments. As stated earlier, these women have unfeminine body types (small breasts, thick necks). Their body type could cause them, consciously or unconsciously, to exaggerate feminine traits, including eschewing stereotypically masculine cognitive skills. Hier and Crowley's (1982) research on minimal androgen levels examined males with underdeveloped testes. Although the finding that they were poorer on "masculine" tasks goes against the idea that they attempted to compensate for their feminine body type, it does seem likely that they sought certain experiences that would help them adjust to their body type. It is difficult to know how these special experiences affected their cognitive growth.

Differences and Deficiencies

It may be no benefit to society to assume that the two sexes are basically homogeneous
with respect to cognition and that the only heterogeneity
is that imposed by different experience. Zero variation
is not a requirement of equal opportunity.
—Witelson (1988, p. 217)

Many people are concerned that if we concede that there are sex differences in the "underlying hardware" of human thought, then those who are anxious to keep women out of nontraditional occupations will use this finding to justify discrimination. Weisstein (1982) offered a stern caveat when she said, "Biology has always been used as a curse against women" (p. 41). It is important to keep in mind that sex differences are not synonymous with sexism. The empirical research that has been reviewed in this chapter is not antifemale. It is neither misogynist nor antifeminist to report that, on average, males have superior spatial ability and females have superior verbal ability and that some of these differences could be biologically based. It could even be argued that these results are more profemale because verbal abilities are needed in every academic field and every endeavor in life and females, on average, demonstrate higher verbal abilities for important real-world tasks like verbal fluency, spelling, and writing.

It is also important to keep in mind that although the major focus of this book and research in this area is on sex differences, similarities are more often the rule. In McGlone's (1980) review of the cerebral asymmetry literature, she concluded, "Thus, one must not overlook perhaps the most basic conclusion, which is that basic patterns of male and female brain asymmetry seem to be more similar than they are different" (p. 226). Perhaps the most striking finding from all of the neuropsychological research is the overwhelming number of similarities between the sexes and the relatively few sex differences that have emerged.

We know that there are sex differences in cognitive abilities, sex hormone concentrations, and probably patterns of cerebral organization. There are also indisputable sex differences in the reproductive organs and genitals. No one would argue that either sex has the better reproductive organs or genitals. They are clearly different, but neither sex would be considered deficient in these biological organs. However, when cognitive differences are considered, there is sometimes an implicit notion that one sex will be found better than the other. Is it better to be high in verbal skills or spatial skills? This is a moot question. The answer depends on the type of task that needs to be performed, the quantification of how much better, and individual predilection. To argue that female hormones are better than male hormones or that male brains are better than female brains is as silly as arguing which sex has the better genitals. It seems almost embarrassing and obvious to state that neither sex has the better biology for intellectual ability and that differences should not be confused with deficits. When it comes to biological explanations for cognitive processes, we still have more questions than answers. It remains the task of future scientists—both females and males—to ask questions and formulate answers about the mutual influences of biology and cognition.

CHAPTER SUMMARY

Gonadal hormones play an important role in the development and organization of the brain. Although hormones affect brain functioning and neuroanatomy throughout the life span, the most critical periods are during prenatal development, when the brain is forming; infancy, when neural connections are forming at high rates of speed; puberty, when excess neural connections are pruned; and late life, when the brain is reducing in overall volume. New brain research has shown that ovarian hormones are important in determining how the brain develops and functions. Earlier research reported that androgens masculinized the brain, which would develop in a female direction without the addition of masculinizing hormones. Recent research has also recognized the critical importance of experience in shaping and altering brain structures and functions. The finding that female and male brains differ in some ways reflects the interplay of biology and environment.

Cognitive neuroscience is a burgeoning field of study in which performance on cognitive tasks is related to brain activities and anatomy. New imaging techniques are allowing scientists to study intact, normal humans as they perform cognitive tasks. This is an exciting field that is casting new light on our understanding of the brain. It is revealing between-sex differences in many brain systems, including rate of regional cerebral blood flow, areas of the brain activated during cognitive tasks, and the size and shape of some brain structures. For the past 100 years (at least), some scientists have argued that women have smaller and therefore inferior brains. This "size" argument has been used with other groups, including Blacks, to justify discrimination. The idea that "brain power" is directly proportional to overall brain size is simple-minded. Given that females and males achieve the same scores on standardized intelligence tests and on tests that are not written to provide comparable female–male scores (with some subscore differences that reflect differences in cognitive abilities that, overall, cancel), the "small size argument" is clearly wrong. The use of science in service of social agendas is one reason why the study of sex differences is so controversial. Just as modern computers are both smaller and more powerful than earlier models that were large and relatively slow, there is no reason to expect a relationship between overall brain size and intelligence.

Anatomical differences between the sexes are found in some regions of the brain that underlie cognition, in addition to those differences that underlie the biology of reproduction. These structures include the hippocampus, hypothalamus, and corpus callosum. A major theory of sex-related brain differences that are important for cognition involves the specialization of each cerebral hemisphere for cognitive tasks. Although this is an area of intense disagreement, there is ample evidence to conclude that, in general, females are more bilaterally organized for cognitive tasks (i.e., more involvement of both halves of the brain for most cognitive tasks), with at least one portion of the corpus callosum larger in women than in men to reflect the involvement of both hemispheres in most tasks. In addition, there are sex differences within each cerebral hemisphere in the way that different areas are specialized.

Human brains reflect the adaptive pressures of evolution. Not surprisingly, many have suggested that the division of labor in hunter–gatherer societies caused sex differentiation in the way the brain developed. It is undoubtedly true that our brains are the product of evolution, but more direct evidence linking modern sex differences in cognition to brain changes that resulted from this early division of labor is tenuous at best. Information about what an object is and where it is located are processed separately in the brain. We do not yet know if there are sex differences in the way that these two systems operate. This is a fruitful area for future research.

Gay males differ from heterosexual males on those cognitive tasks that usually show sex differences. We also know that there are some brain differences between gay and heterosexual males; however, there are no direct links showing that the anatomical brain differences between gay and heterosexual males can explain performance on the cognitive tasks. We know very little about lesbian subgroup performance on cognitive tasks. It is likely that there are no sexual orientation differences on cognitive tasks for females, but more research is needed before data-based conclusions can be made.

Finally, many weaknesses of biological hypotheses were discussed. Our current knowledge of biological–cognitive linkages remains sketchy and largely incomplete. Even those theories that have received empirical support remain open to criticism on methodological and logical grounds. Readers and researchers are urged to avoid interpreting sex differences as a cognitive deficiency for either sex.

6 Psychosocial Hypotheses Part I: Sex Role Stereotypes Throughout the Life Span

CONTENTS

6

PSYCHOSOCIAL HYPOTHESES PART I: SEX ROLE STEREOTYPES THROUGHOUT THE LIFE SPAN

May you be the mother of a hundred sons.
—traditional Indian blessing (and the title of a book by Bumiller, 1990, that depicts the lives of Indian women)

If you have been reading the chapters in order and just finished the preceding two chapters that examined genetic, hormonal, and brain-based hypotheses about sex differences in cognition, you probably spent much of the time considering alternative hypotheses. Whenever I teach this material to college classes, I always find that there are students who simply cannot wait to point out the ways in which differing life experiences for males and females could be used to explain the data. Hypotheses that favor the nurture side of the nature–nurture controversy are considered in this chapter and the following chapter. In thinking about the way societal effects influence how males and females think, keep in mind the psychobiosocial framework that is used throughout this book. How might biological differences between the sexes be contributing to societal expectations, and how might societal expectations be creating or increasing cognitive sex differences? These two approaches are synthesized and conclusions about the relative merits of each are presented in the concluding chapter.

GENDER AS A SOCIAL CONSTRUCTION

Gender depolarization would ... require a psychological revolution
in our most personal sense of who and what we are as males
and females, a profound alteration in our feelings about the meaning
of our biological sex.
—Bem (1993, p. B2)

Before you left your home this morning, did you smear a waxy, colored substance over your lips? Have you ever shaved the hair on your legs? Do you carry books with your arm extended down your side (as opposed to close to your chest)?

I could make a pretty good guess about whether you are a woman or a man on the basis of how you answered just these three questions. Of course, there are some men who wear lipstick and shave their legs (some swimmers shave their legs to reduce "drag") and many women who don't wear lipstick or shave their legs (especially if we consider a world perspective), but if you answered "yes" to the first two questions, I would most frequently be right in guessing that you are a woman. Similarly, if you said that you carry books with your arm extended, you are probably a man. There is nothing about the biological bases of sex that dictate who wears lipstick, shaves their legs, or carries books in a particular way. These sex differences are societal manifestations of sex—that is, they are social constructions. Proponents of the view that sex differences that are unrelated to reproduction are created by society often prefer to use the term *gender* to emphasize the distinction between biological and sociological influences (e.g., Davis & Gergen, 1997). As Crawford, Chaffin, and Fitton (1995) explained it, *"Gender* is what culture makes out of the 'raw material' of biological sex" (p. 341).

Some of the social constructions of sex are so ingrained in our society that we have come to think of them as "natural," that is, part of the nature, not the nurture, of being male or female. It is only by examining societies that are different from our own that we come to recognize that wearing makeup or shaving the hair off of one's legs is not inherent in being female. Cross-cultural comparisons of cognitive sex differences show both transcultural similarities and important differences. Much of the data available from countries around the world was summarized in chapter 3, in which the data in support of the conclusion that there are sex-related cognitive differences were presented. For example, similar conclusions about sex differences in cognitive abilities were obtained from studies in Sweden (Rosen, 1995), Israel (Cahan & Ganor, 1995; Vakil & Blachstein, 1997), Finland (Portin et al., 1995), New Zealand (Fergusson & Horwood, 1997), and in a cross-cultural meta-analysis of multiple countries (Born, Bleichrodt, & Van der Flier, 1987). Astute readers will notice that some regions of the world are not well represented in the cross-cultural comparisons. Not surprisingly, most of the available data are from North America, Europe, and Asia (Japan and China), with the other parts of the world represented with only a handful of studies. The relative scarcity of psychological information from many parts of the world may be changing as technology opens borders to permit the exchange of information and ideas in ways that never before were possible.

Although there are similarities across countries in the patterns of male and female performance on cognitive tests (e.g., males generally perform better on many visual–spatial tasks and females generally perform better on many memory and verbal tasks), there are important cultural differences. For example, Chinese women perform exceptionally well on the International Mathematics Olympiad, an international mathematics competition that attracts very few female participants (Stanley, 1990). The biology of maleness and femaleness does not change for Chinese students; the exceptional performance of Chinese women in mathematics is related to their intensive course work, coupled with the motivation fueled by the highly competitive examination system for entrance into Chinese colleges.

The Importance of Psychosocial Variables

> *Gender is a complex variable because men and women differ not only biologically, but also in their life experiences. More specifically, men and women's lives tend to differ in ways that at least on the face of it, appear to have relevance to the observed gender differences.*
> —Leibenluft (1996, p. 163)

There can be little doubt that environmental and social factors play a major role in the cognitive development of every member in our society. The crucial question for the purpose of understanding cognitive sex differences is "How, how much, and when in the life span do the socialization practices and other life experiences that differ for males and females influence the ability to perform intellectual tasks?" Of course, this question is based on the assumption that life experiences differ in systematic ways depending on biological sex. I have found that some people are willing to accept this assumption at face value, taking it as a statement of the obvious, and are eager to consider the ramifications of these differences. Others, however, believe that sex-differentiated socialization practices are a thing of the past. Advocates of this point of view believe the magazine and billboard ads that proclaim, "You've come a long way baby!" The underlying message is that contemporary women do the same sorts of things that men do and sex-related differences in life experiences are either inconsequential or nonexistent. It is ironic to note the subtle influence of language as typified in this slogan that supposedly announces sexual equality. If women had, in fact, "come a long way," then they would not be referred to as infants or children, just as Black men are no longer called "boy." (These ads, which you probably recognize, are designed to sell cigarettes. The incidence of lung cancer among women is now almost as high as that among men. The ad is correct with respect to lung cancer. Women have come a long way but, in this case, in the wrong direction.)

If anyone doubts that women and men still tend to live sex-segregated lives in contemporary U.S. society, a casual visit to a parent–teacher association meeting, the restaurant in a large department store midweek, a trade union hall, or a corporate engineering department will attest to the fact that although changes in the societal roles of women and men are occurring, there are still considerable differences in men's and women's experiences. High school cheerleaders are still virtually all female, whereas students in shop classes remain virtually all male. Few girls play in the now "coed" little league games (especially in high school leagues), and few boys elect to take home economics classes. Even college students, whose lives seem like they should be a similar mix of attending class, doing homework, working, and engaging in leisure activities, report large sex-related differences in how they spend their time. For example, Astin et al. (1995) found that female students spend much less time exercising, partying, and watching television and much more time on housework, child care, reading for pleasure, and doing volunteer work than male students. In the Astin et al. study, only 7% of the female students, compared with 37% of the male students, spent more than 1 hour per week playing video games. Despite all of the efforts of those associated with the women's movement, de facto sex-related life differences are alive and well.

Implications of Psychosocial Explanations

If we can use psychological and social explanations to understand cognitive sex differences, then the possibility of reducing or eliminating these differences is quite real. In contrast, if we find that we are unable to explain these differences with psychosocial explanations, then there is little hope of being able to alter them by changing learning environments, attitudes, or educational and employment opportunities. Thus, the primary importance of psychosocial hypotheses is not in their heuristic value nor for the development of some abstract theoretical model but in the promise they hold for changing the status quo. Of course, if you are a champion of the status quo, then they are equally important, but for you, they would represent a threat to your preferred hypothesis. In either case, the implications are clear. Psychosocial hypotheses devised to explain the origin of cognitive sex differences have important ramifications for the ways we want society to change or remain the same.

Nonconscious Ideology

Perhaps one of the reasons for the tendency to underestimate sex-differentiated experiences, messages, and expectations is that these differences are so prevalent and so ingrained in life in the United States that we are often unaware of them. In fact, for most of us, it is hard to imagine a society in which they do not exist. Bem and Bem (1976) coined the term *nonconscious ideology* to describe this situation. We are simply unaware of the pervasiveness of sex-differentiated practices. They said that we all are like fish that are unaware that the water is wet. The clothes we wear, the way we furnish our rooms, the toys we were given as children, the hobbies we pursue, the salaries we receive at our jobs, the magazines we read, the household chores we perform, the language we use, and countless other examples all show differences between the sexes. Part of this nonconscious ideology is an unstated assumption that the male is norm and departures from a male pattern of results are therefore deviant.

There are countless examples of the way U.S. and other Western societies have nonconsciously adopted sex-differentiated practices. We expect to see little girls in the advertisements for Barbie dolls and little boys depicted on boxes that contain train sets and, therefore, never stop to consider the powerful messages they convey about sex-appropriate interests and behavior. For example, I remember receiving a prize for serving as president of my high school's honor society. I was delighted with the bracelet I was given. I knew that all of the previous honor society presidents were male, and all of them had received a six-volume set of books by Winston Churchill. Yet, it had never occurred to me that the choice of this particular gift was an excellent example of sex differences in socialization practices. It wasn't until many years later that I was struck with the irony of the gift. Like most other people, I was simply unaware of the numerous subtle and not so subtle practices in our sex-differentiated society.

Later in life, when my own children were in school, I complained to the principal of our local elementary school when I learned that there would be two winners for a school fund-raiser—the boy and the girl who sold the most raffle tickets. The boy's prize was to be a walkie-talkie set, and the girl's prize was to be a stuffed animal. The principal did not understand my concern. He assured me that boys like walkie-talkies and girls like stuffed animals. I suggested that if he wanted to name two winners, why not let them be the top two children who sold the most raffle tickets, regardless of their sex, and allow each winner to select either a walkie-talkie or a stuffed animal. The principal could not see any merit in my suggestions, and the prizes were awarded as they had been announced. I do not believe that any single act, like this one, has much effect on the cognitive abilities of children, but they become part of a larger pattern of messages and outcomes that can have a powerful cumulative effect.

The Words We Use

Consider, for example, the simple matter of the grammatically correct use of the pronoun *he* to mean *he or she* (or *she or he*). Sometime in junior or senior high school, we were all taught that the grammatically correct singular pronoun when sex is unknown is *he*. Thus, it is grammatically correct to say, "Everyone should do his homework." There have been many objections to the use of *he* to mean *he or she*. The use of *he* to refer to either sex has become known as the "generic *he*" to signify that its use is much like the use of generic labels for supermarket canned goods. One argument against changing from the generic *he* to either *s/he* or novel terms (e.g., *te* or *E*) is that the issue is trivial and of no real significance. Detractors have humorously labeled this debate as a case of "pronoun envy," a humorous take-off on Freud's theory of penis envy as a major determinant of sex differences. Research has shown, however, that the issue is far from trivial. MacKay (1983) studied the use of the generic *he* to determine its psychological significance. He estimated that the generic *he* is used more than 1 million times throughout an individual's lifetime. In addition, he found that people tend to think of a male whenever the pronoun *he* is used. It is clearly not a sex-neutral or generic term, from a psychological perspective. I remember once reading about the hardships encountered by early U.S. pioneers and their wives. The nonconscious implication is that the women were not pioneers in the same sense that the men were. There is now a considerable body of evidence that people tend to think of males, and not males and females, when they encounter terms like the generic *he*.

Consider this example of the subtle biasing effect that masculine pronouns can have:

> Because students are most familiar with the ways of the college professor, many choose academic careers which can range from the research scientist involved with man's search for knowledge to the psychologist trying to help solve his client's problems. ... The average corporate businessman probably earns at least twice the salary of the college prof, yet he probably has half the education. (example taken from a study of gender-biased language by Murdock & Forsyth, 1985, p. 39)

If you still doubt that the English language conveys a strong male bias, try this: Ask several friends to provide the correct singular terms for (a) a married couple, (b) children, (c) siblings, (d) royalty, (e) the first humans named in the Bible, and (f) people who give parties. See how people give you these terms in the word order in which we expect to hear them—that is, the male term first: (a) husband and wife, (b) sons and daughters, (c) brother and sister, (d) king and queen, (e) Adam and Eve, and (f) host and hostess. It must be more than coincidence that most people name the male term first. Similarly, men are addressed as "Mr." throughout their adult lives, irrespective of their marital status, yet women have traditionally been addressed in relation to the men they marry and carry either the title of "Miss" or "Mrs." There are still many people who object to the use of the marriage-irrelevant title of "Ms." for women. There are no feminine-oriented generics for terms like *bachelor's degree, brotherhood, mankind, spokesman,* and *workmanlike.*

Socialization practices are also reflected in what and how much we say. For example, in an investigation of the nature of parents' speech to their toddlers, O'Brien and Nagle (1987) found that when children of both sexes play with dolls (a typical female toy), their parents provide more opportunities to learn and practice language than when they play with trucks and cars (typical male toys) and shape sorters (sex-neutral toys). These authors argued that young girls receive more language practice and encouragement than young boys because girls play with dolls much more often than boys do. Other evidence of sex differences in adults' conversations with children was reported by Wells (1986). Wells found that when adults talk to boys, they encourage "a more free-ranging exploratory manipulation of the physical environment," whereas in discussions with girls, adults emphasize domestic activities (p. 123).

Causal Statements and Psychosocial Research

Critics of research on psychosocial influences on sex differences in cognition are quick to point out that sex differences in language usage cannot be used to infer causality because these data are correlational in nature; that is, we cannot determine if children act in sex-differentiated ways because of the language we use, or if we use sex-differentiated language because children act in sex-differentiated ways. I discussed the limitations of correlational research in chapter 2, and it is instructive to reconsider correlational research in this context. Although it can be more difficult to establish causality with social variables than with biological ones because we cannot assign people at random to different long-term social situations, it is not impossible. We can look to other societies as well as to variations within a particular society to illuminate the relationship between social variables and sex differences. For example, we could compare children who live in the same neighborhood and attend the same school but differ in the way their families encourage or discourage sex-role stereotypic behaviors. As you read about the psychosocial research that has been conducted on cognitive sex differences, be sure to keep these criticisms in mind and be as tough a critic as you undoubtedly were for the biological hypotheses.

SEX ROLES AND SEX ROLE STEREOTYPES

Girls' play involves dressing and grooming and acting out their
future—going on a date, getting married—and boys' play
involves competition and conflict.
—Bozarth (spokesperson for Mattel, Inc.; cited in "Stereotypes 'R' Us," 1990, p. 20)

A *stereotype* is "a relatively rigid and oversimplified conception of a group of people in which all individuals in the group are labeled with the socalled group characteristics" (Wrightsman, 1977, p. 672). As a society, we have stereotypes about racial groups (e.g., "Blacks are musical."), nations (e.g., "The Scots are thrifty."), sports groups (e.g., "Football players are dumb."), people who wear eyeglasses, New Yorkers, redheads, obese people, cellists, Republicans, and so on. Any of these stereotypes can influence interactions, feelings, and expectations. Sex role stereotypes are those stereotypes that relate to differences between the sexes. For the purposes of this discussion, the term *sex role stereotypes* is used to encompass widely held assumptions about what females and males are like, as well as what they ought to be like. Sometimes authors make a distinction between these two components of the term *sex role stereotypes* (e.g., Eagly, 1987). Two questions concerning sex role stereotypes that have been raised are: Is there any evidence that they exist, and if so, can these stereotypes be used to understand sex differences in cognitive abilities?

What are the stereotypes about women and men that exist in North America today? This question has been researched extensively by psychologists, sociologists, and others during the past several decades. In the numerous studies that have been conducted (Broverman et al., 1972; Intons-Peterson, 1988; Maccoby, 1995; Spence, Helmreich, & Stapp, 1974), two distinct clusters of traits have emerged. In general, male stereotypic traits suggest competence and task orientation, a cluster of traits sometimes known as "instrumental," whereas female stereotypic traits suggest warmth and expressiveness.

Most studies of sex role stereotypes have gone beyond the notion that certain traits or characteristics are associated exclusively with being male or female. Deaux (1984), for example, examined the relative frequency with which traits are associated with either sex. As shown in Table 6.1, some characteristics are believed to be found more often in one sex or the other. Consider, for example, the role of "financial provider." According to Deaux's results, we expect about 83% of all males to be financial providers, whereas we expect only about 47% of females to assume this role. These data indicate that sex role stereotypes are alive and well in contemporary U.S. society; however, instead of being attributed in an all-or-none fashion, most people acknowledge that the overlap between the sexes with regard to these characteristics.

A similar approach to understanding the attributes that constitute sex role stereotypes was taken by Intons-Peterson (1988). The purpose of her study was to compare sex role beliefs of Americans with those of the Swedish. In the process, she compiled a list of attributes that Americans believe to be true of females, males, and both sexes. These attributes are shown in the overlapping circles in Fig. 6.1. The attributes that are listed in the overlapping portion are those that are associated with both females and males, for example, "friendly" and "hardworking." The attributes in the outer portions are associated with either females (e.g., "aware

TABLE 6.1
Stereotypes of males' and Females' Probability Judgments

Characteristic	Judgment[a]	
	Men	Women
Trait		
Independent	.78	.58
Competitive	.82	.64
Warm	.66	.77
Emotional	.56	.84
Role behaviors		
Financial provider	.83	.47
Takes initiative with opposite sex	.82	.54
Takes care of children	.50	.85
Cooks meals	.42	.85
Physical characteristics		
Muscular	.64	.36
Deep voice	.73	.30
Graceful	.45	.68
Small-boned.39.62		

[a]Probability that the average person of either sex would possess a characteristic. Copyright (1985) by the American Psychological Association. Reprinted by permission of the author.

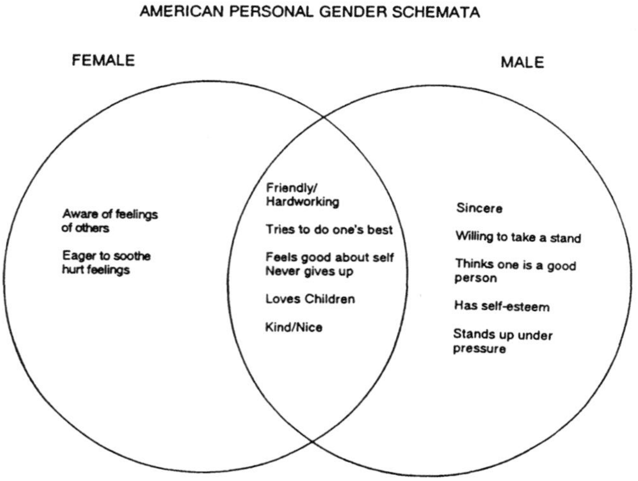

AMERICAN PERSONAL GENDER SCHEMATA

FEMALE   MALE

Aware of feelings
of others

Eager to soothe
hurt feelings

Friendly/
Hardworking

Tries to do one's best

Feels good about self
Never gives up

Loves Children

Kind/Nice

Sincere

Willing to take a stand

Thinks one is a good
person

Has self-esteem

Stands up under
pressure

FIG. 6.1.   Overlapping and distinct traits that are associated with the American Person Gender Schema. From Gender Concepts of Swedish and American Youth (p.
179), by M. G. Intons-Peterson, 1988, Hillsdale, NJ: Lawrence Erlbaum Associates.
Copyright 1988 by Lawrence Erlbaum Associates. Reprinted with permission.

of feelings of others") or males (e.g., "stands up under pressure"). Thus, sex role
stereotypes do not consist of two dichotomous categories, one for females and one
for males. Instead, they are overlapping categories with expectations about different traits and behaviors statistically associated more often with the female or male
sex role.

Repeatedly, the term *sex roles* has come under attack (Lopata & Thorne, 1978).
Those opposed to the term have argued that because we don't use terms like *race
roles* or *class roles,* why should researchers be so concerned with reifying (making a
theoretical concept real or concrete by giving it a label) the concept of sex roles? It
also has been argued that other roles in life, like that of student, factory worker, or
young adult, undergo changes as our life situations change, whereas sex roles don't
change because they are tied to biological sex. It is also frequently argued that the
term *gender roles* is more appropriate than *sex roles* because the term denotes societal rather than biological influences. Despite all of the rhetoric generated by this
term, it is likely to remain in the psychological and sociological literature. One of the
leading journals in the area of sex differences is entitled *Sex Roles,* and the term
seems to have an intuitive meaning for people outside of academia.

It is a widely held belief that sex role stereotypes, those beliefs about behaviors
and dispositions that characterize males and females in our society, exert strong influences on male and female behavior. Eagly (1987) defined them this way: "Gender roles are defined as those shared expectations (about appropriate qualities and

behaviors) that apply to individuals on the basis of their socially identified gender" (p. 12). These stereotypes seem to be narrower or to allow fewer options for males, leaving boys and men fewer choices and dispositional alternatives. Generally, it is far more deviant for a male to engage in traditionally female activities (e.g., home-maker, nurse, secretary) than it is for a female to enter the traditional man's world (e.g., medicine, physics, trucking, plumbing). Many psychologists believe that the female sex role is a devalued role with less self-esteem and prestige than the male sex role (Intons-Peterson, 1988), which may explain why men who assume women's roles are seen as more deviant than women who assume men's roles.

As part of the sex roles we were taught as children, young girls learned that they will be prized for their beauty, and young boys learned that they will be valued for their money and prestige. If you doubt that this is true, find a few friends and tell them that you saw a wealthy, old, pot-bellied man enter an expensive restaurant with a gorgeous young woman "on his arm." Ask them to guess the relationship between these two people. Most will respond in a way that is consistent with the notion that the man traded what is valuable for men (money and prestige) for what is valuable for women (beauty).

Accordingly, it should not be surprising to find that men outnumber women in the "hard" sciences that are both high-paying and prestigious. Mathematics, for example, is a masculine-typed academic subject. One possible explanation for the disparity in sex ratios among mathematically gifted youth is the unwillingness of girls to be identified with mathematics and/or their unwillingness to devote their time to the rigorous demands of mathematics—time that could be spent on "appropriate" female activities like curling their hair and painting their nails. A report in *Time* magazine (Fall, 1990) found that women use 17 to 21 grooming products every morning (e.g., shampoo, cream rinse, lipstick, mascara, face powder, blush, cologne, hand lotion). With so much time spent on grooming, is it any wonder that females are not achieving at the same rate as men?

The impact of sex role stereotypes comes from pervasive lifelong influences to conform to a pattern of behavior that is prescribed by sex. Sex differences in cognitive abilities mirror sex stereotypes about abilities, making it very difficult to determine the extent to which abilities differences and stereotype differences influence each other. The sex role literature is extensive. It contains numerous confirmations of the hypothesis that these stereotypes exert powerful influences on the way we think and behave. For example, in a poll of voters, female politicians were described as "hardworking," "more caring," and "more ethical"; male politicians were described as "tougher" and "emotionally suited for politics" (Skelton, 1990, p. A1). It is difficult to know how these beliefs affect voting patterns, but there is ample evidence that racial and religious stereotypes have affected the outcome of numerous political campaigns. Few would doubt that sex role stereotypes have kept qualified candidates from office.

Consider, for example, a study that investigated the way sex role stereotypes influence memory (Halpern, 1985). High school students were asked to read a fairly bland story about 2 days in the life of a protagonist. For half the high school students, the main character was named Linda; for the other half, the main character was named David. It was hypothesized that errors in memory for stated events and inferences about the main character's goals and motives would be biased toward conformity with sex role stereotypes. In general, the results confirmed the hypothesis that sex role stereotypes influenced the way the students remembered information that was presented in the story. When these results were described to the students who participated in this study, they were surprised. Most of the students were unaware of the extent to which they maintained sex role stereotypes and of the possibility that these stereotypes were influencing how they think and remember. These results were confirmed in a study by Buczek (1986) in which he found that both professional counselors and college students recalled less information from female clients than from male clients. (For a more detailed discussion of the effect of stereotypes on memory and thought processes, see Halpern, 1996c.)

If you doubt whether sex role stereotypes still exist, consider a few of the questions taken from a questionnaire that was designed to show that sex role socialization is alive and well in contemporary society (Jonides & Rozin, 1999, p. 183):

Would you be willing to kill a cockroach by slapping it with your hands?   a) yes b) no

When you are depressed, does washing your hair make you feel better?   a) yes b) no

Do you walk around freely in the nude in a locker room?   a) yes b) no

Can you sew well enough to make clothes?   a)yes b)no

Ask several male and female friends and see if you can detect a sex-related difference in the way your friends answer these questions. How does sex role socialization explain these differences?

Sex Role Identification as a Mediator in Intellectual Development

Many women in our present culture value mathematical ignorance
as if it were a social grace.
—Osen (cited in Burton, 1978, p. 35)

Although there are numerous conceptions of the way sex role stereotypes operate to influence behavior, a modal or typical model assumes that individuals identify with and conform to a particular sex role stereotype. Consider, for example, the fact that mathematical ability is often perceived to be part of the male sex role stereotype. As boys learn their sex roles, they identify with the notion that they should excel at mathematics. Jobs that require an advanced knowledge of mathematics (e.g., accountant, economist, physicist) also tend to have high prestige and to be high-paying, two additional components of the male sex role. Girls, in contrast, learn that mathematical ability is unfeminine and thus avoid advanced mathematics courses. With few females in the field of advanced mathematics, it becomes even more difficult for females to make it in a male-dominated field. In this way, multiple components of sex roles keep different areas of life predominantly single-sex. A man who would consider becoming a preschool teacher or a nurse would face even more resistance because the boundaries for the male sex role are enforced more strictly than those for the female sex role.

Several researchers have proposed more specific models of the way stereotypes influence behaviors (e.g., Deaux & Major, 1987). Let's consider in more detail a model proposed by Eagly (1987). Eagley's model emphasizes the individual as a recipient of social pressures. Each individual reacts in ways that conform to these pressures. Sex differences are a product of the "social rules that regulate behavior in adult life" (Eagly, 1987, p. 7). Eagly used this model to explain why women are better at decoding nonverbal cues than men (a finding reported by Hall & Halberstadt, 1986). Because the female role includes nurturing, women develop a greater sensitivity to nonverbal cues and then, with practice and attention, become better attuned to them. Thus, this sex difference is the result of sex role stereotypes. Although Eagly acknowledged that there may be sex-differentiated biological propensities, she maintained that sex role stereotypes are also important in the creation of sex differences.

Masculine and feminine stereotypes used to be viewed as separate and orthogonal or independent concepts. During the early 1970s, however, several psychologists (Bem, 1974; Constantinople, 1973; Spence et al., 1974) developed a multidimensional conception of the traits that constitute sex role stereotypes and the term *androgynous* became a ubiquitous buzzword in the literature. Individuals of either sex who reported both typical female and male traits were labeled *androgynous*. Some researchers also adopted the term *undifferentiated* to refer to individuals who reported very few feminine or masculine traits. Unlike their androgynous peers who exhibited both masculine and feminine traits, undifferentiated individuals seemed to exhibit very few of the traits associated with either sex role. This type of research introduced a third construct into the literature—*self-concept,* which refers to individuals' beliefs about themselves. According to this view, anyone could believe that she or he does not conform to generalizations about females or males. For example, you might believe that, in general, men are more aggressive than women and also that you are a woman who is more aggressive than most men or a man who is less aggressive than most women. Thus, although most of us maintain sex role stereotypes that we believe apply to most people, we may or may not believe that we conform to them.

A deluge of research followed from the classification of self-reports of sex-typed behaviors and dispositions into masculine, feminine, androgynous, and undifferentiated typological categories. It seems that these categories have been related to almost every conceivable variable. Very often the assumption underlying the research was that "androgyny is good." Androgyny has been examined as a mediating variable that affects success, career choice, psychosomatic problems, locus of control, self-esteem, and sexual behavior (Cook, 1985). Given the immense popularity of sex role stereotypes and self-concept, it should not be surprising that they were also investigated as mediators of intellectual development. Using this framework, Mills (1981) tested the hypothesis that mathematics and verbal skill achievement would be related to sex role identification, or the extent to which someone identifies with the female or male sex role stereotype. She found a positive relationship between mathematical achievement and masculine traits for girls (i.e., the girls who had a more masculine self-identification performed better) and between verbal skills achievement and feminine traits for boys (i.e., the boys who had a more feminine self-identification performed better). On the basis of this study, she concluded that cross-sexed characteristics seemed to be associated with success in traditionally masculine (i.e., mathematics) content areas and traditionally feminine characteristics were associated with success in traditionally feminine (i.e., verbal) content areas.

The hypothesis that sex role identification can explain sex differences on some cognitive tasks has not held up well over the past two decades. For example, Robert (1990) found that a majority of people did not consider the Water-Level Task (the one that requires participants to draw an approximately horizontal line in a picture of a titled glass to indicate their knowledge that the top of the water level will be horizontal regardless of the tilt of the glass) to be either masculine or feminine. You should recall that this is one task that shows consistent sex differences in favor of males. Robert's conclusion that the Water-Level Task is not sex-typed has been replicated by other investigators, showing that between-sex performance differences on this task are unrelated to beliefs about the masculine or feminine nature of the task (Goodrich, Damin, Ascione, & Thompson, 1993).

Several studies have shown that the actual relationship between achievement and personality characteristics is quite complex. There is a vast psychological literature that has addressed the possibility that cognitive sex differences exist as a result of conformity to sex role stereotypes. Signorella and Jamison (1986) summarized the literature in a meta-analytic review of the research. They concluded that there is no evidence that androgyny is associated with better cognitive performance. For spatial and mathematical tasks, they found limited support for the notion that girls who had higher masculine and lower feminine self-concept scores tended to perform well on these masculine sex-typed tasks. However, the proposed relationship was not found for boys on any of the cognitive tasks or for girls on verbal tasks. Thus, the idea that "individuals will perform better on cognitive tasks when the masculinity and femininity of their self concepts is consistent with the gender stereotyping of the tasks" (Signorella & Jamison, 1986, p. 207) has received minimal support. It seems likely that a web of other contributing variables will have to be unraveled before any conclusive statements about the relationship between sex role identification and academic area of achievement can be made.

Interests, Values, and Attitudes.   There are strong and consistent differences in the interests, values, and attitudes of females and males in contemporary Western society, This conclusion is based on studies using the Allport–Vernon–Lindzey Scale of Values (Allport, Vernon, & Lindzey, 1970) assessment instrument over many decades (Lubinski, Schmidt, & Benbow, 1996). The scale yields patterns of interest that are typical of either males or females. These differences in interest reflect the differences that are found in male-typical and female-typical vocational choices. In fact, scales of this sort are frequently used in career counseling. Recently, Lippa (1998) examined sex differences along a personality dimension anchored at one end with *people*-oriented interests and at the other end with *thing*-oriented interests. The *people-thing* dimension is an index of the extent to which individuals prefer work that involves interpersonal tasks (teaching, taking care of, or directing others) or impersonal tasks (working with machines or tools). He found a strong relationship between sex and scores on this scale. With participants from three separate studies, females showed a strong preference for the *people* end of the dimension, and males showed a strong preferences for the *things* end of the dimension.

Differences in values and interests were also reported in a study of secondary school students in London (Lightbody, Siann, Stocks, & Walsh, 1996). In general, the girls in this study reported that they liked school more than the boys did. The girls also showed greater liking for English, French, German, history, drama, music, and home economics classes. The boys preferred the sciences, craft and design technology, physical education, and information technology. The girls believed that working hard and having a teacher who liked you were important for success in school, whereas the boys believed that cleverness, talent, and luck were more important for success in school. When considering complex social variables like preferences and beliefs, it is difficult to determine what is causal. We don't know if the differences in the girls' and boys' beliefs reflect sex-related differences in their experiences or in their perceptions of similar experiences. Regardless of the direction of the causal arrow, it is easy to see how greater liking will lead to higher motivation, more course work in a particular subject area, and expectations about success, followed by increased knowledge and skill. The interwoven web of variables operates in ways that support beliefs about the differences between the sexes.

Are Sex Role Stereotypes Changing?

Gender is a biologically based social category.
—Hood, Draper, Crockett, and Petersen (1987, p. 65)

I have frequently been told by my students that "this sex role stereotype stuff is old hat." Many people believe that sex roles have little relevance for today's young adults. The data that provide an answer to the question of whether sex role stereotypes are changing provide a mixed picture. Like all complex questions, it seems that the answer depends on exactly what comparisons are being made and whether you view the results from the perspective of a "glass half empty or half full." For example, Lewin and Tragos (1987) compared the attitudes of adolescents toward sex role stereotyping in 1956 with those of adolescents in 1982. In 1956, the United States was in the midst of the postwar baby boom. Women were pressured to leave the jobs they held during the war so that the returning GIs could find employment. (Many women served valiantly in World War II, but in comparison with the number of men, the number of women who served in World War II is small.) The women, of course, were to get married, stay home, and have babies, in that order. You're probably thinking that U.S. sex role stereotypes have changed radically since the baby boom years. Well, if that's what you're thinking, you're wrong. Lewin and Tragos found very few differences between the attitudes expressed by adolescents in 1982 and those expressed by adolescents in 1956. They concluded that there is "only modest evidence of the impact of the feminist movement" (Lewin & Tragos, 1987, p. 131). The only difference was that girls in the 1982 survey expressed more satisfaction about being female than their earlier contemporaries. "Contrary to our prediction, sex role stereotyping was not significantly less in 1982 than in 1956" (Lewin & Tragos, 1987, p. 125).

When other measures are used, however, large, meaningful differences are found. Consider the percentage of respondents who agreed with the statement, "The activities of married women are best confined to home and family" (reported in Myers, 1998, p. 566). In 1967, approximately 65% of men agreed, compared with approximately 30% in 1995. For women, approximately 45% agreed in 1967, and less than 20% agreed in 1995. Employment figures also show large changes in some areas, such as the percentage of women who work outside of the home and the number of women entering some formerly traditionally men's fields like law and medicine. But sex differences remain stable in other areas, such as secretarial work, in which more than 90% are women, and engineering, in which the overwhelming majority are men. I have excluded from this list any reference to activities in which body size is an advantage, like moving furniture, where more men might be expected because of their average larger size. Even in areas where physical size might be important, like moving furniture, women who are physically able to do the work are largely absent from that segment of the workforce. Similarly, women can vote in most, but not all, countries that hold popular elections, which is a major change over the past 100 years, but women still are rare among world leaders. Perhaps the best answer to the question about changing sex role stereotypes is that change over the past century has been slow and uneven. In 1946, Eleanor Roosevelt summed it up this way, "Against odds, women inch forward" (quoted in Myers, 1998, p. 566).

Sally Forth cartoon. Reprinted with special permission of North America Syndicate.

HOW STEREOTYPES DIRECT AND REFLECT REALITY

Gender typing must be viewed as multidimensional, encompassing such varied domains as activities and interests (toys, play activities, household roles, and tasks), personal–social attributes (personality characteristics and social behavior, such as aggression, dominance, dependence, and nurturance), social relationships (sex of playmates, friends), and stylistic and symbolic characteristics (gestures and nonverbal behavior, speech, and language patterns).
—Turner and Gervai (1995, p. 759)

People are expected to behave in ways that are consistent with socially defined sex roles (Eagly, Karau, & Makhijani, 1995). Sex role stereotypes provide the "shoulds" for much of our behavior and, for this reason, have limited the possibilities for both men and women. Although much has been written about the deleterious effects of sex roles on women, they have been at least as damaging for men (Levant, 1996; Levant & Pollack, 1995). As explained earlier, women's traits cluster around an expressive–warmth–interpersonal dimension, and men's traits cluster around a competence–object dimension. Asking if it is better to exhibit warmth or competence is like asking if you prefer blue objects or triangles. There is no right answer, except for the possibility that both are desirable.

There is the general perception that stereotypes about girls and women are more negative than those about boys and men (Unger & Crawford, 1992). But Eagly and her colleagues have found that, at least in the United States and Canada, the stereotypes about women often tend to be more positive than those about men (Eagly, Mladinic, & Otto, 1994), with positive and negative aspects associated with both sex roles. I note here that the concern about the negative parts of the female sex role is clearly justified in many other countries in the world. As I write this section, women in Afghanistan are not permitted an education, women are sold as slaves in Sudan, and female infanticide is a horrendous reality in many parts of the world. Even though the data reported are mostly from the United States, Canada, and some countries in Europe, overt discrimination against females, including death, is a harsh reality in some parts of the world, a critical point that I return to in the last chapter.

Where did sex role stereotypes come from? Cross-cultural similarities suggest that they have a biological basis, but cross-cultural differences also show that they have been molded to fit particular societal contexts. Most secretaries are women, and most corporate executives are men. Secretarial jobs are consistent with sex role stereotypes about women's skills and abilities (supportive, neat, follows orders, low professional aspirations, and poorly paid), and executive jobs are consistent with sex role stereotypes about men's skills and abilities (forceful, able to lead, aggressive, smart, and well paid). Differences in the status of some jobs in other parts of the world provide an interesting perspective on the interactive relationship between defining and reflecting reality. In Russia, for example, a physician is a low-status job that does not pay well. Can you guess which sex constitutes the majority of physicians in Russia? If you guessed women, you are correct. Thus, stereotypes both define and reflect reality.

The Threat Is Real: Automatic Activation of Sex Role Stereotypes

There is convincing evidence that categorization on the basis of sex and race (and the activation of associated stereotypes in those categories) occurs prior to conscious awareness, involving information processing and interpretation that are not subject to conscious, controlled, judgment and decision making.
—Human Capital Initiative Coordinating Committee (1998, p. 15)

In an exciting series of studies conducted over the past several years, Steele and his colleagues (Steele, 1997, 1998; Steele & Aronson, 1995) found that when talented students take an advanced test of mathematics with the usual expectations that men will perform better than women, the usual sex differences in average scores are found—men do score higher than women. When talented students take the same test but are led to believe that there will be no overall sex difference in test scores, then, in fact, none occurs. This surprising result has been replicated several times using different groups and different sorts of stereotypes about the performance of each group. Steele (1997, 1998) called this phenomenon stereotype threat. According to Steele, the following conditions must apply for stereotype threat to operate in a way that depresses performance for members of the group with the negative stereotype:

1. Everyone belongs to some group that has a negative stereotype (e.g., Italians, lawyers, old people, the unemployed, Latinos, Catholics, Arabs, cab drivers, the rich, the poor, people from Minnesota, people who wear glasses, golfers). For stereotype threat to affect performance, the negative stereotype about your group must be relevant to the situation. Thus, if an advanced test of mathematics is given, the negative stereotype that women are not good at mathematics would apply. If you are of Scottish descent, the negative stereotype that the Scots are "thrifty" would not be activated in this situation and would not affect performance.

2. The negative stereotype has to be one that the individual cares about. For example, if you were a woman who is planning a career as a singer, then the negative stereotype that women cannot "do math" will not affect performance on an advanced math test because you would not care about the score you achieved on that test. A stereotype cannot be threatening if you don't care about the outcome.

3. The individual does not have to believe that the stereotype is true. You could honestly believe that women are better than men in math, but if you are aware that many people believe in the stereotype, then it is activated.

4. The activation of a relevant and personally important negative stereotype disrupts performance, and it is this disruption that reduces the scores of group members who are working on difficult problems. Stereotype threat would not be expected to affect performance on a simple test of mathematics, but when the material is difficult, its effects are found.

Steele (1997, 1998) provided powerful demonstrations of the way negative group stereotypes can depress performance on difficult and important tasks, with numerous psychologists extending his research in this area. In an interesting study of Asian women, two different stereotypes were pitted against each other (Shih, Pittinsky, & Ambady, 1999). In one condition, the stereotype that Asians excel at mathematics was made salient by first asking questions that would make the participants aware of their Asian heritage (e.g., Do your parents speak languages other than English?). In another condition, the participants' sex was made salient (e.g., What are some advantages to living in a single-sex dorm?). Relative to a control condition that did not make either of these stereotypes salient, the Asian women answered more questions correctly in the Asian-salient condition than the control and fewer in the sex-salient condition than the control.

Does stereotype threat affect performance on "high stakes" tests such as those administered for college placement or for determining if an advanced placement course in high school can be used for college credit? (Stricker, 1998). Stricker & Ward (1998) examined this possibility. In one study, high school test-takers indicated their sex and ethnicity before taking an Advanced Placement Test in Calculus (Stricker, 1998). A matched-control group answered questions about sex and ethnicity after taking the test. Stricker found no differences between the groups and no evidence of stereotype threat. He also found no evidence that making one's sex or ethnicity salient before a test affected a college-level placement test (Stricker & Ward, 1998).

Stereotype threat is a relatively new line of research that will undoubtedly undergo careful scrutiny and replication in the near future. It provides another demonstration of the way in which stereotypes can both reflect and create reality. It will be interesting to see how the concept develops as various researchers test it in different contexts with different groups.

The Implicit, Automatic, Unconscious Nature of Stereotypes

You may be thinking that none of this discussion about the power of stereotypes is relevant for you because you don't believe in stereotypes. You tend to see each person as an individual and do not have expectations based on an individual's sex or other group membership (e.g., race, religion, type of employment, accent). Well, guess what? You're wrong! There is good evidence that categorization is an essential component in information processing, and we all use group membership categories when we interact with people. We may have different stereotypes and other beliefs, but stereotypes are fundamental to the thought process. Furthermore, they operate without our conscious awareness; they operate automatically (we can't stop them), and sometimes we can't articulate the categories that we are using (they operate implicitly).

There are several lines of research investigating how people think that show the importance of stereotypes, even in simple cognitive tasks. Here is one example: Banaji and Hardin (1996) studied reaction times. When psychologists use reaction times, they are measuring the time it takes to make certain judgments about words or figures that are flashed very briefly on a screen. The reaction times are in the order of 0.5 to 1.5 seconds, so fast that participants cannot "fake" a response. In this study, the experimenters flashed some words on a screen for less than 1 second. Participants then saw a pronoun and had to press a key if the pronoun could apply to the word that was just on the screen. It was a very simple task, but it provided interesting results. Participants were much slower in responding to the pronoun *she* when it followed a male-typical noun like *doctor* than when it followed a female-typical word like *nurse.* Cognitive psychologists use results like these to make inferences about the way information is stored in memory. These results show that in the early stages of information processing, many people do not think of doctors as "she" even though they are consciously aware that many doctors are women.

Here is another example from a study that I conducted with a graduate student, Mary Kevari (Halpern & Kevari, 1997). Our participants were adults who had worked for at least 6 months in a place that employed at least 25 people. We first had every participant write out a list of the names of everyone they worked with, in any order that they were remembered. Why not stop now and try this experiment on yourself? Think of a group you belong to that has at least 25 people in it. It could be a church group, your high school graduating class, or perhaps the members of a club. Take a piece of paper and write the names down the left-hand column in any order that you can recall them. Don't go on until you try this for yourself. Now, go back over the list and next to each name put the sex of each person in one column, then continue using race, age (guess if you have to), and other relevant group information. Look over the order in which you recalled the people in your group. Did you first name your closest friends? That is a common recall strategy that is unrelated to the hypothesis. What happened when you started to slow down in your naming? Do the names cluster by sex or by race? By clustering, I mean that several female names appear one after the other, then several male names appear together. If so, then you showed "clustering in free recall," a phenomenon that had been studied for decades when psychologists gave lists of words to participants to understand what happens in learning and memory when participants are required to learn lists of words. Psychologists learned that people recall items in a category at the same time (e.g., all furniture items, then all animals) because remembering one item in the category acts as a recall aid for the other items in that category. Look over the order in your list. Is there a "run" of women's or men's names? Did you tend to recall people from one ethnic category together? If so, then your list tells you something about how you store information about people in your memory. It does not mean you are a sexist, racist, ageist, or other "ist," but it should be an interesting look into your own memory system. In the study by Halpern and Kevari, we found that the workers showed runs by sex and by race. This means that our participants, unknown to them, stored information about the people they worked with by the sex and race of the individual and used this information as a recall aid. When we explained the results to the participants, they were surprised because none reported that they consciously used these groupings in their recall. (The statistical analysis we used to reach this conclusion is beyond the scope of this discussion, because the actual analysis is done by comparing the number of runs with what would be expected if nothing more than chance were operating.)

The Question of Accuracy

Understanding stereotype accuracy and inaccuracy is much more interesting and complicated than simpleminded accusations of racism or sexism would seem to imply.
—Jussim, McCauley, and Lee (1995, p. 3)

If, as assumed here, stereotypes both define and reflect reality, then it would be expected that stereotypical beliefs about what is true about men and women have, at least, a "kernel of truth." In fact, recent studies of the accuracy of common stereotypes have shown them to be surprisingly accurate. In Eagly's (1995) review of the literature, she concluded that "on the whole, people do not exaggerate sex differences" (p. 145). Most people realize that the sexes show considerable overlap on most traits and skills and reflect the degree of overlap in their stereotypes (Swim, 1994). Furthermore, most people take the context into account when they make their judgments about men and women, showing considerable sensitivity to the situational dependency of behavior. For example, in a large study of teachers' beliefs about their students in sixth-grade math classes (942 girls and 847 boys), the teachers reported that the girls were performing slightly better in math than the boys but that the two sexes were equal in mathematical talent (Jussim & Eccles, 1995). In fact, the girls did have slightly better grades than the boys in their fifth-grade math classes, and there were no sex differences in their scores on standardized math tests. The researchers reported that the teachers did not evidence any bias against girls and that they were very accurate in their assessments. (The teachers said that the girls were achieving higher than the boys despite having equal talent because the girls were trying harder.)

The finding that most people have fairly accurate perceptions about sex differences was surprising and upsetting to those psychologists who believed that common stereotypes ascribe greater dissimilarity to females and males than actually exists. This remains a hot area of contention among some researchers because it "runs against the theoretical Zeitgeist" (Lee, Jussim, & McCauley, 1995, p. xiii).

SEX-LINKED SOCIALIZATION PRACTICES
THROUGH THE LIFE SPAN

If gender is socially constructed, then how are these messages about what males and females are and should be like taught and learned by society members? A common theme among the theories of sex role acquisition is that these messages are conveyed in multiple ways, with positive feedback loops increasing the strength of the message. It is clear that the socialization practices we receive vary with age; therefore, a developmental perspective is assumed in examining this issue. For the purposes of this topic, the life span is broken up into four broad stages: (a) infancy and preschool, (b) middle childhood, (c) adolescence and young adulthood, and (d) middle adulthood and old age. The most salient aspects of sex role socialization practices in each of these broad stages are considered. In keeping with the underlying theme that biological and psychosocial influences are inextricably intertwined, readers are reminded of the possibility of biological–behavioral bidirectional effects at every stage of development. The effects may not be equal at each developmental period, but both operate simultaneously throughout the course of human development.

Infancy and Preschool

The infant departments of retail stores are small worlds divided into colors of pink and blue. Perhaps it is not surprising that the infants
for whom we purchase pink or blue booties, rattles, and diaper bags, grow into children who apply gender schemata to organize the world around them into male and female categories.
—Liben and Bigler (1987, p. 89)

Without the trappings of pink or blue booties, it is extremely difficult to tell if an infant is female or male as long the infant in question is suitably wrapped in a diaper. Perhaps it is because there are so few observable cues that signal the sex of a baby that infants' clothes come color-coded for sex. If you doubt that strong messages about expected behaviors and traits are communicated for boy and girl infants, stop at the "new arrival" card section of any store and look over the words and pictures that announce the birth of a girl or a boy. These messages and images are repeated in cards that are sent to congratulate the new parents. When you visit the home of an infant, look in the baby's room. I have yet to find one where the sex of the infant was not immediately apparent from the furnishings, use of colors, toys, and style of accessories (e.g., frilly vs. plain blankets and bedding). Few parents take it kindly if you mistake their infant son for a daughter, or vice versa.

By the end of the 1st year of life, infants are beginning to categorize people according to their sex (Fagot & Leinbach, 1993). Other group categorizations, such as race, do not occur for several more years. The preference for sex-typed toys is well established in the early preschool years. In a study of 3- to 5-year-olds in Israel, 92% of the children chose a truck as a present for a boy and a doll as a present for a girl (Lobel & Menashri, 1993). These preferences for sex-typed toys are generally found throughout Europe and Japan. As noted in an earlier chapter, girls who are exposed to abnormally high levels of male hormones (because of abnormalities in their adrenal glands) also tend to prefer male-typical toys (Berenbaum & Hines, 1992; Berenbaum & Snyder, 1995). The male-typical toys are more active, and it is probably the preference for activity that underlies some of these results. Parents and other socializing agents also purchase sex-typed toys for young children because it is what the children prefer for play, it is what parents believe their children should prefer, it is what toy marketing departments have told parents that their children prefer, or some interaction of marketing, parent, and child-driven effects.

Many sex differences in cognitive abilities can be found during the infancy and preschool years. For example, in a study that attempted to identify children who were gifted in mathematics at this young age, Robinson et al. (1996) reported that sex differences were apparent in every analysis. The boys' scores were significantly higher than the girls' scores on 8 of the 11 mathematical tests used in their study. For the boys, verbal and visual–spatial factors were more highly correlated, even though the relationships among the cognitive factors were similar for boys and girls. What is unknown is whether boys in preschool or kindergarten have more math-related experiences that allow them to develop these abilities at an earlier age than girls.

Numerous studies have shown that parents respond differently to male and female babies, probably from birth (Rubin, Provenzano, & Luria, 1974). Stewart (1976), for example, found that in the first 6 weeks of life, male infants are handled more than female infants, and female infants receive more vocalizations. It is very possible that these early differences in home experiences provide the basis for later cognitive differences. Life experiences are reflected in brain structures, with life experiences in infancy especially important for neural development. In a controversial article, Rauscher et al. (1997) reported that children who had listened to and studied the music of Mozart (and other complex musical pieces) developed their spatial intelligence more than a comparable control group. They hypothesized that the complex neural-firing pattern in response to the music was responsible for brain development. Regardless of whether these particular findings with music are substantiated over time, it is clear that early life experiences are critical to brain development.

Middle Childhood

61% of all parents believe that differences in behavior between boys and girls are not inborn, but a result of the way they're raised.
—Peyser and Underwood (1997, p. 60)

Childhood is the time in life when multiple socializing forces enter the child's life. Although almost any person or institution with which children come into contact can be considered socializing agents, we'll briefly examine three major forces during middle childhood: parents and peers, television and other media, and teachers and schools.

Sex differences in life experiences are particularly striking among children during the middle childhood years, ranging from approximately 6 to 11 or 12 years old. At this age, boys are allowed to travel a greater distance from home than girls (Herman, Heins, & Cohen, 1987). Boys are also much more likely to engage in sports and activities that involve throwing a ball or other object. Recall that large sex differences favoring boys are found in tasks like throwing accuracy and in judging the speed of moving targets. Even though researchers who study these tasks control for experience with the task, often by selecting participants who report the same amount of experience in aiming at a target or some similar experiential variable, I have wondered if, on average, the boys in these studies don't really have more experience, despite assurances to the contrary (Watson & Kimura, 1991). There must be some advantage in judging moving objects that is accrued from the hundreds of hours boys spend on baseball diamonds, basketball courts, and football fields. Of course, there are girls who also engage in these activities, but overall, more boys are spending more time playing ball sports than girls are.

As expected, there is an association between participation in spatial activities and spatial abilities (Newcombe, Bandura, & Taylor, 1983). If you are thinking critically (and I hope that you are), you won't be too quick to conclude from these findings that boys necessarily become better at spatial skills because they participate in more sports. Although this seems to be a possibility, it is also possible that more boys engage in throwing sports because they are better at spatial skills or for a reason that is unrelated to cognition, such as boys' tendency to have greater upper body strength than girls. The same criticism can be made about a study that found that girls who play with traditional boys' toys tend to perform better on spatial tasks (Serbin, cited in Adler, 1989). It is possible that these girls are able to develop their spatial abilities by playing with traditional boys' toys, but it is also possible that the girls who chose boys' toys are the ones with better spatial abilities. These studies do not explain why boys engage in spatial activities and sports more often than girls do, illustrating the intractable problem of determining cause and effect from naturalistic studies. In a meta-analytic review of the literature that linked spatial activity participation with spatial ability, Baenninger and Newcombe (1989) concluded that there is a weak relationship and that the magnitude of the effect is the same for females as for males. Thus, according to these authors, both sexes benefit about equally from participation in spatial activities. Even though we cannot conclude that boys score higher on tests of aiming abilities and spatial skills because of their childhood play activities, there are enough reasons to conclude that some amount of sports involvement is a good childhood activity. The social and health-related benefits alone should convince even the greatest couch potatoes to help children develop an interest in some active (safe and supervised) sport, even if we cannot conclude that participation in sports improves spatial skills.

Parents and Peers

Parental behaviors have no effect on the psychological characteristics their children will have as adults.
—Harris (1995, p. 458)

Parents in Western societies believe that they play a major role in shaping their children's lives. It is easy to understand why parents feel strongly about their importance in their children's lives. Parenting is the most difficult job there is. (Okay, I acknowledge that this is a value judgment—one that is shared by millions of parents who have made their commitment to being good parents their highest priority.) Dedicated parents spend much of their lives caring for their children, working hard to support them in multiple ways and often sacrificing their own careers and leisure time for the good of their children. Parenting is hard, demanding work that offers rich rewards for many adults. Thus, it is not hard to understand the firestorm of protest that angry parents lobbied against an influential book and journal article written by Harris (1995, 1998b) in which she concluded that parents have little effect on the psychological characteristics of their children beyond the genetic material they contributed at conception. When *Newsweek* magazine ran a cover story on Harris' (1998a) conclusion about the puny significance of parents, the magazine received a huge number of angry responses, many from parents who found the very idea that they were not important in shaping their children's personalities to be an anathema. Like other complex issues, the real question cannot be answered with a simple yes or no as to whether parents are important in shaping their children's lives, but when, how much, and what types of effects do parents have on their children (in addition to inherited predispositions)? I assume that Harris (1995, 1998b) meant that parents are relatively unimportant as long as they are acting within a wide range of "normal" parenting behaviors. There can be no doubt that abusive or neglectful parents will have disastrous effects on their children, ranging from

Baby Blues cartoon. Reprinted with special permission of King Features Syndicate.

physical harm to severe mental and emotional reactions. Variables like appropriate schooling, creating a secure and safe environment, and providing adequate nutrition are critically important to the cognitive growth of children, and it is the parents who ensure these essentials for the good of their children.

One reason why so many parents are convinced that they have had a major effect on their children's personalities is that children tend to be similar to their parents in many ways. Harris (1995) noted that these similarities reflect "gene–environment" correlations, not the outcomes of parenting behavior. Parents and their biological offspring share some genetic traits and an environment that is responsive to inherited traits. For example, parents who like to read tend to have children who like to read, but not necessarily because the children learned to love books from their parents. Both parents and children may be good readers, with a preference for sedentary activities like reading. Children of parents who love to read will grow up in an environment filled with books and parents who respond to their children's enjoyment of reading with more books. This theoretical position recognizes that children actively shape their own environment. If, according to Harris (and others who favor a behavioral genetic perspective), parents are not important socializing agents, then how do children learn about sex role stereotypes and other socially mediated roles and rules?

Harris (1995) believes that the peer group is important in transmitting these cultural expectations to children. Sex-typed behaviors, consistent with sex role stereotypes, are fostered through peer group pressures. The sexual composition of children's peer groups is always important, with sex segregation especially critical in middle childhood. Harris believes that the single-sex peer groups that are common across many cultures during middle childhood enforce rigid standards about appropriate behaviors for girls and boys. Children are often more concerned than their parents about maintaining sex-typed behaviors because assimilation into their sex-segregated peer groups requires children to conform to group norms. This theory is supported by Lytton and Romney's (1991) conclusion from a meta-analytic review of 172 studies showing that parents engage in surprisingly few sex-differentiated socialization practices. Distinctions between the groups become exaggerated, and belief in the superiority of one's own group is a necessary component of self-esteem for the group. Appropriate areas of cognitive pursuit and excellence are learned and enforced in similar ways by the peer group. Peer groups in middle childhood operate in the same ways that other groups do—members of the "in-group" achieve a favored status, whereas members of the other group, in this case the other sex, are viewed with some hostility and in ways that exaggerate between-sex differences. To maintain the separatism of the two groups so that girls and boys know what is appropriate for their sex, members of each group must conform to their own group's norms.

A major premise of Harris' (5) position is that parents' role in creating and maintaining sex role stereotypes is relatively small. A growing number of psychologists agree with her general conclusion that the nurturing role of parents has a relatively minor effect on children's psychological development, especially with regard to sex role stereotypes (O'Boyle et al., 1994). Jacklin and Baker (1993), for example, stated that the empirical studies do not confirm the generally accepted idea that children are socialized differently depending on their sex. They went on to explain that we resort to stereotypes for people we do not know well, and parents know their children very well. Parents believe that they are not treating their children in sex-differentiated ways that encourage sex stereotypic behaviors. The extent to which parents influence the sex role stereotypic beliefs and behaviors of their children is a hotly debated topic in contemporary psychology. Keenan and Shaw (1997) concluded that there are early differences in the parenting of boys and girls, although it is difficult to make direct links from parenting behaviors to the development of sex role stereotypes or sex differences in cognition in children.

One thing is certain—children are not learning about sex role stereotypes by spending time with their fathers. A survey taken in 1995 asked about the average number of hours per day that mothers, fathers, and both parents together spend with their 4-year-olds (Owen, 1995). As shown in Fig. 6.2, fathers in the United States spend an average of 42 minutes a day in the care of their children, compared with the 10.7 hours that mothers spend with their children, and the 54 minutes that both parents spend together with their children. It may be that parents are teaching about sex role-appropriate behaviors without their conscious awareness. If these figures are even approximately accurate, then parents' actions may speak louder than words. The large disparity in child care, with mothers spending much more time than fathers with their preschool children, should send a message to the children about women's and men's priorities, even if the boys and girls are treated in similar ways by the parents. Parenting is such an emotional topic, with data that run counter to commonly held assumptions about the importance of parents and adult socializing agents, that there will undoubtedly be much more research on this question as we struggle to understand how to raise our children the best ways we can.

Television and Other Media

When it comes to stereotyped sex behavior, children more and more put on the cultural cloak that is provided by the society they are growing up in. They use the basic categories "male" and "female" as hooks on which to hang a great deal of cumulative information.
—Maccoby (1990, p. 5)

Many people are amazed to learn that by age 4, most children have spent between 2,000 and 3,000 hours watching television (Stewart, 1976). What are they learning about males and females during all of these hours? With only a few exceptions (e.g., *Sesame Street*), media depictions of females and males parallel commonly held sex role stereotypes (Deaux, 1985). Overwhelmingly, men and boys are shown as active, hardworking, goal-oriented individuals, whereas women and girls are depicted as housewives and future housewives. Numerous studies have noted that men on television are characterized as "dominant, aggressive, autono-

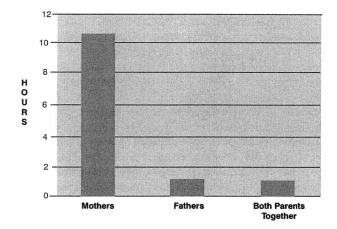

FIG. 6.2.   Average number of hours spent per day caring for preschool children by mothers, fathers, and both parents together for U.S. Sample. Data from Owen (1995).

mous and active while female characters are passive and defiant" (Calvert & Huston, 1987, p. 78). In an analysis of 300 television commercials, Hoyenga and Hoyenga (1979) reported that more than 90% of the following activities or occupations were portrayed by females: caring for a baby, residing in a nursing home, cleaning the house, washing clothes and dishes, shopping, and cooking and serving food. Compare these with the following activities and occupations that were portrayed by males more than 90% of the time: farming, engaging in sports, driving a vehicle, working in an office (not as a secretary), serving as a soldier, and working in a service station.

Television images of the lives of females and males differ dramatically. Women appear in a narrower range of roles, and they are significantly more often depicted on the receiving end of violent attacks. Another message that is conveyed is that marriage and parenthood are of greater significance in females' lives than in males' lives (Gerber 1987). Two recent reviews (Allan & Coltrane, 1996; Signorelli & Bacue, 1999) of the way females and males are depicted on television concluded that although there have been changes over the past 3 decades, "Gender images remain stereotypical" (Allan & Coltrane, 1996, p. 185).

According to the theory of social modeling, which is discussed more fully in chapter 7, children learn about sex roles by observing the activities and occupations of the female and male characters they view on television and in other settings. The prediction that children are more likely to imitate same-sex models than opposite-sex models has been difficult to demonstrate in the laboratory, possibly because of some of the constraints imposed by the nature of laboratory investigations. A typical laboratory study of this phenomenon might consist of exposing children to male and female models who engage in different sorts of activities. The researchers then observe the girls and boys to see if they are more likely to exhibit the activities of the same-sex model than they are to exhibit the activities of the opposite-sex model. It is likely, however, that observational learning followed by imitation of a same-sex model occurs more frequently in real life when a child may have frequent contact with a model and a wider range of opportunities to demonstrate imitation.

Perry and Bussey (1979) provided evidence in support of social modeling theory. They hypothesized that children learn sex-typed behavior by observing differences in the frequencies of sex-typed activities by female and male models. In a test of their hypothesis, they provided children with several male and female models. They found that children were more likely to imitate behaviors of same-sex models than they were to imitate behaviors of other-sex models. Perry and Bussey concluded that "children are most likely to imitate persons whom they perceive to be good examples of their [own] sex role" (p. 1708). If, as Perry and Bussey suggested, repeated observations of the frequency of sex-typed behavior is the mechanism by which social modeling operates, then television should provide an optimal situation for such learning. Given the immense number of hours children and adults spend watching television, it is clear that television is a major socializing agent in modern U.S. society. The sex-stereotyped characterizations it depicts serve to reinforce sex role stereotypes.

A recent study of television viewing habits found that young boys who have achieved the cognitive milestone known as gender constancy, the awareness that they are male and will always remain male, watch more television programs that show a greater percentage of male characters than boys of the same age who do not yet understand that being male is an unchanging physical characteristic (Luecke-Aleksa, Anderson, Collins, & Schmitt, 1995). Additional information about this study is presented in chapter 7 in which theories of sex typed learning are presented. This study showed that children make television choices that provide insights into their understanding of sex-typed behaviors.

Although it is possible to limit or avoid television shows, advertisements in other forms of media are ubiquitous and inescapable (Plous, 1997). Advertisements on billboards, on the screens of Internet search engines, on the food baskets in supermarkets, in magazines and newspapers, in hospital waiting rooms, and, increasingly, in public schools provide a continuous image of a marketer's idea of what life should be like. Plous found disturbing trends in the advertisements in fashion magazines over the past 10 years. He reported that in more than 40% of the advertisements in which women were depicted, the women had portions of their breasts exposed. Seventeen percent of the ads depicted White women, and 9% of the ads depicted Black women, and women of all races were depicted in low-status positions, such as being on their knees. He concluded that both racial and gender bias in advertising may be increasing. It is difficult to estimate how many ads like these children see during their childhood years, but it surely a large number. The cumulative message is loud and clear, even if it is nonverbal—sex role stereotypes are alive and well at the start of the new millennium.

Teachers and Schools

It would be preposterously naïve to suggest that a B.A. Degree
can be made as attractive to girls as a marriage license.
—Kirk (former president of Columbia University)

Schools are the only institution in our society charged with the exclusive responsibility of educating our children. It is there that the intellectual abilities of all girls and boys should be nurtured so that every individual can develop to his or her full potential. Sadker and Sadker (1985) set out to find if there is any evidence that cognitive abilities are being differentially developed for girls and boys in schools. In a 3-year study of 100 4th-, 6th-, and 8th-grade classes in four states and the District of Columbia, they found ample evidence of sex biases. At all grade levels in all subjects, boys dominated classroom discussions. Teachers paid more attention to the boys and praised them more often. "While girls sit patiently with their hands raised, boys literally grab teacher attention. They are eight times more likely than girls to call out answers" (Sadker & Sadker, 1985, p. 56). They reported that boys also received more dynamic and informative feedback to their classroom comments than girls did. Other studies have come up with similar findings: "Boys receive more of the teacher's attention, teachers interact with boys, particularly high achieving boys, more than with girls, and boys are more active in providing answers, particularly unsolicited answers, than are girls" (Kimball, 1989, p. 201). If these sex-differentiated patterns of classroom interactions is pervasive, then, sex-differentiated treatment in the classroom could be directly responsible for or contributing to sex differences in mathematics and science achievement. If girls are taught that they will receive fewer rewards for scholastic success than boys will, learning theory suggests that they will seek success in other areas in which rewards are more probable.

All of the teachers observed by Sadker and Sadker (American Association of University Women [AAUW], 1992) reported that they treated boys and girls the same, yet observations conducted in their classrooms showed that their beliefs about their actions were not accurate. Recall that earlier in this chapter I discussed a study in which high school students showed the influence of sex role stereotypes in a memory task for a dull story. When the students were told these results, they also denied that they were influenced by sex role stereotypes. Thus, although students and teachers are denying that they are influenced by sex role stereotypes, all of the data suggest that they are not even aware of the pervasive and intransigent nature of sex role stereotypes. They have become part of our nonconscious ideology.

Sex role messages pervade the school experience. Conformity to school regulations is more important for girls than boys. In Grades 6 through 10, girls ranked "getting good grades" as their primary aspiration at school (Butcher, 1986). Recall that girls do, in fact, get higher grades than boys in school. Even at the college level, females continue to maintain overall higher grade point averages than males (with the mean difference estimated at 0.17 on a 4.0 scale; Cordes, 1986).

Although schools can no longer require students to take separate courses in drafting and home economics, in fact, most of these classes are still segregated by sex. Despite egalitarian rhetoric (at least in some school districts), some curriculum choices are not real. Although I am certain that every reader has his or her own personal examples, I cannot help but recall what happened when my daughter registered for eighth grade (in a Vancouver, Canada, public school). She was told that she could pick either drafting or home economics, but if she chose drafting, she would be the only girl in the class, and she might find some "resistance" from the boys and their teacher. (Similarly, there were no boys in home economics.) The question is not whether it is better to take drafting or home economics, because both are valuable, but whether one's biological sex should be the determinant. Why doesn't everyone need to know about cooking, nutrition, food storage, and how machines work? (If you were wondering about my daughter's choice, get real. There are very few eighth graders who would risk peer status by doing anything as deviant as taking a sex role-inappropriate course.) This is only one of many examples for which the rhetoric does not match the reality.

It seems that all of the major socializing agents of childhood act in ways that encourage sex-differentiated cognitive development. It also seems that few of us are aware of the multitudinous pressures to conform to traditional sex roles and of the diverse ways these pressures are communicated to children. Notwithstanding this conclusion, there is much disagreement about the cognitive effects of these subtle and not-so-subtle sex-differentiated messages.

Change and Shortchange: Are Current School Practices Detrimental to Girls or Boys?

In a report issued by AAUW (1992), the authors discussed the many ways that "schools shortchange girls." They noted many behaviors that teachers engage in, without conscious awareness, that negatively affect the girls in their classes. The report drew heavily on the research of Sadker and Sadker (1985) that showed that boys get more of the teacher's attention, usually for disruptive behavior; boys call out answers more often than girls; teachers give boys more "thinking time" when they call on them in class; and teachers provide more encouragement to boys in terms of positive comments. The authors of the AAUW report concluded that these behaviors negatively affect girls by limiting their horizons and expectations, leading to occupational segregation and a lifetime of lower earning for women. These data and conclusions have not gone unchallenged. An observational study of teachers and children in science classes found that many of the teachers did call on boys more often than would be expected by the percentage of boys in class, as documented in the AAUW report, but this differential pattern was related to the fact that boys volunteered more often (Altermatt, Jovanovic, & Perry, 1998). The authors of this study emphasized the way children direct classroom interactions and faulted earlier studies for not considering the role of the child in creating and maintaining sex differences in teacher–child interactions.

In an angry response to the AAUW (1992) report, Kleinfeld (1998) wrote, "The idea that the 'schools shortchange girls' is wrong and dangerously wrong" (p. 1). She characterized the AAUW report as "false political propaganda" (p. 3). Kleinfeld argued that the fact that girls, on average, get higher grades in school in all subjects, obtain higher scores on most achievement tests in the early elementary school years and on selected tests in later years, are less likely to be diagnosed as dyslexic or as "slow readers," and now comprise a majority of the enrollments in college (at the undergraduate level) shows that girls are advancing academically at a higher rate than boys. Kleinfeld concluded that the schools are not shortchanging girls. She urged that more attention be paid to the achievement of boys, particularly minority boys, because they are dropping out of U.S. schools at an alarming rate, often failing to achieve even basic work skills. Kleinfeld acknowledged that females are seriously underrepresented in some academic disciplines, including physics, chemistry, computer science, and engineering, but she dismissed the importance of this disparity because only a small proportion of the population is employed in these scientific and technical areas compared with the larger number of boys who are not completing high school.

The Angst of Adolescence

The pre-adolescent peer group tends to reject a girl who appears
to be too smart or too successful.
—Noble (1987, p. 371)

Adolescence covers that time in the life span when boys and girls begin to develop secondary sex characteristics and ends when physical maturity is achieved. Considering the variety of individual differences in the timing of these developmental milestones, it can be roughly operationalized as beginning as early as age 10 and extending to as late as age 18, recognizing, of course, that a few individuals begin puberty before age 10 and a few continue physical maturity after age 18. Adolescence has already been identified in earlier chapters as a critical period in the development of cognitive sex differences. It is during adolescence that boys begin to take the lead in standardized tests of mathematics (usually mathematical problem solving) and girls lose their lead in mathematical computation. At the same time, girls begin to lose their self-confidence in mathematical ability and enroll in the optional advanced classes in mathematics in smaller numbers than their male peers (Dunham, 1998). In a study of sex differences in course selection, the authors found that starting at 7th grade and continuing through high school, girls and boys, on average, took different courses despite the fact that there were no sex differences in academic achievement that could explain the sex-differentiated pattern of course selection (Wilson, Stocking, & Goldstein, 1994).

Several biological hypotheses have been proposed that link the biological events of puberty to the emergence of cognitive sex differences during this time of life. However, along with the tremendous biological changes that occur during these years, there are also numerous and powerful psychosocial changes that occur during the preteen and teen years. Researchers who favor the nurture side of the nature–nurture controversy believe that the etiology of the cognitive sex differences is firmly rooted in the psychosocial forces that dominate the adolescent years. On the basis of this belief, Schwartz and Hanson (1992) recommended three ways to make mathematics education "equal" for female students: (a) change attitudes—parents and teachers need to believe that girls can succeed in math, (b) change teaching methods—use cooperative learning strategies that are more girl friendly and use mathematical examples that are meaningful to girls, and (c) eliminate gender bias in career counseling. These seem to be reasonable recommendations, but there is little evidence that by making these changes, more girls will succeed in mathematics. As already presented, several psychologists think that parents' attitudes (and behaviors) are relatively unimportant to the psychological development of their children, whereas others think that girls are doing well in school, a conclusion that is supported by the fact that girls tend to get better grades in all courses, so they seem to be learning the material that teachers are testing. It is difficult to understand the multiple processes at work during adolescence. One conclusion is clearly warranted: Neither psychosocial variables, like parents' attitudes, nor biological ones, like hormone changes, can explain all of the data regarding cognitive sex differences. A more holistic account that includes a variety of types of variables is needed.

Body Type and Developing Sexuality

Decades after the feminist movement sought to reduce the emphasis
on girls' looks, guess which type pageant—scholarship or beauty—
is most popular?
—Darling (1998, p. E6)

Although biological definitions of puberty usually cite the development of adult patterns of body hair (the word *puberty* is derived from a Latin word meaning fine, downy hair), psychosocial definitions of adolescence are more likely to stress romantic interest and concern with one's changing body. There are profound psychological consequences of the biology of adolescence. The biological events that symbolize the ability to reproduce—menarche for girls and ejaculation for boys—have intense psychological significance. For each sex, these biological events signify that for the first time, the individual, along with a partner, can create life. Friendships with members of the other sex and preadolescent romances assume a new potential meaning when young adults develop sexually.

The biological changes associated with physical maturation have tremendous psychosocial significance. There is ample evidence to suggest that girls and boys who attain puberty at an early age and develop adult-like body types before most of their peers are treated differently than their later maturing friends. As described in the preceding chapter, one biological theory to explain cognitive sex differences is that early maturers don't develop spatial skills as well or as fully as later maturing adolescents, possibly because of the effect of sex hormones on brain organization. It is also possible, however, that early maturers differ from late maturers for psychosocial reasons. Early maturing boys are more muscular and taller than later maturing ones; therefore, they experience greater peer group prestige (Hamburg & Lunde, 1966). There are numerous secondary gains from their physical stature. Their height gives them a competitive edge in sports such as basketball, volleyball, long jump, and soccer. The early growth of body hair allows them to cultivate a moustache while still in junior high school, and their developing biceps are likely to receive positive comments.

Puberty rate differences are even more pronounced for girls, who soon learn that their "hourglass" figures and growing breasts make them desirable dates and mates. They undoubtedly receive more attention from males, especially older males, than their less shapely girlfriends. Girls learn about the importance of being beautiful at an early age. One reporter estimated that there are at least 250 beauty pageants a year in the United States, with the fastest growing segment of the beauty pageant market catering to girls under 8 years old (Frerking, 1997). Adolescent girls receive social and cultural messages about what their bodies should be, and on finding that their own bodies fall short of the "ideal," many girls develop a passionate and consuming hatred for their bodies (Jacobs, 1998).

It seems that early and late maturers have different social environments and receive different rewards. Early maturers are less concerned with academic pursuits than late maturers, who still rely on good grades in school and teachers' praise as a major source of reward. Mazur and Robertson (1972) revealed the feelings of an anonymous girl who had experienced early puberty: "Sure, after I bloomed I always dressed so people could see how big my breasts were. After all, a pair of 48's can make a girl feel like a real person. Everybody pays attention" (p. 115). A psychosocial explanation of the sex-related cognitive differences that emerge during puberty would suggest that both the different life experiences that result from the hormonal events that trigger maturation and the hormonal events per se underlie cognitive differences.

In one of the few examinations of commonly held stereotypes about early and late-maturing girls and boys, Faust (1983) asked college students to describe individuals in these four categories. Early maturing girls were described as "attracted to the opposite sex, egocentric, absolutely boy crazy, and theatrical." By comparison, late-maturing girls were described as "afraid of the opposite sex, unassuming, friends of both boys and girls, and exhibiting normal behavior." Early maturing boys were described as "liking football, sexy and outgoing, macho, slow learner, and a typical jock." Late-maturing boys were described as "would rather read, fast learner, unmacho, and popular only with own friends." It seems that many people would agree with the research showing that early maturers have poorer intellectual skills than later maturers.

Gender Intensification Hypothesis

Adolescence is a special time for gender, a time when gender-related beliefs may become intensified or transcended.
—Alfieri, Ruble, and Higgins (1996, p. 1129)

Adolescence has been identified as the time when boys and girls, but especially girls, respond to environmental pressures to conform to appropriate sex role behavior (Hill & Lynch, 1983). The psychological aspects of being female or male are intensified, hence the term *gender intensification.* Adherence to traditional sex role stereotypes seems particularly important when boys and girls begin to interact in ways that are more characteristic of young women and men. Adolescence is a transitional period in life during which children undergo a metamorphosis from which they emerge as adults. Peer interactions are especially important, and there are strict sanctions against sex role-inappropriate behavior. The need to be "just like everyone else" is high. Strict conformity to sex role stereotypes would also require boys and girls to conform to sex-typed cognitive activities (e.g., avoiding mathematics and science course work for girls and avoiding poetry and literature for boys).

In a study of developmental changes in sex role stereotypes, Alfieri et al. (1996) found that these beliefs about females and males were most flexible in the year following the transition to junior high school (usually seventh grade), a time when children encounter a wide range of new peers with a variety of personality types. However, sex role stereotypes become increasingly rigid over the next several years as the high school students prepared for adult life. Throughout the high school years, boys maintained less flexibility in their sex role stereotypes than girls did. These researchers suggested that programs designed to reduce sexism need to take advantage of the transition year in junior high school when children are most open to the possibility that sex role stereotypes can allow for a wide range of acceptable behaviors for girls and boys.

Many investigators believe that the intensification of sex role stereotypes throughout the high school years can explain the small percentage of girls who score in the highest ranges of the SAT–M. Consider how increasingly rigid sex roles in high school are relevant to our interpretation of the report from Johns Hopkins University on the Study of Mathematically Precocious Youth (Benbow & Stanley, 1980, 1981, 1983). As reported in chapter 3, a national search for mathematically precocious youth identified more males than females, with large sex ratios among the most highly gifted group. If adolescent girls learn that it is unfeminine to succeed at mathematics, then it is likely that a large proportion of mathematically gifted girls either declined to participate in the search or never pursued advanced mathematics courses. Tomizuka and Tobias (1981) noted that such statistics are unfair because it may be difficult to identify the most gifted girls in such a talent search because of the social ostracism they would surely face for such inappropriate behavior during a time in life when sex role adherence is of particular importance.

Evidence of adolescent intellectual decline is seen most dramatically among the elite group of adolescents who are identified as "gifted." At least half of all elementary school children who are identified as gifted, talented, or highly capable are female, but by junior high school, less that one fourth of this elite group are female (Noble, 1987). It is difficult to imagine that there is any biological system that operates such that exceptionally able females become average over a short time period. Sex role stereotyping pressures, which intensify during adolescence, are a much more likely cause for this distressing phenomenon. Gottfried, Gottfried, Bathurst, and Guerin (1994) reported that gifted boys are the most popular of the four ability–sex groups (gifted boys, gifted girls, average boys, and average girls), and gifted girls are the least popular. Gifted girls were perceived as being moody and melancholy, whereas their male counterparts were perceived as being funny and upbeat. It is little wonder why gifted girls begin to disappear at ages when these messages become painfully clear. As a society, we simply cannot afford to lose so many exceptionally talented minds.

Video Games, Sports, and Other Adolescent Activities

U.S. female and male adolescents have always engaged in sex-differentiated activities ranging from hunting and gathering in early civilizations to barn raising and quilting bees in the colonial United States. Even recent attempts at legislation to end sex segregation in groups such as Boy and Girl Scouts and their adolescent counterparts, Explorer and Junior Scouts, and little league and Babe Ruth league have, for the most part, failed. Either the courts have ruled that sex segregation is legal, as in the case of scouting, or the lifting of sex restrictions has not in fact changed much, as in the case of adolescent baseball leagues, which typically enroll few girls. Even in instances in which there is no formal sex segregation, boys and girls often self-segregate. Modern-day examples of this are billiards and video games, which tend to attract a much higher percentage of boys than girls. (The next time you pass or enter a pool hall or arcade, count the number of males and females. I have been doing this for years and am still surprised at how very sex-segregated these public facilities are.)

Both billiards and video games seem to require spatial skills. It seems likely that repeated practice at these activities would lead to improvement in some spatial skills. In an experimental test of these possibilities, Subrahmanyam and Greenfield (1994) trained girls and boys on action-type video games that required the manipulation of shapes on a computer monitor. Both the boys and girls improved by the same amount on tests of spatial ability, showing, as numerous other experimenters have, that spatial ability improves with training, although the boys still scored higher than the girls after training. Similar results have been reported by other investigators (McClurg & Chaillé, 1987). Because numerous surveys have shown that boys play more video games than girls, this is another way in which spatial skills are differentially developed in boys. Of course, as in earlier sections that addressed differences in the activities and interests of girls and boys, we cannot use these data to determine if boys play more video games because they tend to excel at them or whether they tend to excel at them because they play more video games.

The computer explosion has changed our lives in many ways. Computer knowledge is already an essential skill for countless occupations and is likely to become increasingly important in the next decade. Are the sexes participating equally in technologically rich fields? As we have already seen, there are large discrepancies in the use of "entertainment software." Much of the software that is written for children's entertainment has the potential to develop eye and hand coordination and to make the user more comfortable with computers. If you haven't played a computer game in a while, stop in an arcade, and after counting the males and females, look at the nature of the games. A majority of the games involve acts of aggression, such as bombing an assortment of objects and killing enemies. (The enemies are easy to spot—they are usually uglier than the other beings.) Boys seem to prefer the aggressive nature of these games far more than girls do. Not only are boys more likely to use computers in play, but they also are more likely to use them in learning environments (Linn, 1985).

Adolescent boys also engage in more organized sports than adolescent girls. Football, a virtually exclusively male sport, requires considerable spatial analysis, especially if it includes carefully planned "plays" for passing. There are some spatial activities that girls are more likely to engage in than boys. Embroidery, especially embroidery without a preprinted pattern, would seem to be an excellent spatial skill, as would sewing without a pattern. However, these are activities that probably attract few girls, especially in relation to the number of boys who participate in traditionally male activities that contain spatial components. Reading is a somewhat sex-typed female activity. In fact, some toy stores keep their books in the section that is labeled *girls' toys*. We really don't know what the majority of girls are doing while adolescent boys are engaged in sports. It seems likely that adolescent girls probably do read more, talk on the phone more, and watch more daytime television (e.g., soap operas) than adolescent boys. Typically, girls are required to perform more household chores. It is difficult to imagine how household chores could improve intellectual growth. For example, the type of mathematics used in recipes is arithmetic conversions and isn't likely to require any mathematical skills beyond addition, subtraction, and fractions. In general, typical adolescent activities seem to favor the development of cognitive skills for males over females.

Adulthood and Old Age

*The average American woman spends 17 years raising children
and 18 years helping aging parents.*
—*Newsweek* (1990, cover)

The bulk of our lives is spent as adults and later as older adults. There are numerous psychosocial factors that maintain the sex role stereotypic behaviors we learned in our youth. Below is a brief survey of some of the factors that have implications for cognitive functioning.

Sex-Related Power Differential

Even when both spouses work, wives perform a disproportionate share of child care and housework tasks, regardless of social class.
—Rodin and Ickovics (1990, p. 1018)

It is possible that psychologists who study cognitive differences are missing the most salient aspect of sex differences in human interactions. Meeker and Weitzel-O'Neill (1977) believe that many sex differences are merely an artifact of power and status differences. Men behave as they do because they hold substantially all of the real power in society, and women behave as they do because they are much less powerful than men. Men gain power and prestige through the status of their occupation and the size of their paycheck (Gould, 1974; Levant, 1996). A recent survey of career choices found that, relative to men, women attribute less importance to making a high salary and more importance to relationships with people when considering career alternatives (Gati, Osipow, & Givon, 1995). Occupations that are typically male are more highly prized by society than occupations that are typically female. Even when a traditionally female job and a traditionally male job require the same level of background or training (e.g., secretary and groundskeeper), the male job will most often pay substantially more.

Most of society's powerful people are men. Virtually all government leaders, corporate officials, leading scientists, bankers, and stockbrokers are men. Society's power differential continues in most households. Even if men are no longer the sole breadwinner, in the vast majority of U.S. households, they earn more than their wives. In most marriages, the husband not only earns more money but also is better educated, taller, and heavier than the wife. Thus, the power differential extends beyond money and prestige of occupation; it also includes the physical power associated with larger stature.

The occupations that require spatial and mathematical abilities frequently offer higher prestige, power, and salaries. Children learn that if they want to become physicians, pharmacists, engineers, computer analysts, accountants, scientists, or veterinarians, they have to excel in mathematics and sciences. Because these are examples of the high-paying, prestigious occupations that are primarily filled by men, boys learn that success in the academic areas that are prerequisites for these occupations is necessary if they are to fulfill their adult sex role. Occupations that are traditionally female, such as teachers, secretaries, and homemakers, typically do not require excellent mathematical or spatial skills. Good communication or verbal skills are needed in these occupations, which is exactly the academic area in which most females excel.

Although there have been significant increases in the number of women in law, medicine, and business schools, other traditionally male areas have seen much less change. Female participation remains particularly low in chemistry, physics, mathematics, and engineering. The number of males entering traditional female domains is still relatively low (U.S. Bureau of the Census, 1998). If you are a young college student, you may be getting a false impression about sexual equality from your experiences in college. Are you surprised to learn that since 1970 approximately 4 million women have entered the workforce, and of these, 3.3 million are working as secretaries, nurses, bookkeepers, cashiers, and other female-dominated support occupations (e.g., social work; Hacker, cited in Eccles, 1987)? The world of work is still segregated by sex for a large proportion of working adults (AAUW, 1992; Bridges, 1989).

It is difficult to determine cause and effect when sex differences in occupations are considered. Females could dominate selected fields that require verbal ability because they are inherently better in verbal ability, or they could be better than males in verbal ability because they are educated for careers in these areas. The problem with this sort of explanation is that there are few differences between the sexes in verbal abilities for the majority of the population. (Recall that the largest differences are found for those with very low verbal abilities, such as reading difficulties and stuttering, and for the majority of the population only in fluency and ability to generate synonyms.) Similar problems arise when considering the relationship between male abilities and male occupational preferences. The only conclusion that can be reached is that many prestigious, high-paying jobs require mathematical and spatial skills and that these jobs tend to be filled primarily by men. However, it is important to remember when considering the relationship among ability, occupation, and sex that more than ability is involved in determining who fills the high-status occupations. Traditionally, other demographic indicators like race, socioeconomic status, religion, and country of origin, independent of ability, have determined who will succeed in high-status positions. The fact that females exhibit superior performance on some tests of verbal ability (e.g., fluency) has not translated into occupational success in high-verbal fields like academia or journalism that are associated with high prestige and/or high salaries. This demonstrates the importance of psychosocial variables in determining occupational success. Even high-status positions that primarily require verbal ability, such as lawyers and politicians, are overwhelmingly male. Furthermore, it is difficult to think of any important occupation that does not require verbal ability because the ability to communicate is essential in all endeavors.

Performance Evaluations

Individuals' reactions to women leaders are tempered by their expectations about the role of women and men in contemporary society.
—Forsyth, Heiney, and Wright (1997, p. 98)

One possible explanation for cognitive sex differences is that they don't really exist. We are misled into believing that they exist because we live in a sex-biased society that evaluates female and male performance and products differently. There is some evidence that performance or a product is evaluated differently depending on whether the evaluator believes that it was created by a man or a woman. (See Goldberg, 1968, and Pheterson, Kiesler, & Goldberg, 1971, for pioneering studies on this topic.) In a meta-analytic review of the research literature on sex biases in evaluation, the authors concluded that average differences in the rating of male and female accomplishments is "negligible" (Swim, Borgida, Maruyama, & Myers, 1989). They determined that people still use stereotypes but the stereotypes are more complex than simple female–male distinctions. Subtypes of stereotypes are more important in evaluations (e.g., businesswoman and housewife stereotypes).

Although the meta-analytic review of the literature pertaining to performance evaluations suggested that the effects are negligible, once again it seems that large effects are sometimes found, depending on the context in which the effect is investigated. In Etaugh's (1989) review of evaluation bias, she found that "males of low competence are evaluated more poorly than females of low competence. In the middle range of average competence, which includes most people, antifemale bias is the rule" (p. 125). Thus, overall results can appear as negligible when males are evaluated more harshly when their level of competence is below average and females are evaluated more harshly when their level of competence is average. What about evaluations for above average competence? Etaugh (1989) summarized the literature this way:

> Some studies have found that women who are portrayed as being highly successful in traditionally male occupations are judged more competent than males in the same occupation. This has been called the "talking platypus phenomenon": i.e., it makes little difference what the platypus says; the amazing thing is that it can talk at all. But even when the competence of a successful woman is recognized, the explanations offered for her success may differ markedly from those offered to explain a man's success. His successful performance generally is attributable to the stable, internal attribute of skill, while the same performance is attributed to such unstable or external factors as luck, effort, or ease of task. (pp. 124–125)

What about performance evaluations for leaders? Do judgments about leadership differ depending on the sex of the leader? It seems that leadership is such a prototypical male domain that females are judged differently when they act as leaders, even if sex differences in performance evaluations are less clear in other domains. Despite an assortment of measures and manipulations that show no sex differences in actual performance for male and female leaders, women are judged as less effective as leaders when they provide leadership in an area that is male sex-typed (e.g., construction) and when the majority of their subordinates are male (Eagly et al., 1995).

Biased evaluations may explain some of the data in subjective areas like what makes a competent leader or a fine artist, but it is more difficult to apply the notion of sex-differentiated evaluation criteria to standardized tests of mathematics and spatial ability. Some have argued that if a test reveals consistent sex differences, then the test should be declared invalid and a new test should be found. This line of reasoning begins with the assumption that sex differences cannot truly exist; therefore, the fault must lie in the test. Although it is always possible that any between-sex differences are due to some bias in the test itself (e.g., the test uses examples that are unfamiliar to one sex), the standardized tests of spatial, mathematical, and verbal ability that have been used in a majority of the studies reviewed in this book are unlikely to contain many of these biases. The largest between-sex difference is found on the SAT–M, a multiple-choice test that is machine-graded. The Educational Testing Service has come under extreme criticism because of the male advantage on this test. In response to the criticism, every test item that is answered correctly more often by either sex is examined for bias. There is no obvious bias in the content of the questions. (For example, they are as likely to be about cooking as sports, and no knowledge of the content area is needed to answer the questions; Educational Testing Service, 1987). Thus, although sex-differentiated performance evaluations can account for some of the sex differences in success rates in certain occupations, they cannot account for the sex differences found with many standardized ability tests.

Because so many lives are affected by SAT scores, the controversy concerning their use and the possibility of sex bias against women is a topic of considerable concern. Recall from chapter 3 that although women tend to score lower than men on the SAT, women get higher grades in college. Because of this, the SAT underestimates women's success in college and overestimates men's success in college. Furthermore, the issue of bias is far from resolved. In a review of the SAT by the AAUW (1988), it found that "an analysis of 24 passages from the SATs reading comprehension sections contained 34 references to famous men, but only one reference to a famous woman—Margaret Mead—and that was in a passage criticizing her work" (p. 2). Thus, many scholars still maintain that the SAT is biased against women. In a lengthy response to criticisms about sex bias in the SAT, Willingham and Cole (1997) reviewed the extensive data bank of tests produced by the Educational Testing Service. For the most part, they reported that many of the between-sex differences are "small," but just as important, these differences mirror the sex differences found on an assortment of other measures. The authors also pointed out numerous reasons why sex differences would be expected on some tests. For example, if males take more advanced mathematics courses than females do, then higher average scores for males on tests of advanced mathematics would be expected. In fact, something would be wrong with the test if it did not reflect the many differences in the lives of males and females.

As noted earlier in this book, tests of writing are being added to several different assessments of abilities, including a new test of writing for the GRE, the test most frequently used in decisions about admissions to graduate school. The fact that women tend to score higher than men on tests of writing should help to equalize the overall scores obtained by men and women.

Achievement Motivation

Another possible explanation for the cognitive sex differences that are typically found is that they don't represent ability differences. Instead, it is possible that they are indicators of motivational differences. It is possible, for example, that women and men are equally able to learn higher level mathematical concepts, but for some reason, men are more motivated to put in the hard work needed to learn the concepts or are more motivated to demonstrate their knowledge. This is an older hypothesis that was extremely popular in the late 1960s and 1970s. Horner (1969) examined the possibility of sex differences in academic motivation. She asked college students to complete the following story, which concerned a protagonist named either Anne or John: "At the end of first-term finals, Anne [John] finds herself [himself] at the top of her [his] medical school class." She found that college students wrote about many more negative consequences of academic success for the female protagonist than for the male protagonist. Examples of some of the negative consequences that followed Anne's success were: "Everyone hates and envies Anne," and "Anne feels unhappy and unfeminine." It seems that the female protagonist had become unsexed by success. These results led Horner to hypothesize that in addition to the usual motivational tendencies that are found in both men and women, women possess a fear of success or a motive to avoid success because success often has negative consequences for women.

Although Horner's (1969) research on fear of success captured media headlines, it has not held up in replications. Like most psychological constructs, success motivation is more complex than a simple approach–avoid continuum. It seems that we also need to be concerned with "success at what?" Later research showed that there was little negative imagery when Anne was successful in traditional female occupations like nursing. In addition, males also have been found to be concerned with negative consequences of success. More recent research suggests that if fear of success is a valid motivational tendency, then it exists about equally in men and women. It seems that whereas many women may want to become more than just a "sex object," many men want to become more than just a "success object." Thus, the well-publicized fear-of-success motivation cannot be used to understand cognitive sex differences. (See Spence & Helmreich, 1983, and Fogel & Paludi, 1984, for reviews of the literature.)

Other examinations of achievement motivation have considered the multidimensional nature of this construct. Spence and Helmreich (1978, 1983) examined sex differences in achievement concerns in the areas of work (the desire to work hard and to do a good job), mastery (the preference for challenging tasks and high performance standards), and competition (the enjoyment of interpersonal competition and the desire to do better than others). They found that, in general, women are more concerned with work achievement and men are more concerned with achievement in competitive and mastery situations. Similar sex differences in competition are sometimes found with children (Halpern & Kagan, 1984). If males are more aggressive, more competitive, and more concerned with mastery throughout the life span, they might be expected to excel in the more competitive aspects of school and work. It is possible that a "competitive edge" or motivational achievement factor is underlying some of the cognitive sex differences. If you read the want ads, you'll find that many of the job advertisements use masculine or aggressive language. The ads often claim that the job needs to be filled by "a strong deal-closer," "an aggressive negotiator," or a "dominant personality." Sometimes the ads sound more like a job description for a soldier than a salesperson. Because achievement is a major component of the male sex role stereotype, it should not be surprising to find that males are more achievement-oriented, at least in competitive and mastery situations.

Family Life

As much as women want to be good scientists or engineers, they want first and foremost to be womanly companions of men and to be mothers.
—Bruno Bettleheim (1965)

The overwhelming majority of adults marry and become parents. It is also true that despite recent social changes, women and men perform different roles and functions in most U.S. homes. Although a majority of mothers now work outside of the home, most of these mothers still retain primary responsibility for child care and housework (Allgeier, 1983). It is still true that mothers receive criticism for their involvement in paid work and fathers receive criticism for their involvement in the home (Deutsch & Saxon, 1998). The result is severe strain and fatigue for women who want to maintain serious, demanding professional careers and a balanced family life. When the Public Broadcasting Service aired a series exploring the lives of creative people, a startling fact was revealed. The diverse list of creative women they included all had one thing in common—none had children. This was, of course, not true for the creative men, most of whom had children. This result was replicated with a less stellar group. In a phone survey of working women "a larger than expected proportion of women with managerial positions are divorced or separated, and as the level of commitment and preparation required for a job rises, there is an increase in the proportion of childless women and a decrease in the proportion with three or more children under age 18" (Valdez & Gutek, 1986, p. 157).

Although many people regard children as an important asset in their lives and would gladly trade other forms of success for parenthood, one conclusion is that children require mothers to prioritize their time and effort in ways that are not required of many fathers. It does seem that traditional family life mitigates against academic and other professional success for women, although the number of women who have successfully combined motherhood, marriage, and demanding occupations is growing. Family life commitments can explain sex differences in demanding occupations that require years of preparation, such as physicists, mathematicians, and engineers. They also can explain the cognitive sex differences that arise during puberty if we assume that teens direct their energies and select their course work to prepare for their anticipated adult life roles. Marriage and family are viewed by employers as an asset for a man's career and as a hindrance for a woman's career. Surveys have shown the obvious: When mothers work outside the home, they are much more likely to be called at work to care for a sick child than a father who works outside the home (Valdez & Gutek, 1986). It is not surprising to find that women's work is concentrated in low-paying, dead-end jobs (Diamond, 1986).

There was an uproar in the business community when Schwartz (1989) suggested that corporations give working mothers the option of a career track that allows more time for family and other home commitments. Her rationale for this suggestion was that the superwoman myth is just that. It is not physically possible to work a 60–80-hour corporate week (which is the norm in some law firms, corporate offices, and medical internship programs) and still have time and energy for the demanding job of parenting. Presumably, men also would be given this option, but in reality, child care remains overwhelmingly (sometimes quite literally) the responsibility of mothers, and if such career options were available, more women would be involved than men. Is this a good idea? On the pro side, it would allow women to keep working but at less than full speed (which in some occupations might mean 40 to 45 hours a week) if they choose to do so. Women also could opt to remain on the career track. It seems to take into account some harsh realities and offer help for women who are dragging themselves from work, to preschool, to the pediatrician, to the play group, to piano lessons, to parent–teacher association meetings, and so on. On the con side, it would institutionalize a lower career track for women and make all mothers "suspect" of job neglect. This concept has been disparagingly nicknamed the "mommy track"—a separate, less career-oriented track for mothers.

Old Age

Older women are more likely to be widowed, to live alone, and to live in poverty. One person in six may be an older woman.
—Gist and Velkoff (1997, p. 1)

When we consider old age, it is accurate to say that the future is female. Women live an average of 7 years longer than men. If you are not yet a "golden ager," then you will find it informative to visit a community that caters to older people, such as a "retirement village," an "elders' day center," or a nursing home. The participants are overwhelmingly females who are cared for primarily by their daughters (Beck, 1990). This fact has led to the naming of yet another special track for women—the "daughter track." Women at midlife have been described as "a sandwich" because they are wedged between child-care responsibilities and parent-care responsibilities. Perhaps the answer to questions like "Why are there so few outstanding female mathematicians and research scientists?" can be found in the caregiver role in which so many women engage.

Older adult differences in cognitive abilities are similar in many ways to sex differences in cognitive abilities. Verbal abilities tend to remain high into old age, with spatial abilities showing a more precipitous decline. As reviewed in chapter 5, the brains of older men show physical signs of decline at an earlier age than those of women, with men showing declines in brain volume in their 50s, a decade or so earlier than women (Cowell et al., 1994). But when Meinz and Salthouse (1998) conducted a meta-analytic review of 25 studies, they did not find any evidence of a female advantage in cognitive aging. It is likely that they relied on tests that do not show the greatest advantage for females, including the absence of tests of writing and verbal fluency. It is difficult to argue against a female advantage in old age when the majority of people living to an old age are female. The caretaker role of some older adults may provide a protective effect for older women whose household and child-care skills are often valued. There is a genuine lack of experimental data regarding the way psychosocial factors affect cognitive sex differences. As large numbers of baby boomers enter their older adult years, this is likely to become an area of increasing interest.

CHAPTER SUMMARY

A psychosocial perspective assumes that the psychological differences in the lives of women and men are arbitrarily created by society. Proponents of psychosocial explanations often prefer the term *gender* to the term *sex* to signify the societal origins of sex differences that are unrelated to the biology of reproduction. Psychosocial explanations of cognitive sex differences are important because of their implications for change. If sex differences in cognitive abilities can be attributed to psychosocial variables, then these changes can be reduced or eliminated with appropriate societal changes. One of the difficulties in identifying the relevant psychosocial variables is the pervasiveness of sex role stereotypes in our society and the inability to make causal statements from correlational data. Another difficulty is created by the nonconscious ideology that may have blinded us to many of the sex-differentiated attributes and expectations that have become ingrained in contemporary society.

Sex role stereotypes, those beliefs about the ways females and males differ, do not represent two distinct categories. Instead, they consist of traits, behaviors, and dispositions that are more or less statistically associated with being male or female. The stereotypes show considerable overlap on many dimensions. In addition, there is considerable evidence that the stereotypes are frequently accurate in that they correctly assess the statistical differences between females and males and are sensitive to context variables.

There are many differences in the interests, values, and activities of males and females in contemporary Western society. At every age, the sexes spend a large portion of their time in sex-differentiated activities, including experiences and expectations in infancy, type of play in childhood, courses selected in high school, career choices in early adulthood, time spent in child and elder care in adulthood, and life expectancy into old age. In general, females are more concerned with relationships, and males are more concerned with objects. There is intense disagreement among psychologists and others about the role and relative importance of socializing agents in the creation and maintenance of sex role stereotypes. In general, parents believe that children learn sex role behaviors and that they, the parents, do not treat their sons and daughters very differently. Yet, despite these beliefs, there are many indicators that sex role expectations are communicated by parents and others in a variety of subtle and not-so-subtle ways. Stereotypes can depress performance for members of any group associated with a negative stereotype when that negative stereotype is activated. Activation occurs when the negative stereotype is made salient, when performance on the task is important to the individual, and when the task is difficult. Recent research has also shown that stereotypes may affect performance without conscious awareness, but failures to confirm this finding means that any conclusions about "stereotype threat" are still tentative. These two new aspects of stereotypes show that stereotypes may be powerful forces that are difficult to counteract because they can operate automatically, without the belief that the stereotype is true and without conscious awareness.

A developmental life-span approach was used to show how each age has particular implications for learning and using sex role stereotypes and the way these beliefs can be influencing cognitive sex differences. Sex role stereotypic messages and pressures can be found throughout the life span.

7

Psychosocial Hypotheses Part II: Theoretical Perspectives for Understanding the Role of Psychosocial Variables

CONTENTS

7

PSYCHOSOCIAL HYPOTHESES PART II: THEORETICAL PERSPECTIVES FOR UNDERSTANDING THE ROLE OF PSYCHOSOCIAL VARIABLES

Gender roles mandate different primary activities for women and men. Women are supposed to support their husband's careers and raise their children; men are supposed to compete successfully in the occupational world in order to confirm their worth as human beings and to support their families.
—Eccles (1994, p. 600)

A wide variety of psychosocial variables implicated in creating, maintaining, or increasing sex differences in cognitive abilities were presented in chapter 6. The belief that psychosocial variables are (primarily) responsible for the differences in the lives of males and females has been referred to as the "nurture assumption" (Harris, 1998b). Part of the appeal of assuming that differences in sex roles are caused by variables near the nurture end of the nature–nurture continuum is that nurture variables are rooted in societal practices and societies can change. Would females and males become more similar if they were treated the same way? For example, parents who spank their son for some misbehavior but send their daughter to her room without supper for the same misbehavior are sending a strong sex role stereotypic message to all of the members of the household—even when the behavior is the same, girls and boys are treated differently. There are different expectations for girls and boys, different beliefs about what is appropriate, and different consequences for the same actions. This message is reinforced with viewing tens of thousands of hours of television shows, seen over many years, that depict sex-typed characters and themes. Outside the home, children encounter teachers who pay attention to girls and boys for different reasons and peers who enforce different rules for girls and boys. Evidence of sex role stereotypes can be found throughout the life span. But how do sex role stereotypes arise? Why do they per-

279

sist if they are arbitrarily created by the members of society? How easily or quickly could they be changed? What would a society be like if the lives of women and men became more similar? Many theorists have used questions like these as a starting point for theories that can help us to understand, predict, and perhaps even manipulate those psychosocial variables that are implicated in cognitive sex differences.

A THEORY OF THEORIES

Although debates arise among psychologists working from differing perspectives, each addresses important questions.
—Myers (1998, p. 4)

Making sense of the host of psychosocial variables that could be influencing the cognitive development of males and females in sex-differentiated ways is a tough job because many different types of variables are interwoven into the fabric of society. There are multiple possible perspectives for organizing the psychosocial world. A "theory of theories" is needed to organize the many theories applied to the many questions about cognitive sex differences. I like to think about the quest to understand cognitive sex differences as analogous to the well-known parable of the three blind men and the elephant. It is a story that is probably familiar to most readers (Wade & Tavris, 1998). In this parable, each blind man attempts to "know" what an elephant is like by the only way he can—by feeling it. One blind man is certain that an elephant is broad and strong like a tree; he is feeling the elephant's leg. Another blind man is certain that it is small and thin like a reed; he is feeling the elephant's tail. The third blind man cannot understand how the others can be so blind, when the elephant is surely flexible like a hose; he is feeling the elephant's trunk. Which of these blind men is correct? In part, they all are correct, and of course, in part they are all wrong. Perhaps this is a good metaphor for understanding the varying theoretical perspectives on cognitive sex differences. Each of the psychosocial theories frames the question of cognitive sex differences in a somewhat different way, and each takes a different view of what is important and how and why the differences came about. Not surprisingly, each provides a "piece of the answer."

Several different theoretical positions are considered in this chapter: the psychoanalytic view associated with Sigmund Freud; learning theories that posit general mechanisms for learning; social learning theories that emphasize the importance of appropriate role models; the expectancies–values–motives perspective, in which motivation and individual choice are of primary importance; a "bent twigs" theory, in which biological predispositions are enhanced by society; social ecology, an approach that emphasizes the contextual nature of sex role behaviors; cognitive schema and social cognition theories that highlight the thinking processes; and performance and strategy variables that explain cognitive sex differences as being more similar to habits than abilities. These diverse perspectives mirror the many subfields of psychology—each with a different emphasis and a different view of what is important in understanding the complexity of human nature.

THE PSYCHOANALYTIC PERSPECTIVE

The psychic development of the individual is a short repetition
of the course of development of the race.
—Freud (cited in Bartlett, 1980, p. 678)

Approximately 100 years ago, Sigmund Freud (1920) proposed an influential theory that encompassed developmental psychology, psychopathology, psychotherapy, and personality. Freud is probably the most famous psychologist who ever lived, in part because his views were so radical, and in part because he influenced many of psychology's subdisciplines with a single broad theory known as "psychoanalytic theory." The foundation of Freud's psychoanalytic theory was built on the biological differences between the sexes, thereby representing a strong form of the belief that "biology is destiny." He was a prolific and popular writer, with much to say about a wide range of topics, including the ways in which girls and boys develop in psychologically sex-differentiated ways. Unlike the other psychologists whose research is reviewed in this book, Freud did not conduct research to determine if his theories were supported with data. For this reason, most psychologists who emphasize the scientific bases of the discipline see Freud as a historical figure who has little relevance to modern psychology. Others argue that Freud's profound influence on the early development of psychology cannot be minimized and that his views need to be understood within the historical context in which he lived.

Psychosexual Stages of Development

One of the major tenets of Freud's psychoanalytic theory is that girls and boys proceed sequentially through a series of developmental stages, each important in shaping sex-differentiated behaviors and feelings. These stages were called *psychosexual* because female and male differences in sexual nature were primary determinants of psychological development. These stages highlight the importance of early life experiences on adult development, a major contribution of Freudian theory. According to Freud, if an individual could not resolve important issues in any of the stages, he or she would develop lifelong personality characteristics that were associated with the unresolved issues in that stage.

The core concept in Freudian psychoanalytic theory is that children come to identify with their same-sex parent and through identification, they imitate the appropriate sex role behaviors of their mothers or fathers. The first of these stages, the *oral stage* of development, begins at birth and continues until age 2. In the first 2 years of life, infants learn the pleasures of oral activity by sucking, first for nourishment and later for the pleasure it brings. Between the ages of 2 and 4, children pass through the *anal stage,* in which they learn the pleasures of urination and defecation. The third psychosexual stage is particularly important in understanding sex-differentiated behaviors that occur later in life. Freud maintained that all children at approximately 4 to 5 years of age enter a developmental period known as the *phallic stage,* so named because of children's preoccupation with their genitals. (Freud used the term *phallic stage* to refer to the development of both girls and boys, even though the term *phallic* is derived from a Greek word meaning *penis.*) Children in the phallic stage go through a fairly involved sequence of parental alliances and jealousies that follows different paths depending on whether the child is a girl or a boy. It is during this developmental period that children resolve their early feelings of love and hate for their parents and ultimately identify with the same-sex parent.

Let's first consider how this process proceeds for boys because it is somewhat less complicated than the process Freud attributed to girls. The impetus for boys to identify with their same-sex parent is the *Oedipus complex,* named for a 5th century B.C. play by Sophocles entitled *Oedipus Rex.* In this play, Oedipus unknowingly commits the unspeakable crime of killing his father and later marrying his mother and fathering children with her. (He did not know they were his parents until after he had committed these acts.) Freud believed that this story represented a universal theme of all boys' sexual longing for their mothers. During the phallic stage, the young boy's newly discovered erotic feelings are vaguely directed toward his mother (or mother substitute) because she has been the source of pleasure in the past. At the same time, he also begins to feel jealous of his father, a "rival" for his mother's love. This is also the time in his development when he learns that girls do not have a penis, leading him to conclude that it must have been cut off for some terrible reason. Whatever the reason, the inference is that the female genitalia are lacking something important. He then reasons that the same thing could happen to him because of his sexual desire for his mother and his jealousy of his father. All boys at this age must resolve the problem of *castration anxiety* (an unconscious fear of being castrated). Boys resolve this dilemma the only way possible; they repress their erotic feelings for their mothers and identify with their fathers.

How do girls come to identify with their mothers according to Freudian theory? There is a roughly analogous version of the Oedipus complex known as the *Electra complex.* Electra was the heroine in a Greek tragedy who convinced her brother to kill their mother, also a supposedly universal theme. During the preschool years that comprise the phallic stage of development, girls discover that they do not have a penis and immediately develop *penis envy,* an intense desire to have male genitals. For reasons never clearly explained, the girl concludes that she must have once had a penis, which was removed for some unknown reason. She holds the mother responsible for this sad state of affairs when she realizes that the mother also lacks the prized organ. Girls then turn to their fathers and, like their brothers, have to resolve feelings of hatred and jealousy. Because of fear of reprisal from jealous mothers, girls shift their identification back to their mothers and imitate female sex role behaviors.

Thus, for Freud, the key to sex role identification was the presence or absence of a penis during critical years of child development (approximately 4 to 6 years old) and the appropriate resolution of the Oedipus or Electra complex. Freudian theory is actually much more complex than this, but these are the basic assumptions underlying sex role identification. There are numerous problems with this aspect of Freudian theory. Most notably, research has shown that a large proportion of children in this age range don't have a conscious understanding about the anatomical differences between women and men (Katcher, 1955). Psychoanalytic theory has also been criticized for its antifemale (penis-centered) orientation, especially for its assumption that children of both sexes immediately perceive the superiority of male genitals over female genitals. In addition, it implies that children who are raised in homes without a same-sexed parent will fail to develop sex role-appropriate behaviors. Research with children in single-parent families has shown this prediction to be false (Lynn, 1974).

At the end of the phallic stage, children of both sexes enter a *latency stage* during which time their sexuality is dormant, and children focus their energies on the learning tasks that are important in middle childhood. At puberty, the sexual desires that marked the phallic stage reemerge, but at this stage, sexual desire is focused on opposite-sex peers instead of the opposite-sex parent. Thus, it is identification with the same-sex parent that causes boys to emulate their fathers' behaviors and girls to emulate their mothers' behavior. According to Freudian theory, the most critical developmental period for identification with the same-sex parent occurs during the preschool years.

LEARNING THEORIES

In almost every case, exposure to spatial test materials, or training on related materials, raises spatial ability test scores.
—Baenninger and Newcombe (1995, p. 365)

In the generic sense of the term, all of the theories being described in this chapter can be described as *learning theories* because they all are concerned with understanding the way sex role stereotypes are learned. Learning theory, however, has a very specific meaning in psychology. It refers to the theory that most learning is contingent on the rewards and punishments that follow behavior. Although terms like *reward* and *punishment* have an intuitive everyday meaning, they have a precise meaning in the jargon of learning theory. A reward is anything that increases the probability of a particular behavior, and a punishment is anything that decreases the probability of a particular behavior. Learning theorists explain the acquisition of sex roles by positing that children are rewarded when they evince appropriate sex role behaviors and attitudes and punished for behaviors and attitudes that do not conform to the sex-appropriate roles. We're all familiar with sex role statements like "boys don't cry" and "lady-like behavior." It's easy to imagine how rewards and punishments could function to reinforce sex role-appropriate behavior.

Rewards and Punishments Shape Future Behaviors

Rewards and punishments can assume many different forms. A smile, a pat on the back, an award, or some candy could all functionally serve to increase desired behavior. Similarly, a frown, scolding, physical punishment, or public humiliation could all serve to discourage or decrease the likelihood of some behavior. As children grow, they receive numerous rewards and punishments from parents and other socializing agents who want to influence their behaviors.

In a learning theory conceptualization of the origins of cognitive sex differences, the emphasis is on the overt behaviors that children engage in and their consequences. Children and adults receive rewards and punishments for certain intellectual activities, repeating those that are rewarded and avoiding those that are punished. In this way, we all learn from repeated experiences. Mathematics, for example, is a highly sex-typed academic subject (Sherman, 1983). One way that children come to learn that mathematics is a male domain is through differential rewards and punishments. Numerous studies have shown that boys are more likely than girls to receive encouragement to work through difficult mathematics problems and girls receive less praise than boys for correct answers in mathematics classes (AAUW, 1992; Stage & Karplus, 1981). It is also likely that a sex-differentiated pattern of rewards and punishments could be used to explain sex differences in verbal and spatial ability, with girls encouraged to read more often than boys and boys encouraged to engage in spatial activities (blocks, erector sets, etc.) more often than girls. Thus, according to learning theory, through sex-differentiated rewards and punishments, children learn that mathematical and spatial activities are more appropriate for boys and that reading and other verbal activities are more appropriate for girls.

Practice and Feedback

Learning is an inevitable consequence of living. If we could not learn, we would die. With appropriate instruction and experience, everyone (except, perhaps, profoundly retarded individuals) improves in all of the areas in which sex differences in cognitive abilities are found. These are all educable areas of human cognition. There are many studies showing that both females and males, at every age, can improve their cognitive performance on any task if they receive appropriate instruction. For example, Law et al. (1993) found the usual sex differences, with males performing more accurately than females, in tests of spatiotemporal reasoning, which included making time-of-arrival and velocity judgments about a moving figure. With practice and feedback, both females and males improved on this task. Although the female–male difference in performance was not eliminated with training in this study, both groups showed improved performance. Law et al. believe that the ability to make judgments about moving objects is increasingly im-

Baby Blues cartoon. Reprinted with special permission of King Features Syndicate.

portant because of the growth in the use of technology, often with moving arrays depicted on computer monitors. This skill is valuable in multiple work and other applied settings. They urged that educators and psychologists consider the experiential histories of their students with different types of cognitive tasks, the rate at which the students can learn a skilled task, and the absolute level of performance needed to successfully accomplish a particular task. Given what we know about the life experiences of males and females, it is likely that most males have more spatial experience than most females. If both can learn at a rapid rate and attain a high level of performance after training, then any initial differences between males and females could be meaningless in terms of expected skill levels after training. This is an important point because it addresses the real-world implications of sex differences in an important skill and the way training can be used to improve the skill level of most people regardless of sex. Very similar results were reported by Subrahmanyam and Greenfield (1994) in a study that used a spatial video game as a way of improving visual–spatial skills. Like Law et al., they found that for the 10- and 11-year-olds who served as participants in the study, the boys initially performed better than the girls on several spatial ability measures. They then provided training in the form of video games. Both the boys and the girls improved their performance after the training, but the improvement was the same for both groups, which means that the boys were still outperforming the girls after the training, with everyone performing at a higher level.

The result that both sexes improve their performance on cognitive tests with training has been widely replicated with different age groups (e.g., very old populations; Fernández-Ballesteros & Calero, 1995), with different visual–spatial tasks (e.g., mental rotation tasks; Peters et al., 1995), for a variety of computer games (McClurg & Chaillé, 1987), and even with male and female rats who demonstrated their improved performance on a water maze task (Perrot-Sinal, Kostenuik, Ossenkopp, & Kavaliers, 1996).

Differential Life Experiences

Sex role stereotypes could be indirectly influencing the development of spatial skills by providing each sex with different amounts and types of spatial and other cognitive-related experiences. The underlying idea is that each sex has more prac- tice with different sorts of tasks, resulting in the enhanced development of differ- ent cognitive skills. This possibility was considered in the last chapter when video games and billiards were discussed as common adolescent activities among boys but not among girls. Boys' and girls' lives differ in many ways. For example, in an observation of preschool children, Adams and Bradford (1985) found that boys touched unfamiliar objects more often than girls did and girls touched familiar ob- jects more often than boys did. It is possible that early life exploration of the unfa- miliar provides a head start in spatial skills learning. In a meta-analytic review of the literature that linked spatial activity participation with spatial ability, Baenninger and Newcombe (1989) concluded that there is a weak relationship and that the magnitude of the effect is the same for females as for males. Thus, accord- ing to these authors, both sexes benefit about equally from participation in spatial activities. All of these studies point to the same conclusion: Spatial ability can be improved with appropriate training.

Despite the multiplicity of positive results that implicate environmental factors in the development of spatial skills, there are still some nagging inconsistencies that remain unexplained by appeals to learning theory. The principle that the top edge of water remains horizontal when a glass is tipped seems particularly difficult for girls to comprehend (or perhaps to demonstrate). The large sex differences that have been reported for many decades on the Water-Level Test cannot be explained by positing that females have less experience with glasses of water or receive less encouragement or fewer rewards in working and playing with liquids. An interest- ing article offered some hope in understanding why females perform less accu- rately on the Water-Level Task. Hecht and Proffitt (1995) reported that people in occupations that required that they work with liquids (e.g., bartenders, waiters, and waitresses) were less accurate in their knowledge that the water line remains hori- zontal in a tilted container. This finding presented an intriguing possibility for un- derstanding why females, who probably have more experience with liquids than males do, might have had detrimental learning experiences. However, this possi- bility needs to be rejected at this time because the results did not hold up under rep- lication (Vasta et al., 1997).

It is possible, although unproven, that boys learn spatial principles more easily or readily than girls. It also seems reasonable to conclude that we should be provid- ing all children with visual–spatial and building toys that are typically labeled *boys' toys*. There is enough evidence to suggest that experience with these toys may be useful in the development of spatial skills. We may be shortchanging the intellectual development of girls by providing them with only traditional sex-ste- reotyped toys. Another important implication of this research is the finding that spatial skills are trainable. Very few schools incorporate spatial skills training into their curriculum. One way to be certain that all individuals develop their spatial abilities to their fullest capacity is to routinely provide such training to all students from their preschool through their high school years. Empirical results have shown that both girls and boys would benefit from such instruction.

SOCIAL LEARNING THEORY

Math class is tough; I love dressing up; Do you want to braid my hair?
—Teen-Talk Barbie's first words

Attack the Cobra Squad with heavy fire power; when I give the orders, listen or get captured.
—GI Joe (cited in Viner, 1994, p. 105).

Several prominent theorists have proposed that sex-typed behaviors are learned in multiple ways (Bandura & Walters, 1963). They believe that although direct rewards and punishments can produce sex role learning, imitation learning or modeling may be the more important mechanism for producing sex role-appropriate behaviors. This theoretical perspective is many decades old and has a large research literature. Because of the importance psychologists attach to imitation or modeling in social situations, this theory is sometimes called *social learning* or *social modeling*. In addition to receiving rewards and punishments for behaviors that are either consistent or inconsistent with sex roles, children are told in numerous ways that they are either a girl or a boy. Children also notice similarities among other girls and among other boys. A list of possible examples would be quite long: Girls may wear bows and barrettes in their hair but boys may not. Girls may wear almost any color clothing, whereas boys may not wear pink clothes. Very few boys own doll carriages, a common girl's toy. Combat dolls like GI Joe and play guns and rifles are appropriate for boys but not for girls. In fact, these "dolls" are frequently called "action figures" so that they are distinguished from the sort of dolls that elicit care-taking play. GI Joe, "The Hulk," and similar action figures are not designed to encourage the same play activities as "Betsy Wetsy," a doll that sucks from bottles and needs to have her diapers changed, and "Chatty Cathy," a doll that talks all the time. (These are the real names of popular dolls. I leave it to the reader to consider whether The Hulk is as demeaning as dolls that eat, urinate, and talk nonstop.)

There are also obvious differences among adults who model grown-up behaviors. Women may wear high-heeled shoes, girdles, make-up, nail polish, and dresses, while any man who wears these items is considered deviant. Men may wear wing-tipped shoes and men's style clothing. Anyone who doubts that there are strong sanctions about something as simple as clothing type should try to shop for shoes in the shoe department reserved for the other sex. The message that some shoe styles are appropriate only for women or men was probably never stated explicitly, but it was made clear just by observing. If you are a woman, you did not have to try to purchase shoes in the men's shoe department, or if you are a man, you did not have to try to purchase shoes in the women's shoe department to learn what is appropriate for your sex.

Observational Learning

Ask yourself how you would respond to a "math freak" adolescent son and a "math freak" adolescent daughter.
—Braine (1988, p. 186)

According to social modeling theory, children learn about sex role behaviors by observing between-sex differences as they are played out in the lives of the other children and adults with whom they interact and in the media. They then imitate the behaviors and attitudes of same-sex models. Social modeling theory differs from learning theory in that it does not assume that rewards and punishments must be received to shape behavior or that the child personally engages in the behavior. Sex role learning can occur from observing others and imitating them. Appropriate imitation is likely to be rewarded, as in the case of a young girl who dresses up in her mother's shoes and old dresses. Inappropriate imitation is likely to be punished, as in the case of a young boy who dresses up in his mother's shoes and old dresses. Thus, through a combination of observational learning, appropriate modeling, and rewards and punishments received by both the role models and the children in their attempts to imitate the models, boys and girls learn society's sex roles.

An interesting implication of social learning theory is that much of the learning is done by watching others, which means that sex role messages can come from a variety of sources outside of the home. Even if parents did not differentially socialize their children on the basis of each child's sex, there are still many opportunities for children to learn about sex-typed behaviors, including those presented on television, in school classrooms, on the playground, and in the homes of others. These messages can even be learned from Barbie dolls and GI Joes and the various characters found in video games, books, and other media. With messages about appropriate female and male behavior coming from so many different sources, these messages would be almost impossible to ignore.

Social modeling is not restricted to the acquisition of sex roles in childhood. As adults, we also observe how each sex should act, imitate appropriate models, and receive rewards and punishments for these actions. We are social animals who frequently look to others to determine how we should act and what we should think and feel. We are most likely to adopt the behaviors and attitudes of those who are similar to us. Social influences to conform to behaviors deemed appropriate by society are extremely strong, even for adults. Few women would feel comfortable as the only female in an all-male class on motor repair, and few men would feel comfortable in an all-female nursing class, for example. In this theoretical framework, it would be extremely important for women and men considering careers in these traditionally "sex-inappropriate" fields to have female mathematicians to serve as models for women and male nurses to serve as models for men.

EXPECTANCIES–VALUES–MOTIVES

The superwomen are weary; ... in the 80's American women learned
that "having it all" meant doing it all.
—Wallis (1989, p. 80)

The most comprehensive theoretical model designed to explain sex differences in academic achievement was proposed by Eccles (Parsons) et al. (1983) and more recently by Eccles (1987, 1994) and Wigfield and Eccles (1992). It is a variation of a more general model called an Expectancy × Value model. The underlying idea is that the outcome of a cognitive task depends on how much the individual doing the task expects to succeed or fail and how much she or he values the outcome. Note that this model is expressed as a mathematical equation in which the relationship between expectancy and value is multiplicative. Thus, if either the expectancy of success or the value of the outcome is zero, then, regardless of what the other variable is, together, they are mathematically equal to zero. If a task has no value to an individual (it is mathematically equal to zero in value) or if an individual believes that he or she has no chance of success (expectancy of success is mathematically equal to zero), then the multiplicative relationship is zero. Similarly, if both expectancy and value are high, their multiplied combination will be high, and if both are low, their multiplied combination will also be low.

Models of this type are really models of achievement motivation and thus have a broad research literature that addresses many questions in addition to those about sex differences. They can be used to understand the capabilities and behaviors that are involved in situations in which people are evaluated—situations like college entrance examinations, tests in school, and performance on cognitive tasks for which someone will be grading the performance on the task. The underlying idea is that individuals persist at tasks in which they expect success and avoid tasks in which they expect failure. Similarly, individuals persist at tasks when they value the goal and avoid tasks when they do not value the goal. Thus, expectations and values combine in ways that more or less motivate individuals to achieve at a task.

Self-Efficacy

Self-efficacy is a classic theory in the psychological literature on motivation (Bandura, 1986). It explains the origins and operation of self-confidence, the belief that we can achieve a goal. The belief that an individual can or can't achieve a particular goal may not be related to actual ability, but it is likely to have an effect on whether the goal is actually achieved. In general, people are willing to put more effort and resources into attempts to achieve a goal if they believe that they will ultimately be successful. Self-efficacy is a core belief in the ability to achieve a desired outcome from an action. It is essentially a cognitive theory in that beliefs about one's ability are seen as the core that determines the actions an individual is willing to take to reach a goal. The underlying idea of self-efficacy is that people's beliefs about their ability to achieve a goal influence their actual ability to achieve that goal because they work harder and longer and the increase in effort improves their ability to achieve the goal. Self-efficacy is reflected in the expectancy component of the values–expectancy–motivation model. This chain of events is depicted in Fig. 7.1.

The underlying idea in the concept of self-efficacy is that an individual's beliefs about his or her academic abilities determine what that individual does when faced with learning or performance tasks that utilize the abilities. For example, consider a recent study of third-, fourth-, and fifth-grade girls and boys (Pajares, Miller, & Johnson, 1999). In this study, each child's writing ability was assessed by the teacher, a writing sample was rated by judges, and the children in each grade responded to questions about their writing abilities. There was a high degree of consistency in the results: The teachers judged the girls to be better writers than the boys, and the judges who rated the writing samples agreed that the girls were better writers than the boys. When the children answered questions about their own writing ability relative to other children, the girls, overall, rated themselves to be better writers than the boys rated themselves. Thus, all three groups—teachers, raters, and children—agreed that the girls were better at writing than the boys. The authors of this study discussed how these beliefs can have long-lasting effects, which are especially important when the children face obstacles in their writing. The authors used the concept of self-efficacy to explain why children with similar ability levels often have widely differing levels of achievement.

Models of Academic Achievement

How does the idea that values and the expectancy of success are important determinants to success at any task apply more specifically to cognitive sex differences?

High Self-Efficacy:

1. Belief that "I can achieve this goal" ———▶ 2. High effort + More resources toward goal attainment + Greater persistence to achieve the desired goal ———▶3. Improved ability to actually achieve the goal ———▶ 4. Greater probability of successfully achieving a goal.

Low Self-Efficacy:

1. Belief that "I cannot achieve this goal"———▶ 2. Little effort + Few resources toward goal attainment + failing to try or quitting soon after starting ———▶ 3. No learning or gains in ability ———▶ 4. Low probability of successfully achieving a goal.

FIG. 7.1.   Self-efficacy model of achievement success. Individuals with high self-efficacy believe that they can achieve a goal, and because of this belief, they act in ways that enhance their ability to achieve the goal (e.g., hard work and persistence). Individuals with low self-efficacy do not believe that they can achieve a goal and therefore expend little or no effort, sometimes quitting soon after an initial attempt. These individuals do not improve in their goal-related abilities and have a low probability of success.

Let's consider some of the ways values and expectancies could be operating to depress female achievement in advanced mathematics. The same sort of determination could be made for the other cognitive abilities that are presented in this text, but it is easiest to apply this model to achievement in mathematics because there is a large research and theoretical literature that pertains to sex differences in advanced mathematics.

Benbow (1988) listed many of the psychosocial hypotheses that have appeared in the literature to explain sex differences in mathematics. I summarize, embellish on, and borrow from her listing. Interested readers should consult Benbow's article along with the many comments on it. There are approximately 500 references to related studies in mathematics that the author and commentators used to support their points and to refute those that they didn't agree with. I keep this section relatively brief because those of you who want to delve further into the topic can consult Benbow's excellent article and its related commentaries and rebuttal.

1. *Females maintain more negative attitudes toward mathematics.* As with every area of research, the literature is not entirely consistent in reporting these findings, but the vast majority of times when differences are found, they are in the predicted direction, with females more negative than males. (See, e.g., Hyde, Fennema, Ryan, Frost, & Hopp, 1990.)

2. *Females perceive mathematics to be less important for career goals than males do.* Again, although there are some failures to confirm this hypothesis (e.g., Singer & Stake, 1986), when differences are found, they tend to support this contention. This is important because it relates directly to motivation. At least some of the time, most students have to exert time and effort to comprehend advanced mathematical concepts. If females, in general, believe that mathematics is less useful to their future careers, then they are less likely to exert much effort to learn the concepts. This belief is sometimes seen in the popular media. I remember sitting in a movie theater several years ago watching the movie *Peggy Sue Got Married*. In this fantasy film, a grown woman has the opportunity to return to high school with the knowledge and experience she had accumulated in her adult life. In her mathematics class, she assured the teacher that she would never need to know the mathematics he wanted her to learn. A spontaneous cheer went up from the movie audience, many of whom seemed to agree with her pronouncement about the uselessness of mathematics for women's lives.

3. *Females have less confidence in their ability to learn mathematics.* This is an interesting hypothesis because although females expect to receive lower course grades in mathematics than males do, females, in fact, receive higher course grades even in advanced mathematics courses (Elmore & Vasu, 1986; Willingham & Cole, 1997). Although females may be less confident, they are performing better in virtually all mathematics courses. Of course, this comparison may be unfair because there are fewer

females than males in advanced mathematics courses, so they may represent a more select group of females. Females are also more likely to attribute success in mathematics to effort than to ability (Ryckman & Peckham, 1987). In a study of academic self-confidence, Bennett (1996, 1997) found that among college students in England, the men estimated their IQ scores to be higher than the estimates that women gave for their own IQ scores. Recall that, by design, the scores of men and women are identical. The British male college students also estimated their ability in mathematics and spatial tasks to be significantly higher than the estimates the women provided for their abilities in these areas. Thus, even when women perform as well as men, women are less confident in their abilities than men are in their abilities.

4. *Mathematics is a male-stereotyped cognitive domain.* In general, the disproportionate number of males in advanced mathematics courses suggests that this is true. If you doubt this, show a few friends Fig. 7.2, which is an artist's rendition of the stereotypical female mathematician. Ask your friends to guess the college major of the woman depicted. The stereotype that females who succeed in mathematics and the sciences are masculine can be vicious and demeaning. Again, I provide a personal example that brought this fact home to me in a much more vivid manner than any of the research that I have read. A male college student was showing me around the very large campus at the University of California, Los Angeles. We went to the portion of the campus that housed the engineering school, mathematics, and physical sciences departments. He told me that there was a derogatory name for the female students on that part of campus ("science dog"). The message was quite strong that being an attractive female and studying mathematics and the sciences are not compatible. This ugly moniker saddened and angered me. Name-calling designed specifically to denigrate females who study mathematics and the sciences provides strong support for the notion that mathematics is a male-stereotyped domain.

5. *Females receive less encouragement and support for studying advanced mathematics.* In a survey of the parents of junior high school students, Yee and Eccles (1988) found that parents believe that mathematics is more difficult for their daughters than for their sons. These beliefs would presumably translate into giving their daughters less support for studying advanced mathematics than their sons.

6. *Females take fewer mathematics courses than males; therefore, they score lower on tests of mathematical reasoning ability.* This is a prediction that is difficult to disagree with, but it is not as straightforward as it may seem. It is true that fewer females are enrolled in advanced mathematics courses, with the proportion decreasing as the level of the course increases. But there have been studies that have controlled for number of mathematics courses taken, and sex differences are still found favoring males (e.g., Gallagher, 1998; Meece et al., 1982; Willingham & Cole, 1997).

FIG. 7.2.   An artist's conception of the stereotypical "woman mathematician" as described by Professor Martha Smith: "Many people on hearing the words 'female mathematician' conjure up an image of a six-foot, gray-haired, tweed suited oxford clad woman. ... This image, of course, doesn't attract the young woman who is continually being bombarded with messages, direct and indirect, to be beautiful, 'feminine' and catch a man" (cited in Ernest, 1976, p. 14).

Even if some of these hypothesized reasons to explain sex differences in advanced mathematics are weak or even wrong, the effect of socialization on females and males comes from the totality of experiences and not any one of them in isolation. Several more complex models to explain mathematics sex differences have been proposed. Sherman (1982), for example, identified confidence in learning mathematics, perceived usefulness of mathematics, and attitudes of one's mother, father, and teacher toward learning mathematics as important determinants of mathematics achievement. It seems intuitively obvious that these are important variables in understanding success in mathematics. Few people would persist in higher mathematics course work if they believed that they did not have the ability to learn the material, if they felt that it was of little value, or if they were routinely discouraged by their parents and teachers.

Eccles' Model of Career-Related Choices

Using the variables reviewed by Benbow (1988), which showed that mathematics is a male-stereotyped domain, women expect that advanced mathematics will be less valuable to them in their careers, and women receive multiple negative messages about success in mathematics, it is easy to see how a combined model of expectancies for success and the perceived value of achieving at advanced mathematics would predict that females achieve at a lower rate than males. This is the basis for Eccles' (1987, 1994) Expectancy × Value model of career-related choices.

In Eccles' (1987, 1994) model, she delineated the relationships among several important determinants of academic choices in general and career decisions. She posited a theoretical network composed of the following variables (which are described in ways that link them to the preceding discussion in this chapter and chap. 6): sex role stereotypes, beliefs and behaviors of parents and teachers, individual aptitude, previous experiences, the way the individual perceives these variables, and the individual's goals and expectations of success. Eccles' model is shown in Fig. 7.3.

Figure 7.3 explains how sex differences in the pattern of educational and occupational choices arise from an array of psychosocial variables. Take some time to look over the variables that are shown in Fig. 7.3 and the way they connect to each other. Recall earlier discussions about the role that women play as primary caretaker for their children, their home, and, later, for their aging parents. The ideal mother–daughter spends much time and effort caring for others and maintaining a clean, orderly home. In this social context, it is easy to understand why we find fewer women in society's most demanding, prestigious, and highly paid careers, such as surgeon, high-level politician (state and national level), research scientist, and chief corporate officer.

Eccles' (1987, 1994) model differs from most of the others in that it includes the issue of choice. Everyone makes choices all of the time; what this model attempts

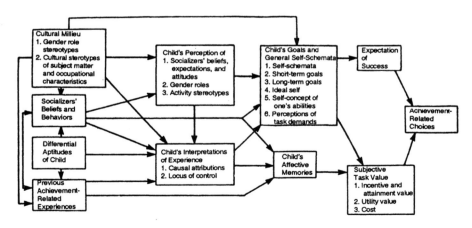

FIG. 7.3.   Model devised to explain how an interdependent network of values and expectations influence academic and career choices. From Eccles, 1987. Gender Roles and Women's Achievement-Related Decisions. *Psychology of Women Quarterly, 11*, p. 135–172. Reprinted with permission.

to do is delineate the variables that shape the choices we make and suggests that for many of the so-called choices, there really are few alternatives. In this context, women and men (on average) have different values, and in the context of one's own values, women and men would be expected to make different achievement-related choices. Women and men also would have different experiences which led to different evaluations about the likelihood of success at different tasks. As Eccles described, there is a complex web of psychosocial causative factors that all work against female excellence in achievement-related positions. This is a powerful model backed with a considerable body of research (e.g., Eccles, 1994; Wigfield & Eccles, 1992). From this perspective, it is easy to understand why many researchers in this area have been highly critical of any claim that sex differences in cognitive performance or career choices can be traced to a biological etiology (Fox, Tobin, & Brody, 1979; Sherman, 1979). The large number of psychosocial explanations that have been used both logically and empirically to explain the data provide a powerful addition to the research on biological underpinnings of these differences.

BENT TWIGS

Tis education forms the common mind. Just as the twig is bent,
the tree's inclined.
—Pope (cited in Bartlett, 1980, p. 335)

Sherman (1967) proposed a theory to explain female superiority in language memory and usage. It has come to be known as the "bent twig hypothesis" in reference to an old saying that goes something like this: "As the twig is bent, so the tree shall grow." Sherman began with the assumption that girls talk at an earlier age than boys. The reasons why girls talk at an earlier age are not as important as the consequence. Because of their early advantage with language, girls rely more on verbally and socially mediated approaches in their interactions with people and objects in their world. Boys, in contrast, rely on their better developed musculature to interact with people and objects; thus, they move around more, a fact that could contribute to the development of their spatial skills. Each sex develops somewhat fixed patterns or preferences for interacting, with the result that early developmental differences guide later actions. In this way, a small initial difference in abilities between the sexes grows larger over time. It is interesting to note that the bent twig hypothesis does not explain the initial sex differences with respect to verbal, motor, or other abilities. These could be due to early differential reinforcement patterns for infant vocalizations, to biologically based readiness to produce language, or to some interaction of these two possibilities.

If, as Sherman (1967) suggested, girls tend to rely on verbal skills instead of using spatial ones, then the finding that females' brains may be organized more bilaterally could, in fact, reflect strategy differences and not biological differences. In other words, the sex differences in brain lateralization that were discussed in the biological chapters could be an artifact of verbal strategy preferences among females and not reflective of "hard-wired" neurological differences. Suppose, for example, that females use verbal strategies or modes of information processing when faced with the Embedded Figures Test, the test in which the contours of a smaller figure are obscured by the contours of a larger figure that encompasses the smaller one. The task is to find the smaller figure in the visual display. A verbal strategy would be less efficient than a spatial approach to this problem. Females would then be expected to perform less well than males, who rely on spatial modes of information processing when taking this test. If this hypothesis is true, then cognitive sex differences could be explained by the perseverative use of verbal strategies by females, which leaves them at a disadvantage when performing spatial tasks.

Biological Propensities and Beneficial Environments

Casey and her colleagues (Casey & Brabeck, 1990; Casey, Brabeck, & Nuttall, 1995; Casey, Nuttall, et al., 1995; Pezaris & Casey, 1991) developed a program of research that explores the way biological predispositions, especially small ones, can interact with social influences, like parental encouragement, to create fairly large sex differences in cognitive abilities. She identified girls with biological correlates of mathematical giftedness. (Recall from chap. 4 and 5 that left-handedness is statistically associated with extreme mathematical giftedness.) If these girls also had mothers who encouraged non-sex-typed behaviors, the biologically talented girls were more likely to achieve at the highest levels of mathematics than girls who did not have this combination of biological and environmental factors. Casey described her research approach as an example of the bent twig hypothesis because initial differences in abilities, which arise from the biological basis of sex differences. are magnified by differential experiences.

In another study that typifies the bent twig approach, Casey, Nuttall, and Pezaris (1997) examined the way confidence in one's ability to succeed in math and an opposite construct, math anxiety, relate to performance on the SAT–M for a sample of high-performing adolescents. These measures are in the tradition of the self-efficacy and achievement motivation literature because they assess expectations of success at math tasks. In addition, Casey et al. (1997) obtained measures of the spatial abilities (i.e., a mental rotation test like the one described in chap. 3) of their participants because spatial ability has already been established as a moderator in the differences between males and females on the SAT–M (Casey, Nuttall, et al., 1995). These investigators controlled for a variety of other variables that might affect the results, such as the number and type of mathematics courses that the participants had taken. The actual statistical procedures that Casey et al. (1997) used to analyze their data are beyond the scope of this book, so I explain their conclusions and leave it to readers with advanced statistical knowledge to review the data analytic techniques for themselves. The investigators found clear evidence that spatial skills are important in SAT–M scores, perhaps because the participants who scored well on the SAT–M used spatial strategies to solve problems. Furthermore, they found that confidence in one's ability to solve math problems was also an important factor in determining SAT–M scores, although it was not as important as spatial ability. Thus, both spatial ability and self-confidence are involved in determining SAT–M scores. What is particularly appealing about this approach to studying sex differences in cognitive abilities is that it includes a variety of different sorts of measures and looks to both abilities and beliefs to provide an explanation of complex phenomena.

SOCIAL ECOLOGY

Humans carry the imprint of their particular social worlds.
—Elder (1995, p. 101)

The social ecology perspective is a more recent conceptualization of the multitude of variables that influence the way we grow and the abilities we develop than the other perspectives considered in this chapter. The beginning premise for the theory of social ecology is that people's lives can be understood only by understanding the context in which they occur. Sometimes, social ecology is called "life review" because of the way proponents of this theoretical perspective view and re-view entire lives in terms of the social and historical periods—the contexts—in which they are lived. It is most often associated with the pioneering work of Uri Bronfenbrenner (1994), an influential developmental psychologist. Bronfenbrenner and his adherents view each individual as an active agent who contributes to his or her own development. They recognize the reciprocal ways in which life events change people and people, in turn, change their environment, thereby altering the trajectories of subsequent life events. In this sense, social ecology shares the active participant ideas found in choice models, but it also recognizes the importance of biology in influencing the choices that people make. It differs from a traditional interactionist view of heredity and environment in that social ecologists emphasize the way the environment unlocks the genetic potential of individuals, the way intellect unfolds in a particular context (Ceci & Hembrooke, 1995). An important component of this theoretical approach is recognition of the way social environments are constructed by and for children as they grow (Maccoby, 1995).

Development in Context

It makes sense that generations raised with different expectations
and in different historical circumstances may age differently.
—Stewart and Ostrove (1998, p. 1185)

The theoretical perspective of social ecology is predicated on the interplay among the characteristics of individuals, the social context in which they find themselves, developmental processes, and the way these components change over time (Moen, 1995). Human development depends on the reciprocal influences of development and context. According to Maccoby (1995), the importance of one's sex waxes and wanes throughout the life span. In infancy and during the toddler years, boys and girls are treated in very similar ways, with the only documented difference being that boys are treated more roughly during this period than girls are and girls are talked to more about emotions than boys are. But, in childhood, a new social structure emerges that is dependent on one's peers. It is a developmental period when children actively construct the social structures that help to define middle childhood. It is at this developmental stage that boys' and girls' lives begin to differ in important ways. Children in middle childhood self-segregate by sex, with boys showing much more preoccupation with dominance and aggression. In adolescence, children begin the process of disengaging from their nuclear family, with girls kept much closer to the family than boys in societies that delay marriage beyond the adolescent years.

An important difference between this perspective and the others is its emphasis on historical events and the way in which one's age and sex determine the effect of a historical event on the individual. It assumes, for example, that the large numbers of women who entered the labor force en masse during World War II experienced a clash in the values they were brought up with as children and adolescents in the 1930s. Their younger siblings also were influenced by this historical event, but they were changed in different ways because they were at a different developmental stage at the time of this historical event. Certainly, we can see how this would be true for young men in the United States at the start of World War II. They went to war and to the many horrific and sometimes heroic experiences of war, while their younger siblings, who were too young for war, and their older siblings, who were too old for war, watched from the physical safety of their homes. Being a young adult male during those war years changed the life course for many of these young men compared with women of the same age and men of different ages at that time in history. Differences between those who went to war and those who stayed at home in areas that were not subject to fighting remain the same regardless of which war we consider. Thus, the importance of being male or female depends on one's age and the historical context (Stewart & Ostrove, 1998).

In applying the perspective of social ecology to the many questions about sex differences in cognitive abilities, it assumes that individuals have multiple cognitive abilities and the potential to develop some or all of them in many ways. The abilities that are developed depend on one's biological propensities, the context that is shared with the rest of society, the context that is altered by the individual, one's stage of development, and the sociohistorical context. Consider this contemporary example: Women now comprise a majority of all students enrolled in college, which is a major change over earlier enrollment patterns. The skills and abilities that large numbers of women are developing at the turn of the 21st century are very different than those developed by the majority of women at the turn of the 20th century. Similarly, the lives of men who go to war or have other sex-differentiated life experiences determine how their cognitive abilities are developed and the subsequent course of their lives. Young men who go off to war because of historical events may develop certain physical or aiming skills that they would not have developed if they had gone to college or worked at a local factory instead. Similarly, advanced conceptual skills in abstract scientific thinking or the analysis of literature will probably not be developed, or their development will be delayed, for these hypothetical young soldiers.

COGNITIVE SCHEMA THEORY

Gender schemas are "networks of characteristics associated with males and females."
—Serbin, Powlishta, and Gulko (1993, p. 3)

Cognitive theories are a general class of theories that are based on the primary importance of children's and adults' knowledge of sex-differentiated behaviors. Kohlberg (1966) proposed a cognitive development theory to explain the acquisition of sex-typed behavior by children. A different sort of cognitive theory that explains sex role maintenance among adults is gender schema theory, which was proposed by Bem (1981). The most recent and promising areas of study are broadly known as social cognition. Because each theory is designed for a different purpose, they are considered separately.

Cognitive Development Theory

Kohlberg's (1996) cognitive development theory began with the notion that children's conceptions about the nature of the world change as they go through various developmental stages. Just as children's understanding of numerical concepts changes at different ages, so does their understanding of sex roles and sex-appropriate behaviors. Around 3 years of age, children begin to label themselves as either a girl or a boy, and sometime during the next 2 years, they learn to label other people's sex. During this developmental period, they also develop "gender constancy," which is the idea that gender or sex is an immutable part of one's identity. Once the child has developed a notion of his or her own sex, the child models the behaviors of same-sex models. In Serbin and Sprafkin's (1986) review of the literature in this area, they concluded that "it appears that learning about sex roles may be a universal phenomenon based on the early tendency to classify according to the gender dimension" (p. 1198). Knowledge about sex role stereotypes precedes and promotes sex differences in behavior (Serbin et al., 1993). Apparently this knowledge appears very early in life. Servin, Bohlin, and Berlin (1999) found that children as young as 12 months make sex-typed toy choices, so whatever processes are involved, they develop very early in life.

In distinguishing the basic differences between social modeling or social learning theory and cognitive development theory, Kohlberg (1966) said, "The social-learning syllogism is: 'I want rewards, I am rewarded for doing boy things, therefore I want to be a boy.' In contrast, a cognitive theory assumes this sequence: 'I am a boy, therefore I want to do boy things, therefore the opportunity to do boy things (and to gain approval for doing them) is rewarding'" (p. 89). The basic difference between these two theories is that social modeling assumes that children conform to sex role stereotypes and acquire a sex role identity because they imitate sex role-consistent behaviors that are reinforced, whereas cognitive development theory assumes that children first develop an awareness of sex categories and then they form a sexual identity as part of their self-concept (I am a girl, or I am a boy). After a sexual identity is formed, they perform sex role-consistent behaviors that get rewarded. Children do not begin to value sex-appropriate behaviors and values until after they understand that being either a female or a male is a permanent part of one's identity that will never change (Maccoby, 1990).

Gender Schema Theory

Bem (1981) proposed that our knowledge about sex differences forms a *schema,* or an organizing framework in which we process, interpret, and organize information. The term *schema* comes from cognitive psychology, the branch of psychology concerned with how we think, learn, and remember. The notion of a schema is very close to what we mean when we talk about stereotypes. It refers to the way we store information in memory and use that information. Hyde (1985) described it this way: "A schema is a general knowledge framework that a person has about a particular topic. A schema organizes and guides perception" (p. 76). Gender schemata are "a set of ideas that define as appropriate for men and women particular skills, preferences, personalities and self-concepts, and that act as filters shaping our perceptions and interpretations of events" (Goodnow, 1985, p. 19). The categories of female and male form a framework that allows children to organize and interpret information about sex roles.

When we interact with people, we use our schemata first to understand and then to remember what transpired. For example, Koblinsky, Cruse, and Sugawawa (1978) showed that 10-year-old children remembered the masculine behaviors of

Calvin and Hobbes   by Bill Watterson

CALVIN AND HOBBES © 1990 Watterson. Reprinted with permission of Universal Press Syndicate. All rights reserved.

boy characters and the feminine behaviors of girl characters better than sex-reversed behaviors. A similar effect was found by Liben and Signorella (1980) using a picture recognition task with first- and second-grade children. Furthermore, children with the most rigidly defined sex role stereotypes showed the greatest recall and recognition memory for pictures that were consistent with stereotypes (Signorella & Liben, 1984) and showed a proclivity to distort information that was inconsistent with their schemata into consistent information (Levy, 1989).

The organization and structure of information is a normal cognitive process with important consequences for how we think and remember (Bardach & Park, 1996; Halpern, 1985). The propensity to interpret and remember information that is consistent with our schemata serves to perpetuate these schemata (Levy & Fivush, 1993). Gender schema theory addresses the issue of why sex roles (as opposed to other categories) are such an important organizer of information even at a young age. Thus, once these cognitive categories are established, they resist change because information that is inconsistent tends to be either forgotten or changed. In this way, our stereotypes or gender schemata bias the way we interpret behavior.

Social Cognition

Social cognition is a general term for understanding the way cognitive factors (thinking, learning, remembering, and perceiving) and social factors (the way people interact in groups) mutually influence each other. When this perspective is applied to cognitive sex differences, it blends some of the topics already presented in this chapter—beliefs about oneself and one's attitudes toward academic domains—and a topic discussed more fully in chapter 6—knowledge of common stereotypes. In an attempt to present a unified theory of social cognition, Greenwald et al. (in press) examined the relationship among self-concept, sex role stereotypes (they used the term *gender stereotypes*), and attitudes toward math. Unlike the other studies on confidence in one's ability or beliefs about success that were described earlier in this chapter, in which the participants answered questions about these topics, Greenwald et al. used reaction time measures to study the way cognitive and social processes reflect self-concept and self-attitudes. If you have been reading these chapters in order, then you already know that one way to measure how people think is to have them respond very quickly to stimuli that are presented on a computer (or other) screen or to auditory stimuli. The response times are usually in the range of 0.5 to 2.0 seconds, so participants cannot "fake" a response or provide a "socially desirable" response because they cannot consciously make one response fractions of a second shorter or longer than another. One of the underlying ideas in using reaction time measures is that concepts that are closely associated in memory are responded to more quickly when they are presented together than ones that are not closely associated.

Suppose, for example, that you are a participant in one of these studies. You are seated at a computer and have been given instructions about how to respond to stimuli that will be presented on the screen. The task is to press one key if the letters flashed on the screen form a word and another key if they do not form a word. If you are like most people, you will respond more quickly when *bread* is flashed on the screen if the word immediately before it was *butter* than if the word immediately before it was conceptually unrelated to *bread,* such as *office.* (There also would be control trials in which the letters do not form a word.) Researchers would compare how quickly you responded to *bread* when it followed *butter* with how quickly you responded to *bread* when it followed *office* to determine how closely *bread* and *butter* are conceptually related. You may be wondering how this discussion turned to *bread* and *butter.* Well, that is just an example of the principles used to determine how closely concepts are related.

Nosek, Banaji, and Greenwald (1998, cited in Greenwald et al., in press) applied this basic experimental paradigm (setup) to examine the relationship among attitudes toward math, stereotypes about males and females, and self-concept. The responses they used in their study were simple reaction times to different categories of items—items that pertained to either oneself or others (*I* and *me* vs. *they* and *them*), math or the arts (*calculus* and *numbers* vs. *poetry* and *dance*), male or female (*brother* and *father* vs. *sister* and *mother*), and positive or negative terms (*joy* and *warmth* vs. *pain* and *stink*). Admittedly, these sorts of measures may seem like a long way from understanding sex differences on tests of math ability, but they have the advantage of being "unfakeable," and they are supported by a long history of research on human cognition. In this study, the researchers found that males had positive attitudes toward math and strong associations between the male terms and the math terms. For the females, those with strong positive associations between math and the male terms also had more negative attitudes toward math. In other words, when the males thought of math as a male-stereotyped domain, they also had positive attitudes toward math. By contrast, when the females thought of math as a male-stereotyped domain, they had more negative attitudes toward math. Thus, with this single model (and somewhat complex paradigm), both sex role stereotypes and attitudes toward math came together in a single explanatory framework.

PERFORMANCE AND STRATEGY VARIABLES

The idea behind appeals to performance and strategy variables is that sex differences in cognitive abilities are not really reflecting different levels of abilities but instead are indicators of differences in the way males and females approach and solve problems or take tests. The idea that performance and strategy variables underlie cognitive sex differences is not a coherent theory of development like psychoanalytic theory or social ecology theory; rather, it is an explanation that would apply only to cognitive sex differences. Why males and females would develop and use different strategies for solving problems or taking tests is not clear. Nor is this perspective a single coherent point of view; it is a loose categorization of reasons that have been offered to explain why the sexes perform differently on cognitive tasks. Let's consider these explanations. There are several different indicators that show, in fact, men and women do use different strategies for some cognitive tasks. For example, in a study of how people navigate through space, Lawton (1996) found that women tend to use a route strategy (room numbers and signs) and men tend to use an orientation strategy (knowledge of directions). The men's strategy was more spatial in nature, whereas the women's strategy was more verbal in nature, a finding that seems to also apply to other sorts of cognitive problems, including advanced problems in mathematics (Gallagher, 1998).

Speed–Accuracy Trade-Offs

A difference in speed of problem solving is not a sufficient explanation of the sex difference on Mental Rotations Test.
—Resnick (1993, p. 71)

The SAT is important in determining college admissions, and because it is so critical in determining who goes to college, which college is likely to find an applicant acceptable, and what someone is likely to study, this test is considered in several places in this book. This test also has excellent statistical properties (psychometrics) and is available for research purposes to many researchers. Thus, we know a good deal about performance on the SAT. Both the verbal and mathematics sections are taken under timed conditions. Suppose females, on average, respond to timed pressures in a different way from males. Furthermore, suppose that there are no real differences in these cognitive abilities between the sexes (or the differences are too small to be consequential), but females take a more cautious approach to selecting answers. If there is not enough time to complete the test, and females routinely take more time to select answers because of a bias to respond more slowly, then we would have a situation in which females score significantly lower than males.

This hypothetical scenario served as the basis for several studies. There are some indicators that at least part of the sex differences that are found in timed tests are due to differences in response styles. In a study of sex differences on the National Assessment of Educational Progress in Science, Linn, De Benedictis, Delucchi, Harris, and Stage (1987) found consistent sex differences for children 13 to 17 years old, with males answering about 5% more questions correctly than females. This corresponded to $d = 0.27$. But when they went through the types of answers picked by females and males, they found that the females were more likely to use the "I don't know" alternative than the males were. It seems that females have less confidence in their science knowledge or ability.

In another study of sex differences in mode of responding, Goldstein, Haldane, and Mitchell (1990) found the usual male advantage on a mental rotation test, but when they analyzed their data using the ratio of correct responses to the number of items attempted, the male advantage on this test was eliminated. What this means is that the females did not attempt to solve as many problems as the males (perhaps the females worked more slowly and cautiously), but they answered correctly the same proportion of attempted problems as the males did. In a second test of the hypothesis that sex differences would be eliminated when time constraints were removed, these researchers found no sex differences in untimed administrations of the mental rotation test. These results provide strong support for the idea that cautiousness or some other response bias was responsible for a large portion of the sex differences found in cognitive abilities (Gallagher, 1989, 1998). However, as you probably guessed by now, there is also evidence that sex differences cannot be explained by differences in speed of responding. There are no simple or single answers to the many questions of cognitive sex differences.

There is a test of verbal abilities that is known as the Stroop test. In the Stroop test, the stimuli are color names (e.g., the words *green, blue,* and *red*) that are printed in different color ink. For example, the word *red* might be printed in blue ink, and the word *blue* might be printed in yellow ink. The task for the participant is to name the ink color as quickly as possible while ignoring the word that the letters form. Although this may seem like a simple task, it is surprisingly difficult to ignore the printed word and name the ink color. Nayak and Dash (1987) found that "girls are superior to boys in response speed" (p. 88) in the Stroop test. Thus, at least under some testing situations, girls respond faster than boys. If females are more cautious in responding, and therefore slower to respond, then we would expect this response bias in any timed task. The fact that girls were faster at responding to verbal stimuli suggests that a generalized tendency to respond cautiously cannot be the cause of all of the sex differences found in reaction times.

Of course, by now you should be able to recognize how the conclusion that longer reaction times for females are creating a false appearance of cognitive sex differences on some tasks could be questioned. Recall that reaction time is one measure of intelligence or cognitive functioning. Psychologists who use reaction time measures as an ability index are not going to accept untimed versions of the same test as a measure of intellectual prowess. If reaction time really reflects "thinking time," then it is a measure of cognitive speed or cognitive ability. One possible way around this problem is to determine if reaction time is related to the time needed for thinking or whether it is being influenced by some secondary variable that cognitive psychologists don't care as much about—something like the time it takes to indicate the response. Some psychologists have examined the possibility that reaction time data might not be really measuring thinking time. For example, Welford (1980) examined whether sex differences in reaction time were due to the actual time needed to move the hand to make the response (motor time) or the "premotor time"—the time between exposing the stimulus and the initiation of the response. Welford concluded that sex differences are due to differences in premotor time rather than musculature (movement) factors—that is, differences in thinking time, not movement time. "The longer mean time for women than men for completing the entire testing session could be explained in terms of longer premotor times of women" (Rammsayer & Lustnauer, 1989). In other words, most cognitive psychologists are comfortable with the idea that reaction time is a good measure of cognitive abilities and that differences in reaction times reflect differences in abilities.

Several researchers have objected to the idea that sex differences can be reduced by computing the ratio of the number of problems solved correctly to the number of problems attempted as being nonsensical (Masters, 1998). For example, if in a given time period, say 3 minutes, one person attempts only one mental rotation problem and gets it correct, then this person's ratio is $1/1 = 1$. For this person, 100% of all of the attempted problems were solved correctly. By contrast, suppose another person attempted eight mental rotation problems in the same 3-minute period and got seven of them correct. This person's ratio of the number of problems solved correctly to the number of problems attempted would be $7/8$, which is less than 100% correct. By the logic of ratio scoring, the first person would be judged to have better mental rotation skills than the second, which seems to make no sense, because the first person got only one problem correct in 3 minutes and the second got seven correct in 3 minutes. In addition to the conceptual problems raised with the use of ratio scores, other researchers did not find that unspeeded versions of mental rotation tests reduced the size of the sex difference (Masters, 1998; Resnick, 1993). More recent studies have also reported that males and females are about equal in their reluctance or readiness to guess when they are not sure about the correct answer, so confidence and willingness to take a risk are probably not causing cognitive sex differences (Delgado & Prieto, 1996). In a test with four different types of visual–spatial tasks, the error rates for each of the tasks were comparable between women and men, but the men were significantly faster (all ds between 0.63 and 0.77; Loring-Meier & Halpern, 1999). Thus, the idea that women work more slowly, but perhaps more accurately, cannot be used to account for cognitive sex differences.

The question of whether we should be using reaction times as an index of intelligence or cognitive abilities is important. Some psychologists have argued for the use of reaction times because they are relatively "culture-free"; that is, they are less dependent on life experiences such as an enriched education than other measures, so there is little advantage for the rich (e.g., Jensen, 1980). Psychologists study the relationship between speed of responding and accuracy of the responses by constructing "speed–accuracy curves" in which the speed of responding is plotted as a function of accuracy (e.g., proportion correct). Let's consider the rationale of speed–accuracy curves. Suppose that you responded very, very quickly to a series of questions. In an extreme example, suppose that you never read the questions but picked answers at random. What would happen to your accuracy? It would be very low if responding were very, very fast. Alternatively, suppose that you were very slow and cautious about responding. Accuracy would be high, but speed would be slow. Thus, within limits, there is a reciprocal relationship between speed and accuracy. Lohman (1986) conducted an interesting study in which he examined speed–accuracy curves for different groups. He reported that participants with low spatial ability produce different speed–accuracy curves than people with high spatial ability. (He used the mental rotation paradigm in this example.) Furthermore, Lohman reported that the speed–accuracy curves for females were different than those for males, with the female speed–accuracy curves very similar to those found for females and males with low spatial abilities. Thus, he argued that the finding that females take longer to respond than males is good evidence that, on average, females are poorer at this task than males are.

Learning Styles

One suggestion is that boys have more autonomous learning styles, which means that they prefer more self-directed learning. According to this hypothesis, girls learn better when they are given directives. Perhaps another way of thinking about this possibility is that girls rely more heavily on strategies or skills learned in school, which could be a reflection of better memory for these learned strategies (Gallagher, 1998). Therefore, males perform better than females when the test is not similar to the topics that are taught in school (as in standardized tests), and females perform better than males when they are tested on material that is similar to that taught in class (as in school exams; Kimball, 1989). Although this is an interesting possibility, there are no independent confirmations that males and females have different learning styles or that girls perform better under directed conditions.

An important part of the mathematics sex differences debate is which is the better measure of mathematical abilities. Is it grades, which reflect achievement on multiple tests over the course of a semester or a year, or is it single-session tests like the SAT–M? The SAT–M is not closely tied to any particular instruction; course grades are. Some will argue that cognitive tests that are independent from the learning setting and the teacher are "fairer" because they are not influenced by teacher bias or by factors unrelated to ability, like working neatly or behaving well and smiling in class. Others will argue that the cognitive test may include material that favors one sex or the other because they have not had the same learning opportunities to prepare for it. It seems that this question is like many of the others posed in this book. The answer is not one or the other, but both are important, depending on what you want to know about mathematical abilities.

A COMPARISON OF THE THEORIES

A theory is an explanation. It is a way of understanding something; in this case, the "something" is the complicated findings related to sex differences in cognitive abilities. A good theory can account for a wide range of data and can be used to make predictions that are testable. Good theories also allow experimenters to design interventions and manipulations that will bring about a predicted change. Let's consider the eight theoretical perspectives presented in this chapter with these criteria in mind. As you probably noticed, I have not called all of the alternative explanations "theories" because not all of them are well developed. Some explanations were designed to explain all of personality (e.g., psychoanalytic theory), and others are narrow in the scope of variables they attempt to explain (e.g., performance and strategy variables), but what they share is a way of thinking about the *why* of cognitive sex differences in which the *why* variables are mostly found in psychological effects of societal practices and values.

Each of the theoretical perspectives begins with a different notion about the nature of the forces that cause humans to conform to sex role stereotypes or to develop in ways that favor some cognitive abilities and not others. Salient points about each of these perspectives are summarized in Table 7.1, in which the origins, basic mechanisms of action, secondary influences, and outcomes are compared. In comparing these nine theoretical perspectives, it is difficult to determine which is "best" because there are areas of overlap among them, they each begin with a different starting point, and they attempt to solve a different part of the puzzle. Nor do they necessarily represent mutually exclusive categories. It is likely that rewards and punishments, imitation of same-sex models, and gender schemata all operate in the establishment and maintenance of sex role stereotypes. It seems obvious that expectancies and values would play a role in determining cognitive development and the results of any specific test. Yet, none of these is a sufficient explanation for the pervasive patterns of cognitive sex differences. As you might probably guess, psychoanalytic theory has been most heavily criticized because of its "penis-centered" orientation. An alternative explanation is that the male role is preferred not because males have a penis but because males have greater power and greater freedom in our society. Of course, each of the theoretical perspectives might have a "small piece of the best explanation" for the way psychosocial variables operate in sex-differentiated ways that create and maintain cognitive sex differences.

CHAPTER SUMMARY

Nine different theoretical perspectives were presented on the question of "Why are there are sex differences in cognitive abilities?" These perspectives differ from those presented in earlier chapters in that they are predicated on the belief that the reason for these differences lies either exclusively or primarily in the way societies define and prescribe roles for males and females or the way biology directs societal influences. There are major differences among these perspectives, despite the fact that each emphasizes the nurture end of the nature–nurture continuum.

The oldest theory is Freud's psychoanalytic theory, which was proposed approximately 100 years ago as an all-encompassing theory of development, psychotherapy, personality, and psychopathology. As applied to the questions of cognitive sex differences, it places the origin of these differences in the biological differences between females and males, but environmental reactions to these differences are important. A major premise is that the way individuals resolve psychosexual conflicts during the preschool years has lifelong effects on personality. If these conflicts are resolved well, the developing child will identify with the same-sex parent and conform to the sex role expectations associated with one's own sex. This perspective can be contrasted with that of learning theory, which is a general theory of learning that applies beyond the issues involved in understanding cognitive sex differences. The basic principles of reward and punishment deter-

TABLE 7.1

A Comparison of Nine (Primarily) Psychosocial Perspectives

Theoretical Perspective	Origin	Mechanism of Action	Secondary Influences	Outcome
Psychoanalytic	In the child's understanding of visible differences between female and male genitals	Resolution of sexual urges during preschool developmental period	Rewards and punishments for appropriate sex-typed actions	Identification with same-sex parent and subsequent adoption of sex-appropriate roles and behaviors
Learning theory	In sex-differentiated rewards and punishments	Basic principles of reinforcement	Could include alternative ways of learning	Rewarded behaviors increase in probability and punished behaviors decrease in probability
Social learning theory	In the multiple ways males and females exhibit different behaviors and receive different outcomes	Observational learning—learn from observing models who are similar to oneself and knowledge of one's sex	Could include direct rewards and punishments	Children learn to match their behaviors to same-sex model
Expectancies-values-motives	Early learning experiences create expectations of success or failure and determine values for some outcomes	Individuals exercise choices that are based on multiplicative relationships between expectancies for success and value of outcomes	Expectations and values are based on prior learning	Individuals develop abilities for which they exert effort and value the outcomes and not for which failure is expected or the outcome is not valued
Bent twigs	In general, males and females have different initial propensities	The environment encourages development in areas in which initial talent is evident	Initial biologically based differences are recognized	Small initial between-sex differences are magnified by sex-differentiated environmental experiences

Social ecology	Sex, like age, influences development depending on sociohistorical context	Context variables are responsible for many of life's outcomes, including development of cognitive abilities	Social expectations as a function of sex change with historical period	Males and females at different ages in different historical periods develop different cognitive abilities
Cognitive schema theory	Cognitive sex differences begin with the cognitive principles that underlie how we think	Understanding that one's sex is permanent and that each sex engages in different activities	Reinforcement principles can play a secondary role after the establishment of "gender constancy"	Children adhere to sex-appropriate activities to maintain cognitive constancy
Social cognition	Individuals learn common stereotypes that interact with knowledge of one's own sex	Knowledge of stereotypes gains positive or negative associations based on whether they apply or do not apply to self	Strength of common sex role stereotypes interacts with knowledge of one's own sex	One's own sex is important in determining attitudes toward stereotyped relationships (math–male) if the stereotype is strong
Performance and strategy variables	Cognitive sex differences are not differences in abilities but in the way females and males perform cognitive tasks	Females are more concerned with accuracy and each sex uses different cognitive strategies	Different initial use of some strategies could be experiential or biological in origin	Inefficient strategies are not synonymous with less ability

mine which behaviors will be repeated, and in this way, children learn sex-appropriate behaviors. Social learning theory recognizes that learning also occurs by observing the behaviors of appropriate models. Individuals do not need to receive the rewards and punishments themselves; a great deal can be learned through a combination of observation and modeling.

Motivation and the role of individual choice come into play in expectancies–values–motives theories, which posit that individuals learn to expect success or failure at different tasks on the basis of their past experiences. They also come to value different sorts of outcomes on the basis of the perceived usefulness of the outcome to their own lives. Implicitly, each individual computes his or her own expectancies of success or failure, multiplied by the value of an outcome, and then decides how much effort to expend in achieving a goal. For example, if an individual expects to be successful in map reading and values that skill, she or he will work hard to learn it. In return for the hard work, success becomes more likely, further fueling the cycle of expectations and success. Similarly, low expectations of success will result in little or no effort and the increased probability of failure, which in turn lowers subsequent expectations of success.

The bent twigs hypothesis assumes that individuals are different with regard to their abilities. For example, if an individual has a small advantage in a certain area, let's say mathematical ability, and this individual receives encouragement or enriched mathematical experiences, the small advantage will grow larger. The small advantage in mathematical ability would also bias this hypothetical individual to seek additional opportunities in mathematics. This hypothesis further assumes that there are some initial differences, on average, between males and females and that these small advantages grow larger through differential learning opportunities and encouragement. The social ecology perspective also centers on the way society treats males and females differently, but this perspective emphasizes the importance of sociohistorical context. The cognitive abilities that we develop, along with critical changes in many other life variables, depend on one's age and sex at different periods in history. Today's young men and women receive much more education that any previous cohort because of the technological era in which we live, a fact that supports the importance of sociohistorical period on cognitive abilities.

Cognitive schema theories are rooted in the thinking processes that enable us to understand those behaviors and attitudes that are associated with femaleness and maleness. One variant of this perspective was proposed by Kohlberg (1966), who viewed children's understanding of gender as a cognitive milestone. Once children understand that they will always be the same sex, they then seek sex-appropriate rewards and engage in those behaviors that will result in the rewards. Another variant is that the categorization of activities as male-typical and female-typical is inherent in how people make sense of the world. By creating female and male categories, we reduce uncertainty. This essential categorization process underlies human cognition and directs how we process information. A more recent social cognition perspective takes into account the way people think about common sex role stereotypes (e.g., males are good at math and females are good in the arts) and whether we are female or male. Thus, self-concept is an important contributor to way we process information about sex role stereotypes. Data in support of this perspective tend to come from reaction time studies in which researchers make inferences about underlying cognitive processes from how quickly participants respond to simple questions.

The final theoretical perspective discussed in this chapter is the idea that females and males differ in the strategies they use when approaching cognitive tasks. For example, several psychologists have posited that females are more cautious in how they approach novel problems, so they work more slowly than males, even when they are equally able. Another suggestion is that females use a less efficient strategy on those tasks on which males excel, for example, mental rotation tasks. This theoretical perspective is more easily tested than the global theories like psychoanalytic theory. Although there are some supporting data, in general, it has not held up well as an explanation of cognitive sex differences.

8 Using a Psychobiosocial Perspective to Understand Cognitive Sex Differences

CONTENTS

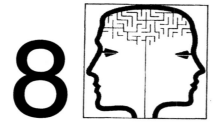

8

USING A PSYCHOBIOSOCIAL PERSPECTIVE TO UNDERSTAND COGNITIVE SEX DIFFERENCES

Like first-year medical students, we have dissected the body of knowledge that pertains to the immensely complex system we are trying to understand. But medical science could not proceed unless the students can comprehend the way the pieces work together and can see the connectiveness and interrelatedness of all of the systems. Similarly, we need to put the biological and psychosocial theories and research together because, in reality, they are as connected as the mind and brain.

MYOPIA USA

[There are] wide variations among groups in what is defined
as appropriate behaviors for the genders.
—Doyle (1995, p. 111)

As presented in the preceding chapters, biological and psychosocial hypotheses provide two frameworks for studying sex differences in cognitive abilities. But this division, like any other scheme for dissecting the multiple determinants of human development, is artificial because these two types of influences are inextricably entwined—we all are biological organisms that develop within a cultural environment. In North American society, for example, males receive more spatial toys as children and more rewards and encouragement for engaging in spatial activities like playing with building toys, joining various ball teams, and traveling on their own. They also have the male chromosome configuration, a preponderance of male hormones, and other biological indexes that define them as male. At birth, they are classified by the shape of their genitals and, on average, are somewhat more active and physically aggressive than females. Because biological sex and psychosocial environment are confounded, it is impossible to ascertain the independent contribution of any of these variables. All of the methods that have been

315

discussed, such as examining medical anomalies, correlating twin data, and providing specific educational experiences to selected groups of participants can suggest only an approximation of the relative importance of each of the variables under investigation. Another technique for approximating the relative contributions of biological and psychosocial variables is to look to other cultures.

The underlying rationale of cross-cultural research in this area is that all females, everywhere in the world, share a similar biology, as do all males. Although there are obvious differences among people in their skin color, hair texture and curl, eye shape, and so on, the biology of femaleness and maleness is the same everywhere. Except for medical anomalies, members of each sex have the same chromosome configuration for determining sex, internal reproductive organs, gonads (sex glands), genitals, and sex hormone balance. In addition, cognitive abilities are universal in that everyone must learn, use information, make decisions, represent and communicate meaning, navigate through space, reason with quantities, create, decide, solve problems, and so on. In a seminal book, Cole and Scribner (1974) concluded, "We are unlikely to find cultural differences in basic component cognitive processes" (p. 193).

However, societal and environmental milieus differ from culture to culture. Consider, for example, the implications of cognitive sex differences research conducted in a society in which sex roles are very different from those in Western cultures. Suppose that some hypothetical society existed in which sex role stereotypes were the reverse of those in North America, such that girls were encouraged to succeed in mathematics and science areas and boys were encouraged to be nurturant and to engage in more quiet activities like reading and sewing. If we were to find the same cognitive sex differences that we typically find in North American studies, then we would have strong support for the importance of sex-related biological variables in the determination of cognitive abilities. Conversely, if we were to find the reverse or a different pattern of cognitive sex differences, or no differences at all, then the psychosocial variables would have received a strong endorsement. Thus, one of the major advantages of cross-cultural research is that it allows the possibility of, at least partly, unraveling biological and psychosocial contributions to cognitive sex differences.

Unfortunately, high-quality cross-cultural research that has used comparable measures in a wide variety of cultures is rare. More than 30 years ago, Fairweather (1976) used the term *myopia USA* to describe the relative paucity of cross-cultural data designed to investigate the origins of cognitive sex differences. Although there is much more cross-cultural research available now than when Fairweather coined the phrase "myopia USA," much of it is still conducted in industrialized societies that share many similarities with North America and Europe. There are several reasons why researchers have been so nearsighted in their search for answers to sex differences and other psychological questions. One of the primary reasons for the paucity of research is that cross-cultural data are difficult and expensive to collect. Unlike anthropologists, who tend to examine cross-cultural issues, few psychologists have the necessary connections in other countries to arrange for data collection.

They also lack the requisite language skills to converse with foreign participants and foreign researchers. Subtle differences among languages and nuances that are lost in literal translation can render a research instrument that is valid in one culture invalid or even ludicrous when administered in another culture. There are also numerous experimental controls that are necessary in cross-cultural research. For example, much of the early research designed to compare Mexican youth with U.S. youth used poor Mexicans and middle-class Americans as participants. Not surprisingly, large cultural differences emerged; however, these so-called cultural differences were really created by differences in socioeconomic status.

The Politics of Cross-Cultural Investigations

The majority of knowledge about cognitive sex differences comes from research conducted with participants in Western industrialized nations by researchers living in those nations. Very little sex differences research is conducted in Majority (sometimes called Third) World countries. Sex differences research is simply not a priority in underdeveloped countries struggling to provide enough food for their citizens and fighting for economic and political survival.

There are also political ramifications to research of this sort because beliefs about the roles that men and women should and do play in any society are always embedded in a historical, religious, and political context. For example, the "emancipation of women" was one of the tenets of communism as defined by Marx and Engels. The Russian newspaper, *Pravda,* interpreted the failure of Americans to pass the Equal Rights Amendment as tantamount to endorsing sex discrimination. In fact, there are large numbers of women in the scientific community in Russia and the other countries of the former Soviet Union. Detractors are quick to point out, however, that Russia cannot claim to be a sex-egalitarian society because there are still very few women in positions of power in the government or in the newly created countries. In fact, sexism is so blatant in many of the newly formed countries that emerged from the breakup of the Soviet Union that employment advertisements, even for professional positions like accountants or business managers, often specify that a young, attractive woman with "good legs" is desired. (See Halpern & Voiskounsky, 1997, for a comparison of Western and post-Soviet psychology.) Whatever your political persuasion, the fact that a high proportion of engineers and scientists in the Soviet Union are women shows that if women are encouraged by society, they can demonstrate the ability to succeed in what has been construed by Western society as "traditional men's fields."

Cross-cultural research is complicated by the possibility that although biological indicators of sex are nonvariant, other concomitant variables could vary by sex between ethnic and racial groups. For example, it is likely that different ethnic groups mature at somewhat different rates. (Differences in the average age at puberty could be due to genetically programmed ethnic differences and/or environmental variables such as nutrition, sanitation, and working conditions.) If maturation rate were an important determinant of cognitive sex differences, as some researchers believe, then between-group sex differences could be due to maturation rate differences and not sex per se.

Unfortunately, the hypothetical example of a culture that differs from our own only in terms of its sex roles has never been found. In early research, world-renown anthropologist Margaret Mead (1961) studied societies with radically different sex roles for women and men. Her findings, based on data from three different cultures, used to be routinely included in classes on the psychology of sex differences, but soon after her death, her research was questioned by another noted anthropologist (Freeman, 1983) who believes that she misinterpreted the cultures she visited. (His actual criticism of Mead was much stronger—he implied that she was "duped" or perhaps even falsified or exaggerated her findings.) Freeman also believes that the finding of societies with radically different sex role stereotypes was too coincidental to be real. Unfortunately, these allegations were made after Mead's death, so she was unable to respond to them. Thus, we are left with no strong data comparing societies with fundamental differences in their sex role stereotypes. It seems that cross-cultural research, like all of the other research that has been reviewed, cannot provide us with "the definitive answer" about the etiology of cognitive sex differences, although it can provide support for or against any particular hypothesis.

Outcomes of Cross-Cultural Research

Williams and Best (1982) reported the results of an extensive cross-cultural project whose objective was "to identify the beliefs commonly held in many cultures about the psychological characteristics associated with men and women and to examine these sex-trait stereotypes for evidence of cross-national similarities and differences" (p. 13). They examined the sex role stereotypic beliefs of adults and children in 39 different countries selected from 6 different areas of the world (Africa, Asia, Europe, North America, South America, and Oceania). They found a surprisingly high degree of similarity in sex role stereotypes. Williams and Best coined the term *pancultural generality* to describe the finding that instrumental or goal-oriented traits tend to be associated with being male and expressive or interpersonal traits tend to be associated with being female in all of the cultures they studied.

Western Industrialized Nations.   Perhaps not surprisingly, when we look at other countries with sex roles similar to those in the United States, we find congruence between their patterns of sex-differentiated cognitive abilities and the ones discussed in this book. A London newspaper (*The London Times,* 1984), for example, reported on the low level of participation by girls in science and technology courses. There are more than four times as many boys as girls studying college preparatory physics in high school in England. Research on schools in England has shown the same sex-differentiated pattern of classroom interactions that was revealed by Sadker and Sadker (1985) in their research on U.S. schools conducted in four states and the Washington, DC area. Like their U.S. counterparts, English boys are asked more questions by teachers; receive most of the teachers' attention. and; according to the report in *The London Times* (1984), "monopolise science laboratory equipment, consistently depriving girls of practical experience." It seems inevitable that classroom experiences reflect societal biases about what is appropriate behavior for girls and boys, although I note here that some psychologists have criticized this conclusion because it does not control for other variables such as how often the children volunteer answers (Kleinfeld, 1998).

One country that offers the possibility of assessing societal influences on sex-related cognitive differences is Sweden. Sweden has a government policy that institutionalized sexual equality, including a parental leave policy for fathers as well as for mothers. In a comparison of sex role stereotypes between children, adolescents, and adults in the United States and Sweden, Intons-Peterson (1988) found that there is less sex role stereotyping in Sweden. Have Sweden's more egalitarian attitudes manifested themselves by changing the sex-differentiated pattern of cognitive abilities? Stage (1988) examined this question by investigating sex differences on the Swedish Scholastic Aptitude Test. This test has been used to select candidates for higher education in Sweden since 1977. Although it has a similar name to the SAT that is produced in New Jersey by the Educational Testing Service, it is a different test. The Swedish test provides six subscores: Vocabulary; Quantitative Reasoning; Reading Comprehension; Interpretation of Diagrams, Tables, and Maps; General Knowledge; and Study Ability. Stage reported that the largest sex differences favoring males are found on the subtests of Quantitative Reasoning and Interpretation of Diagrams, Tables, and Maps. Females have a slight advantage on the Vocabulary subtest, with no differences on the other subtests. This pattern of results is highly reminiscent of the one found with the SAT in the United States.

Although results from the Swedish Scholastic Aptitude Test suggest that sex role stereotypes may not play a substantial role in establishing and/or maintaining cognitive sex differences, critics will point out that it is not a fair test of the hypothesis. Swedish society is more egalitarian only in its sex role stereotypes than is North American culture, but the stereotypes that exist in Sweden are similar to the ones with which most North Americans are familiar. A strong test of the contribution of sex role stereotypes to cognition requires that we examine societies that are much more different from our own.

The Israeli kibbutz is another culture that was founded on a basis of social and sexual equality (all property is jointly owned), and sex differences are "less pronounced" for children raised in the kibbutz than for Israeli children raised in the traditional family setting (Safir, 1986). But, as in Sweden, the sex role stereotyping is a matter of degree, not of kind. In Israel, every male is a future soldier, and there is greater emphasis on scholastic success for boys than for girls (in keeping with Jewish tradition). Safir examined cognitive sex differences in Israeli youth and concluded that when they are found, they tend to favor males on all cognitive measures. More recent research with Israeli samples (Birenbaum et al., 1994) was reviewed in chapter 3. In general, the patterns of cognitive sex differences found in Israel parallel those reported for the United States and other industrialized countries, despite the cultural differences and expectations that kibbutzim and other communal living arrangements would have resulted in reduced differences in sex-related cognitive outcomes.

A study of the cognitive achievement of White children and their parents in South Africa (Afrikaans) mirrors the Swedish and Israeli results (Visser, 1987). Both mothers and fathers reported that they regarded mathematics as more important for their sons than for their daughters. Correspondingly, more White South African males persist in advanced mathematics courses in high school, more males are identified at the highest levels of mathematics achievement (the Math Olympiad), and males score significantly higher on tests of spatial abilities.

You are probably wondering about Black South Africans—does the same pattern occur? I could not find any research on cognitive sex differences among the Black majority of South Africa. This is not surprising because such research would not tell us much. Black children in South Africa continue to receive less education than the White children, and they receive it in seriously overcrowded, substandard schools (Wright, 1990). Any sex differences would be lost amid the massive other influences on academic achievement—crushing poverty, discrimination, disease, and poor nutrition.

The countries that were formed from the breakup of the Soviet Union provide an interesting backdrop for contrasting the effects of socialization on the way cognitive abilities develop. In the early part of this century, a large number of American immigrants came from the countries that comprised the former Soviet Union. During the years following World War II, U.S. women were pressured to leave their war jobs, marry, and have children. The situation in the Soviet Union was very different. World War II claimed the lives of a substantial number of young males in the Soviet Union. Whereas large numbers of U.S. males returned home after the war, the Soviet Union was left with an entire generation of males that had been decimated by war. In 1994, I was fortunate to receive a Fulbright Award to teach courses in the psychology of sex differences and similarities and critical thinking at Russia's premier university, Moscow State University, and to study cognitive sex differences in post-Soviet Russia, so this is one region of the world where I have been personally involved in cross-cultural research.

The relative absence of old men in Russia is particularly striking. According to an official Russian guide, in the years immediately after the war, the proportion of males in the population was approximately 35%. Thus, many women never married because of the demographics of postwar Russia. Postwar Russia was left in rubble, and the reconstruction effort still continues. For this reason, women assumed many of the physically demanding jobs that were traditionally men's jobs, such as plastering and building construction and reconstruction. Women also assumed the majority of the jobs in medicine. Unfortunately, the assumption of work in traditional men's fields by women did not lead to sexual equality. The status of physicians in Russia and the other countries formed from the former Soviet Union is much lower than in Western nations. And, as mentioned earlier, women are still underrepresented in high-paying professions and government positions. The role that women and men will play in the future as Russia attempts to recover from severe economic hardship is unknown, but it seems that Russia will need to rely on its cadre of educated women to make the economic recovery it so badly needs.

In general, cross-cultural studies find that although there are differences among cultures, the relative skills and abilities of males and females within each culture are fairly similar. Consider, for example, a study that compared female and male performance on two tests of spatial ability—mental rotation and space relations (Silverman et al., 1996). The performances of comparable samples of adults from Canada and Japan were compared on these two tests. As you may recall from earlier chapters, the mental rotation test typically yields very large effect sizes, that is, large differences between females and males, with the advantage on this test shown for males. The space relations test tends to yield medium effect sizes when the sexes are compared. The size of an effect is usually given in terms of standard deviation units (as explained in chap. 2). In this comparison, both the Japanese and Canadian samples showed large sex differences for the mental rotation test ($d = 1.36$ in Japan and $d = 1.19$ in Canada) and medium sex differences for the space relations test ($d = 0.31$ in Japan and $d = 0.46$ in Canada). It is interesting to also note that, overall, the Japanese performed much better than the Canadians on both tests, so culture was an important variable, but within each culture, the relative performance of females and males was almost identical. Thus, both culture and one's sex are important determinants of performance on spatial tests.

More Isolated Majority World Ethnic Groups.   Although we live in a large world, you would never know it by perusing the literature on cognitive sex differences. It is only by looking at a variety of cultures that we can understand how psychosocial factors interact with the biology of femaleness and maleness to create each of us as unique humans. One study that is frequently cited as an exception to the usual shortsightedness is a study by Berry (1966) that compared Canadian Eskimos from the Baffin Islands with the Temne tribe in Africa on a variety of spatial tasks. Overall, the Eskimos outperformed the Temne on every spatial test. Most interesting from the perspective of the sex differences literature, there were no differences between females and males in the Eskimo sample; whereas among the Temne, the males scored higher on the spatial abilities tests than the females. One interpretation of these data is that for the Eskimos, the males and females tend to lead similar lives. For both sexes, traveling from home and hunting are important and frequent activities, and both of these activities should help to develop spatial skills. Among the Temne, traveling far from home is largely a male prerogative, and the sexes tend to be more segregated in their daily activities. Although these results seem to favor environmental explanations of differences in spatial abilities, proponents of the biological position would be quick to point out that there may be genetic differences among isolated groups, which have a restricted gene pool.

Another early study that is of particular interest in examining the nature–nurture controversy compared two different New Zealand ethnic groups, the Maori and Pakeha, on eight different cognitive tasks (Brooks, 1976). Brooks found that male children in one ethnic group performed better on two different spatial tests, whereas female children in the other ethnic group performed better on the same two spatial tests. Brooks concluded that cultural differences through different patterns of socialization develop unique ability patterns for each sex. With respect to verbal abilities, the Pakeha seemed to have a clear-cut advantage. Brooks concluded from this finding that verbal ability is the most sensitive to cultural influences of the cognitive abilities. It is interesting to note that this is the same conclusion that was reported in previous chapters on the basis of correlational research with twin and nontwin siblings.

Other reports from more isolated tribal groups are not easily interpreted. For example, it is difficult to know what to conclude from reports that in rural Kenya, girls score higher academically in Grades 1, 2, and 3 and boys score higher academically in Grades 6, 7, and 8, with no differences during the transition years of 4th and 5th grades (Arap-Maritim, 1987), or the report that among the Mizo children in India, males get more items correct on the Embedded Figures Test (Srivastava, 1989). The lives of females and males differ in every world society, with many of the psychosocial differences occurring at the same time that biological differences become most pronounced. Even if we were to find a worldwide cross-cultural advantage for males on some tests of spatial abilities (a conclusion that is favored by many psychologists, such as Harris, 1978, and Silverman et al., 1996), we still would not know whether females would score as high or higher if they were exposed to male life experiences.

The Devalued Female.   One truth that seems to hold up across cultures is the relative devaluation of what is female. In a newspaper article on helping couples select the sex of a child they are about to conceive, a physician in this field warned, "If we had 1,000 women coming to us in the next year, and all were going to have their first baby, and if all could easily select the sex, there's a substantial chance that we'd have 800 boys" (Barry May, Chief of Obstetrics and Gynecology at the Women's Hospital in Laguna Hills, cited in *The Los Angeles Times,* 1990, p. E2). This is a frightening thought as we quickly approach a time when sex selection techniques will be widely and easily available. The excess number of males in many countries of the world was documented in the first chapter of this book. It is important to return to this theme again at the end of this book because we need to consider the state of females and males throughout the world when we consider cognitive performance. The cognitive focus of this book needs to be interpreted within a larger framework of sex differences and similarities because cognition is only one of many variables that varies as a function of one's sex.

Equal participation in education by males and females is still a widespread myth. In 1979, women became the majority on college campuses in the United States, with the enrollment gap between women and men increasing almost every year since then (US On-Line News, 1999, http://usnews.com/usnews/is-sue/990208/8gap1.html). Many college campuses are 60% to 70% female. But what these data fail to note is that the large female enrollment is still found primarily in education, nursing, and other helping professions, which have less prestige and lower pay than the male-dominated fields. These data also change radically when we examine other cultures. For example, one of the first proclamations when the religious-based government in Afghanistan assumed power in 1997 was that females would not be allowed to attend school. Women were also forbidden to work, thereby leaving begging as the only way single women of any age could obtain enough money for food and other necessities. Perhaps even more shocking to Western readers, and largely ignored by the Western press, is the fact that girls as young as 12 can be and are bought as slaves in Sudan and other countries for as little as $50 (Jacobs, 1998). When a worldwide perspective is assumed, it becomes clear that whether someone is male or female remains a major determinant in many aspects of one's life.

CHANGING DATA, CHANGING MINDS

Please try this important experiment:

> Take a few minutes and reflect on the theories and research results presented in the hundreds of pages in this book. Think about your beliefs when you first picked up this book and compare them with what you now believe to be true. Have your beliefs changed in any way? If so, how? What information was most influential in changing your beliefs? If you have not changed what you believe to be true about sex differences in cognitive abilities, think about the reason for the lack of change. Did you fairly evaluate the information? Did you maintain both the open mind and the amiable skepticism of a scientific thinker?

If you are like most people, then you are already thinking that you're not like most people. In other words, most people like to think that only "other people" are average, but we are unique and not like the average others. But, like it or not, as you read the chapters in this book, you probably examined the evidence for and against each hypothesis with a bias for information that supported your own preferred views of what, where, why, and how the sexes differ and are the same with respect to cognitive abilities. This tendency is not surprising, because the preference for information that supports what we believe to be true helps us maintain a consistent set of beliefs and a fairly constant worldview (Halpern, 1996b, 1996c). The data concerning cognitive sex differences have been accumulating at a rapid rate, and there are not only new data (e.g., new cross-cultural studies like the one conducted by Silverman et al., 1996) but also new kinds of data (e.g., brain imaging techniques that show areas of brain activity while normal people engage in different types of cognitive tasks) that provide support for new conclusions about cognitive sex differences. Shouldn't you rethink your beliefs about cognitive sex differences on the basis of this new information?

Confirmation Bias

The tendency to look for and use information that confirms what we believe to be true is a powerful and pervasive effect. It operates in a wide range of settings, and few of us are even aware of the many times that our own thinking is influenced by this bias (Halpern & LaMay, 1999). Confirmation bias is the predilection to seek and utilize information that supports or confirms one's hypotheses or premises while ignoring or discounting disconfirming evidence. It involves building a case to justify a conclusion that has already been made. When we reason, we evaluate evidence to reach a conclusion. In contrast, when we rationalize, we begin with a conclusion and then look for evidence that will support it (Nickerson, 1998). In building your own conclusions about cognitive sex differences, did you use reason or rationalization?

Consistency Is the Hobgoblin of Closed Minds

Attitudes about controversial topics like cognitive sex differences are highly resistant to change because these attitudes are embedded in a system of values (e.g., suppose you believe that all people should have the same abilities), a social identity (as a female or a male), and other related beliefs (e.g., all the girls you know are good in mathematics). This web of beliefs creates a kind of barrier that makes new information that runs counter to the beliefs very difficult to assimilate (Kendrick, Neuberg, & Cialdini, 1999). The unwillingness to consider new information is the hallmark of a "closed mind." Given all of the information you now know about the topic of cognitive sex differences, have you changed your thinking about this topic in any way? If not, was it because you closed your mind to information that did not conform to your prior beliefs?

Note that in this attempt to get you, the reader, to reflect on what and how you think about the controversial topics presented in this book, I have not tried to tell you how to think. Instead, I have presented the information in the fairest way that I can and have asked that you consider the strength and consistency of the evidence and theories that were presented and that you remain open to new information and ideas while also using the rules of critical thinking and scientific understanding as a guide. This is a difficult task.

What's the Answer?

> In the search for factors that influence achievement levels,
> single explanations cannot adequately account for the observed performance
> differences.
> —Sue and Okazaki (1990, p. 913)

Any reader who picked up this book in the hope of finding easy answers is certainly frustrated by now. At one moment the data seem to favor one conclusion, yet on reflection or the accumulation of contradictory data, each theory seems inadequate, subject to alternative explanations, or completely wrong. This state of affairs is not unique to cognitive sex differences. It seems to be the norm in all areas of psychology and in the other sciences that are trying to understand the what, when, where, why, and how of complex phenomena. In the search for understanding why the sexes differ in some abilities, we have amassed a considerable quantity of information, although we still have many questions without answers and answers for which we haven't yet formulated the questions.

One thing that we clearly know is that there is no simple or single answer for the many questions about cognitive sex differences. The answers we have are as complex as the questions we are asking. This will come as a disappointment to some readers who want a simple answer that can explain how and why females and males differ on cognitive abilities. The disappointment is not surprising because even sophisticated scientists who work in this area want a simple answer. I recently sat in a small auditorium with approximately 100 department chairs from graduate programs in psychology. Claude Steele, a distinguished psychologist from Stanford University, described his research on "stereotype threat" to this group. I hope that you can recall that his research showed that the fear that one might confirm negative stereotypes associated with one's group (e.g., female or male) actually lowered performance on difficult exams (Steele, 1997; Steele & Aronson, 1995). This is exciting and powerful research, and the audience responded enthusiastically, so enthusiastically that several were quick to proclaim that Steele's research proved that biological factors are not important in determining performance on difficult tests. Similarly, I also attended a meeting of biological psychologists where Doreen Kimura, a respected psychologist from the University of Western Ontario in Canada, presented research that showed the cyclical nature of performance on several cognitive tests as a function of the proportion of testosterone and estrogen in one's blood (Hampson & Kimura, 1988). Her research was described in chapter 4. This is also an exciting and powerful finding about the role of hormones in cognitive performance for normal adult women. In this audience of biological psychologists, many were quick to conclude that biological variables are clearly the most important determinants of male and female cognitive abilities. I hope that you can see that both explanations are, in part, true and that the need to declare either nature or nurture as the winner" is a false dichotomy.

With some reflection, it should not be surprising that there is no single correct answer to complex questions. There is a lore among college professors that freshmen enter college wanting to know the correct answer to life's difficult questions. As freshmen turn into sophomores, juniors, and then seniors, the search for the right answer also changes. As students mature, they come to understand that not only do we not know the right answer, but we may not even be asking the right questions. This state of affairs is not particular to psychology because all of the difficult questions in the other sciences—chemistry, biology, and physics, for example—are intricate and multifaceted. The ability to accept uncertainty and ambiguity is a sign of cognitive development because questions about complex phenomena do not have simple answers.

What's the Question?

The kinds of answers that we can accept will depend on what we want to know and, correspondingly, the questions we ask. There are different levels of analysis for different sorts of questions. We know that there are average differences for males and females on some types of tests, for some types of abilities, and for different portions of the abilities distribution. There are numerous differences in brain activity for males and females for some tasks, but the link between the brain indexes and performance are still indirect and weak. Females perform better, on average, than males on some measures, with the reverse being true for other measures. Learning histories are always important (at least within educable ranges of intelligence), but learning is a biological and social phenomenon, and although everyone can (probably) improve on any cognitive task; some people will improve more quickly than others. There are multiple research questions whose answers depend on the age and developmental phase of the participants, the type of data collected, and the level of analysis (e.g., brain recordings, self-reports, test performance, beliefs about group and individual abilities).

It remains the task of future research to come up with creative new ways of finding and answering questions that may be as old as the human race. The number of questions posed by researchers is increasing as rapidly as new data are being collected. If the maturity of a field is measured by the number of unanswered and unasked questions, then cognitive sex differences is maturing well as an area of inquiry.

A PSYCHOBIOSOCIAL PERSPECTIVE

Biology and culture are isomorphic.
—Barta (1999, p. 56)

The nature–nurture dichotomy has created a framework that has guided much of the research on cognitive sex differences. As noted in numerous places throughout this book, there are problems inherent in this dichotomy. A dichotomy requires an "either/or" answer or, at best, a "more or less" type answer. Instead, we need to change the framework in which we are thinking. This framework was created, in part, by our data analytic techniques. If you are familiar with the data analytic technique known as analysis of variance, then you already know that psychologists think of the effects on what we are measuring as being explained by independent variables and their interaction. Thus, it is common to think of environmental and biological influences as acting independently and their joint effect as an interaction. With a psychobiosocial perspective, we cannot partition variables into those that are environmental and those that are biological because all humans are biological organisms developing in an environment. Thus, biology and environment cannot be conceptualized as independent effects. The psychobiosocial perspective eliminates the nature–nurture dichotomy because within this framework, there are no variables that are distinctly biological or environmental.

In psychobiosocial models, cause and effect are circular, and we cannot tell where biology ends and environment begins. Consider, for example, the findings that portions of the human brain that are unrelated to reproduction are sexually dimorphic. Although this may seem like biological evidence of cognitive sex differences, recall that both the structural and functional differences in the anatomy and physiology of the brain could result from different environmental experiences and cause individuals to select different experiences from their environment or to alter the environment to which they are exposed. Original research by Greenough et al. (1987) showed that intellectually enriching environments caused neural growth in the brain and created new connections among neurons in the brain. More recently, Ungerleider (1995) used brain imaging techniques to show changes in cortical representations that occurred after specific experiences. What people learn influences brain structures such as dendritic connections and cell size; brain architectures, in turn, support selected skills and abilities, which may lead people to seek additional similar experiences, thus completing the circle of variables.

Similarly, the prenatal and postnatal hormones that are critical in brain and other nervous system development also respond to internal and external stimuli and the genetic messengers that direct development. Although this may seem like a clearly biological process, people respond to environmental experiences with changes in hormone levels. Individuals will then alter their environment in a variety of ways—for example, they may decide to flee from a fearful situation or to engage in an aggressive response. Environments are not experienced randomly. To some extent, we make selections from our environment, and we alter our environment in ways that correspond to biological states. Any model of the multiple, sequentially interacting variables that cause and effect changes in hormone levels, brain structures and organization, the environments we select, and those that are correlated with our genetic predispositions must recognize the way psychological, biological, and social variables operate reciprocally on each other. Nature–nurture is a false dichotomy; they are as inseparable as conjoined twins who share a common heart.

Although laws of parsimony require researchers to accept the simplest explanation of a phenomenon, there is little likelihood that we will be able to respond to the many questions regarding cognitive sex differences with a simple answer. Like most researchers, I find beauty and elegance in simple answers—a single explanation for all of the differences. However, I do not believe that cognitive abilities are simply determined, nor do I believe that a single answer like "It's all in the hormones" or "It's all because of mothers' attitudes" will ever emerge as the origin of all sex differences in cognitive abilities.

The most important component of any psychobiosocial model is the reciprocal and simultaneous effects that biology, psychology, and socialization have on each other. A developmental psychobiosocial model has been proposed by Petersen (1980). Petersen's model takes into account the relative contributions of hormonal influences, family, peers, and broader society throughout the life span. Petersen's model is depicted in Fig. 8.1.

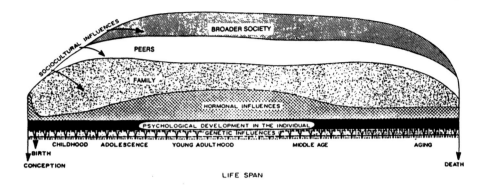

FIG. 8.1.   A hypothetical model for biopsychosocial development over the life span. From "Biopsychosocial Processes in the Development of Sex-Related Differences" (pp. 31–55), by A. C. Petersen, 1980, in J. E. Parsons (Ed.), *The Psychology of Sex Differences and Sex Roles,* Washington, DC: Hemisphere. Copyright 1980 by Hemisphere. Reprinted with permission.

As you can see in Fig. 8.1, hormones have the greatest impact during the prenatal and perinatal periods and through adolescence and middle age. By contrast, family influences are greatest during childhood. Peers and broader society assume a proportionally greater importance late in childhood and have a fairly constant influence into old age. Although the relative importance of these types of variables fluctuates throughout the life span, they all operate simultaneously and exert mutual effects on each other.

Nature Needs Nurture

In a review article on sex differences in the rhesus monkey, Wallen (1996) concluded that "nature needs nurture" (p. 364). His conclusions fit well with the psychobiosocial perspective assumed here. Wallen noted that male rhesus monkeys exhibited more "rough and tumble play" than females, but when the monkeys were raised without their mothers, the males were more aggressive than normally raised males, and the females were more submissive than normally raised females. By comparison, when prenatal androgen was suppressed in male monkeys who were reared in their normal family groups, they did not appear different from control males on any of the sex-typed measures. Wallen concluded from these and other studies that the expression of a host of sex-typed behaviors is biologically possible, but the ones that actually emerge and the extent to which they emerge are shaped by the social environment. Development is always in a context, and it is the totality of variables, both inside and outside the body, that determines what develops.

INTO THE FUTURE

Unfortunately, there are no crystal balls to tell us about the changing nature of cognitive sex differences. No one believes that conclusions based on today's cognitive sex differences literature will remain unchanged even a few years from now. But where the changes will be and when they will occur are, of course, unknown. Predictions about future research results are always risky and sometimes humorous when viewed with the benefit of hindsight; yet, I believe that we will find that the magnitude of all of the sex differences will diminish as we learn new ways to teach and learn, because all of cognitive abilities can improve with appropriate experiences. Future technology may, however, create new sex differences. We know, for example, that many more males than females are pursuing careers in computer-related fields and males are scoring substantially higher than females on advanced placement tests in computer science and physics (Stanley & Stumpf, 1996). The nature of the skills required for success in computer-related occupations varies with different jobs. Some computer jobs, like documentation analyst or writer, require high verbal ability. Others, like programming in "low-level languages," require mathematical ability, and still others, like computer graphic designer, require spatial ability. It would seem that almost everyone could find a niche in a computer field. Yet, computer science majors are predominantly male. If a major field of study becomes predominantly male or female, it seems likely that the skills stressed in that academic area will soon show sex differences.

In 1999, two anthropologists published very different texts on the future of women and men. In one book, Helen Fisher (1999) sees a better world because of the feminizing of corporate America—a world where personal relationships are strengthened, greater compassion is found, and enhanced interpersonal skills enrich the gathering and processing of information. According to Fisher, these benefits will accrue from the increased participation of women in all aspects of the workplace. By contrast, Lionel Tiger (1999) sees the decline of males because women can now control contraception, a state of affairs that has allowed women to exclude men from the family unit. For Tiger, "the sex war is real" (cited in McDonald, 1999, p. A17); for Fisher, "women are more interested in balancing work and family, so they much more regularly do not strive for the top" (cited in McDonald, 1999, p. A17). Fisher adds that men are, on average, better at mechanical and engineering skills, an advantage that will continue to be critically important in the coming decades. Thus, Fisher believes that men will continue as leaders of most of the world's large, traditional, and hierarchically organized corporations and governments. These books provide two very different views of how the future will unfold because of the changing roles and differing abilities of men and women. Predicting the future is risky business. Maybe one of them will be right, maybe neither.

Suppression of Knowledge Poses the Greatest Danger

The ideological suppression of scientific knowledge is nothing new.
—Hunt (1999, p. 7)

It is not surprising that I return in the last chapter to themes that I introduced in the beginning of this book. It is critically important to a free society and to science to be able to investigate questions that may have unpopular answers. Research into the many questions about sex differences in cognitive abilities is fraught with political minefields and emotional rhetoric from every corner of the political spectrum. Flynn (1999), a New Zealand philosopher and political scientist, recently wrote about the many moral and ethical dilemmas associated with studies of group differences. He eloquently explained how his own beliefs about social justice were tested along with his commitment to the highest scientific ideals as he pursued questions about race differences in intelligence. It is inspiring reading for anyone who is thinking about research on a controversial topic.

But it is not just scientists and philosophers who need to struggle with conflicting values. I believe that all educated citizens have an obligation to support honest research on any scientific topic, especially ones that are controversial. Informed citizens also have obligations that extend into the way the data are being interpreted and used, the way numbers are translated into conclusions, and the way conclusions from social science research are used to determine public policies. Of course, I am talking about you, the reader. Despite the risks of misusing research data for political purposes—social correctness or biological politics—the greatest risk is in the failure to seek answers for the most controversial questions. It is these questions that are most in need of honest inquiry. The greatest danger lies in censorship, even self-censorship, not in the open scientific study of controversial issues.

Education for the 21st Century

Today's young people are tomorrow's citizens, and the future is in their hands. How can we best prepare them for life in the 21st century and ensure that every individual develops her or his unique abilities to their fullest? Here are some suggestions for educators, parents, and other concerned citizens (Halpern, 1997):

1. Separate the fact that there are·average differences between males and females in some cognitive abilities from the tendency to evaluate these differences as "better" or "worse." This is an important distinction regardless of the nature of the group. Do not permit the misuse of data for the advancement of biological politics, political correctness, or any other ideology. The truth about sex differences in cognitive abilities depends on the nature of the cognitive task, the range of ability that is tested, the age and education of the participants, and numerous other modifying and context

variables. There are intellectual areas in which females excel and others in which males excel; these data do not support the notion of a smarter sex, nor do they mean that the differences are immutable.

2. The research summarized here is based on group averages, and no one is average. These results cannot be applied to any individual because there is a great deal of overlap in all of the distributions of abilities. For example, even though boys outnumber girls among those who are in the most gifted abilities range on standardized tests of mathematical achievement, there are many girls in this elite group. Similarly, boys excel in some tests of language usage, even though there are many more verbal tasks that show an average advantage for girls. We cannot afford to write off anyone or allow group membership to limit talent development.

3. Recent research has shown that beliefs about group differences exert powerful effects on thoughts and behaviors that occur without conscious awareness. These results highlight the importance of understanding stereotypes and offer a pessimistic outlook for the ease with which prejudice can be attenuated. For this reason, all of the stakeholders in education need to examine school texts for possible bias and speak to teachers and counselors about the nature of their group-based messages. We cannot pretend that children will select options that are best suited for their individual abilities and interests if we do not give them real choices.

4. The hormone-like chemicals that are polluting our environment are having negative effects on the animals that live in and near the polluted areas. Alterations to the hormone-sensitive reproductive organs of those animals provide reason to believe that these chemicals can affect the hormone-sensitive regions of the brain that support human cognitive functioning. No one can predict the long-term consequences of dumping chemicals, particularly pesticides, that mimic the actions of sex hormones. It is possible that they will alter the intelligence of humans who are exposed to them, a hypothesis that remains untested.

5. Support research on human cognition. We may be close to genuine breakthroughs in cognitive aging. New reports show that estrogen therapy can delay or reduce the occurrence of Alzheimer's disease in elderly women. Although the research on the effects of testosterone replacement therapy is decades behind that of estrogen replacement, both offer the possibility of great hope to an aging society.

6. Boys mature later than girls. Be sure that flexible criteria are used when making assignments to low-ability groups in the primary grades, especially in reading. Some of the boys will catch up with their peers, if they are not allowed to fall too far behind.

7. We have remedial instruction for reading and mathematics, but spatial reasoning, a skill that might benefit more girls, is virtually never taught in school. There is ample evidence that training with spatial tasks leads to

improved achievement on spatial tests (Vasta et al., 1996). Researchers and others need to provide all children with opportunities to develop spatial reasoning skills.

8. Most of the standardized tests that are used for admissions to college, graduate and professional schools, programs for gifted youth, and scholarships underpredict female performance and overpredict male performance. Be sure that multiple measures of ability and achievement are used in these decisions, especially course grades and tests of writing, which tend to favor females.

9. There are no cognitive reasons to support sex-segregated education. The fact that girls get better grades in every subject shows that they are learning at least as well as boys. For those concerned with increasing the number of females in science and math, the problem lies in convincing more females that "math counts" and to make academic and career choices that are "math-wise."

10. Interpret research findings with an amiable skepticism, and examine conclusions to determine if they are data-based. Conclusions about a topic as complex as cognitive sex differences will rest on the cumulative results of many studies. Although each person has social–political preferences for particular types of explanations, it is also necessary to strive to maintain an open-minded fairness when assessing a variety of theoretical and empirical findings, including the conclusions presented in this book. Explain the many pitfalls of this sort of research whenever you hear simple statements like "It's all in the hormones," or "It's all in the mother's attitude" are being made.

11. Remember that the brain remains plastic throughout life, which means that it is altered in response to experiences even into very old age. Work to keep old age a time of useful activity. This is one benefit that you personally can reap when you enter your own old age.

Sex Differences, So What!

There are hundreds of observable sex differences that we, as intuitive scientists, try to explain.
—Valian (1998, p. 109)

What are the applied and practical implications of cognitive sex differences? Consider the following applied problem: It seems safe to assume that most Americans and American allies would agree that the U.S. Air Force should have highly qualified officers. To ensure that this is so, prospective officers take a test (U.S. Air Force Officers Qualifying Test) that measures their verbal, quantitative, and spatial ability. In general, results obtained with this test agree with the sex differences literature in these areas, with females scoring higher on verbal ability and males scoring higher on quantitative and spatial ability. Because spatial ability seems particularly important for air force officers, who often need to rely on aerial landmarks and spatial co-ordinates, it is likely that many women are disqualified on the basis of this test. In fact, 98% of all student aviators are male (Gordon & Leighty, 1988).

In an examination of the question of whether females can, on average, become as qualified for air force officer duties as men, McCloy and Koonce (1982) trained women and men on standard simulated flight maneuvers. They found that men were faster on learning the flight tasks than the women were. But, as they pointed out, is this the right question? The more important question concerns the level of ability after training. Were women as good as men? The dependent measure in this study was the number of trials to criterion. In other words, the women required more training trials than the men did to learn a particular task. Perhaps the most important point is that the women apparently were as good as the men when they completed the training. These results are in accord with the general finding that spatial skills are trainable. If we rely on tests of abilities to decide who may enter training programs, we will miss able candidates who can learn to perform as well as their peers who scored higher on these tests prior to instruction.

We do not know why the women in McCloy and Koonce's (1982) experiment required more trials to learn the same flight maneuvers as the men. It could be due to biological or psychosocial reasons, or both, or some other yet undiscovered difference between the sexes. Although the etiology of cognitive sex differences is very important from a theoretical perspective, it is irrelevant in most applied settings. With appropriate training, the sex differences in this study disappeared. We also do not know if the women who received this training will be able to transfer their new spatial ability to other novel spatial tasks as quickly as the men can. In other words, if they are faced with a new and different spatial task, will they now perform it as quickly as their male counterparts? This remains another important question for future research.

The example of the air force officers applies in other settings as well. Every teacher knows that some students will take longer to learn certain concepts than others. If one student takes a half hour to complete a homework assignment and another student takes 45 minutes, the difference is unimportant in most contexts. The important fact is that both students now know and understand something that they did not know before and, after training, both are able to perform tasks that require the use of the newly acquired knowledge.

It is important to keep in mind a point that has been reiterated throughout this book. The experimental results that have been reviewed concern average differences obtained from groups of men and women, and no one is average. The data reviewed in this text are largely irrelevant when making decisions about individuals. They should never be used to justify or predict anyone's success or failure. There is considerable between-sex overlap with respect to these abilities.

The literature on sex differences has been proliferating in recent years because the questions are of profound human interest. A firestorm of interest is ignited every time the media carries headlines like those associated with Harris' (1995, 1998b) report that parents' behaviors have little effect on the psychological outcomes of their children or Shayowitz et al.'s (1999) study showing that when women take hormone replacement therapy they show different patterns of brain activation than when they take a placebo. Both of these reports made front-page news in the country's largest newspapers and were the subject of television and radio news programs. I hope that every reader of this text will understand the complexities, limitations, and implications of research of this sort. The next time you read or hear about research findings on cognitive sex differences, you have all the rights and obligations of informed consumers. This knowledge should empower you.

References

Adams, R. P., & Bradford, M. R. (1985). Sex differences in preschool children's tactual exploration of novel and familiar objects with parents and strangers. *Journal of Genetic Psychology, 146,* 567–569.

Adelman, C. (1991). *Woman at thirtysomething: Paradoxes of attainment.* Washington, DC: U.S. Department of Education.

Adkins-Regan, E. (1988). Sex hormones and sexual orientation in animals. *Psychobiology, 16,* 335–347.

Adler, T. (1989, June). Early sex hormone exposure studied. *APA Monitor,* p. 9.

Adler, T. (1993, January). Separate gender norms on tests raise questions. *APA Monitor,* p. 6.

Aiken, L. (1986–1987). Sex differences in mathematical ability: A review of the literature. *Educational Research Quarterly, 10,* 25–35.

Allan, K., & Coltrane, S. (1996). Gender display in television commercials: A comparative study of television commercials in the 1950s and 1980s. *Sex Roles, 35,* 185–203.

Alfieri, T., Ruble, D. N., & Higgins, E. T. (1996). Gender stereotypes during adolescence: Developmental changes and the transition to junior high school. *Developmental Psychology, 32,* 1129–1137.

Allen, L. S., Richey, M. F., Chai, Y. M., & Gorski, R. A. (1991). Sex differences in the corpus callosum of the living human being. *Journal of Neuroscience, 11,* 933–942.

Allgeier, E. R. (1983). Reproduction, roles and responsibilities. In E. R. Allgeier & N. B. McCormick (Eds.), *Changing boundaries: Gender roles and sexual behavior* (pp. 163–181). Palo Alto, CA: Mayfield.

Allport, G. W., Vernon, P. E., & Lindzey, G. (1970). *Manual for the study of values* (3rd ed.). Boston: Houghton Mifflin.

Altermatt, E. R., Jovanovic, J., & Perry, M. (1998). Bias or responsivity? Sex and achievement level effects on teachers' classroom questioning. *Journal of Educational Psychology, 90,* 516–527.

American Association of University Women. (1988). *College admission tests: Opportunities or roadblocks?* Washington, DC: Author.

American Association of University Women. (1992). *How schools shortchange girls: The AAUW report.* New York: Marlowe.

American Psychiatric Association. (1994). *Diagnostic and statistical manual of mental disorders* (4th ed.). Washington, DC: Author.

Anderson. J. R. (1990). *Cognitive psychology and its implications* (3rd ed.). San Francisco: Freeman.

Andrews, G., Morris-Yates, A., Howie, P., & Martin, N. G. (1991). Genetic factors in stuttering confirmed. *Archives of General Psychiatry, 48,* 1034–1035.

Angier, N. (1990, July). Scientists find sex differentiation gene. *International Herald Tribune,* p. 3.

Annett, M. (1988). Comments on Lindesay: Laterality shift in homosexual men. *Neuropsychologia, 26,* 341–343.

Annett, M. (1994). Handedness as a continuous variable with dextral shift: Sex, generation, and family handedness in subgroups of left- or right-handers. *Behavior Genetics, 24,* 51–63.

Arap-Maritim, E. K. (1987). Developmental analysis of sex differences in class rank of primary-grade children. *Psychological Reports, 60,* 155–158.

Ardila, A., & Rosselli, M. (1994). Development of language, memory, and visuospatial abilities in 5– to 12–year-old children using a neuropsychological battery. *Developmental Neuropsychology, 10,* 97–120.

Arenson, K. W. (1998, January). A revamped student test reduces the gap between the sexes. *The New York Times,* p. B7.

Asaro, C. (1990, January). We need to know why women falter in math. *The Chronicle Of Higher Education,* p. B4.

Astin, A., Sax, L., Korn, W., & Mahoney, K. (1995). *The American freshman: National norms for fall 1995.* Los Angeles: Higher Education Research Institute.

Astur, R. S., Ortiz, M. L., & Sutherland, R. J. (1998). A characterization of performance by men and women in a virtual Morris water maze: A large and reliable sex difference. *Behavioural Brain Research, 93,* 185–190.

Bachevalier, J., & Hagger, C. (1991). Sex differences in the development of learning abilities in primates. *Psychoneuroendocrinology, 16,* 177–188.

Backman, M. E. (1979). Patterns of mental abilities of adolescent males and females from different ethnic and socioeconomic backgrounds. In L. Willerman & R. G. Turner (Eds.), *Readings about individual and group differences* (pp. 261–265). San Francisco: Freeman.

Baenninger, M., & Newcombe, N. (1989). The role of experience in spatial test performance: A meta-analysis. *Sex Roles, 20,* 5–6.

Baenninger, M., & Newcombe, N. (1995). Environmental input to the development of sex-related differences in spatial and mathematical ability. *Learning and Individual Differences, 7,* 363–382.

Baenninger, M., & Newcombe, N. (1996). Sauce for the goose, sauce for the gander. *Learning and Individual Differences, 8,* 65–82.

Bakan, P. (1990). Nonright-handedness and the continuum of reproductive casualty. In S. Coren (Ed.), *Advances in Psychology: Vol 67. Left-handedness: Behavioral implications and anomalies.* (pp. 33–74). New York: North-Holland.

Baker, L. A., Ho, H., & Reynolds, C. (1994). Sex differences in genetic and environmental influences for cognitive abilities. In J. C. DeFries & R. Plomin (Eds.), *Nature and nurture during middle childhood* (pp. 181–200). Oxford, England: Blackwell.

Baker, M. A. (1987a). Sensory functioning. In M. A. Baker (Ed.), *Sex differences in human performance* (pp. 5–36). New York: Wiley.

Baker, M. A. (Ed.). (1987b). *Sex differences in human performance.* New York: Wiley.

Banaji, M. R., & Hardin, C. D. (1996). Automatic stereotyping. *Psychological Science, 7,* 136–141.

Bandura, A. (1986). The explanatory and predictive scope of self-efficacy theory. *Journal of Social and Clinical Psychology, 4 ,* 359–373.

Bandura, A., & Walters, R. H. (1963). *Social learning and personality development.* New York: Holt, Rinehart & Winston.

Banich, M. T., & Heller, W. (1998). Evolving perspectives on lateralization of function. *Current Directions in Psychological Science , 7,* 1–2.

Bannatyne, A. (1976). *Language, reading, and learning disabilities: Psychology, neuropsychology, diagnosis, and remediation.* Springfield, IL: Thomas.

Bardach, L., & Park, B. (1996). The effect of in-group/out-group status on memory for consistent and inconsistent behavior of an individual. *Personality and Social Psychology Bulletin, 22,* 169–178.

Bar-Haim, G., & Wilkes, J. M. (1989). A cognitive interpretation of the marginality and underrepresentation of women in science. *Journal of Higher Education, 60,* 371–387.

Barta, W. (1999). Gardner Murphy's double-aspect psychology. *Review of General Psychology, 3,* 55–79.

Bartlett, J. (1980). *Bartlett's familiar quotations* (15th ed.). Boston: Little, Brown.

Baucom, D. H., & Welsh, G. S. (1978). In support of extreme groups design for studying masculinity–femininity and intelligence. *Intelligence, 2,* 6–10.

Baumeister, R. F. (1988). Should we stop studying sex differences altogether? *American Psychologist, 42,* 756–757.

Beck, A. (1990, July). The daughter track. *Newsweek,* 48–64.

Becker, J. T., Bass, S. M., Dew, M. A., Kingsley, I., Selnes, O. A., & Sheridan, K. (1992). Hand preference, immune system disorder, and cognitive function among gay/bisexual men: The Multicenter AIDS Cohort Study (MACS). *Neuropsychologia, 30,* 229–236.

Beeman, M. J., & Chiarello, C. (1998). Complementary right- and left-hemisphere language comprehension. *Current Directions in Psychological Science, 7,* 2–8.

Begley, S. (1999, January 4). Into the gene pool. *Newsweek,* 68–69.

Belenky, M. F., Clinchy, B. M., Goldberger, N. R., & Tarule, J. M. (1986). *Women's ways of knowing.* New York: Basic Books.

Beller, M., & Gafni, N. (1996). The 1991 International Assessment of Educational Progress in Mathematics and Sciences: The gender differences perspective. *Journal of Educational Psychology, 88,* 365–377.

Bem, S. L. (1974). The measurement of psychological androgyny. *Journal of Consulting and Clinical Psychology, 42,* 155–162.

Bem, S. L. (1981). Gender schema theory: A cognitive account of sex-typing. *Psychological Review, 88,* 354–364.

Bem, S. L. (1993). The meaning of gender. *The Chronicle of Higher Education.*

Bem, S. L., & Bem, D. J. (1976). Training the woman to know her place: The power of a nonconscious ideology. In S. Cox (Ed.), *Female psychology: The emerging self* (pp. 180–190). Chicago: Science Research Associates.

Benbow, C. P. (1988). Sex differences in mathematical reasoning ability in intellectually talented preadolescents: Their nature, effects, and possible causes. *Behavioral and Brain Sciences, 11,* 169–232.

Benbow, C. P., & Lubinski, D. (1993). Psychological profiles of the mathematically talented: Some sex differences and evidence supporting their biological basis. In Ciba Foundation (Ed.), *The origins and development of high ability* (pp. 44–66). New York: Wiley.

Benbow, C. P., & Stanley, J. C. (1980, December). Sex differences in mathematical ability: Fact or artifact? *Science, 210,* 1262–1264.

Benbow, C. P., & Stanley, J. C. (1981). Mathematical ability: Is sex a factor? *Science, 212,* 118–121.

Benbow, C. P., & Stanley, J. C. (1983, December). Sex differences in mathematical reasoning ability: More facts. *Science, 222,* 1029–1031.

Benderly, B. L. (1989, November). Don't believe everything you read. *Psychology Today, 23,* 67–69.

Bennett, C. K. (1969). *Bennett Mechanical Comprehension Test.* New York: Psychological Corporation.

Bennett, M. (1996). Self-estimates of intelligence in men and women. *Journal of Social Psychology, 136,* 411–412.

Bennett, M. (1997). Self-estimates of ability in men and women. *Journal of Social Psychology, 137,* 540–541.

Berenbaum, S. A. (1999). Effects of early androgens on sex-typed activities and interests in adolescents with congenital adrenal hyperplasia. *Hormones and Behavior, 35,* 102–110.

Berenbaum, S. A., & Hines, M. (1992). Early androgens are related to childhood sex-typed toy preferences. *Psychological Science, 3,* 203–206.

Berenbaum, S. A., Korman, K., & Leveroni, C. (1995). Early hormones and sex differences in cognitive abilities. *Learning and Individual Differences, 7,* 303–322.

Berenbaum, S. A., & Snyder, E. (1995). Early hormonal influences on childhood sex-typed activity and playmate preferences: Implications for the development of sexual orientation. *Developmental Psychology, 31,* 31–42.

Berrebi, A. S., Fitch, R. H., Ralphe, D. L., Denenberg, J. O., Freidrich, V. L., Jr., & Denenberg, V. H. (1988). Corpus callosum: Region specific effects of sex, early experience, and age. *Brain Research, 438,* 216–224.

Berry, J. W. (1966). Temne and Eskimo perceptual skills. *International Journal of Psychology, 1,* 207–229.

Bettencourt, B. A., & Miller, N. (1996). Gender differences in aggression as a function of provocation: A meta-analysis. *Psychological Bulletin, 119,* 422–447.

Bigler, E. D., Blatter, D. D., Anderson, C. V., Johnson, S. C., Gale, S. D., Hopkins, R. O., & Burnett, B. (1997). Hippocampal volume in normal aging and traumatic brain injury. *American Journal of Neuroradiology, 18,* 11–23.

Bilous, F. R., & Krauss, R. M. (1988). Dominance and accommodation in the conversational behaviours of same- and mixed-gender dyads. *Language & Communication, 8,* 183–194.

Birenbaum, M., Kelly, A. E., & Levi-Keren, M. (1994). Stimulus features and sex differences in mental rotation test performance. *Intelligence, 19,* 51–64.

Bishop, K. M., & Wahlsten, D. (1997). Sex differences in the human corpus callosum: Myth or reality? *Neuroscience and Biobehavioral Reviews, 12,* 581–601.

Bleier, R. (1978). Bias in biological and human sciences: Some comments. *Signs, 5,* 159–162.

Bleier, R. (1984). *Science and gender: A critique of biology and its theories on women.* Elmsford, NY: Pergamon.

Bleier, R. (1991). *Gender ideology and the brain: Sex differences research.* Washington, DC: American Psychiatric Press.

Block, J. H. (1976). Issues, problems, and pitfalls in assessing sex differences: A critical review of the psychology of sex differences. *Merrill Palmer Quarterly, 22,* 283–308.

Block, R. A., Arnott, D. P., Quigley, B., & Lynch, W. C. (1989). Unilateral nostril breathing influences lateralized cognitive performance. *Brain and Cognition, 9,* 181–190.

Block, R. A., Hancock, P. A., & Zakay, D. (1999). *Sex differences in duration judgments: A meta-analytic review.* Manuscript submitted for publication.

Bock, R. D., & Kolakowski, D. (1973). Further evidence of sex-linked major-gene influence on human spatial visualizing ability. *American Journal of Human Genetics, 25,* 1–14.

Boles, D. B. (1980). X-linkage of spatial ability: A critical review. *Child Development, 51,* 625–635.

Boliek, C. A., & Obrzut, J. E. (1995). Perceptual laterality in developmental learning disabilities. In R. J. Davidson & K. Hugdahl (Eds.), *Brain asymmetry* (pp. 637–658). Cambridge, MA: MIT Press.

Boomsma, D., Anokhin, A., & deGeus, E. (1997). Genetics of electrophysiology: Linking genes, brain, and behavior. *Current Directions in Psychological Science, 6,* 106–110.

Born, M. P., Bleichrodt, N., & Van der Flier, H. (1987). Cross-cultural comparison of sex-related differences on intelligence tests: A meta-analysis. *Journal of Cross Cultural Psychology, 18,* 283–314.

Bouchard, T. J., Jr., & McGee, M. G. (1977). Sex differences in human spatial ability: Not an X-linked recessive gene effect. *Social Biology, 24,* 332–335.

Bowers, C. A., & LaBarba, R. C. (1988). Sex differences in the lateralization of spatial abilities: A spatial component analysis of extreme group scores. *Brain and Cognition, 8,* 165–177.

Braddick, O. (1993). Computing "where" and "what" in the visual system. In N. Elian & R. A. McCarthy (Eds.), *Spatial representation: Problems in philosophy and psychology* (pp. 340–355). Oxford, England: Blackwell.

Bradshaw, J. L., & Bradshaw, J. A. (1988). Reading mirror-reversed text: Sinistrals really are inferior. *Brain and Language, 33,* 189–192.

Braine, L. G. (1988). Sex differences in mathematics: Is there any news here? *Behavioral and Brain Sciences, 11,* 185–186.

Bridgeman, B., & McHale, F. (1996). *Gender and ethnic group differences on the GMAT analytical writing assessment* (Report No. RR-96-2). Princeton, NJ: Educational Testing Service.

Bridgeman, B., & Moran, R. (1996). Success in college for students with discrepancies between performance on multiple-choice and essay tests. *Journal of Educational Psychology, 88,* 333–340.

Bridgeman, B., & Wendler, C. (1991). Gender differences in predictors of college mathematics course grades. *Journal of Educational Psychology, 83,* 275–284.

Bridges, J. S. (1989). Sex differences in occupational values. *Sex Roles, 20,* 3–4.

Brody, N. (1992). *Intelligence* (2nd ed.). New York: Academic Press.

Bromley, S. M., & Doty, R. L. (1995). Odor recognition memory is better under bilateral than unilateral test conditions. *Cortex, 31,* 25–40.

Bronfenbrenner, U. (1994). A constant frame of reference for sociometric research: Part II. Experiment and inference. *Sociometry, 7,* 40–75.

Brooks, I. R. (1976). Cognitive ability assessment with two New Zealand ethnic groups. *Journal of Cross Cultural Psychology, 7,* 347–356.

Brooks-Gunn, J., Klebanov, P. K., & Liaw, F.-R. (1992). Effects of early intervention on cognitive functions of low birth weight preterm infants. *Journal of Pediatrics, 120,* 350–359.

Broverman, D. M., Klaiber, E. L., Kobayashi, Y., & Vogel, W. (1968). Roles of activation and inhibition in sex differences in cognitive abilities. *Psychological Review, 75,* 23–50.

Broverman, I. K., Vogel, S. R., Broverman, D. M., Clarkson, F. E., & Rosenkrantz, P. S. (1972). Sex-role stereotypes: A current appraisal. *Journal of Social Issues, 28,* 59–78.

Brown, G. R., & Dixson, A. F. (1999). Investigation of the role of postnatal testosterone in the expression of sex differences in behavior in infant rhesus macaques (*Macaca mulatta*). *Hormones and Behavior, 35,* 186–194.

Brown, H. D., & Kosslyn, S. M. (1995). Hemispheric differences in visual object processing: Structural versus allocation theories. In R. J. Davidson & K. Hugdahl (Eds.), *Brain asymmetry* (pp. 77–97). Cambridge, MA: MIT Press.

Brush, F. R., & Levine, S. (1989). Preface. In F. R. Brush & S. Levine (Eds.), *Psychoendocrinology* (pp. xiii–xiv). New York: Academic Press.

Bryden, M. P. (1977). Measuring handedness with questionnaires. *Neuropsychologia, 15,* 617–624.

Bryden, M. P. (1986). Dichotic listening performance, cognitive ability, and cerebral organization. *Canadian Journal of Psychology, 40,* 445–456.

Bryden, M. P. (1988). An overview of the dichotic listening procedure and its relation to cerebral organization. In K. Hugdahl (Ed.), *Handbook of dichotic listening* (pp. 1–43). New York: Wiley.

Bryden, M. P., McManus, I. C., & Bulman-Fleming, M. B. (1994). Evaluating the empirical support for the Geschwind–Behan–Galaburda model of cerebral lateralization. *Brain and Cognition, 26,* 103–167.

Buckwalter, J. G., Sobel, E., Dunn, M. E., & Diz, M. M. (1993). Gender differences on a brief measure of cognitive functioning in Alzheimer's disease. *Archives of Neurology, 50,* 757–760.

Buczek, P. A. (1986). A promising measure of sex bias: The incidental memory task. *Psychology of Women Quarterly, 10,* 127–140.

Bumiller, E. (1990). *May you be the mother of a hundred sons.* New York: Random House.

Burnham, D. (1977). Biology and gender: False theories about women and Blacks. *Freedomways, 17,* 8–13.

Burton, G. M. (1978). Why Susie can't—or doesn't want to—add. In J. E. Jacobs (Ed.), *Perspectives on women and mathematics* (pp. 35–57). Columbus, OH: ERIC Clearinghouse for Science, Mathematics and Environmental Education.

Buss, D. M. (1995). Evolutionary psychology: A new paradigm for psychological science. *Pschyological Inquiry, 6,* 1–30.

Butcher, J. (1986). Longitudinal analysis of adolescent girls' aspirations at school and perceptions of popularity. *Adolescence, 21,* 133–143.

Butler, S. (1984). Sex differences in human cerebral function. In G. J. DeVries (Ed.), *Progress in brain research* (pp. 443–454). New York: Elsevier.

Byrne, R. (1988). *One thousand nine hundred eleven best things anybody ever said.* New York: Fawcett.

Cahan, S., & Ganor, Y. (1995). Cognitive gender differences among Israeli children. *Sex Roles, 32,* 469–484.

Calvert, S. L., & Huston, A. C. (1987). Television and children's gender schemata. In L. S. Liben & L. S. Signorella (Eds.), *Children's gender schemata* (pp. 75–88). San Francisco: Jossey-Bass.

Caplan, P. J., MacPherson, G. M., & Tobin, P. (1985). Do sex-related differences in spatial abilities exist? *American Psychologist, 40,* 786–799.

Carter, C. O. (1972). Sex-linkage and sex-limitation. In C. I. Ounsted & D. Taylor (Eds.), *Gender differences: Their ontogeny and significance* (pp. 1–12). Edinburgh, Scotland: Churchill-Livingstone.

Casey, M. B. (1996). Understanding individual differences in spatial ability within females: A nature/nurture interactionist framework. *Developmental Review, 16,* 241–260.

Casey, M. B., & Brabeck, M. M. (1990). Women who excel on a spatial task: Proposed genetic and environmental factors. *Brain and Cognition, 12,* 73–84.

Casey, M. B., Brabeck, M. M., & Nuttall, R. L. (1995). As the twig is bent: The biology and socialization of gender roles in women. *Brain and Cognition, 27,* 237–246.

Casey, M. B., Nuttall, R. L., & Pezaris, E. (1997). Mediators of gender differences in mathematics college entrance test scores: A comparison of spatial skills with beliefs and anxieties. *Developmental Psychology, 33,* 669–680.

Casey, M. B., Nuttall, R., Pezaris, E., & Benbow, C. P. (1995). The influence of spatial ability on gender difference in mathematics college entrance test scores across diverse samples. *Developmental Psychology, 31,* 697–705.

Cattell, R. B. (1963). Theory of fluid and crystallized intelligence. *Journal of Educational Psychology, 54,* 1–22.

Ceci, S. J., & Hembrooke, H. A. (1995). A bioecological model of intellectual development. In P. Moen, G. H. Elder, Jr., & K. Luscher (Eds.), *Examining lives in context: Perspectives on the ecology of human development* (pp. 303–345). Washington, DC: American Psychological Association.

Chabris, C. F., & Kosslyn, S. M. (1998). How do the cerebral hemispheres contribute to encoding spatial relations? *Current Directions in Psychological Science, 7,* 8–14.

Christiansen, K. (1993). Sex hormone-related variations of cognitive performance in !Kung San hunter–gatherers of Namibia. *Neuropsychobiology, 27,* 97–107.

Christiansen, K., & Knussmann, R. (1987). Sex hormones and cognitive functioning in men. *Neuropsychobiology, 18,* 27–36.

Clarkson-Smith, L., & Halpern, D. F. (1983). Can age-related deficits in spatial memory be attenuated through the use of verbal coding? *Experimental Aging Research, 9,* 179–184.

Cohen, J. (1969). *Statistical power analysis for the behavioral sciences.* New York: Academic Press.

Cohen, J. (1977). *Statistical power analysis for the behavioral sciences* (Rev. ed.). Hillsdale, NJ: Lawrence Erlbaum Associates.

Cohen, J. (1994). The earth is round ($p < .05$). *American Psychologist, 49,* 997–1003.

Cohen, J., & Cohen, P. (1983). *Applied multiple regression/correlational analysis for behavioral sciences.* Hillsdale, NJ: Lawrence Erlbaum Associates.

Cole, M., & Scribner, S. (1974). *Culture and thought: A psychological introduction.* New York: Wiley.

Collaer, M. L., & Hines, M. (1995). Human behavioral sex differences: A role for gonadal hormones during early development? *Psychological Bulletin, 118,* 55–107.

College Entrance Examination Board. (1997). *National report on college-bound seniors, various years.* New York: Author.

Colvin, R. L. (1996, November 21). Global study finds U.S. students weak in math. *Los Angeles Times,* pp. A1, A24–A25.

Constantinople, A. (1973). Masculinity–femininity: An exception to a famous dictum? *Psychological Bulletin, 80,* 389–407.

Cook, E. P. (1985). *Psychological androgyny.* Elmsford, NY: Pergamon.

Cooper, L. A., & Mumow, R. J. (1985). Spatial aptitude. In R. F. Dillman (Ed.), *Individual differences in cognition* (2nd ed., pp. 67–94). New York: Academic Press.

Corballis, M. C., & Beale, I. L. (1983). *The ambivalent mind: The neuropsychology of left and right.* Chicago: Nelson-Hall.

Cordes, C. (1986, June). Test tilt: Boys outscore girls on both parts of SAT. *APA Monitor,* pp. 30–31.

Coren, S. (1990). *Left handedness: Behavioral implications and anomalies.* New York: Elsevier.

Coren, S., & Halpern, D. F. (1991). Left-handedness: A marker for decreased survival fitness. *Psychological Bulletin, 109,* 90–106.

Coren, S., & Halpern, D. F. (1993). A replay of the baseball data. *Perceptual and Motor Skills, 76,* 403–406.

Cornell, D. G. (1997). Post hoc explanation is not prediction: Commentary on J. Archer. *American Psychologist, 52,* 1380.

Courtney, S. M., Ungerleider, L. G., Keil., K., & Haxby, J. V. (1996). Object and spatial visual working memory activate separate neural systems in human cortex. *Cerebral Cortex, 39–49.*

Cowell, P. E., Turetsky, B. I., Gur, R. C., Grossman, R. I., Shtasel, D. L., & Gur, R. E. (1994). Sex differences in aging of the human frontal and temporal lobes. *Journal of Neuroscience, 14,* 4748–4755.

Crawford, M., Chaffin, R., & Fitton, L. (1995). Cognition in social context. *Learning and Individual Differences, 7,* 341–362.

Crawford, M., & Kimmel, E. (1999). Promoting methodological diversity in feminist research. *Psychology of Women Quarterly, 23,* 1–6.

Crawford, M. C., & Kimmel, E. B. (Guest Eds.). (1999). Innovations in feminine research (special ed.). *Psychology of Women Quarterly, 23*(2).

Dalton, K. (1976). Prenatal progesterone and educational attainments. *British Journal of Psychiatry, 129,* 438–442.

Daly, M., & Wilson, M. I. (1999). Human evolutionary psychology and animal behavior. *Animal Behaviour, 57,* 509–519.

Daniel, J. M., Fader, A. J., Spencer, A. L., & Dohanich, G. P. (1997). Estrogen enhances performance of female rats during acquisition of a radial arm maze. *Hormones and Behavior, 32,* 217–225.

Darling, J. (1998, January 13). Drug lords tainting beauty pageants. *Los Angeles Times.* Part A, 1.

Davidson, R. J., & Hugdahl, K. (1995). *Brain asymmetry.* Cambridge, MA: MIT Press.

Davis, H., & Gergen, P. J. (1997). Self-described weight status of Mexican-American adolescents. *Journal of Adolescent Health, 15,* 407–409.

Dawes, R. M. (1994). *House of cards: Psychology and psychotherapy built on myth.* New York: The Free Press.

Deaux, K. (1984). From individual differences to social categories: Analysis of a decade's research on gender. *American Psychologist, 39,* 105–116.

Deaux, K. (1985). Sex and gender. *Annual Reviews of Psychology, 36,* 49–81.

Deaux, K., & Major, B. (1987). Putting gender into context: An interactive model of gen-der-related behavior. *Psychological Review, 94,* 369–389.

DeFries, J. C., & Gillis, J. J. (1993). Genetics of reading disability. In R. Plomin & G. E. McClearn (Eds.), *Nature, nurture, and psychology* (pp. 121–145). Washington, DC: American Psychological Association.

DeFries, J. C., Vandenberg, S. G., & McClearn, G. E. (1976). Genetics of specific cognitive abilities. *Annual Review of Genetics, 10,* 179–207.

deLacoste-Utamsing, C., & Holloway, R. L. (1982, June). Sexual dimorphism in the human corpus callosum. *Science, 216,* 1431–1432.

Delgado, A. R., & Prieto, G. (1996). Sex differences in visuospatial ability: Do perfor-mance factors play such an important role? *Memory and Cognition, 24,* 504–510.

De Lisi, R., Parameswaran, G., & McGillicuddy-DeLisi, A. (1989). Age and sex differ-ences in representation of horizontality among children in India. *Perceptual and Motor Skills, 68,* 739–746.

Denenberg, V. H., Berrebi, A. S., & Fitch, R. H. (1988). A factor analysis of the rat's corpus callosum. *Brain Research, 497,* 271–279.

Desmond, D. W., Glenwick, D. S., Stern, Y., & Tatemichi, T. K. (1994). Sex differences in the representation of visuospatial functions in the human brain. *Rehabilitation Psychol-ogy, 39,* 3–14.

Deutsch, D. (1980). Handedness and memory for tonal pitch. In J. Herron (Ed.), *Neuropsychology of left-handedness.* New York: Academic Press.

Deutsch, F. M., & Saxon, S. (1998). The double standard of praise and criticism for mothers and fathers. *Psychology of Women Quarterly, 22,* 665–683.

de Waal, F. (1996). *The Chronicle of Higher Learning,* p. B1.

Diamond, E. E. (1986). Theories of career development and the reality of women at work. In B. A. Gutek & L. Larwood (Eds.), *Women's career development* (pp. 15–27). Newbury Park, CA: Sage.

Diamond, M. C. (1988). *Enriching heredity: The impact of the environment on the anatomy of the brain.* New York: The Free Press.

Diamond, M. C. (1999). Enrichment response of the brain. In G. Adelman & J. DePasquale (Eds.), *Elsevier's encyclopedia of neuroscience* (pp. 655–657). New York: Elsevier Sci-ence.

Dollinger, S. A. C. (1995). Mental rotation performance: Age, sex, and visual field differ-ences. *Developmental Neuropsychology, 11,* 215–222.

Dorries, K. M., Schmidt, H. J., Beauchamp, G. K., & Wysocki, C. J. (1989). Changes in sensitivity to the odor of androstenone during adolescence. *Developmental Psychobiology, 22,* 423–435.

Doty, R. L., Shaman, P., Applebaum, S. L., Giberson, R., Siksorski, L., & Rosenberg, L. (1984, December). Smell identification ability: Changes with age. *Science, 226,* 1441–1443.

Dowker, A. (1996). How important is spatial ability to mathematics? *Behavioral and Brain Sciences, 19,* 251.

Doyle, J. A. (1995). *The male experience* (3rd ed.). Madison, WI: Brown & Benchmark.

Dror, I., & Kosslyn, S. M. (1994). Mental imagery and aging. *Psychology of Aging, 9,* 90–102.

Dunham, P. H. (1998). Procedures to increase the entry of women in mathematics-related careers. *Science Education Digest, 3.*

Eagly, A. H. (1987). *Sex differences in social behavior: A social-role interpretation.* Hillsdale, NJ: Lawrence Erlbaum Associates.

Eagly, A. H. (1990). On the advantages on reporting sex comparisons. *American Psychologist, 45,* 560–562.

Eagly, A. H. (1994). On comparing women and men. *Feminism & Psychology, 4,* 513–522.

Eagly, A. H. (1995). The science and politics of comparing women and men. *American Psychologist, 50,* 145–158.

Eagly, A. H. (1996). Differences between women and men: Their magnitude, practical importance, and political meaning. *American Psychologist, 51,* 158–159.

Eagly, A. H., Karau, S. J., & Makhijani, M. G. (1995). Gender differences in career decision making. *Psychological Bulletin, 42,* 204–216.

Eagly, A. H., Mladinic, A., & Otto, S. (1994). Are women evaluated more favorably than men? An analysis of attitudes, beliefs, and emotions. *Journal of Experimental Social Psychology, 15,* 203–216.

Eagly, A. H., & Wood, W. (1999). The origins of sex differences in human behavior. *American Psychologist, 54,* 408–423.

Eals, M., & Silverman, I. (1994). The hunter–gatherer theory of spatial sex differences: Proximate factors mediating the female advantage in recall of object arrays. *Ethology and Sociobiology, 15,* 95–105.

Eaton, W. O., & Enns, L. R. (1986). Sex differences in human motor activity level. *Psychological Bulletin, 100,* 19–28.

Eccles, J. S. (1987). Gender roles and women's achievement-related decisions. *Psychology of Women Quarterly, 11,* 135–172.

Eccles, J. S. (1994). Understanding women's educational and occupational choices: Applying the Eccles et al. model of achievement-related choices. *Psychology of Women Quarterly, 18,* 585–609.

Eccles (Parsons), J. S., et al. (1983). Expectancies, values, and academic behaviors. In J. T. Spence (Ed.), *Achievement and achievement motives: Psychological and sociological approaches* (pp. 75–146). San Francisco: Freeman.

Educational Testing Service. (1987). *Manual of information for test committees members.* Princeton, NJ: Author.

Educational Testing Service. (1996). *1996 annual report: Building equity since 1947.* Princeton, NJ: Author.

Ehrhardt, A. A., & Meyer-Bahlburg, H. F. L. (1979). Prenatal sex hormones and the developing brain: Effects on psychosexual differentiation and cognitive function. *Annual Review of Medicine, 30,* 417–430.

Elder, G. J., Jr. (1995). The life course paradigm: Social change and individual development. In P. Moen, G. H. Elder, Jr., & K. Luscher (Eds.), *Examining lives in context* (pp. 101–140). Washington, DC: American Psychological Association.

Eliot, J., & Fralley, J. S. (1976). Sex differences in spatial abilities. *Young Children, 31,* 487–497.

Elliot, R. (1961). Interrelationship among measures of field dependence, ability, and personality traits. *Journal of Abnormal and Social Psychology, 63,* 27–36.

Elmore, P. B., & Vasu, E. S. (1986). A model of statistics achievement using spatial ability, feminist attitudes and mathematics-related variables as predictors. *Educational and Psychological Measurement, 46,* 215–222.

Ernest, J. (1976). *Mathematics and sex.* Berkeley: University of California Press.

Erwin, R. J., Gur, R. C., Gur, R. E., & Skolnick, B. (1992). Facial emotion discrimination: I. Task construction and behavioural findings in normal subjects. *Psychiatry Research, 42,* 231–240.

Erwin, R. J., Mawhinney-Hee, M., Gur, R. C., & Gur, R. E. (1989). Effects of task and gender on EEG indices of hemispheric activation. *Neuropsychiatry, Neuropsychology, and Behavioral Neurology, 2,* 248–260.

Etaugh, C. (1989). Evaluation bias. In H. Tierney (Ed.), *Women's studies encyclopedia* (pp. 124–125). Westport, CT: Greenwood.

Evans, S. H., & Anastasio, E. J. (1968). Misuse of analysis of covariance when treatment effect and covariate are confounded. *Psychological Bulletin, 69,* 225–234.

Fagot, B. I., & Leinbach, M. D. (1993). Gender-role development in young children: From discrimination to labeling. *Developmental Review, 13,* 205–224.

Fairweather, H. (1976). Sex differences in cognition. *Cognition, 4,* 231–280.

Faust, M. S. (1977). Somatic development of adolescent girls. *Monographs of the Society for Research in Child Development, 42,* 1–90.

Faust, M. S. (1983). Alternative constructions of adolescent growth. In J. Brooks-Gunn & A. C. Petersen (Eds.), *Girls at puberty: Biological and psychosocial perspectives* (pp. 105–125). New York: Plenum.

Fausto-Sterling, A. (1985). *Myths of gender: Biological theories about woman and man.* New York: Basic Books.

Feingold, A. (1988). Cognitive gender differences are disappearing. *American Psychologist, 43,* 95–103.

Feingold, A. (1993). Cognitive gender differences: A developmental perspective. *Sex Roles, 29,* 91–112.

Feingold, A. (1996). Cognitive gender differences: Where are they and why are they there? *Learning and Individual Differences, 8,* 25–32.

Fennema, E., & Sherman, J. (1977). Sex-related differences in mathematics achievement, spatial visualization, and sociocultural factors. *Journal of Educational Research, 14,* 51–71.

Fennema, E., & Sherman, J. (1978). Sex-related differences in mathematics achievement and related factors: A further study. *Journal for Research in Mathematics Education, 9,* 189–203.

Fergusson, D. M., & Horwood, L. J. (1997). Gender differences in educational achievement in New Zealand birth cohort. *New Zealand Journal of Educational Studies, 32,* 83–96.

Fernández-Ballesteros, R., & Calero, M. D. (1995). Training effects on intelligence of older persons. *Archives of Gerontology and Geriatrics, 20,* 135–148.

Fisher, H. (1999). *The first sex: The natural talents of women and how they are changing the world.* New York: Random House.

Fitch, R. H., & Denenberg, V. H. (1998). A role for ovarian hormones in sexual differentiation of the brain. *Behavioral and Brain Sciences, 21,* 311–352.

Flynn, J. R. (1998). Israeli military IQ tests: Gender differences small; IQ gains large. *Journal of Biosocial Science, 30,* 541–553.

Flynn, J. R. (1999). Searching for justice: The discovery of IQ gains over time. *American Psychologist, 54,* 5–20.

Foertsch, J., & Gernsbacher, M. A. (1997). In search of gender neutrality: Is singular they a cognitively efficient substitute for generic he? *Psychological Science, 8,* 106–111.

Fogel, R., & Paludi, M. A. (1984). Fear of success and failure or norms for achievement? *Sex Roles: A Journal of Research, 10,* 431–434.

Foote, D., & Seibert, S. (1999, Spring/Summer). The age of anxiety. *Newsweek (Special Edition: Health for Life)*, 68–72.

Forsyth, D. R., Heiney, M. M., & Wright, S. S. (1997). Biases in appraisals of women leaders. *Group Dynamics: Theory, Research, and Practice, 1*, 98–103.

Fox, L. H., Tobin, D., & Brody, L. (1979). Sex role socialization and achievement in mathematics. In M. A. Wittig & A. C. Petersen (Eds.), *Sex related differences in cognitive functioning* (pp. 303–332). New York: Academic Press.

Freeman, D. (1983). *Margaret Mead and Samoa: The making and unmaking of an anthropological myth*. Cambridge, MA: Harvard University Press.

Frerking, B. (1997, January 13). Looking sexy beyond their years. *Los Angeles Times*, p. B1.

Freud, S. (1920). *A general introduction to psychoanalysis*. New York: Boni & Liveright.

Frick, R. W. (1996). The appropriate use of hull hypothesis. *Psychological Methods, 1*, 379–390.

Friedman, L. (1995). The space factor in mathematics: Gender differences. *Review of Educational Research, 65*, 22–50.

Frisch, R. E. (1983). Fatness, puberty, and fertility: The effects of nutrition and physical training on menarche and ovulation. In J. Brooks-Gunn & A. C. Petersen (Eds.), *Girls at puberty: Biological and psychosocial perspectives* (pp. 29–50). New York: Plenum.

Galea, L. A. M., & Kimura, D. (1993). Sex differences in route learning. *Personality & Individual Differences, 14*, 53–65.

Gallagher, S. A. (1989). Predictors of SAT mathematics and scores of gifted male and gifted female adolescents. *Psychology of Women Quarterly, 13*, 191–203.

Gallagher, A. M. (1998). Gender and antecedents of performance in mathematics testing. *Teachers College Record, 100*, 297–314.

Gallagher, A., M., DeLisi, R., Holst, P.C., McGillicuddy-DeLisi, A. V., Morley, M., & Cahalan, C. (1999). *Matching solution strategies to problem demands in advanced mathematical problem solving*. Manuscript submitted for publication.

Gardner, H. (1983). *Frames of mind*. New York: Basic Books.

Gati, I., Osipow, S. H., & Givon, M. (1995). Gender differences in career decision making: The content and structure of preferences. *Journal of Counseling Psychology, 42*, 204–216.

Gaulin, S. J. C. (1995). Does evolutionary theory predict sex differences in the brain? In M. S. Gazzaniga (Ed.), *The cognitive neurosciences* (pp. 1211–1225). Cambridge, MA: MIT Press.

Gaulin, S. J. C., & Fitzgerald, R. W. (1989). Sexual selection for spatial learning ability. *Animal Behavior, 37*, 322–331.

Gaulin, S. J. C., Fitzgerald, R. W., & Wartell, M. S. (1990). Sex differences in spatial ability and activity in two vole species. *Journal of Comparative Psychology, 104*, 88–93.

Gaulin, S. J. C., & Wartell, M. S. (1990). Effects of experience and motivation on symmetrical-maze performance in the prarie vole. *Journal of Comparative Psychology, 104*, 183–189.

Gazzaniga, M. S. (Ed.). (1995). *The cognitive neurosciences*. Cambridge, MA: MIT Press.

Gazzaniga, M. S., Ivry, R. B., & Mangun, G. R. (1998). *Cognitive neuroscience: The biology of the mind*. New York: Norton.

Geary, D. C. (1988, November). *Sex-dimorphic behavior patterns, maturational timing, and gender differences in spatial ability*. Paper presented at the 29th annual meeting of the Psychonomic Society, Chicago.

Geary, D. C. (1995). Reflection of evolution and culture in children's cognition: Implications for mathematical development and instruction. *American Psychologist, 50,* 24–37.

Geary, D. C. (1996). Response: A biosocial framework for studying cognitive sex differences. *Learning and Individual Differences, 8,* 55–60.

Geary, D. C. (1998). *Male, female: The evolution of human sex differences.* Washington, DC: American Psychological Association.

Geary, D. C. (1999). Evolution and developmental sex differences. *Current Directions in Psychological Science, 8,* 115–120.

Gee, H. (1997). Available on-line: http://www.nature.com/nature2/

Geffen, G., Moar, K. J., O'Hanlon, A. P., Clark, C. R., & Geffen, L. B. (1990). Performance measures of 16– to 86–year-old males and females on the Auditory Verbal Learning Test. *The Clinical Neuropsychologist, 4,* 45–63.

Gelman, D., Carey, J., Gelman, E., Malamud, P., Foote, D., Lubenow, G. C., & Contreras, J. (1981). Just how the sexes differ. *Newsweek,* 77–83.

Gerber, G. L. (1987). Sex stereotypes among American college students: Implications for marital happiness, social desirability, and marital power. *Genetic, Social, & General Psychology Monographs, 113,* 413–431.

Gersh, E. S., & Gersh, I. (1981). *Biology of women.* Baltimore: University Park Press.

Geschwind, N. (1974). The anatomical basis of hemisphere differentiation. In S. J. Dimond & J. G. Beaumont (Eds.), *Hemisphere function in the human brain.* New York: Wiley.

Geschwind, N. (1983). Biological associations of left-handedness. *Annals of Dyslexia, 33,* 29–40.

Geschwind, N. (1984). Cerebral dominance in biological perspective. *Neuropsychologia, 22,* 675–683.

Geschwind, N., & Behan, P. (1982). Left-handedness: Associations with immune disease, migraine, and developmental learning disorders. *Proceedings of the National Academy of Sciences, 79,* 5097–5100.

Geschwind, N., & Behan, P. (1984). Laterality, hormones and immunity. In N. Geschwind & A. M. Galaburda (Eds.), *Cerebral dominance: The biological foundations* (pp. 211–224). Cambridge, MA: Harvard University Press.

Geschwind, N., & Galaburda, A. M. (1987). *Cerebral lateralization: Biological mechanisms, associations, and pathology.* Cambridge, MA: MIT Press.

Gill, H. S., & O'Boyle, M. W. (1997). Sex differences in matching circles and arcs: A preliminary EEG investigation. *Laterality, 2,* 33–48.

Gilligan, C. (1982). *In a different voice: Psychological theory and women's development.* Cambridge, MA: Harvard University Press.

Gilovich, T. (1991). *How we know what isn't so: The fallability of human reason in everyday life.* New York: The Free Press.

Gist, Y. J., & Velkoff, V. A. (1997). International brief: Gender and aging: Demographic dimensions. *U.S. Department of Commerce,* 1–8.

Gittler, G., & Vitouch, O. (1994). Empirical contribution to the question of sex-dependent inheritance of spatial ability. *Perceptual and Motor Skills, 78,* 407–417.

Gladue, B. A. (1994). The biopsychology of sexual orientation. *Current Directions in Psychological Sciences, 3,* 150–154.

Gladue, B. A., Beatty, W. W., Larson, J., & Staton, R. D. (1990). Sexual orientations and spatial ability in men and women. *Psychobiology, 18,* 101–108.

Goldberg, P. (1968, April). Are some women prejudiced against women? *Transaction,* 28–30.

Goldstein, D., Haldane, D., & Mitchell, C. (1990). Sex differences in visual–spatial ability: The role of performance factors. *Memory & Cognition, 18,* 546–550.

Golub, S. (1976). The effect of premenstrual anxiety and depression on cognitive function. *Journal of Personality and Social Psychology, 34,* 99–104.

Goodnow, J. (1985). Topics, methods and models: Feminist challenges in social science. In J. Goodnow & C. Pateman (Eds.), *Women, social science and public policy.* Sydney, Australia: George Allen & Unwin.

Goodrich, G. A., Damin, P. B., Ascione, F. R., & Thompson, T. M. (1993). Gender difference in Piagetian visual–spatial representation of verticality and horizontality. *Journal of Genetic Psychology, 154,* 449–458.

Goolkasian, P. (1980). Cyclic changes in pain perception: An ROC analysis. *Perception and Psychophysics, 27,* 499–504.

Goolkasian, P. (1985). Phase and sex effects in pain perception: A critical review. *Psychology of Women Quarterly, 9,* 15–28.

Gordon, H. W. (1980). Cognitive asymmetry in dyslexic families. *Neuropsychologia, 18,* 645–656.

Gordon, H. W., & Leighty, R. (1988). Importance of specialized cognitive function in the selection of military pilots. *Journal of Applied Psychology, 73,* 38–45.

Gorski, R. A., Gordon, J. H., Shryne, J., & Southam, A. (1978). Evidence for a morphological sex difference within the medial preoptic area of the rat brain. *Brain Research, 148,* 333–346.

Gotestam, K. O., Coates, T. J., & Ekstrand, M. (1992). Handedness, dyslexia, and twinning in homosexual men. *International Journal of Neuroscience, 63,* 179–186.

Gottesman, I. I. (1997, June). Twins: En route to QTLs for cognition. *Science, 276,* 1522–1523.

Gottfried, A. W., Gottfried, A. E., Bathurst, K., & Guerin, D. W. (1994). *Gifted IQ: Early developmental aspects, the Fullerton longitudinal study.* New York: Plenum.

Gouchie, C., & Kimura, D. (1991). The relationship between testosterone levels and cognitive ability patterns. *Psychoneuroendocrinology, 16,* 323–334.

Gould, J. S. (1978). Women's brains. *Natural History, 87,* 44–50.

Gould, R. E. (1974). Measuring masculinity by the size of a paycheck. In J. H. Pleck & J. Sawyer (Eds.), *Men and masculinity* (pp. 96–100). Englewood Cliffs, NJ: Prentice-Hall.

Goy, R. W., Bercovitch, F. B., & McBrair, M. C. (1988). Behavioral masculinization is independent of genital masculinization in prenatally androgenized female rhesus macaques. *Hormones and Behavior, 22,* 552–571.

Grace, S. (1992, July 7). Whites, women dominate teaching corps. *Los Angeles Times,* p. A6.

Graves, L. M., & Powell, G. N. (1994). Effects of sex-based preferential selection and discrimination on job attitudes. *Human Relations, 47,* 133–157.

Green, R., Roberts, C. W., Williams, K., Goodman, M., & Mixon, A. (1987). Specific cross-gender behaviour in boyhood and later homosexual orientation. *British Journal of Psychiatry, 151,* 84–88.

Greenough, W. T. (1986). What's special about development? Thoughts on the bases of experience-sensitive synaptic plasticity. In W. T. Greenough & J. M. Juraska (Eds.), *Developmental neuropsychobiology* (pp. 387–407). Orlando, FL: Academic Press.

Greenough, W. T., & Black, J. E. (1992). Induction of brain structure by experience: Substrates for cognitive development. In M. Gunnar & C. A. Nelson (Eds.), *Minne-*

sota Symposia on Child Psychology: Vol. 24. Behavioral developmental neuroscience (pp. 35–52). Hillsdale, NJ: Lawrence Erlbaum Associates.

Greenough, W. T., Black, J. E., & Wallace, C. S. (1987). Experience and brain development. *Child Development, 58,* 539–559.

Greenwald, A. G., Banaji, M. R., Rudman, L. A., Franham, S. D., Nosek, B. A., & Rosier, M. (in press). Prologue to a unified theory of attitudes, stereotypes, and self concept. In J. P. Forgas (Ed.), *Feeling and thinking: The role of affect in social cognition and behavior.* New York: Cambridge University Press. http://weber.u.washington.edu/~agg/Prologue/prologue.060398.html

Grimshaw, G. M., Sitarenios, G., & Finegan, J. K. (1995). Mental rotation at 7 years: Relations with prenatal testosterone levels and spatial play experiences. *Brain and Cognition, 29,* 85–100.

Grisham, W., Kerchner, M., & Ward, I. L. (1991). Prenatal stress alters sexually dimorphic nuclei in the spinal cord of male rats. *Brain Research, 551,* 126–131.

Guilford, J. P. (1967). *The nature of human intelligence.* New York: McGraw-Hill.

Gunter, N. C., & Gunter, B. G. (1990). Domestic division of labor among working couples. *Psychology of Women Quarterly, 14,* 335–370.

Gur, R. C., Gur, R. E., Orbrist, W. D., Hungerbuhler, J. P., Younkin, D., Rosen, A. D., Skolnick, B. E., & Reivich, M. (1982, August 13). Sex and handedness differences in cerebral blood flow during rest and cognitive activity. *Science, 217,* 659–661.

Gur, R. C., Mozley, L. H., Mozley, P. D., Resnick, S. M., Karp, J. S., Alavi, A., Arnold, S. E., & Gur, R. E. (1995, January 27). Sex differences in regional cerebral glucose metabolism during a resting state. *Science, 267,* 528–531.

Gur, R. C., Mozley, P. D., Resnick, S. M., Gottlieb, G. L., Kohn, M., Zimmerman, R., Herman, G., Atlas, S., Grossman, R., Berretta, D., Erwin, R., & Gur, R. E. (1991). Gender differences in age effect on brain atrophy measured by magnetic resonance imaging. *Proceedings of the National Academy of Sciences, 88,* 2845–2849.

Gur, R. E., & Gur, R. C. (1990). Gender differences in cerebral blood flow. *Schizophrenia Bulletin, 16,* 247–254.

Hagen, R. L. (1997). In praise of the null hypothesis statistical test. *American Psychologist, 52,* 15–24.

Hall, J. A. (1985). *Nonverbal sex differences: Communication accuracy and expressive style.* Baltimore: Johns Hopkins University Press.

Hall, J. A., & Halberstadt, A. G. (1986). Smiling and gazing. In J. S. Hyde & M. C. Linn (Eds.), *The psychology of gender: Advances through meta-analysis* (pp. 136–158). Baltimore: Johns Hopkins University Press.

Hall, J., & Kimura, D. (1995). Performance by homosexual males and females on sexually-dimorphic motor tasks. *Archives of Sexual Behavior, 24,* 395–407.

Halpern, D. F. (1984). Age differences in response time to verbal and symbolic traffic signs. *Experimental Aging Research, 10,* 201–204.

Halpern, D. F. (1985). The influence of sex-role stereotypes on prose recall. *Sex Roles, 12,* 363–375.

Halpern, D. F. (1986a). A different response to the question "Do sex differences in spatial abilities exist?". *American Psychologist, 41,* 1014–1015.

Halpern, D. F. (1986b). *Sex differences in cognitive abilities.* Hillsdale, NJ: Lawrence Erlbaum Associates.

Halpern, D. F. (1988). Sex differences in mathematical reasoning ability: Let me count the ways. *Behavioral and Brain Sciences, 11,* 191–192.

Halpern, D. F. (1989). The disappearance of cognitive gender differences: What you see depends on where you look. *American Psychologist, 102,* 1156–1158.

Halpern, D. F. (1996a). Public policy implications of sex differences in cognitive abilities. *Psychology, Public Policy, and Law, 2,* 561–574.

Halpern, D. F. (1996b). *Thought & knowledge: An introduction to critical thinking* (3rd ed.). Mahwah, NJ: Lawrence Erlbaum Associates.

Halpern, D. F. (1997). Sex differences in intelligence: Implications for education. *American Psychologist, 52,* 1091–1102.

Halpern, D. F. (1998). Recipe for a sexually dimorphic brain: Ingredients include ovarian and testicular hormones. *Behavioral and Brain Sciences, 21,* 330–331.

Halpern, D. F., & Cass, M. (1994). Laterality, sexual orientation, and immune system functioning: Is there a relationship? *International Journal of Neuroscience, 77,* 167–180.

Halpern, D. F., & Coren, S. (1988). Do right-handers live longer? *Nature, 333,* 213.

Halpern, D. F., & Coren, S. (1990). Laterality and longevity: Is left-handedness associated with a younger age at death? In S. Coren (Ed.), *Left-handedness: Behavioral implications and anomalies* (pp. 509–545). New York: Elsevier.

Halpern, D. F., & Coren, S. (1991). Laterality and life span. *New England Journal of Medicine, 324,* 998.

Halpern, D. F., & Crothers, M. (1997). The sex of cognition. In L. Ellis & L. Ebertz (Eds.), *Sex, sexual orientation and cognition* (pp. 181–197). Westport, CT: Praeger.

Halpern, D. F., Haviland, M. G., & Killian, C. D. (1998). Handedness and sex differences in intelligence: Evidence from the Medical College Admission Test. *Brain and Cognition, 38,* 87–101.

Halpern, D. F., & Kagan, S. (1984). Sex, age and cultural differences in individualism. *The Journal of Genetic Psychology, 145 ,* 23–25.

Halpern, D. F., & Kevari, M. (1997, August). *With whom do you work? Clustering by sex and race in free recall.* Paper presented at the 105th Annual Convention of the American Psychological Association, Chicago.

Halpern, D. F., & LaMay, M. L. (1999). Confirmation Bias. In PsychologyPlace [on-line]. Available: http://www/psychplace.com.

Halpern, D. F., & Voiskounsky, A. (Eds.). (1997). *States of mind: American and post-Soviet perspectives on contemporary issues in psychology.* New York: Oxford University Press.

Halpern, D. F., & Wright, T. (1996). A process-oriented model of cognitive sex differences [Special issue]. *Learning and Individual Differences, 8,* 3–24.

Hamburg, D. A., & Lunde, D. T. (1966). Sex hormones in the development of sex differences in human behavior. In E. E. Maccoby (Ed.), *The development of sex differences* (pp. 1–24). Stanford, CA: Stanford University Press.

Hamer, D. (1997). The search for personality genes: Adventures of a molecular biologist. *Current Directions in Psychological Science, 6,* 111–114.

Hamer, D., & Copeland, P. (1998). *Living with our genes: Why they matter more than you think.* Garden City, NY: Doubleday.

Hamilton, M. C. (1988). Using masculine generics: Does generic he increase male bias in the user's imagery? *Sex Roles, 19,* 11–12.

Hampson, E. (1990a). Estrogen-related variations in human spatial and articulatory–motor skills. *Psychoneuroendocrinology, 15,* 97–111.

Hampson, E. (1990b). Variations in sex-related cognitive abilities across the menstrual cycle. *Brain and Cognition, 14,* 26–43.

Hampson, E. (1998). Is the size of the human corpus callosum influenced by sex hormones? *Behavioral and Brain Sciences, 21,* 331–332.

Hampson, E., & Kimura, D. (1988). Reciprocal effects of hormonal fluctuations on human motor and perceptual–spatial skills. *Behavioral Neuroscience, 102,* 456–495.

Hancock, P. A., Arthur, E. J., Chrysler, S. T., & Lee, J. (1994). The effects of sex, target duration, and illumination on the production of time intervals. *Acta Psychologica, 86,* 57–67.

Hancock, P. A., Vercruyssen, M., & Rodenburg, G. J. (1992). The effect of gender and time-of-day on time perception and mental workload. *Current Psychology: Research & Reviews, 11,* 203–225.

Hardyck, C., Goldman, R., & Petrinovich, L. (1975). Handedness and sex, race, and age. *Human Biology, 47,* 369–375.

Hare-Mustin, R. T., & Maracek, J. (1994). Asking the right questions: Feminist psychology and sex differences. *Feminism & Psychology, 4,* 531–537.

Harris, D. R., Bisbee, C. T., & Evans, S. H. (1971). Further comments–misuse of analysis of covariance. *Psychological Bulletin, 75,* 220–222.

Harris, J. R. (1995). Where is the child's environment? A group socialization theory of development. *Psychological Review, 102,* 458–489.

Harris, J. R. (1998a, September). Do Parents Matter? *Newsweek,* cover.

Harris, J. R. (1998b). *The nurture assumption: Why children turn out the way they do.* New York: The Free Press.

Harris, L. J. (1978). Sex differences in spatial ability: Possible environmental, genetic, and neurological factors. In M. Kinsbourne (Ed.), *Asymmetrical functions of the brain* (pp. 405–522). Cambridge, England: Cambridge University Press.

Harshman, R. A., & Hampson, E. (1987). Normal variation in human brain organization: Relation to handedness, sex, and cognitive abilities. In D. Ottoson (Ed.), *Duality and unity of the brain* (pp. 83–99). New York: Plenum.

Harshman, R. A., Hampson, E., & Berenbaum, S. A. (1983). Individual differences in cognitive abilities and brain organization: Part I. Sex and handedness differences in ability. *Canadian Journal of Psychology, 37,* 144–192.

Hays, W. L. (1963). *Statistics for psychologists.* New York: Holt, Rinehart & Winston.

Hays, W. L. (1981). *Statistics.* New York: Holt, Rinehart & Winston.

Hecht, H., & Proffitt, D. R. (1995). The price of expertise: Effects of experience on the water-level task. *Psychological Science, 6,* 90–95.

Hedges, L. V., & Nowell, A. (1995, July). Sex differences in mental test scores, variability, and numbers of high-scoring individuals. *Science, 269,* 41–45.

Hegarty, M., & Sims, V. K. (1994). Individual differences in mental animation during mechanical reasoning. *Memory & Cognition, 22,* 411–430.

Heilman, M. E. (1995). Sex stereotypes and their effects in the workplace: What we know and what we don't know. *Journal of Social Behavior and Personality, 10,* 3–26.

Heister, G., Landis, T., Regard, M., & Schroeder-Heister, P. (1989). Shift of functional cerebral asymmetry during the menstrual cycle. *Neuropsychologia, 27,* 871–880.

Helleday, J., Bartfai, A., Ritzen, E. M., & Forsman, M. (1994). General intelligence and cognitive profile in women with congenital adrenal hyperplasia (CAH). *Psychoneuroendocrinology, 19,* 343–356.

Heller, W., Nitschke, J. B., & Miller, G. A. (1998). Lateralization in emotion and emotional disorders. *Current Directions in Psychological Science, 7,* 26–32.

Hellige, J. B. (1993). *Hemispheric asymmetry: What's right and what's left.* Cambridge, MA: Harvard University Press.

Hendricks, B., Marvel, M. K., & Barrington, B. L. (1990). The dimensions of psychological research. *Teaching of Psychology, 17,* 76–82.

Henning-Stout, M., & Close-Conoley, J. (1992). Gender: A subtle influence in the culture of the school. In F. J. Medway & T. P. Cafferty (Eds.), *School psychology: A social psychological perspective* (pp. 113–135). Hillsdale, NJ: Lawrence Erlbaum Associates.

Herlitz, A., Nilsson, L.-G., & Baeckman, L. (1997). Gender differences in episodic memory. *Memory & Cognition, 25,* 801–811.

Herman, J. F., Heins, J. A., & Cohen, D. S. (1987). Children's spatial knowledge of their neighborhood environment. *Journal of Applied Developmental Psychology, 8,* 1–15.

Herring, S. L., & Reitan, R. M. (1992). Gender influences on neuropsychological performance following unilateral cerebral lesions. *Clinical Neuropsychologist, 6,* 431–442.

Herrnstein, R. J., & Murray, C. (1994). *The bell curve: Intelligence and class structure in American life.* New York: The Free Press.

Hier, D. B., & Crowley, W. F., Jr. (1982). Spatial ability in androgen-deficient men. *New England Journal of Medicine, 306,* 1202–1205.

Hier, D. B., Yoon, W. B., Mohr, J. P., Price, T. R., & Wolf, P. A. (1994). Gender and aphasia in the stroke data bank. *Brain Language, 47,* 155–167.

Hill, J. P., & Lynch, M. E. (1983). The intensification of gender-related role expectations during early adolescence. In J. Brooks-Gunn & A. C. Petersen (Eds.), *Girls at puberty: Biological and psychosocial perspectives* (pp. 201–228). New York: Plenum.

Hill, R. D., Grut, M., Wahlin, A., Herlitz, A., Winblad, B., & Backma, L. (1995). Predicting memory performance in optimally healthy very old adults. *Journal of Mental Health & Aging, 7,* 55–65.

Hilton, T. L., & Berglund, G. W. (1974). Sex differences in mathematics achievement—A longtudinal study. *The Journal of Educational Research, 67,* 231–237.

Hines, M. (1982). Prenatal gonadal hormones and sex differences in human behavior. *Psychological Bulletin, 92,* 56–80.

Hines, M. (1990). Gonadal hormones and human cognitive development. In J. Balthazart (Ed.), *Brain and behaviour in vertebrates 1: Sexual differentiation, neuroanatomical aspects, neurotransmitters and neuropeptides* (pp. 51–63). Basel, Switzerland: Karger.

Hines, M., Chiu, L., McAdams, L. A., Bentler, P. M., & Lipcamon, J. (1992). Cognition and the corpus callosum: Verbal fluency, visuospatial ability, and language lateralization related to midsagittal areas of callosal subregions. *Behavioral Neuroscience, 106,* 3–14.

Hines, M., & Collaer, M. L. (1993). Gonadal hormones and sexual differentiation of human behavior: Developments from research on endocrine syndromes and studies of brain structure. *Annual Review of Sex Research, 4,* 1–48.

Hines, M., & Sandberg, E. C. (1996). Sexual differentiation of cognitive abilities in women exposed to diethylstilbestrol (DES) prenatally. *Hormones and Behavior, 30,* 354–363.

Holding, C. S., & Holding, D. H. (1989). Acquisition of route network knowledge by males and females. *Journal of General Psychology, 116,* 29–41.

Holland, J. H., Holyoak, K. J., Nisbett, R. E., & Thagard, P. R. (1986). *Induction: Processes of inference, learning, and discovery.* Cambridge, MA: MIT Press.

Holloway, R. L. (1998). Relative size of the corpus collosum redux: Statistical smoke and mirrors? *Behavioral and Brain Sciences, 21,* 333–335.

Hollway, W. (1994). Beyond sex differences: A project for feminist psychology. *Feminism & Psychology, 4,* 538–546.

Holtzen, D. W. (1994). Handedness and sexual orientation. *Journal of Clinical and Experimental Neuropsychology, 16,* 702–712.

Hood, K. F., Draper, P., Crockett, L. J., & Petersen, A. C. (1987). The ontogeny and phylogeny of sex differences in development: A biopsychosocial synthesis. In D. B. Carter (Ed.), *Current conceptions of sex roles and sex typing: Theory and research* (pp. 49–77). New York: Praeger.

Horgan, D. M. (1975). *Language development*. Ann Arbor: University of Michigan.

Horner, M. S. (1969). Fail: Bright women. *Psychology Today, 3*, 36–38, 62.

Horvath, T. L., & Wikler, K. C. (1999). Aromatase in developing sensory systems of the rat brain. *Journal of Neuroendocrinology, 11*, 77–84.

Howell, D. C. (1992). *Statistical methods for psychology* (3rd ed.). Boston: PWS-Kent.

Hoyenga, K. B., & Hoyenga, K. T. (1979). *The question of sex differences: Psychological, cultural, and biological issues*. Boston: Little, Brown.

Huang, J. (1993). An investigation of gender differences in cognitive abilities among high school students. *Personality and Individual Differences, 15*, 717–719.

Hugdahl, K. (1995). Dichotic listening: Probing temporal lobe functional integrity. In R. J. Davidson & K. Hugdahl (Eds.), *Brain asymmetry* (pp. 123–156). Cambridge, MA: MIT Press.

Hughes, J. (1999, April 30). Increase projected in female merit scholars. *The Chronicle of Higher Education*, p. A2.

Human Capital Initiative Coordinating Committee. (1998). Social cognition and stereotyping [Special issue]. *Observer, 15*.

Humphreys, L. F., Lubinski, D., & Yao, G. (1993). Utility of predicting group membership and the role of spatial visualization in becoming an engineer, physical scientist, or artist. *Journal of Applied Psychology, 78*, 250–261.

Humphreys, L. G. (1978). Research on individual differences requires correlational analysis, not ANOVA. *Intelligence, 2*, 1–5.

Hunt, E. (1985). Verbal ability. In R. J. Sternberg (Ed.), *Human abilities: An information processing approach* (pp. 31–58). San Francisco: Freeman.

Hunt, E., Pellegrino, J. W., Frick, R. W., Farr, S. A., & Alderton, D. (1988). The ability to reason about movement in the visual field. *Intelligence, 12*, 77–100.

Hunt, M. (1999). *The new know-nothings*. New Brunswick, NJ: Transaction.

Hunter, J. E., & Schmidt, F. L. (1996). Intelligence and job performance: Economic and social implications. *Psychology, Public Policy, and Law, 2*, 447–472.

Huttenlocher, J., Haight, W., Bryk, A., Seltzer, M., & Lyons, T. (1991). Early vocabulary growth: Relation to language input and gender. *Developmental Psychology, 27*, 236–248.

Hyde, J. S. (1981). How large are cognitive gender differences? *American Psychologist, 36*, 892–901.

Hyde, J. S. (1985). *Half the human experience: The psychology of women*. Lexington, MA: Heath.

Hyde, J. S. (1986). Gender differences in aggression. In J. S. Hyde & M. C. Linn (Eds.), *The psychology of gender: Advances through meta-analysis* (pp. 51–66). Baltimore: Johns Hopkins University Press.

Hyde, J. S., Fennema, E., & Lamon, S. J. (1990). Gender differences in mathematics performance: A meta-analysis. *Psychological Bulletin, 107*, 139–153.

Hyde, J. S., Fennema, E., Ryan, M., Frost, L. A., & Hopp, C. (1990). Gender comparisons of mathematics attitudes and affect: A meta-analysis. *Psychology of Women Quarterly, 3*, 299–324.

Hyde, J. S., & Linn, M. C. (Eds.). (1986). *The psychology of gender: Advances through meta-analysis*. Baltimore: Johns Hopkins University Press.

Hyde, J. S., & Linn, M. C. (1988). Gender differences in verbal ability: A meta-analysis. *Psychological Bulletin, 104,* 53–69.

Hynd, G. W., & Semrud-Clikeman, M. (1990). Dyslexia and brain morphology. *Psychological Bulletin, 106,* 447–482.

Innocenti, G. M. (1994). Some new trends in the study of the corpus callosum. *Behavioral Brain Research, 64,* 1–8.

Intons-Peterson, M. G. (1988). *Gender concepts of Swedish and American youth.* Hillsdale, NJ: Lawrence Erlbaum Associates.

Ippolitov, F. W. (1973). Interanalyser differences in the sensitivity-strength parameter for vision, hearing, and cutaneous modalities. In V. D. Nebylitsym & J. A. Gray (Eds.), *Biological bases of individual behavior* (pp. 43–61). New York: Academic.

Jacklin, C. N. (1989). Female and male: Issues of gender. *American Psychologist, 44,* 127–133.

Jacklin, C. N., & Baker, L. A. (1993). Early gender development. In S. Oskamp, & M. Costanzo (Eds.), *Claremont symposium on applied social psychology: Vol. 6. Gender issues in contemporary society* (pp. 41–57). Newbury Park, CA: Sage.

Jacklin, C. N., Wilcox, K. T., & Maccoby, E. E. (1988). Neonatal sex-steroid hormones and intellectual abilities of six year old boys and girls. *Developmental Psychobiology, 21,* 567–574.

Jacobs, C. (1998, December 28). In Sudan, a 12-year-old girl can be bought for $50. *Los Angeles Times,* p. B5.

Jacobs, D. M., Tang, M. X., Stern, Y., Sano, M., Marder, K., Bell, K. L., Schofield, P., Dooneief, G., Gurland, B., & Mayeux, R. (1998). Cognitive function in nondemented older women who took estrogen after menopause. *Neurology, 50,* 368–373.

Jacobs, J. A. Ed. (1995). *Gender inequality at work.* Thousand Oaks, CA: Sage.

Jacobs, L. F., Gaulin, S. J. C., Sherry, D. F., & Hoffman, G. E. (1990). Evolution and spatial cognition: Sex-specific patterns of spatial behavior predict hippocampal size. *Proceedings of the National Academy of Sciences, USA, 87,* 6349–6352.

Jaeger, J. J., Lockwood, A. H., Van Valin, R. D., Jr., Kemmerer, D. L., Murphy, B. W., & Wack, D. S. (1998, August 24). *Neuroreport, 9,* 2803–2807.

James, T. W., & Kimura, D. (1997). Sex differences in remembering the location of objects in an array: Location-shifts versus location-exchanges. *Evolution and Human Behavior, 18,* 155–163.

James, W. H. (1989). Fetal testosterone levels, homosexuality, and handedness: A research proposal for jointly testing Geschwind's and Dorner's hypotheses. *Journal of Theoretical Biology, 136,* 177–180.

James, W. H. (1992). The sex ratios of dyslexic children and their sibs. *Developmental Medicine and Child Neurology, 34,* 530–533.

Jancke, L., & Steinmetz, H. (1994). Interhemispheric transfer time and corpus callosum size. *Neuroreport, 5,* 2385–2388.

Janowsky, J. S. (1989). Sexual dimorphism in the human brain: Dispelling the myths. *Developmental Medicine and Child Neurology, 31,* 257–263.

Janowsky, J. S., Oviatt, S. K., & Orwoll, E. S. (1994). Testosterone influences spatial cognition in older men. *Behavioral Neuroscience, 108,* 325–332.

Jensen, A. R. (1969). How much can we boost IQ and scholastic achievement? *Harvard Educational Review, 39,* 1–123.

Jensen, A. R. (1980). Chronometric analysis of intelligence. *Journal of Social and Biological Structures, 3,* 103–122.

Jensen, A. R. (1998). *The g factor: The science of mental ability.* New York: Praeger.

Johnson, E. S., & Meade, A. C. (1987). Developmental patterns of spatial ability: An early sex difference. *Child Development, 58,* 725–740.

Jones, L. V. (1984). White–Black achievement differences: The narrowing gap. *American Psychologist, 39,* 1207–1213.

Jonides, J., & Rozin, P. (1999). *Study guide: Gleitman, Fridlund, Reisberg psychology* (5th ed.). New York: Norton.

Jovanovic, J., & Lerner, R. (1994). Individual contextual relationships and mathematical performance: Comparing American and Serbian young adolescents. *Journal of Early Adolescence, 26,* 37–48.

Juraska, J. M. (1991). Sex differences in "cognitive" regions of the rat brain. *Psychoneuroendocrinology, 16,* 105–119.

Jussim, L. J., & Eccles, J. (1995). Are teacher expectations biased by students' gender, social class, or ethnicity? In Y.-T. Lee, L. J. Jussim, & C. R. McCauley (Eds.), *Stereotype accuracy: Toward appreciating group differences* (pp. 245–271). Washington, DC: American Psychological Association.

Jussim, L. J., McCauley, C. R., & Lee, Y. T. (1995). Why study stereotype accuracy and inaccuracy? In Y.-T. Lee, L. J. Jussim, & C. R. McCauley (Eds.), *Stereotype accuracy: Toward appreciating group differences* (pp. 3–27). Washington, DC: American Psychological Association.

Kalat, J. W. (1998). *Biological psychology* (6th ed.). Monterey, CA: Brooks/Cole.

Kalichman, S. C. (1989). The effects of stimulus context on paper-and-pencil spatial task performance. *Journal of General Psychology, 116,* 133–139.

Kampen, D. L., & Sherwin, B. B. (1996). Estradiol is related to visual memory in healthy young men. *Behavioral Neuroscience, 110,* 613–617.

Katcher, A. (1955). The discrimination of sex differences by young children. *Journal of Genetic Psychology, 87,* 131–143.

Kaufman, A. S., Kaufman-Packer, J. L., McLean, J. E., & Reynolds, C. R. (1991). Is the pattern of intellectual growth and decline across the adult life span different for men and women? *Journal of Clinical Psychology, 47,* 801–812.

Kaye, J. A., DeCarli, C., Luxenberg, J. S., & Rappoport, S. I. (1992). The significance of age-related enlargement of the cerebral ventricles in healthy men and women measured by quantitative computed X-ray tomography. *Journal of the American Geriatric Society, 40,* 225–231.

Keane, M. M., Gabrieli, J. D. E., Mapstone, H. C., Johnson, K. A., & Corkin, S. (1995). Double dissociation of memory capacities after bilateral occipital-lobe or medial temporal-lobe lesions. *Brain, 118,* 1129–1148.

Kee, D. W., & Cherry, B. (1990). Lateralized interference in finger tapping: Initial value differences do not affect the outcome. *Neuropsychologia, 28,* 313–316.

Keenan, K., & Shaw, D. (1997). Development and social influences on young girls' early problem behavior. *Psychological Bulletin, 121,* 95–113.

Keeton, W. T. (1967). *Biological science.* New York: Norton.

Kendrick, D. T., Neuberg, S. L., Cialdini, R. B. (1999). *Social psychology: Unraveling the mystery.* Boston: Allyn & Bacon.

Kenrick, D. T. (1988). Biology: Si, hard-wired ability: Maybe no. *Behavioral and Brain Sciences, 11,* 199–200.

Kerchner, M., & Ward, I. L. (1992). SDN-MPOA volume in male rats is decreased by prenatal stress, but is not related to ejaculatory behavior. *Brain Research, 581,* 244–251.

Kimball, M. M. (1989). A new perspective on women's math achievement. *Psychological Bulletin, 105,* 198–214.

Kimmel, D. C., & Weiner, I. B. (1985). *Adolescence: A developmental transition.* Hillsdale, NJ: Lawrence Erlbaum Associates.

Kimura, D. (1985, November). Male brain, female brain: The hidden difference. *Psychology Today, 19,* 50–52, 54, 55–58.

Kimura, D. (1987). Are men's and women's brains really different? *Canadian Psychology, 28,* 133–147.

Kimura, D. (1989, November). How sex hormones boost—or cut—intellectual ability. *Psychology Today, 23,* 62–66.

Kimura, D. (1993). *Neuromotor mechanisms in human communication.* New York: Oxford University Press.

Kimura, D. (1996). Sex, sexual orientation and sex hormones influence human cognitive function. *Current Opinion in Neurobiology, 6,* 259–263.

Kimura, D. (1999). *Sex and cognition.* Cambridge, MA: MIT Press.

Kimura, D., & Hampson, E. (1994). Cognitive pattern in men and women is influenced by fluctuations in sex hormones. *Current Directions in Psychological Science, 3,* 57–61.

Kite, M. E., Deaux, K., & Miele, M. (1991). Stereotypes of young and old: Does age outweigh gender? *Psychology and Aging, 6,* 19–27.

Kitterle, F. L., & Kaye, R. S. (1985). Hemispheric symmetry in contrast and oventation sensitivity. *Perception & Psychophysics, 37,* 391–396.

Kitzinger, C. (1994). Sex differences: Feminist perspectives. *Feminism & Psychology, 4,* 501–506.

Kleinfeld, J. (1998). *The myth that schools shortchange girls: Social science in the service of deception.* Washington, DC: The Women's Freedom Network.

Koblinksy, S. G., Cruse, D. F., & Sugawawa, A. I. (1978). Sex role stereotypes and children's memory for story content. *Child Development, 49,* 452–458.

Koelega, H. S., & Koster, E. P. (1974). Some experiments on sex differences in odor perception. *Annals of the New York Academy of Sciences, 237,* 234–246.

Kogan, N. (1973). Creativity and cognitive style: A life-span perspective. In P. G. Baltes, & K. W. Schaie (Eds.), *Life-span developmental psychology: Personality and socialization.* New York: Academic Press.

Kohlberg, L. (1966). A cognitive-developmental analysis of children's sex-role concepts and attitudes. In E. E. Maccoby (Ed.), *The development of sex differences* (pp. 82–172). Stanford, CA: Stanford University Press.

Konner, M. (1988). She and he. In A. L. Hammond & P. G. Zimbardo (Eds.), *Readings on human behavior* (pp. 33–40). Glenview, IL: Scott, Foresman.

Kramer, J. H., Delis, D. C., Kaplan, E., O'Donnell, L., & Prifitera, A. (1997). Developmental sex differences in verbal learning. *Neuropsychology, 11,* 577–584.

Krull, D. S., & Anderson, C. A. (1997). The process of explanation. *Current Directions in Psychological Science, 6,* 1–5.

Lach, J. (1997, Spring/Summer). Cultivating the mind. *Newsweek Special Edition Your Child,* 38–39.

LaHoste, G. J., Mormede, P., Rivet, J. M., & LeMoal, M. (1988). New evidence for distinct patterns of brain organization in rats differentiated on the basis of inherent laterality. *Brain Research, 474,* 296–308.

Larrabee, G. J., & Crook, T. H., III. (1993). Do men show more rapid age-associated decline in simulated everyday verbal memory than do women? *Psychology and Aging, 8,* 68–71.

Law, D., Pellegrino, J. W., & Hunt, E. B. (1993). Comparing the tortoise and the hare: Gender differences and experience in dynamic spatial reasoning tasks. *Psychological Science, 4,* 35–41.

Lawton, C. A. (1996). Strategies for indoor wayfinding: The role of orientation. *Journal of Environmental Psychology, 16,* 137–145.

Lee, Y.-T., Jussim, L. J., & McCauley, C. R. (1995). Preface. In Y.-T. Lee, L. J. Jussim, & C. R. McCauley (Eds.), *Stereotype accuracy: Toward appreciating group differences* (pp. xii–xiv). Washington, DC: American Psychological Association.

Lehrke, R. G. (1974). *X-linked mental retardation and verbal disability.* New York: Intercontinental Medical Book Company.

Lehrner, J. P. (1993). Gender differences in long-term odor recognition memory: Verbal versus sensory influences and the consistency of label use. *Chemical Sciences, 18,* 17–26.

Leibenluft, E. (1996). Women with bipolar illness: Clinical and research issues. *American Journal of Psychiatry, 153,* 163–173.

Levant, R. F. (1996). The new psychology of men. *Professional Psychology: Research and Practice, 27,* 259–265.

Levant, R. F., & Pollack, W. S. (1995). *A new psychology of men.* New York: Basic Books.

LeVay, S. (1991). A difference in hypothalamic structure between heterosexual and homosexual men. *Science, 253,* 1034–1037.

LeVay, S. (1993). *The sexual brain.* Cambridge, MA: MIT Press.

LeVay, S. (1996). *Queer science: The use and abuse of research into homosexuality.* Cambridge, MA: MIT Press.

Levy, G. D. (1989). Developmental and individual differences in preschoolers' recognition memories: The influences of gender schematization and verbal labeling of information. *Sex Roles, 21,* 305–324.

Levy, G. D., & Fivush, R. (1993). Scripts and gender: A new approach for examining gender-role development. *Developmental Review, 13,* 126–146.

Levy, J. (1974). Psychobiological implications of bilateral asymmetry. In S. Dimond & J. G. Beaumont (Eds.), *Hemispheric function in the human brain* (pp. 121–183). London: Elek.

Levy, J. (1976). Cerebral lateralization and spatial ability. *Behavior Genetics, 6,* 171–188.

Levy, J., & Heller, W. (1992). Gender differences in human neuropsychological function. In A. A. Gerall & H. Moltz (Eds.), *Sexual differentiation: Handbook of behavioral neurobiology* (pp. 245–274). New York: Plenum.

Levy, J., & Nagylaki, T. (1972). A model for the genetics of handedness. *Genetics, 72,* 117–128.

Levy, J., & Reid, M. (1978). Variations in cerebral organization as a function of handedness, handposture in writing, and sex. *Journal of Experimental Psychology: General, 107,* 119–144.

Levy-Agresti, J., & Sperry, R. W. (1968). Differential perceptual capacities in major and minor hemispheres. *Proceedings of the National Academy of Science U.S.A., 61,* 1151.

Lewin, M., & Tragos, L. M. (1987). Has the feminist movement influenced adolescent sex role attitudes? A reassessment after a quarter century. *Sex Roles, 16,* 125–135.

Lewis, R. S., & Harris, L. J. (1990). Handedness, sex, and spatial ability. In S. Coren (Ed.), *Left-handedness: Behavioral implications and anomalies* (pp. 319–342). New York: Elsevier.

Liben, L. S. (1995). Psychology meets geography: Exploring the gender gap on the national geography bee. *Psychological Science Agenda, 8,* 8–9.

Liben, L. S., & Bigler, R. S. (1987). Reformulating children's gender schemata. *New Directions for Child Development, 38,* 89–105.

Liben, L. S., & Signorella, M. L. (1980). Gender-related schemata and constructive memory in children. *Child Development, 51,* 11–18.

Lightbody, P., Siann, G., Stocks, R., & Walsh, D. (1996). Motivation and attribution at secondary school: The role of gender. *Educational Studies, 22,* 13–25.

Lim, T. K. (1994). Gender-related differences in intelligence: Application of confirmatory factor analysis. *Intelligence, 19,* 179–192.

Lindesay, J. (1987). Laterality shift and homosexual men. *Neuropsychologia, 25,* 965–969.

Linn, M. C. (1985). Gender equity in computer learning environments. *Computers and the Social Sciences, 1,* 19–27.

Linn, M. C., DeBenedictis, T., Delucchi, K., Harris, A., & Stage E. (1987). Gender differences in National Assessment of Educational Progress science items: What does "I don't know" really mean? *Journal of Research and Science Teaching, 24,* 267–278.

Linn, M. C., & Petersen, A. C. (1985). Emergence and characterization of sex differences in spatial ability: A meta-analysis. *Child Development, 56,* 1479–1498.

Linn, M. C., & Petersen, A. C. (1986). A meta-analysis of gender differences in spatial ability: Implications for mathematics and science achievement. In J. S. Hyde & M. C. Linn (Eds.), *The psychology of gender: Advances through meta-analysis* (pp. 67–101). Baltimore: Johns Hopkins University Press.

Lippa, R. (1998). Gender-related individual differences and the structure of vocational interests: The importance of the people–things dimension. *Journal of Personality and Social Psychology, 74,* 996–1009.

Lobel, T. E., & Menashri, J. (1993). Relations of conceptions of gender-role transgressions and gender constancy to gender-typed toy preferences. *Developmental Psychology, 29,* 150–155.

Loehlin, J. C., Sharan, S., & Jacoby, R. (1978). In pursuit of the "spatial gene": A family study. *Behavior Genetics, 8,* 27–41.

Logie, R. H. (1995). *Visuo-spatial working memory.* Hillsdale, NJ: Lawrence Erlbaum Associates.

Lohman, D. F. (1986). The effect of speed–accuracy tradeoff on sex differences in mental rotation. *Perception & Psychophysics, 39,* 427–436.

Lohman, D. F. (1988). Spatial abilities as traits, processes, and knowledge. In R. J. Sternberg (Ed.), *Advances in the psychology of human intelligence* (Vol. 4, pp. 181–248). Hillsdale, NJ: Lawrence Erlbaum Associates.

Lopata, H. Z., & Thorne, B. (1978). On the term "sex roles." *Signs, 3,* 718–721.

Loring-Meier, S., & Halpern, D. F. (1999). Sex differences in visual–spatial working memory: Components of cognitive processing. *Psychonomic Bulletin and Review, 6,* 464–471.

Los Angeles Times. (1990, September 5). For many, picking a child's gender is a fertile field. pp. E1–E2.

Lott, B. (1985). The potential enrichment of social/personality psychology through feminist research and vice versa. *American Psychologist, 40,* 155–164.

Lott, B. (1996). Politics or science? The question of gender sameness/difference. *American Psychologist, 51,* 155–156.

Lubinski, D., Schmidt, D. B., & Benbow, C. P. (1996). A 20-year stability analysis of the study of values for intellectually gifted individuals from adolescence to adulthood. *Journal of Applied Psychology, 81,* 443–451.

Luchins, E. H. (1979). Women and mathematics: Fact and fiction. *American Mathematical Monthly, 88,* 413–419.

Luecke-Aleska, D., Anderson, D. R., Collins, P. A., & Schmitt, K. L. (1995). Gender constancy and television viewing. *Developmental Psychology, 31,* 773-780.

Luine V. N., Richards, S. T., Wu, V. Y., & Beck, K. D. (1998). Estradiol enhances learning and memory in a spatial memory task and effects levels of monoaminergic neurotransmitters. *Hormones and Behavior, 34,* 149–162.

Luszcz, M. A., Bryan, J., & Kent, P. (1997). Predicting episodic memory performance of very old men and women: Contributions from age, depression, activity, cognitive ability, and speed. *Psychology of Aging, 12,* 340–351.

Lynn, D. (1974). *The father: His role in child development.* Monterey, CA: Brooks/Cole.

Lynn, R. (1987). The intelligence of the Mongoloids: A psychometric, evolutionary, and neurological theory. *Personality and Individual Differences, 8,* 813–844.

Lynn, R. (1994). Sex differences in intelligence and brain size: A paradox resolved. *Personality and Individual Differences, 17,* 257–271.

Lynn, R. (1996). Differences between males and females in mean IQ and university examination performance in Ireland. *Personality and Individual Differences, 20,* 649–652.

Lytton, H., & Romney, D. M. (1991). Parents' differential socialization of boys and girls: A meta-analysis. *Psychological Bulletin, 109,* 267–296.

Maccoby, E. E. (1966). Sex differences in intellectual functioning. In E. E. Maccoby (Ed.), *The development of sex differences* (pp. 25–55). Stanford, CA: Stanford University Press.

Maccoby, E. E. (1990). Maccoby: Children are "ruthless stereotypers." *APS Observer, 3,* 5–7.

Maccoby, E. E. (1995). The two sexes and their social systems. In P. Moen, G. H. Elder, Jr., & K. Luscher (Eds.), *Examining lives in time: Perspectives on the ecology of human development* (pp. 347–364). Washington, DC: American Psychological Association.

Maccoby, E. E., & Jacklin, C. N. (1974). *The psychology of sex differences.* Stanford, CA: Stanford University Press.

MacKay, D. G. (1983). Prescriptive grammar and the pronoun problem. In B. Thorne, C. Kramarae, & N. Henley (Eds.), *Language, gender, and society* (pp. 38–53). Rowley, MA: Newbury House.

MacLusky, N. J., & Naftolin, F. (1981). Sexual differentiation of the central nervous system. *Science, 211,* 1294–1303.

Mann, V. A., Sasanuma, S., Sakuma, N., & Masaki, S. (1990). Sex differences in cognitive abilities: A cross-cultural perspective. *Neuropsychologia, 28,* 1063–1077.

Marshall, S. P., & Smith J.D. (1987). Sex differences in learning mathematics: A longitudinal study with item and error analyses. *Journal of Educational Psychology, 79,* 372–383.

Martell, R. F., Lane, D. M., & Emrich, C. (1996). Male–female differences: A computer simulation. *American Psychologist, 51,* 157–158.

Martin, D. J., & Hoover, H. D. (1987). Sex differences in educational achievement: A longitudinal study. *Journal of Early Adolescence, 7,* 65–83.

Martin, G. N. (1998). *Human Neuropsychology.* London: Prentice-Hall Europe.

Mascie-Taylor, C. G. N. (1993). How do social, biological, and genetic factors contribute to individual differences in cognitive abilities? In T. J. Bouchard, Jr. & P. Propping (Eds.), *Twins as a tool of behavioral genetics: Life sciences research report* (pp. 53–65). New York: Wiley.

Masters, M. S. (1998). The gender difference on the mental rotations test is not due to performance factors. *Memory & Cognition, 26,* 444–448.

Masters, M. S., & Sanders, B. (1993). Is the gender difference in mental rotation disappearing? *Behavior Genetics, 23,* 337–341.

Matlin, M. W. (1996). *The psychology of women.* Ft. Worth, TX: Harcourt Brace College Publishers.

Mazur, A., & Robertson, L. S. (1972). *Biology and social behavior.* New York: The Free Press.

McCauley, E., Kay, T., Ito, J., & Treder, B. (1987). The Turner syndrome: Cognitive deficits, affective discrimination, and behavior problems. *Child Development, 58,* 464–473.

McClearn, G. E., Johansson, B., Berg, S., Pederson, N. L., Ahern, F., Petrill, S. A., & Plomin, R. (1997, June). Substantial genetic influence on cognitive abilities in twins 80 or more years old. *Science, 276,* 1560–1563.

McClintock, M. K., & Herdt, G. (1996). Rethinking puberty: The development of sexual attraction. *Current Directions in Psychological Science, 5,* 178–183.

McCloy, T. M., & Koonce, J. M. (1982). Sex as a moderator variable in the selection and training of persons for a skilled task. *Aviation, Space, and Environmental Medicine, 53,* 1170–1172.

McClurg, P. A., & Chaillé, C. (1987). Computer games: Environments for developing spatial cognition? *Journal of Educational Computing Research, 3,* 95–111.

McCormick, C. M., & Witelson, S. F. (1991). A cognitive profile of homosexual men compared to heterosexual men and women. *Psychoneuroendocrinology, 16,* 459–473.

McCormick, C. M., Witelson, S. F., & Kingstone, E. (1990). Left-handedness in homosexual men and women: Neuroendocrine implications. *Psychoneuroendocrinology, 15,* 69–76.

McDonald, K. A. (1999, May 21). Citing the rising influence and power of women, 2 anthropologists ponder the future of men. *The Chronicle of Higher Education,* pp. A17–A18.

McEwen, B. S. (1981). Neural gonadal steroid actions. *Science, 211,* 1303–1311.

McEwen, B. S., Alves, S. E., Bulloch, K., & Weiland, N. G. (1997). Ovarian steriods and the brain: Implications for cognition and aging. *American Academy of Neurology, 48,* S8–S15.

McGee, M. G. (1979). Human spatial abilities: Psychometric studies and environmental, genetic, hormonal, and neurological influences. *Psychological Bulletin, 86,* 889–918.

McGivern, R. F., Huston, J. P., Byrd, D., King, T., Siegle, G. J., & Reilly, J. (1997). Sex differences in visual recognition memory: Support for a sex-related difference in attention in adults and children. *Brain & Cognition, 34,* 323–336.

McGlone, J. (1980). Sex differences in human brain asymmetry: A critical survey. *Behavioral and Brain Sciences, 3,* 215–227.

McGoodwin, W. (1998, July 3). Executive Director, Council for Responsible Genetics. *The Chronicle of Higher Education,* p. B8.

McGuiness, D. (1976). Sex differences in the organization of perception and cognition. In B. Lloyd & J. Archer (Eds.), *Exploring sex differences* (pp. 123–156). New York: Academic Press.

McHugh, M. C., Koeske, R. D., & Frieze, I. H. (1986). Issues to consider in conducting nonsexist research: A guide for researchers. *American Psychologist, 41,* 879–890.

Mead, M. (1961). *Coming of age in Samoa: A psychological study of primitive youth for Western civilization.* New York: Morrow.

Mebert, C. J., & Michel, G. F. (1980). Handedness in artists. In J. Herron (Ed.), *Neuropsychology of left handedness* (pp. 273–278). New York: Academic Press.

Mecklinger, A., & Müller, N. (1996). Dissociations in the processing of "what" and "where" information in working memory: An event-related potential analysis. *Journal of Cognitive Neuroscience, 8,* 453–473.

Meece, J. L., Eccles-Parsons, J., Kaczala, C. M., Goff, S. B., & Futterman, R. (1982). Sex differences in math achievement: Toward a model of academic choice. *Psychological Bulletin, 91,* 324–348.

Meehan, A. M. (1984). A meta-analysis of sex differences in formal operational thought. *Child Development, 55,* 1110–1124.

Meeker, B. F., & Weitzel-O'Neill, P. A. (1977). Sex roles and interpersonal behavior in task-oriented groups. *American Sociological Review, 42,* 91–104.

Meinz, E. J., & Salthouse, T. A. (1998). Is age kinder to females than to males? *Psychonomic Bulletin & Review, 5,* 56–70.

Merritt, R. D., & Kok, C. J. (1995). Attribution of gender to a gender-unspecified individual: An evaluation of the people = male hypothesis. *Sex Roles, 33,* 145–155.

Messick, S. (1995). Validity of psychological assessment: Validation of inferences from persons' responses and performance as scientific inquiry into score meaning. *American Psychologist, 50,* 741–749.

Meyer-Bahlburg, H. F. L., & Ehrhardt, A. A. (1977). Effects of prenatal hormone treatment on mental abilities. In R. Gemme & C. C. Wheeler (Eds.), *Progress in sexology* (pp. 85–92). New York: Plemun.

Miles, C., Green, R., Sanders, G., & Hines, M. (1998). Estrogen and memory in a transsexual population. *Hormones and Behavior, 34,* 199–208.

Mills, C. J. (1981). Sex roles, personality, and intellectual abilities in adolescents. *Journal of Youth and Adolescence, 10,* 85–112.

Moen, P. (1995). Introduction. In P. Moen, G. H. Elder, Jr., & K. Luscher (Eds.), *Examining lives in time: Perspectives on the ecology of human development* (pp. 1–13). Washington, DC: American Psychological Association.

Moffat, S. D., & Hampson, E. (1996). A curvilinear relationship between testosterone and spatial cognition in humans: Possible influence of hand preference. *Psychoneuroendocrinology, 21,* 323–337.

Molfese, D. L. (1990). Auditory evoked responses recorded from 16–month-old human infants to words they did and did not know. *Brain and Language, 38,* 345–363.

Money, J. (1986). *Lovemaps: Clinical concepts of sexual/erotic health and pathology, paraphilia, and gender transposition in childhood, adolescence, and maturity.* New York: Irvington.

Money, J. (1987). Propaedutics of ducious G-I/R: Theoretical foundations for understanding dimorphic gender-identity/role. In J. M. Reinisch, L. A. Rosenblum, & S. A. Sanders (Eds.), *Masculinity/femininity: Basic perspectives* (pp. 13–34). New York: Oxford University Press.

Money, J., & Ehrhardt, A. A. (1972). *Man & woman, boy & girl.* Baltimore: Johns Hopkins University Press.

Mong, J. A., Kurzweil, R. L., Davis, A. M., Rocca, M. S., & McCarthy, M. M. (1996). Evidence for sexual differentiation of glia in rat brain. *Hormones and Behavior, 30,* 553–562.

Moore, T. (1967). Language and intelligence: A longitudinal study of the first eight years. *Human Development, 10,* 88–106.

Morisset, C. E., Barnard, K. E., & Booth, C. L. (1995). Toddlers' language development: Sex differences within social risk. *Developmental Psychology, 31,* 851–865.

Morrell, C. H., Gordon-Salant, S., Pearson, J. D., Brant, L. J., & Fozard, J. L. (1996). Age- and gender-specific reference ranges for hearing level and longitudinal changes in hearing level. *Journal of the Acoustical Society of America, 100,* 1949–1967.

Morrison, P. (1995, June 18). Girl trouble. *Los Angeles Times Magazine,* p. 5.

Mullen, M. K. (1994). Earliest recollections of childhood: A demographic analysis. *Cognition, 52,* 55–79.

Mullis, I. V. S., & OTHERS. (1993). *NAEP 1992—Reading report card for the nation and the states: Data from the national and trial state assessments.* Princeton, NJ: National Assessment of Educational Progress.

Murdock, K. R., & Forsyth, D. R. (1985). Is gender-biased language sexist? A perceptual approach. *Psychology of Women Quarterly, 9,* 39–49.

Murphy, D. G. M., Allen, G., Haxby, J. V., Largay, K. A., Daly, E., White, B. J., Powell, C. M., & Schapiro, M. B. (1994). The effects of sex steroids, and the X chromosome, on female brain function: A study of the neuropsychology of adult Turner syndrome. *Neuropsychology, 32,* 1309–1323.

Murphy, K. R. (1990). If the null hypothesis is impossible, why test it? *American Psychologist, 45,* 403–404.

Myers, D. G. (1998). *Psychology* (5th ed.). New York: Worth.

Nash, M. (1997, February 3). Fertile minds. *Time, 149*(5), 48–56.

Nayak, R., & Dash, A. S. (1987). Effects of grade, sex, nutritional status and time of testing on children's Stroop scores. *Psycho-Lingua, 17,* 87–93.

Neisser, U., Boodoo, G., Bouchard, T. J., Jr., Boykin, A. W., Brody, N., Ceci, S. J., Halpern, D. F., Loehlin, J. C., Perloff, R., Sternberg, R. J., & Urbina, S. (1996). Intelligence: Knowns and unknowns. *American Psychologist, 51,* 77–101.

Nelson, C. A. (1999). Neural plasticity and human development. *Current Directions in Psychological Science, 8,* 42–45.

New Woman. (1990, January). Stereotypes 'R' Us. P. 20

Newcombe, N. S., & Baenninger, M. (1989). Biological change and cognitive ability in adolescence. In G. R. Adams, R. Montemayor, & T. P. Gullota (Eds.), *Biology of adolescent behavior and development* (pp. 168–191). Newbury Park, CA: Sage.

Newcombe, N., Bandura, M., & Taylor, D. G. (1983). Sex differences in spatial ability and spatial activities. *Sex Roles, 9,* 377–386.

Newcombe, N., & Dubas, J. S. (1987). Individual differences in cognitive ability: Are they related to timing of puberty? In R. M. Lerner & T. T. Foch (Eds.), *Biological–psychosocial interactions in early adolescence: A lifespan perspective* (pp. 249–302). Hillsdale, NJ: Lawrence Erlbaum Associates.

Newsweek. (1990, July). *The Average American Woman Spends 17 Years Raising Childrren and 18 Years Helping Aging Parents,* p. cover.

Nicholson, K., & Kimura, D. (1996). Sex differences for speech and manual skill. *Perceptual and Motor Skills, 82,* 3–13.

Nickerson, R. S. (1998). Confirmation bias: A ubiquitous phenomenon in many guises. *Review of General Psychology, 2,* 175–220.

Nikolova, P., Stoyanova, Z., & Negrev, N. (1994). Functional brain asymmetry, handedness and menarcheal age. *International Journal of Psychophysiology, 18,* 213–215.

Nisbett, R. E., & Gurwitz, S. B. (1970). Weight, sex, and the eating behavior of human newborns. *Journal of Compatative and Physiological Psychology, 73,* 245–253.

Noble, K. D. (1987). The dilemma of the gifted woman. *Psychology of Women Quarterly, 11*, 367–378.

Nyborg, H. (1983). Spatial ability in men and women: Review and new theory. *Advances in Behaviour Research and Therapy, 5*, 89–140.

Nyborg, H. (1984). Performance and intelligence in hormonally different groups. In G. J. DeVries, J. DeBruin, H. Uylings, & M. Cormer (Eds.), *Progress in brain research* (pp. 491–508). New York: Elsevier.

Nyborg, H. (1988). Mathematics, sex hormones, and brain function. *Behavioral and Brain Sciences, 11*, 206–207.

Nyborg, H. (1990). Sex hormones, brain development and spatio–perceptual strategies in Turner syndrome. In D. B. Berch & B. G. Bender (Eds.), *Sex chromosome abnormalities and human behavior* (pp. 100–128). Washington, DC: American Association for the Advancement of Science.

O'Boyle, M. W., & Benbow, C. P. (1990). Handedness and its relationship to ability and talent. In S. Coren (Ed.), *Left-handedness: Behavioral implications and anomalies* (pp. 343–372). New York: Elsevier.

O'Boyle, M. W., Gill, H. S., Benbow, C. P., & Alexander, J. E. (1994). Concurrent finger-tapping in mathematically gifted males: Evidence for enhanced right hemisphere involvement during linguistic processing. *Cortex, 30*, 519–526.

O'Boyle, M. W., & Hoff, E. J. (1987). Gender and handedness differences in mirror-tracing random forms. *Neuropsychologia, 25*, 977–982.

O'Boyle, M. W., Hoff, E. J., & Gill, H. S. (1995). The influence of mirror reversals on male and female performance in spatial tasks: A componential look. *Personality and Individual Differences, 18*, 693–699.

O'Brien, M., & Nagle, K. J. (1987). Parents' speech to toddlers: The effect of play context. *Journal of Child Language, 14*, 269–279.

Ohkura, T., Isse, K., Akazawa, K., Hamamoto, M., Yaoi, Y., & Hagino, N. (1995). Long-term estrogen replacement therapy in female patients with dementia of the Alzheimer type: 7 case reports. *Dementia, 6*, 99–107.

O'Keefe, J., & Nadel, L. (1978). *The hippocampus as a cognitive map.* New York: Oxford University Press.

O'Kelly, C. G. (1980). *Women and men in society.* New York: Van Nostrand.

Orwin, R. G., & Cordray, D. S. (1985). Effects of deficient reporting on meta-analysis: A conceptual framework and reanalysis. *Psychological Bulletin, 97*, 134–147.

Ostatnikova, D., Laznibatova, J., & Dohnanyiova, M. (1996). Testosterone influence on spatial ability in prepubertal children. *Studia Psychologica, 38*, 237–245.

Owen, K. (1995, July 20). Social issues; US dads lag in child-care duties, global study finds; but American moms are with kids more than other mothers. *Los Angeles Times,* Part A, 1.

Owen, K., & Lynn, R. (1993). Sex differences in primary cognitive abilities among Blacks, Indians and Whites in South Africa. *Journal of Biosocial Science, 25*, 557–560.

Packard, M. G. (1998). Posttraining estrogen and memory modulation. *Hormones and Behavior, 34*, 126–139.

Paganini-Hill, A., Buckwalter, J. G., Logan, C. G., & Henderson, V. W. (1993). Estrogen replacement and Alzheimer's disease in women. *Society for Neuroscience Abstracts, 19*, 1046.

Pajares, F., Miller, M. D., & Johnson, M. J. (1999). Gender differences in writing self-beliefs of elementary school students. *Journal of Educational Psychology, 91*, 50–61.

Patlak, M. (1990, March 19). Starting point. *Los Angeles Times*, p. B2.

Pearson, G. A. (1996, October 18). Of sex and gender. *Science, 274,* 330–331.

Perrot-Sinal, T. S., Kostenuik, M. A., Ossenkopp, K.-P., & Kavaliers, M. (1996). Sex differences in performance in the Morris Water Maze and the effects of initial nonstationalry hidden platform training. *Behavioral Neuroscience, 110,* 1309–1320.

Perry, D. G., & Bussey, K. (1979). The social learning theory of sex differences: Imitation is alive and well. *Journal of Personality and Social Psychology, 37,* 1699–1712.

Peters, M., & Campagnaro, P. (1996). Do women really excel over men in manual dexterity? *Journal of Experimental Psychology, 22,* 1107–1112.

Peters, M., Laeng, B., Latham, K., Jackson, M., Zaiyouna, R., & Richardson, C. (1995). A redrawn Vandenberg and Kuse mental rotations test: Different versions and factors that affect performance. *Brain and Cognition, 28,* 39–58.

Petersen, A. C. (1976). Physical androgyny and cognitive functioning in adolescence. *Developmental Psychology, 12,* 524–533.

Petersen, A. C. (1980). Biopsychosocial processes in the development of sex-related differences. In J. E. Parsons (Ed.), *The psychology of sex differences and sex roles* (pp. 31–55). Washington, DC: Hemisphere.

Petersen, A. C., & Crockett, L. J. (1985, August). *Factors influencing sex differences in spatial ability across the lifespan.* Symposium conducted at the 93rd Annual Convention of the American Psychological Association, Los Angeles.

Petersen, A. C., & Crockett, L. J. (1987). Biological correlates of spatial ability and mathematical performance. In J. A. Sechzer & S. M. Pfafflin (Eds.), *Psychology and educational policy* (pp. 69–86). New York: New York Academy of Sciences.

Petersen, A. C., & Hood, K. E. (1988). The role of experience in cognitive performance and brain development. In G. M. Vroman (Ed.), *Genes and gender: V women at work: Socialization toward inequity* (pp. 52–77). New York: Gordian Press.

Petrill, S. A. (1997). Molarity versus modularity of cognitive functioning? A behavioral genetic perspective. *Current Directions in Psychological Science, 6,* 96–99.

Peyser, M., & Underwood, A. (1997). Shyness, sadness, curiosity, joy. Is it nature or nurture? *Newsweek Special Edition Your Child,* 60–63.

Pezaris, E., & Casey, M. B. (1991). Girls who use "masculine" problem-solving strategies on a spatial task: Proposed genetic and environmental factors. *Brain and Cognition, 17,* 1–22.

Phelps, J. A., Davis, J. O., & Schartz, K. M. (1997). Nature, nurture, and twin research strategies. *Current Directions in Psychological Science, 6,* 117–121.

Pheterson, G. I., Kiesler, S. B., & Goldberg, P. A. (1971). Evaluation of the performance of women as a function of their sex, achievement, and personal history. *Journal of Personality and Social Psychology, 19,* 114–118.

Phillips, K., & Silverman, I. (1997). Differences in the relationship of menstrual cycle phase to spatial performance on two- and three-dimensional tasks. *Hormones and Behavior, 32,* 167–175.

Piaget, J., & Inhelder, B. (1956). *The child's conception of space.* London: Routledge & Kegan Paul.

Plake, B. S., Loyd, B. H., & Hoover, H. D. (1981). Sex differences in mathematics components of the Iowa Test of Basic Skills. *Psychology of Women Quarterly, 5,* 780–784.

Plomin, R. (1990). *Nature and nurture: An introduction to human behavioral genetics.* Monterey, CA: Brooks/Cole.

Plomin, R. (1997). Current directions in behavioral genetics: Moving into the mainstream. *Current Directions, 6,* 58.

Plomin, R., Fulker, D. W., Corley, R., & DeFries, J. C. (1997). Nature, nurture, and cognitive development from 1 to 16 years: A parent–offspring adoption study. *Psychological Science, 8,* 442–447.

Plous, S. (1997). Racial and gender biases in magazine advertising: A content-analytic study. *Psychology of Women Quarterly, 21,* 627–644.

Pontius, A. A. (1989). Color and spatial error in block design in stone-age Auca Indians: Ecological underuse of occipital–parietal system in men and of frontal lobes in women. *Brain and Cognition, 10,* 54–75.

Poole, C., & Stanley, G. (1972). A factorial and predictive study of spatial abilities. *Australian Journal of Psychology, 24,* 317–320.

Porac, C., & Coren, S. (1981). *Lateral preference and human behavior.* New York: Springer-Verlag.

Portin, R., Saarijärvi, S., Joukamaa, M., & Salokangas, R. K. R. (1995). Education, gender, and cognitive performance in a 62–year-old normal population: Results from the Turva Project. *Psychological Medicine, 25,* 1295–1298.

Posner, M. I., & Raichle, M. E. (1994). *Images of mind.* San Francisco: Freeman.

Postma, A., Izendoorn, R., & De Haan, E. H. F. (1998). Sex differences in object location memory. *Brain and Cognition, 36,* 334–345.

Postma, A., Winkel, J., Tuiten, A., & van Honk, J. (1999). Sex differences and menstrual cycle effects in human spatial memory. *Psychoneuroendocrinology, 24,* 175–192.

Psychological Corporation. (1990). *The mechanical reasoning test of the differential aptitudes test.* New York: Author.

Ramist, L., & Arbeiter, S. (1986). *Profiles: College bound seniors 1985.* New York: College Entrance Examination Board.

Rammsayer, T., & Lustnauer, S. (1989). Sex differences in time perception. *Perceptual and Motor Skills, 68,* 195–198.

Rauscher, F. H., Shaw, G. L., Levine, L. J., Wright, E. L., Dennis, W. R., & Newcombe, R. L. (1997). Music training causes long-term enhancement of preschool children's spatial–temporal reasoning. *Neurological Research, 19,* 2–8.

Ray, W. J., Newcombe, N., Semon, J., & Cole, P. M. (1981). Spatial abilities, sex differences and EEG functioning. *Neuropsychologia, 19,* 719–722.

Rebok, G. W. (1987). *Life-span cognitive development.* New York: Holt, Rinehart & Winston.

Reinisch, J. (1981, March). Prenatal exposure to synthetic progestins increases potential for aggression in humans. *Science, 211,* 1171–1173.

Reinisch, J. M., Rosenblum, L. A., & Sanders, S. A. (1987). Masculinity/ femininity: An introduction. In J. M. Reinisch, L. A. Rosenblum, & S. A. Sanders (Eds.), *Masculinity/femininity: Basic perspectives* (pp. 3–10). New York: Oxford University Press.

Reinisch, J. M., & Sanders, S. A. (1992). Prenatal hormonal contributions to sex differences in human cognitive and personality development. In A. A. Gerall, H. Moltz, & I. I. Ward (Eds.), *Handbook of behavioral neurobiology: Vol. 2. Sexual differentiation* (pp. 221–243). New York: Plenum.

Reiss, A. L., Mazzocco, M. M. M., Greenlaw, R., Freund, L. S., & Ross, J. L. (1995). Neurodevelopmental effects of X monosomy: A volumetric imaging study. *Annals of Neurology, 38,* 731–738.

Resnick, S. M. (1993). Sex differences in mental rotations: An effect of time limits? *Brain and Cognition, 21,* 71–79.

Resnick, S. M., Berenbaum, S. A., Gottesman, I. I., & Bouchard, T. J., Jr. (1986). Early hormonal influences of cognitive functioning in congenital adrenal hyperplasis. *Developmental Psychology, 22,* 191–198.

Resnick, S. M., Maki, P. M., Golski, S., Kraut, M. A., & Zonderman, A. B. (1998). Effects of estrogen replacement therapy on PET cerebral blood flow and neuropsychological performance. *Hormones and Behavior, 34,* 171–182.

Resnick, S. M., Metter, E. J., & Zonderman, A. B. (1997). Estrogen replacement therapy and longitudinal decline in visual memory: A possible protective effect? *Neurology, 49,* 1491–1497.

Richardson, J. T. E. (1991). Gender differences in imagery, cognition, and memory. In R. H. Logie & M. Denis (Eds.), *Mental images in human cognition* (pp. 271–303). New York: Elsevier.

Richardson, J. T. E. (1994). Continuous recognition memory tests: Are the assumptions of the theory of signal detection really met? *Journal of Clinical and Experimental Neuropsychology, 16,* 482–486.

Ricketts, M. (1989). Epistemological values of feminists in psychology. *Psychology of Women Quarterly, 13,* 401–415.

Robert, M. (1990). Sex typing the water-level task: There is more than meets the eye. *International Journal of Psychology, 25,* 475–490.

Robert, M., & Chaperon, H. (1989). Cognitive and exemplary modelling of horizontality representation of the Piagetian water-level task. *International Journal of Behavioral Development, 12,* 453–472.

Robert, M., & Ohlmann, T. (1994). Water-level representation by men and women as a funciton of rod-and-frame test proficiency and visual and postural information. *Perception, 23,* 1321–1333.

Robinson, N. M., Abbott, R. D., Berninger, V. W., & Busse, J. (1996). The structure of abilities in math-precocious young children: Gender similarities and differences. *Journal of Educational Psychology, 88,* 341–352.

Rodin, J., & Ickovics, J. R. (1990). Women's health: Review and research agenda as we approach the 21st century. *American Psychologist, 45,* 1018–1034.

Rose, S. A., & Feldman, J. F. (1995). Prediction of IQ and specific cognitive abilities at 11 years from infancy measures. *Developmental Psychology, 31,* 685–696.

Rosen, M. (1995). Gender differences in structure, means and variances of hierarchically ordered ability dimensions. *Learning & Instruction, 5,* 37–62.

Rosenstein, L. D., & Bigler, E. D. (1987). No relationship between handedness and sexual preference. *Psychological Reports, 60,* 704–706.

Rosenthal, R. (1966). *Experimenter effects in behavioral research.* New York: Appleton-Century-Crofts.

Rosenthal, R., & Rubin, D. B. (1982). Further meta-analytic procedures for assessing cognitive gender differences. *Journal of Educational Psychology, 74,* 708–712.

Rosenthal, R., & Rubin, D. B. (1985). Statistical analysis: Summarizing evidence versus establishing facts. *Psychological Bulletin, 97,* 527–529.

Rosnow, R. L., & Rosenthal, R. (1996). Computing contrasts, effect sizes, and general procedures for research consumers. *Psychological Methods, 1,* 331–340.

Rossi, J. S. (1983). Ratios exaggerate gender differences in mathematical ability. *American Psychologist, 38,* 348.

Rovet, J., & Netley, C. (1979). Phenotypic vs. genotypic sex and cognitive abilities. *Behavior Genetics, 9,* 317–321.

Rovet, J., Szekely, C., & Hockenberry, M. (1994). Specific arithmetic calculation deficits in children with Turner syndrome. *Journal of Clinical and Experimental Neuropsychology, 16*, 820–839.

Rozeboom, W. W. (1960). The fallacy of the null-hypothesis significance test. *Psychological Bulletin, 57*, 416–428.

Rubin, J., Provenzano, F., & Luria, Z. (1974). The eye of the beholder: Parents' views on sex of newborns. *American Journal of Orthopsychiatry, 44*, 512–519.

Ruff, C. B., Trinkhaus, E., & Holliday, T. W. (1997). Body mass and encephalization in Pleistocene Homo. *Nature, 387*, 173–176.

Russett, C. E. (1989). *Sexual science: The Victorian constructions of womanhood.* Cambridge, MA: Harvard University Press.

Ryckman, D. B., & Peckham, P. (1987). Gender differences in attributions for success and failure situations across subject areas. *Journal of Educational Research, 81*, 120–125.

Sadker, M., & Sadker, D. (1985, March). Sexism in the schoolroom of the 80's. *Psychology Today, 19*, 54–57.

Safir, M. P. (1986). The effects of nature or of nurture on sex differences in intellectual functioning: Israeli findings. *Sex Roles, 14*, 581–590.

Sanders, B., & Soares, M. P. (1986). Sexual maturation and spatial ability in college students. *Developmental Psychology, 22*, 199–203.

Sanders, G., & Ross-Fields, L. (1986). Sexual orientation and visual–spatial ability. *Brain and Cognition, 5*, 280–290.

Sanders, G., & Wright, M. (1993). Sexual orientation differences in cerebral asymmetry and in the performance of sexually dimorphic cognitive and motor tasks. *Archives of Sexual Behavior, 26*, 463–480.

Saudino, K. J. (1997). Moving beyond the heritability question: New directions in behavioral genetic studies of personality. *Current Directions in Psychological Science, 6*, 86–90.

Scarr, S. (1997). Rules of evidence: A larger context for the statistical debate. *Psychological Science, 8*, 16–17.

Schab, F. R. (1991). Odor memory: Talking stock. *Psychological Bulletin, 109*, 242–251.

Schaie, K. W. (1987). Aging and human performance. In M. W. Riley, J. D. Matarazzo, & A. Baum (Eds.), *Perspectives in behavioral medicine: The aging dimension* (pp. 29–37). Hillsdale, NJ: Lawrence Erlbaum Associates.

Schaller, M. (1997). Beyond "competing," beyond "compatible": Commentary on J. Archer. *American Psychologist, 52*, 1379–1380.

Schiff, W., & Oldak, R. (1990). Accuracy of judging time to arrival: Effects of modality, trajectory, and gender. *Journal of Experimental Psychology: Human Perception and Performance, 16*, 303–316.

Schlaug, G., Jancke, L., Huang, Y., Staiger, J. F., & Steinmetz, H. (1995). Increased corpus callosum size in musicians. *Neuropsychologia, 33*, 1047–1055.

Schwartz, F. N. (1989, January/February). Executives and organizations: Management women and the new facts of life. *Harvard Business Review, 65–76.*

Schwartz, W., & Hanson, K. (1992). Equal mathematics education for female students. *ERIC/CUE Digest, 78.*

Seligman, D. (1998, April 6). Gender mender. *Forbes, 161*(7), 72–74.

Sells, L. W. (1980). The mathematics filter and the education of women and minorities. In L. H. Fox & D. Tobin (Eds.), *Women and the mathematical mystique* (pp. 66–75). Baltimore: Johns Hopkins University Press.

Serbin, L. A., Bohlin, G., & Berlin, L. (1999). Sex differences in 1–, 3–, and 5–year-olds toy-choice in a structured play-session. *Scandinavian Journal of Psychology, 40,* 43–48.

Serbin, L. A., Powlishta, K. K., & Gulko, J. (1993). *The development of sex typing in middle childhood.* Chicago: University of Chicago Press.

Serbin, L. A., & Sprafkin, C. (1986). The salience of gender and the process of sex typing in three- to seven-year-old children. *Child Development, 57,* 1188–1199.

Seth-Smith, M., Ashton, R., & McFarland, K. (1989). A dual-task study of sex differences in language reception and production. *Cortex, 25,* 425–431.

Shah, P., & Miyake, A. (1996). The separability of working memory resources for spatial thinking and language processing: An individual differences approach. *Journal of Experimental Psychology: General, 125,* 4–27.

Shaywitz, B. A., Shaywitz, S. E., Pugh, K. R., Constable, R. T., Skudlarski, P., Fulbright, R. K., Bronen, R. A., Fletcher, J. M., Shankweiler, D. P., Katz, L., & Gore, J. C. (1995). Sex differences in the functional organization of the brain for language. *Nature, 373,* 607–609.

Shaywitz, S. E., Shaywitz, B. A., Pugh, K. R., Fulbright, R. K., Skudlarski, P., Mencl, W. E., Constable, R. T., Naftolin, F., Palter, S. F., Marchione, K. E., Katz, L., Shankweiler, D. P., Fletcher, J. M., Lacadie, C., Keltz, M., & Gore, J. C. (1999, April 7). Effects of estrogen on brain activation patterns in postmenopausal women during working memory tasks. *Journal of the American Medical Association, 281,* 1197–1202.

Shepard, R. N., & Metzler, J. (1971, February). Mental rotation of three dimensional objects. *Science, 171,* 701–703.

Sherman, J. A. (1967). Problems of sex differences in space perception and aspects of intellectual functioning. *Psychological Review, 74,* 290–299.

Sherman, J. A. (1977). Effects of biological factors on sex-related differences in mathematics achievement. In L. H. Fox, E. Fennema, & J. Sherman (Eds.), *Women and mathematics: Research perspectives for change* (pp. 137–206). Washington, DC: National Institute of Education.

Sherman, J. A. (1978). *Sex-related cognitive differences: An essay on theory and evidence.* Springfield, IL: Thomas.

Sherman, J. A. (1979). Cognitive performance as a function of sex and handedness: An evaluation of the Levy hypothesis. *Psychology of Women Quarterly, 3,* 378–390.

Sherman, J. A. (1980). Mathematics, spatial visualization, and related factors: Changes in girls and boys Grades 8–11. *Journal of Educational Psychology, 72,* 476–482.

Sherman, J. A. (1982). Continuing in mathematics: A longitudinal study of the attitudes of high school girls. *Psychology of Women Quarterly, 72,* 132–140.

Sherman, J. A. (1983). Girls talk about mathematics and their future: A partial replication. *Psychology of Women Quarterly, 7,* 338–342.

Sherry, D. F., Jacobs, L. F., & Gaulin, S. J. C. (1992). Spatial memory and adaptive specialization of the hippocampus. *Trends in Neuroscience, 15,* 298–303.

Sherwin, B. B. (1994). Hormonal restructuring of the adult brain: Basic and clinical perspectives. In V. N. Luine & C. F. Harding (Eds.), *Basic and clinical percpectives* (pp. 213–231). New York: New York Academy of Sciences.

Shields, S. A. (1975). Functionalism, Darwinism, and the psychology of women: A study in social myth. *American Psychologist, 30,* 739–754.

Shields, S. A. (1980). Nineteenth-century evolutionary theory and male scientific bias. In G. W. Barlow & J. Silverberg (Eds.), *Sociobiology: Beyond nature/nurture* (pp. 489–502). Boulder, CO: Westview Press.

Shih, M., Pittinsky, T. L., & Ambady, N. (1999). Stereotype susceptibility: Identity salience and shifts in quantitative performance. *Psychological Science, 10,* 80–83.

Shucard, D. W., Shucard, J. L., & Thomas, D. G. (1987). Sex differences in electrophysiological activity in infancy: Possible implications for language development. In S. U. Philips, S. Steele, & C. Tanz (Eds.), *Language, gender, and sex in comparative perspectives* (pp. 278–295). Cambridge, England: Cambridge University Press.

Signorella, M., & Jamison, W. (1986). Masculinity, femininity, androgyny, and cognitive performance: A meta-analysis. *Psychological Bulletin, 100,* 207–228.

Signorella, M. L., & Liben, L. S. (1984). Recall and reconstruction of gender-related pictures: Effects of attitude, task difficulty, and age. *Child Development, 55,* 393–405.

Signorelli, N., & Bacue, A. (1999). Recognition and respect: A a content analysis of prime-time television characters across three decades. *Sex Roles, 40,* 527–544.

Silverman, I., & Eals, M. (1992). Sex differences in spatial abilities: Evolutionary theory and data. In J. H. Barkow, L. Cosmides, & J. Tooby (Eds.), *The adapted mind: Evolutionary psychology and the generation of culture* (pp. 533–549). New York: Oxford University Press.

Silverman, I., & Phillips, K. (1993). Effects of estrogen changes during the menstural cycle on spatial performance. *Ethology and Sociobiology, 14,* 257–270.

Silverman, I., Phillips, K., & Silverman, L. K. (1996). Homogeneity of effect sizes for sex across spatial tests and cultures: Implications for hormonal theories. *Brain and Cognition, 31,* 90–94.

Simpkins, J. W., Singh, M., & Bishop, J. (1994). The potential role for estrogen replacement therapy in the treatment of the cognitive decline and neurodegeneration associated with Alzheimer's disease. *Neurobiology of Aging, 15,* S195–S197.

Singer, G., & Montgomery, R. B. (1969). Comment on "Role of Activation and Inhibition in Sex Differences in Cognitive Abilities." *Psychological Review, 76,* 325–327.

Singer, J. M., & Stake, J. E. (1986). Mathematics and self-esteem: Implications for women's career choice. *Psychology of Women Quarterly, 10,* 339–352.

Singh, M., & Bryden, M. P. (1994). The factor structure of handedness in India. *International Journal of Neuroscience, 74,* 33–43.

Skelton, G. (1990, April). As women climb political ladder, stereotypes follow. *Los Angeles Times,* pp. A1, A24–A25.

Skinner, P. H., & Shelton, R. L. (1985). *Speech, language, and hearing: Normal processes and disorders* (2nd ed.). New York: Wiley.

Skuse, D. H., James, R. S., Bishop, D. V. Coppin, B., Dalton, P., Aamodt-Leeper, G., Bacarese-Hamilton, M., Creswell, C., McGurk, R. & Jacobs, P. A. (1997). Evidence from Turner's syndrome of an imprinted X-linked locus affecting cognitive function. *Nature, 387,* 652–653.

Smith, G. A., & McPhee, K. A. (1987). Performance on a coincidence timing task correlates with intelligence. *Intelligence, 11,* 161–167.

Smock, T. K. (1999). *Physiological psychology: A neurosciences approach.* Englewood Cliffs, NJ: Prentice-Hall.

Smolak, L. (1986). *Infancy.* Englewood Cliffs, NJ: Prentice-Hall.

Smotherman, W. P., & Robinson, S. R. (1990). The prenatal origins of behavioral organization. *Psychological Science, 1,* 97–106.

Spear, N. E., Spear, L. P., & Woodruff, M. L. (1995). *Neurobehavioral plasticity: Learning, development, and response to brain insults: A volume in honor of Robert L. Isaacson.* Hillsdale, NJ: Lawrence Erlbaum Associates.

Spearman, C. (1927). *The abilities of man: Their nature and measurement.* New York: Macmillan.

Spence, J. T. (1993). Gender-related traits and gender ideology: Evidence for a multifactorial theory. *Journal of Personality and Social Psychology, 64,* 624–635.

Spence, J. T., & Helmreich, R. (1978). *Masculinity and femininity: Their psychological dimensions, correlates, and antecedents.* Austin: University of Texas Press.

Spence, J. T., & Helmreich, R. L. (1983). Achievement-related motives and behaviors. In J. T. Spence (Ed.), *Achievement and achievement motives: Psychological and sociological approaches* (pp. 7–74). San Francisco: Freeman.

Spence, J. T., Helmreich, R. L., & Stapp, J. (1974). The Personal Attributes Questionnaire: A measure of sex role stereotypes and masculinity–femininity. *JSAS Catalog of Selected Documents in Psychology, 4,* 43.

Spiers, P. A. (1987). Acalcalia revisited: Current issues. In G. Deloche & X. Seron (Eds.), *Mathematical disabilities: A cognitive neuropsychological perspective* (pp. 1–25). Hillsdale, NJ: Lawrence Erlbaum Associates.

Springer, S. P., & Deutsch, G. (1998). *Left brain, right brain* (5th ed.). San Francisco: Freeman.

Srivastava, A. K. (1989). A study of field dependence–independence among Mizo children. *Psychological Studies, 34,* 55–58.

Stafford, R. E. (1961). Sex differences in spatial visualization as evidence of sex-linked inheritance. *Perceptual and Motor Skills, 13,* 428.

Stafford, R. E. (1963). *An investigation of similarities in parent–child test scores for evidence of hereditary components* (Report No. RB-63-11). Princeton, NJ: Educational Testing Service.

Stafford, R. E. (1972). Hereditary and environmental components of quantitatve reasoning. *Review Educational Research, 42,* 183–201.

Stage, C. (1988). Gender differences in test results. *Scandinavian Journal of Educational Research, 32,* 101–111.

Stage, E. K., & Karplus, R. (1981). Mathematical ability: Is sex a factor? *Science, 212,* 114.

Stanley, J. (1990, January). We need to know why women falter in math. *The Chronicle of Higher Education,* p. B4.

Stanley, J. C. (1993). Boys and girls who reason well mathematically. In G. R. Bock & K. Acrill (Eds.), *The origin and development of high ability* (pp. 119–138). New York: Wiley.

Stanley, J. C., & Benbow, C. P. (1982). Huge sex ratios at upper end. *American Psychologist, 37,* 972.

Stanley, J. C., Benbow, C. P., Brody, L. E., Dauber, S., & Lupkowski, A. (1992). Gender differences on eighty-six nationally standardized aptitude and achievement tests. In N. Colangelo, S. G. Assouline, & D. L. Ambroson (Eds.), *Talent development, Vol. 1: Proceedings from the 1991 Henry B. and Jocelyn Wallace National Research Symposium on Talent Development* (pp. 42–65). Unionville, NY: Trillium Press.

Stanley, J. C., & Stumpf, H. (1996). Able youths and achievement tests. *Behavioral and Brain Sciences, 19,* 263–264.

Starkweather, C. W. (1987). *Fluency and stuttering.* Englewood Cliffs, NJ: Prentice-Hall.

Steele, C. M. (1997). A threat in the air: How stereotypes shape intellectual identity and performance. *American Psychologist, 52,* 613–629.

Steele, C. M. (1998). Stereotyping and its threat are real. *American Psychologist, 53,* 680–681.

Steele, C. M., & Aronson, J. (1995). Stereotype threat and the intellectual test performance of African Americans. *Journal of Personality and Social Psychology, 69,* 797–811.

Stein, J. F. (1994). Developmental dyslexia, neural timing and hemispheric lateralisation. *International Journal of Psychophsiology, 18,* 241–249.

Steinmetz, H., Staiger, J. F., Schluag, G., Huang, Y., & Jancke, L. (1995). Corpus callosum and brain volume in women and men. *Neuroreport: An International Journal for the Rapid Communication of Research in Neuroscience, 6,* 1002–1004.

Stellman, S. D., Wynder, E. L., DeRose, D. J., & Muscat, J. E. (1997). The epidemiology of left-handedness in a hospital population. *Annals of Epidemiology, 3,* 156–164.

Sternberg, R. J. (1988). *The triarchic mind.* New York: Viking.

Sternberg, R. J. (1996). Myths, countermyths, and truths about human intelligence. *Educational Researcher, 25,* 11–16.

Stewart, A. J., & Ostrove, J. M. (1998). Women's personality in middle age: Gender, history, and midcourse corrections. *American Psychologist, 53,* 1185–1194.

Stewart, V. (1976). Social influences on sex differences in behavior. In M. S. Teitelbaum (Ed.), *Sex differences: Social and biological perspectives* (pp. 138–174). New York: Anchor Books.

Stones, I., Beckmann, M., & Stephens, L. (1982). Sex-related differences in mathematical competencies of pre-calculus college students. *School Science and Mathematics, 82,* 295–299.

Stricker, L. J. (1998). *Inquiring about examinees' ethnicity and sex: Effects on AP Calculus AB Examination performance* (Report No. 98-1). New York: The College Board.

Stricker, L. J., Rock, D. A., & Barton, N. W. (1993). Sex differences in predictions of college grades from Scholastic Aptitude scores. *Journal of Educational Psychology, 85,* 710–718.

Stricker, L. J., & Ward, W. C. (1998). Inquiring about examinees' ethnicity and sex: Effects on computerized placement tests performance (Report No. 98-2). New York: The College Board.

Stumpf, H. (1995). Gender differences in performance on tests of cognitive abilities: Experimental design issues and empirical results. *Learning and Individual Differences, 74,* 275–287.

Stumpf, H., & Eliot, J. (1995). Gender-related differences in spatial ability and the k factor of general spatial ability in a population of academically talented students. *Personality and Individual Differences, 19,* 33–45.

Stumpf, H., & Jackson, D. N. (1994). Gender-related differences in cognitive abilities: Evidence from a medical school admissions testing program. *Personality and Individual Differences, 17,* 335–344.

Stumpf, H., & Stanley, J. C. (1996). Gender-related differences on the College Board's Advanced Placement and Achievement Tests, 1982–1992. *Journal of Educational Psychology, 88,* 353–364.

Stumpf, H., & Stanley, J. C. (1998). Standardized tests: Still gender biased? *Current Directions in Psychological Science, 7,* 192–196.

Subrahmanyam, K., & Greenfield, P. M. (1994). Effect of video game practice on spatial skills in girls and boys. *Journal of Applied Developmental Psychology, 15,* 13–32.

Sue, S., & Okazaki, S. (1990). Asian-American educational achievements: A phenomenon in search of an explanation. *American Psychologist, 45,* 913–920.

Sutaria, S. D. (1985). *Specific learning disabilities: Nature and needs.* Springfield, IL: Thomas.

Swaab, D. F., Zhou, J. N., Fodor, M., & Hofman, M. A. (1996). Sexual differentiation of the human hypothalamus: Differences according to sex, sexual orientation, and transsexuality. In L. Ellis & L. Ebertz (Eds.), *Sexual orientation: Toward biological understanding* (pp. 129–150). New York: Praeger.

Swim, J. K. (1994). Perceived versus meta-analytic effect sizes: An assessment of the accuracy of gender stereotypes. *Journal of Personality and Social Psychology, 66,* 21–36.

Swim, J., Borgida, E., Maruyama, G., & Myers, D. G. (1989). Joan McKay versus John McKay: Do gender stereotypes bias evaluations? *Psychological Bulletin, 105,* 409–429.

Tabachnick, B. G., & Fidell, L. S. (1996). *Using multivariate statistics* (3rd ed.). New York: HarperCollins.

Tan, U., & Tan, M. (1998). The curvilinear correlations between total testosterone level and fluid intelligence in men and women. *International Journal of Neuroscience, 94,* 55–61.

Tanner, J. M. (1962). *Growth and adolescence.* Oxford, England: Blackwell.

Temple, C. M., & Carney, R. A. (1993). Intellectual functioning of children with Turner syndrome: A comparison of behavioral phenotypes. *Developmental Medicine and Child Neurology, 35,* 691–698.

Temple, C. M., & Carney, R. A. (1996). Reading skills in children with Turner's syndrome: An analysis of hyperlexia. *Cortex, 32,* 335–345.

Temple, C. M., & Marriott, A. J. (1998). Arithmetical ability and disability in Turner's syndrome: A cognitive neuropsycholgical analysis. *Developmental Neuropsychology, 14,* 47–67.

Thomas, H., Jamison, W., & Hummel, D. D. (1973). Observation is insufficient for discovering that the surface of still water is invariantly horizontal. *Science, 181,* 173–174.

Thurstone, L. L. (1938). *Primary mental abilities.* Chicago: University of Chicago Press, Psychometric Monographs, No. 1.

Thurstone, L. L., & Thurstone, T. G. (1941). *Factorial studies of intelligence.* Chicago: University of Chicago Press.

Tierney, M. C., & Luine, V. N. (1998). New concepts in hormone replacement: Selective estrogen receptor modulators (SERMS). IV. Effects of estrogens and antiestrogens on the CNS. *Journal of the Canadian Society of Obstetrics & Gynecology, 19,* 46–56.

Tiger, L. (1970). Male dominance? Yes, alas. A sexist ploy? No. *The New York Times Magazine,* pp. 35–37, 124–127, 132–138.

Tiger, L. (1988). Sex differences in mathematics: Why the fuss? *Behavioral and Brain Sciences, 11,* 212.

Tiger. L. (1999). *The decline of males.* New York: Golden.

Time. (1990, Fall). Women the road ahead [Special issue]. New York: Time Magazine.

Tomizuka, C., & Tobias, S. (1981). Mathematical ability: Is sex a factor? *Science, 212,* 114.

Trenerry, M. R., Jack, C. R., Cascino, G. D., Sharbrough, F. W., & Ivnik, R. J. (1996). Sex differences in the relationship between visual memory and MRI hippocampal volumes. *Neuropsychology, 10,* 343–351.

Turner, P. J., & Gervai, J. (1995). A multidimensional study of gender typing in preschool children and their parents: Personality, attitudes, preferences, behavior, and cultural differences. *Developmental Psychology, 31,* 759–772.

Unger, R. K. (1979). *Female and male: Psychological perspectives.* New York: Harper & Row.

Unger, R. K. (1989). *Representations: Social construction of gender.* Amityville, NY: Baywood.

Unger, R. K., & Crawford, M. E. (1992). *Women and gender: A feminist psychology.* Philadelphia: Temple University Press.

Ungerleider, L. G. (1995, November 3). Functional brain imaging studies of cortical mechanisms for memory. *Science, 270,* 769–775.

U.S. Bureau of the Census. (1997). *Statistical abstract of the United States: 1997* (117th ed.). Washington, DC: Author.

U.S. Bureau of the Census. (1998). *Statistical abstract of the United States: 1998* (118th ed.). Washington, DC: Author.

U.S. Committee for UNICEF. (1993). The other apartheid: All over the world, missing girls and missed opportunities. *Thursday's Child: A Publication for the United States Committee for UNICEF, 10*–13.

U.S. Department of Education. (1996). The third international mathematics and science study. Washington, DC: Author. [http://www.ed.gov/nces].

U.S. Department of Education. (1997). National assessment of educational progress (Indicator 32: Writing proficiency: Prepared by the Educational Testing Service). Washington, DC: Author. [http://www.ed.gov/nces].

US On-Line News. (1999, May 31). Available on-line: http://usnews.com/usnews/issue/990208/8gap1.html).

Vakil, E., & Blachstein, H. (1997). Rey AVLT: Developmental norms for adults and the sensitivity of different memory measures to age. *Clinical Neuropsychologist, 11,* 356–369.

Valdez, R. L., & Gutek, B. A. (1986). Family roles a help or a hindrance for working women? In B. A. Gutek & L. Larwood (Eds.), *Women's career development* (pp. 157–169). Newbury Park, CA: Sage.

Valentine, S. Z., & Brodsky, S. L. (1989). Personal construct theory and stimulus sex and subject sex differences. In R. K. Unger (Ed.), *Representations: Social constructions of gender* (pp. 112–125). Amityville, NY: Baywood.

Valian, V. (1998). *Why so slow? The advancement of women.* Cambridge, MA: MIT Press.

Vandenberg, S. G. (1968). Primary mental abilities or general intelligence? Evidence from twin studies. In J. M. Thoday & A. S. Parkes (Eds.), *Genetic and environmental influences on behavior* (pp. 146–160). New York: Plenum.

Vandenberg, S. G. (1969). A twin study of spatial ability. *Multivariate Behavioral Research, 4,* 273–294.

Vandenberg, S. G. (1987). Sex differences in mental retardation and their implications for sex differences in ability. In L. A. Reinisch, L. A. Rosenblum, & S. A. Sanders (Eds.), *Masculinity/femininity: Basic perspectives* (pp. 157–171). New York: Oxford University Press.

Van Goozen, S. H. M., Cohen-Kettenis, P. T., Gooren, L.J. G., Frijda, N. H., & Van De Poll, N. E. (1995). Gender differences in behaviour: Activating effects of cross-sex hormones. *Psychoneuroendocrinology, 20,* 343–363.

Van Strien, J. W., & Boumsa, A. (1995). Sex and familial sinistrality differences in cognitve ability. *Brain and Cognition, 27,* 137–146.

Vasta, R., Knott, J. A., & Gaze, C. E. (1996). Can spatial training erase the gender differences on the water-level task. *Psychology of Women Quarterly, 20,* 549–567.

Vasta, R., & Liben, L. S. (1996). The water-level task: An intriguing puzzle. *Current Directions in Psychological Science, 5,* 171–177.

Vasta, R., Rosenberg, D., Knott, J. A., & Gaze, C. E. (1997). Experience and the water-level task revisited: Does expertise exact a price? *Psychological Science, 8,* 336–339.

Vernon, P. A. (1987). New developments in reaction time research. In P. A. Vernon (Ed.), *Speed of information processing and intelligence* (pp. 1–20). Norwood, NJ: Ablex.

Viner, K. (1994). Live issues. *Cosmopolitan,* 105.

Visser, D. (1987). Sex differences in adolescent mathematics behavior. *South African Journal of Psychology, 17,* 137–144.

Voyer, D. (1995). Effect of practice on laterality in a mental rotation task. *Brain & Cognition, 29,* 326–335.

Voyer, D. (1996). On the magnitude of laterality effects and sex differences in functional lateralities. *Laterality, 1,* 51–83.

Voyer, D., Voyer, S., & Bryden, M. P. (1995). Magnitude of sex differences in spatial abilities: A meta-analysis and consideration of critical variables. *Psychological Bulletin, 117,* 250–270.

Waber, D. P. (1976). Sex differences in cognition: A function of maturation rate? *Science, 192,* 572–574.

Waber, D. P. (1977). Sex differences in mental abilities, hemispheric lateralization, and rate of physical growth at adolescence. *Developmental Psychology, 13,* 29–38.

Wade, C., & Tavris, C. (1998). *Psychology* (5th ed.). New York: Addison-Wesley-Longman.

Wallen, K. (1996). Nature needs nurture: The interaction of hormonal and social influences on the development of behavioral sex differences in rhesus monkeys. *Hormones and Behavior, 30,* 364–378.

Wallis, C. (1989, December 4). Onward, women! *Time, 134,* 80–82, 85–86, 89.

Watson, N. V., & Kimura, D. (1991). Nontrivial sex differences in trowing and intercepting: Relation to psychometrically-defined spatial functions. *Personality and Individual Differences, 12,* 375–385.

Wechsler, D. (1981). *Manual for the Wechsler Adult Intelligence Scale—Revised.* New York: Psychological Corporation.

Wechsler, D. (1991). *WISC–III Wechsler Intelligence Scale for Children manual* (3rd ed.). New York: Psychological Corporation.

Weisstein, N. (1972). Psychology constructs the female. In V. Gornick & B. K. Moran (Eds.), *Women in sexist society* (pp. 207–224). New York: New American Library.

Weisstein, N. (1982, November). Tired of arguing about biological inferiority. *Ms.,* 41–46, 85.

Welford, A. T. (1980). Relationship between reaction time and fatigue, stress, age, and sex. In A. T. Welford (Ed.), *Reaction times* (pp. 321–354). London: Academic Press.

Wells, G. (1986). Variation in child language. In P Fletcher & M. Garman (Eds.), *Language acquisition: Studies in first language development* (pp. 109–139). Cambridge, England: Cambridge University Press.

Wentzel, K. R. (1988). Gender differences in math and English achievement: A longitudinal study. *Sex Roles, 18,* 11–12.

West, R. L. (1996). An application of prefrontal cortex function theory of cognitive aging. *Psychological Bulletin, 120,* 272–292.

Westkott, M. (1979). Feminist criticism of the social sciences. *Harvard Educational Review, 49,* 422–430.

Wigfield, A., & Eccles, J. S. (1992). The development of achievement task values: A theoretical analysis. *Developmental Review, 12,* 265–310.

Williams, C. L., & Meck, W. H. (1991). The organizational effects of gonadal steroids on sexually dimorphic spatial ability. *Psychoneuroendocrinology, 16,* 155–176.

Williams, J. E., & Best, D. L. (1982). *Measuring sex stereotypes: A thirty-nine nation study.* Beverly Hills, CA: Sage.

Williams, J. H. (1983). *Psychology of women: Behavior in a biosocial context* (2nd ed.). New York: Norton.

Willingham, W. W., & Cole, N. S. (1997). *Gender and fair assessment.* Mahwah, NJ: Lawrence Erlbaum Associates.

Willmott, M., & Brierley, H. (1984). Cognitive characteristics and homosexuality. *Archives of Sexual Behavior, 13,* 311–319.

Wilson, J. S., Stocking, V., & Goldstein, D. (1994). Gender differences in motivations for course selection: Academically talented students in an intensive summer program. *Sex Roles, 31,* 349–367.

Winograd, E., & Simon, E. V. (1980). Visual memory and imagery in the aged. In L. W. Poon, J. L. Fozard, L. S. Cermak, D. Arenberg, & L. W. Thompson (Eds.), *New directions in memory and aging: Proceedings of the George A. Talland Memorial Conference* (pp. 485–506). Hillsdale, NJ: Lawrence Erlbaum Associates.

Wisniewski, A. B., Nguyen, T. T., Flannery, T. W., & Dobs, A. S. (1999). Hypogonadal status and functional cerebral lateralization in adult men. *Brain and Cognition, 40,* 276–281.

Witelson, S. F. (1976). Sex and the single hemisphere: Specialization of the right hemisphere for spatial processing. *Science, 193,* 425–427.

Witelson, S. F. (1988). Neuroanatomical sex differences: Of consequence for cognition? *Behavioral and Brain Sciences, 11,* 215–217.

Witelson, S. F. (1989). Hand and sex differences in the isthmus and genu of the human corpus callosum. *Brain, 112,* 799–835.

Witkin, H. A. (1950). Individual differences in case of perception of embedded figures. *Journal of Personality, 19,* 1–15.

Witkin, H. A., Dyk, R. B., Faterson, H. F., Goodenough, D. G., & Karp, S. A. (1962). *Psychological differentiation.* New York: Wiley.

Witkin, H. W., Lewis, H. B., Hertzman, M., Machover, K., Meissner, P. B., & Wapner, S. (1954). *Personality through perception.* New York: Harper & Row.

Wittig, M. A. (1985). Metatheoretical dilemmas in the psychology of gender. *American Psychologist, 40,* 800–811.

Wittig, M. A., & Allen, M. J. (1984). Measurement of adult performance of Piaget's water horizontality task. *Intelligence, 8,* 305–313.

Wolf, M., & Gow, D. (1985). A longitudinal investigation of gender differences in language and reading development. *First Language, 6,* 81–110.

Wolff, P. H. (1969). The natural history of crying and other vocalizations in early infancy. In B. M. Foss (Ed.), *Determinants of infant behavior* (Vol. 3, pp. 113–138). London: Metheun.

Wright, R. (1990, August 19). Black scars, white fears. *Los Angeles Times Magazine,* 10–16, 34–35, 39.

Wright, T. A. (1997). Job performance and organizational commitment. *Perceptual & Motor Skills, 85,* 447–450.

Wrightsman, L. S. (1977). *Social psychology.* Monterey, CA: Brooks/Cole.

Yari, E., & Ambrose, N. (1992). Onset of stuttering in preschool children: Selected factors. *Journal of Speech and Hearing Research, 35,* 782–788.

Yee, D. K., & Eccles, J. S. (1988). Parent perceptions and attributions for children's math achievement. *Sex Roles, 19,* 5–6.

Zakay, D., & Block, R. A. (1997). Temporal cognition. *Current Directions in Psychological Science, 6,* 12–16.

Zappalà, G., Measso, G., Cavarzeran, F., Grigoletto, F., Lebowitz, B., Pizozzolo, F., Amaducci, L., Massari, D., & Crook, T. (1995). Aging and memory: Corrections for age, sex and education for three widely used memory tests. *Italian Journal of Neurological Sciences, 16*, 177–184.

Author Index

A

Aamodt-Leeper, G., 140, *369*
Abbott, R. D., 106, 116, 119, 252, *366*
Adams, R. P., 286, *335*
Adelman, C., 82, 95, 96, *335*
Adkins-Regan, E., 177, *335*
Adler, T., 15, 253, *335*
Ahern, F., 143, *359*
Aiken, L., 117, *335*
Akazawa, K., 176, *363*
Alavi, A., 207, *349*
Alderton, D., 101, *353*
Alexander, J. E., 202, 256, *363*
Alfieri, T., 264, *335*
Allan, K., 257, *335*
Allen, G., 148, 163, *361*
Allen, L. S., 199, *335*
Allen, M. J., 108, *375*
Allgeier, E. R., 272, *335*
Allport, G. W., 243, *335*
Altermatt, E. R., 260, *335*
Alves, S. E., 155, 176, 198, *360*
Amaducci, L., 122, 375
Ambady, N., 248, 368
Ambrose, N., 127*t*, 212, 375
American Association of University
  Women, 259, 260, 261, 268,
  270, 284, 335
American Psychiatric Association, 6, 90,
  95, 127*t*, 212, 335
Anastasio, E. J., 53, 344
Anderson, C. A., 25, 356
Anderson, C. V., 200, 338

Anderson, D. R., 258, 358
Anderson, J. R., 118, 335
Andrews, G., 95, 336
Angier, N., 141, 336
Annett, M., 178, 203, 336
Anokhin, A., 142, 339
Applebaum, S. L., 88, 343
Arap-Maritim, E. K., 322, 336
Arbeiter, S., 127, 365
Ardila, A., 122, 336
Arenson, K. W., 87, 336
Arnold, S. E., 207, 349
Arnott, D. P., 97, 338
Aronson, J., 247, 325, 370
Arthur, E. J., 89, 350
Asaro, C., 40, 336
Ascione, F. R., 243, 347
Ashton, R., 50, 367
Astin, A., 6, 234, 336
Astur, R. S., 105, 336
Atkins, L., 127*t*
Atlas, S., 190, 349

B

Bacarese-Hamilton, M., 140, 369
Bachevalier, J., 91, 336
Backma, L., 106, 352
Backman, M. E., 121, 336
Bacue, A., 257, 368
Baeckman, L., 93, 351
Baenninger, M., 14, 161, 215, 253, 283,
  286, 336, 362

Subject Index